# A Belle of the Fifties

Mrs. Clay of Alabama

# A Belle of the Fifties
## Memoirs of Mrs. Clay of Alabama

Covering Social and Political Life in
Washington and the South, 1853–66
Put into Narrative Form by Ada Sterling

Virginia Clay-Clopton

With Introduction, Annotations, and
Index to the Annotations by
Leah Rawls Atkins, Joseph H. Harrison Jr.,
and Sara A. Hudson

THE UNIVERSITY OF ALABAMA PRESS
Tuscaloosa and London

Published originally in 1905 by Doubleday, Page and Company
Introduction, Annotations, and Index to the Annotations
Copyright © 1999
The University of Alabama Press
Tuscaloosa, Alabama 35487-0380
All rights reserved
Manufactured in the United States of America

1 2 3 4 5 6 7 8 9 • 07 06 05 04 03 02 01 00 99

Cover design by Shari DeGraw

Special thanks to Ellen Garrison, Curator, W. S. Hoole Special Collections,
University of Alabama Libraries, for her assistance with this project.

∞

The paper on which this book is printed meets the minimum requirements of
American National Standard for Information Science–Permanence of Paper for
Printed Library Materials, ANSI Z39.48-1984.

Library of Congress Cataloging-in-Publication Data

Clay-Clopton, Virginia, 1825–1915.
A belle of the fifties : memoirs of Mrs. Clay of Alabama,
covering social and political life in Washington and the South,
1853–66 / Virginia Clay-Clopton ; put into narrative form by Ada
Sterling (d. 1939) ; with an introduction and annotations by Leah Rawls
Atkins, Joseph H. Harrison Jr., and Sara A. Hudson.
p. cm.
Originally published: New York : Doubleday, Page, 1905.
Includes indexes.
ISBN 0-8173-0986-1 (pbk.) (alk. paper)
ISBN 0-8173-1020-7 (cloth) (alk. paper)
1. Southern States—Social life and customs—1775–1865. 2.
Washington (D.C.)—Social life and customs—19th century. 3. United
States—History—Civil War, 1861–1865—Personal narratives,
Confederate. 4. Confederate States of America—Social life and
customs. 5. Clay-Clopton, Virginia, 1825–1915. I. Clay-Clopton,
Virginia, 1825–1915. II. Title.
F213.S84 1999
975'.03—dc21
99-6143

British Library Cataloguing-in-Publication Data available

# CONTENTS

Introduction vii

*A Belle of the Fifties*

# INTRODUCTION

Virginia Caroline Tunstall Clay-Clopton had length of days to match her length of name. When she was born on January 16, 1825, James Monroe was still president; at the time of her death on June 23, 1915, Woodrow Wilson was halfway through his first term. Virginia lived to be a luminary of the women's suffrage movement as well as of the United Daughters of the Confederacy, but it was in the 1850s and 1860s that this born actress played near center stage of American history. A social leader in the Washington of James Buchanan and in the Richmond of Jefferson Davis, Virginia was an astute political observer and a favorite and confidante of the men who held political power. She knew everyone who was important in Washington before and after the war and in the Confederate capital during the war. Her narrative, long considered one of the finest female Southern memoirs from the antebellum period, chronicles, with an extraordinary effort toward historical accuracy on the part of her editor, Ada Sterling, the social and political intrigues of the period—balls and state dinners, romantic entanglements and weddings, manners and fashions, secession and war. She spends but one chapter on her early life and instead focuses on a most tumultuous time—the period from when she and her husband first arrive in Washington in 1853 to when her husband is released from prison in 1866. She led a remarkably active and independent life for a woman of her time, and she owed that situation to a fortunate combination of birth, marriage, and an extraordinary personality.

She was born into the "dominant class" of the nineteenth-century South at a time when "everybody who was anybody

[had] scores of cousins scattered throughout their own and neighboring states."[1] Being somebody, little Virginia Tunstall—who was only three when she lost her mother and would not see much of her father for some years to come—was an object of concern to a formidable network of Tunstalls, Arringtons, Williamses, and Battles. They held solid positions in Virginia and in North Carolina, the two states whose names she bore, were calmly confident of their own status, and would assume leadership, almost as a matter of right, in new Southern states such as Alabama. Most helpful in a practical way were the Battles, the children of her maternal grandmother's first marriage. It was Martha Williams Fort (née Battle) and her husband, Elias B. Fort, who conveyed small Virginia from her native Nash County, North Carolina, to Tuscaloosa, Alabama, where she was deposited with Mrs. Henry Watkins Collier (née Mary Ann Williams Battle) and her husband; the latter would become chief justice of the Alabama Supreme Court and later governor of Alabama. When another move was indicated, she went to Mrs. Collier's brother, Alfred, the owner of a large plantation with nine hundred slaves.[2]

Yet the Tunstall influence on Virginia's imagination was far from negligible. Her paternal uncle Thomas Barker Tunstall, a Baldwin County planter and onetime Alabama secretary of state, gave her a glorified view of that family's past. Especially gratifying was Walter Scott's reference in *Marmion* to "Brian Tunstall, perfect knight" among the English chivalry at Flodden; the Tunstalls of Virginia were assumed to be this hero's descendants.[3] And it was Uncle Tom, along with the father now back in her life, who introduced her to the joys of the theater in Mobile.

That Virginia would marry within her own class was to be expected. Nevertheless, she was fortunate in her choice of Clement Claiborne Clay (1816–1882). "C. C. Clay Jr.," as he was usually called to distinguish him from his eminent father, Clement Comer Clay (1789–1866), was handsome, well educated, of scholarly tastes, and—despite a readiness to fight when he thought honor required it—of an essentially gentle and magnanimous disposition. He could maintain friendship, as his Confederate experience would show, with such people as William Lowndes Yancey and Jefferson Davis, who could not abide each other. He was a gifted orator and politician, yet not consumed by personal ambition. His love for Virginia, whom he married on February 1, 1843, after a very brief courtship, was devoted, admiring, and—so far as the record suggests—unswervingly faithful.

C. C. Clay Jr.'s connections were impressive. His father—a native of Virginia but raised and educated in Tennessee—had made his career from a base in Huntsville, Alabama. Clement Comer Clay had been a leader from the beginning of Alabama's statehood: chief justice, congressional representative, governor, United States senator, unflinching Jacksonian, and owner of a powerful newspaper. The Withers and Comer families, to which young Clement's mother and paternal grandmother, respectively, belonged, were "somebodies" too. Except for an early defeat for Congress at the hands of the amiable demagogue Williamson R. W. Cobb, the younger Clay also enjoyed almost unbroken political success, including election to the Alabama legislature, the United States Senate (where he served from 1853 until secession), and the senate of the Confederacy. To this last office, however, he was defeated for reelection in 1863, largely because of his support of Jefferson Davis.[4]

After his defeat in 1863 Clay accepted the role as a Confederate agent in Canada, which led him to be charged later, on wholly spurious evidence, with complicity in the assassination of President Lincoln. This turn of events brought about his harsh and lengthy imprisonment, without trial, in Fortress Monroe and gave Virginia the great dramatic role of her life. In the lurid

Washington of Andrew Johnson she was the indomitable sup-
pliant, besieging everyone who could help her to free and vindicate her husband. She prevailed, but she could not revitalize
the man or his career. His already delicate health had been further impaired, most of his property was gone, and he had little
future as lawyer or farmer. He tried but failed in the insurance
business and was passed over for the presidency of the University of Alabama. He died in Huntsville in 1882.

As the wife of Senator Clay, Virginia brilliantly exploited the
social opportunities afforded by Washington and Richmond.
She was certainly not a classic beauty. As one historian put it,
"She was tall and strong. Her oval face, blond complexion, light
chestnut hair, and close-set eyes gave her an appearance typical
of many North Carolinians."[5] Nevertheless, she had irrepressible vitality and wit, a huge—and sometimes mischievous—
sense of fun, and an allure that, without offense to decorum,
she was quite ready to exploit.

If her only child had not been stillborn during her first Washington winter, Virginia might not have been tempted to play
the role of belle so long. But she obviously adored Washington
society, cheerfully spent her husband's money (of which he never
had enough) on shoes and dresses, and gloried in the services
of a maid for whom he paid sixteen hundred dollars.

Fairly well educated, a keen newspaper reader, and possessed
of a more natural flair for politics than her husband, she was no
intellectual like her friend Mary Chesnut. And unlike Mrs. John J.
Crittenden, she made no attempt to conciliate Northerners unless they were already pro-Southern, cheerfully ostracizing many
whose help she would need in the grim days of 1865 and 1866.
She could refer in later life, with a nostalgia untouched by irony,
to the "brilliant Buchanan administration"—and socially, thanks
in part to her, it had been that. For the reader who knows how
it all came out, there are overtones of Belshazzar's feast. None-

theless, in Virginia Clay's memory the music continued to play, and she evidently had the gift of making those days live again in conversation.

Virginia's prominence in later years was chiefly local, despite a warm reception in Washington after the Democrats returned briefly to power in 1885. In 1887 she married David Clopton, a former congressional colleague of her husband's, twice a widower, and a judge of the Alabama Supreme Court. He died in 1892, but Mrs. Clay-Clopton, as she called herself in her later years, would live to preside over both the Alabama Daughters of the Confederacy and the Alabama Woman Suffrage Association. She was the second president of the latter and first president, in 1912, of its successor, the Alabama Equal Suffrage Association. Only six months before she died, her beauty and vitality were hailed at a memorable ninetieth birthday party in Huntsville.

The memory of Virginia's vivid personality and her fund of recollections would soon have been lost, however, had she not been persuaded to make these memories part of the published record of the turbulent years of civil conflict. The origin of this project might be re-created in Virginia's dramatic power and perceived as well to be a theme that helps to unify the three parts of *Belle.*

The prelude occurs when, as a young girl, she was taken to a play, her first, in Mobile. As she watched Charles Kean and Ellen Tree on the stage, a remarkable transformation took place. "As the play proceeded," she wrote, "I became so absorbed in the story, so real and so thrillingly portrayed, that from silent weeping I took to sniffling and from sniffling to ill-repressed sobbing."[6] Later, a friend told Clement Clay, after Clay's marriage to Virginia, that he still remembered the occasion, that he had gone to see Ellen Tree but that "not half the house knew what was going on on the stage for watching the little girl in the auditorium! Never till then had I imagined the full power of the drama!"[7]

Following the theme of drama takes us to Washington in the 1850s and the first part of *Belle*. Here Virginia moved in the southern-dominated social and political circles of Washington. Here, too, the theater played a central role in Virginia's life. The climax of her Washington career came at a fancy dress ball given by Senator and Mrs. Gwin when she was given the opportunity to perform a dramatic role before a sophisticated audience. She chose a comic role, Mrs. Ruthy Partington, the popular character created by Benjamin Shillaber in *Life and Sayings of Mrs. Partington* (1854), an American version of Mrs. Malaprop.[8] Virginia not only adopted the dress and voice of this Yankee character but also improvised speech patterns and created life experiences for the role so compellingly that her husband was moved to exclaim that "when she married me America lost its Siddons."[9]

The second part of *Belle* occurs during the war years in Richmond, where Virginia was involved in the social and political lives of the Confederate leadership. Here again, a dramatic performance marked the climax of her Richmond experiences. This time it was as Mrs. Malaprop in a celebrated production of *The Rivals*. Among others who have left written accounts of this memorable occasion, Mary Chesnut notes (in a February 1864 diary entry) that "Mrs. Clay's Mrs. Malaprop was beyond our wildest hopes. . . . The back, even, of Mrs. Clay's head was eloquent as she walked away."[10]

In a sense, too, the climax of the third part of *Belle* is also a drama. After Clement Claiborne Clay is imprisoned along with Jefferson Davis, a passionate Virginia confronts President Johnson repeatedly with fervent pleas for her husband's release. The memoir ends soon after Clay gains his freedom.

In later years, her ability to recollect and dramatize the events of her life orally convinced her friends that her memories must be preserved. Yet this would never have happened if it had not been for two women: Ellalee Chapman Humes, a resident of Huntsville and an old friend of Virginia's, and Ada Sterling, a free-lance writer living in New York who was contacted by Mrs. Humes and who agreed to undertake the production of a book. Sterling is duly credited with editing *Belle,* but her modest preface does not provide much insight into the very substantial role she had in writing the book. Her letters to Mrs. Humes and to Virginia Clay (or rather to Mrs. Clopton, as Sterling addressed her) provide a more detailed, though not complete, account of how the book came into being.[11]

Sometime in 1902, Ada Sterling, then a woman in her early thirties who had to that point published only magazine articles of a miscellaneous kind, began the task ahead of her. The record does not indicate that she received any money from her sponsors, that is, Virginia's friends, and she knew that it was up to her to find a publisher. She was in Huntsville in June 1902 to assess her resources—notably, Virginia herself, in addition to heaps of papers and correspondence, which needed to be organized and mined. Old-time friends of Virginia were solicited for information and support. Once back in New York, Sterling wrote Virginia on August 22, 1902, that she knew "our course was to work at 'Wildwood,'"[12] and she returned to Alabama in October. To Mrs. Humes, Sterling wrote a letter of encouragement that contained a warning as well. "I was sure of the value of a work such as might be made of the recollections. Please observe that phraseology. I mean, quite exactly, a work to be *made* and not one which Mrs. Clopton could herself make unassisted. The bed of ore is solid and rich, but it needs mining. The road to the real gold is [so] thickly interlaced (in the matter already written by her) with impossible metaphor and redundant adjectives as to almost over power one." She concludes this long letter with a characteristic note of enthusiasm: "We are in the midst of wonderful letters, documents galore that will daunt the most malicious who engage to throw doubt on Mrs. C's recital . . . and which, if the worst were to occur today, are sufficient to make a powerful book of history."[13] The references to "matter" already written and "recital" indicate that both oral and written sources were available for the editor's use. The reason for her third journey to Wildwood in February 1903 was to collect additional "recitals."

In general, Ada Sterling's objective was clear enough, as she wrote Virginia in a letter dated July 31, 1902: "The point was made . . . that the book, if done, must be made so accurate and literary, that its interest will command a value, permanent, in the North, even more than in the South, for book-buyers as a rule, are more numerous in the North." She added this interesting comment: "What so greatly lured me in your own great character . . . is the philosophic, large grasp you have of conditions that would have embittered a smaller mind. *This* is what will charge your pages with *permanency*."[14]

This theme continued to be important. In a long letter dated July 14, 1903, Sterling wrote Virginia that she had perceived long ago that Virginia's memoirs "must be one of two things, either light and gay" and thus appeal to a popular audience, or they must compete "boldly, with the most authoritative and permanent of historians." After some inner debate, Sterling concluded that the memoirs "must saunter forth to meet the eye of critics panoplied with the armor against attack." To illustrate her point, she used the example of Joseph Holt, the United States judge advocate general, once a friend of the Clays who became Clement's persecutor. The question was whether to soften the strong accusations that Virginia made against Holt in *Belle* (which would make finding a publisher easier, among other things) or whether to accept Virginia's version. Having discovered information that supported the "hard" version of Holt's behavior, Sterling was determined to publish "unassailable" history, no matter the consequences. To the best of her ability, then, Sterling validated history and corrected Virginia's faulty memory. She organized the material and prepared a text. In this same letter, she wrote Virginia that beginning July 25, she would send her "chapter after chapter of bellum days, for you to read and verify and promptly return to me with such corrections as may occur to you."[15]

The letters from Ada Sterling to Virginia are a study in cultivating a relationship by frequent words of encouragement, admiration, and affection, tempered sometimes by obvious frustration. Nonetheless, finally, or so it seems, there was a sense of resentment, which Sterling did not openly express in her letters. For example, on February 21, 1905, she wrote a revealing letter explaining to Virginia why literary friends of hers had failed to review *Belle*: "They told me . . . that my consent to the allowing of 'A Belle of the Fifties' to go out mislabelled as an *edited* work, was a step which, unless I corrected it, would appear a very *nasty* reflection on my honor as a trained writer. They counselled me that I must at once, for all succeeding editions, correct this mis-apprehension my ultra-delicacy in this matter had created, by inserting a full, careful explanation where only such explanation could ultimately do justice to my work in the book, namely in the form of a second preface."[16] (It is interesting to note that the book, originally published in 1904, was republished in 1905 and did have a slight change in the designation of editor [although no second preface]. In the 1904 edition, the title is followed by the words "Gathered and Edited by Ada Sterling." In the 1905 edition, these words were changed to "Put into narrative form by Ada Sterling." Most scholars regard the 1905 edition as the definitive version because, in addition to this change, some other clarifications within the text were made.)

Sterling was also subjected to frustrating experiences with publishers. The first reference to a publisher appeared in a letter to Ellalee Humes dated July 19, 1902, in which Sterling described her fruitless effort to interest Harper and Brothers in an "unwritten book."[17] Later that month she was writing Virginia that she had approached McClure's and that the representative she talked to was greatly interested already.[18] Nevertheless, this too fell through. The next publisher to be mentioned was Century, but again the result of initial interest was disappointing—and interesting—news. "A partial answer has been given to me verbally," Sterling wrote Virginia on June 24, 1903, "that the sectional feeling—or rather the chief point, that of strong reference to *Joseph Holt,* will *probably* prevent the 'Century' people from handling the MS. They feel, as told in a brief interview, that Joseph Holt did good service to the country; that he did his duty, as he saw it, conscientiously; and, as the firm who launched and worked over the Nicolay-Hay book in which Mr. Holt is praised highly, they are indisposed to admit that he is to be criticised [sic]."[19] There was nothing but failure to report at the beginning of 1904: "Our work has now been turned down by three houses, to wit, the Century people, the A. S. Barnes Co. and, serially, the Harpers." Sterling then outlined various reasons that had been given for the rejections and continued with her encouragement: "My courage, however, is not diminished, nor my faith in the work's value lessened."[20]

Then, in a letter dated March 9, 1904, there is the first reference to a new publisher, though not by name. This time, in spite of the fact that two years earlier Sterling had expressed the hope of a 25 percent royalty, the lower figure of 10 percent was accepted by both, and a definite offer was made by Doubleday, Page and Co.[21] There is no record in the Sterling letters when or by whom the final book title was chosen. Throughout the negotiations with Doubleday the book was referred to either as *Memoirs* or as *Memoirs of Mrs. Clay of Alabama.* Perhaps Sterling (or someone from Doubleday) discovered the final title of *Belle* from a sentence in Sara Rice Pryor's *Reminiscences of Peace and War:* "The belle in the fifties lived in an expansive time."[22] Mrs. Pryor's book had been recently published by Macmillan and of course was highly visible.

In any case, competition was very much on Sterling's mind. The Civil War, like no other event in American history, motivated women to keep diaries and journals. Later, they wrote memoirs, a number of which found publishers in the nineteenth and twentieth centuries and some of which are still being discovered as we approach the twenty-first century. By far the greater proportion of this kind of literature was published by Southern women (or for them by their descendants) for the obvious reason that the war had an impact more or less onerous on virtually every inhabitant of the South. The results of the rude intrusion of public events into the lives of articulate and educated women are an important part of that "remarkable literature [of] speeches and pamphlets, private letters and diaries, personal memoirs and journalistic reports" that, according to Edmund Wilson, flourished in contrast to the dearth of belles lettres.[23]

The closest of these memoirs to *Belle* both in terms of publication date and in scope (in time and place) was Sara Rice Pryor's *Reminiscences of Peace and War.* Mrs. Roger A. Pryor, to use her "authorial" name, had, like Virginia, spent much of the 1850s in Washington. Also, as the wife of a man who was a diplomat and then a congressman, she was acquainted with most of the same persons, including Presidents Pierce and Buchanan, who figure prominently in *Belle*.[24] And as a Virginian, Sara Pryor was equally familiar with the Richmond scene. Mrs. Pryor had noted, as had other observers, that Southern women dominated Washington society in the 1850s and that "the wittiest and brightest of them all was Mrs. Clay, the wife of the Senator from Alabama. She was extremely clever, the soul of every company."[25]

Ada Sterling duly noted this competitor. In a letter dated November 9, 1904, to "My dear sweet Mrs. Clopton," Sterling wrote that a friend "came in yesterday and says *some* paper . . . declares that 'A Belle of the Fifties' *obscures Mrs. Pryor's book,* just out. (I have read it, twice. It is highly interesting, but scattered, and, strangely enough the *Washington* portion lacks the *intime* quality which makes *your* perspective so delightful. It reads as if made up, at least in spots, from old newspaper files and, from the *out*side of things.)" She continued in the same letter, "Think of it, *another* firm here, Appleton & Co., says they have *another* book of Southern reminiscences which will knock *Mrs. Clay's* all to pieces! They won't tell the lady's name, but say she is better known than Mrs. Clay!!!! Upon hearing this I rang *our* publishers up. 'Let 'em come!' was the response. 'Bring on your popular ladies! All you want of them, but we bank on *ours!*'"[26]

This mysterious lady was Mary Boykin Chesnut, as Sterling soon discovered and announced in a postscript of a letter to Virginia dated around March 25, 1905: "Have you seen the announcements of 'A Diary of [sic] Dixie' supposed to be Mrs. Chesnut's diary, edited by *two* women? . . . They *announce* that Mrs. Chesnut was the most *distinguished woman the south ever produced*—They should attach a *bell* to *that* Chesnut. *N'est ce pas?*" Sterling shrewdly added, "I wonder if *her* diary was written *during* or *after* the time it purports to tell of."[27]

Here is another figure who played a part in Virginia Clay's life, and though the purview of Mary Chesnut's *Diary* is the

Civil War only, their acquaintance began in Washington. Indeed, Virginia Clay was so well known that when James Chesnut was elected to the U.S. Senate in 1856, one of his friends suggested "that as Mr. Clay stood sponsor for you in the Senate I hope she [Mrs. Chesnut] and Mrs. Clay will be great friends. I have often heard that Mrs. Clay *was* the first woman in Washington."[28] Virginia did become Mary Boykin Chesnut's friend and remained her friend until Mrs. Chesnut's death in 1886.

Considering their memoirs only, there are obvious and significant differences between these two sophisticated women. Virginia did not have, or at least did not exhibit, any of the introspective habits of mind that illuminate Mary Chesnut's *Diary*, and the tragic perspective eludes Virginia. (Remember that she chose to play comic characters in her public appearances on the "stage.") Mary Chesnut's mind is more richly furnished than Virginia's, thanks to a lifetime of deep reading, and consequently she is able to transcend some of the prejudices of her society. Compare, for example, their opinions on slavery.[29] Yet, in one way at least, Mrs. Clay was more independent than Mrs. Chesnut. Virginia lived as she pleased; Mary Chesnut was at the command of her husband. Both were childless, which enhanced their independence but which also made them much less selfless than women were supposed to be. They both disliked the isolation of country life and found Washington especially civilizing and exhilarating. Mary Chesnut felt this even more keenly than Virginia, the tedium of plantation society falling heavily on her when she was exiled to the family estate, Mulberry.[30] Nonetheless, one also senses an underlying rivalry for center stage, even in Richmond, where the very center was already occupied by Varina Davis. Thus, though Mary Chesnut had been dead for nineteen years when *A Diary from Dixie* appeared, Ada Sterling expressed her own jealousy on behalf of Virginia.

Two more books by women who were much younger than

the Pryor, Clay, Chesnut triumvirate but who also focused on the same political and social world of war time Richmond were published within the next few years. The first was *A Southern Girl in '61: The War-Time Memories of a Confederate Senator's Daughter,* by Mrs. D. Giraud Wright (the daughter of Texas senator Louis Wigfall), published in 1905 also by Doubleday and Page. The second was *Recollections Grave and Gay,* by Mrs. Burton Harrison (Constance Cary), who after the war married Jefferson Davis's secretary. This book was published in 1911 by Charles Scribner's Sons.

This glut undoubtedly affected the demand for *Belle,* and sales figures were a great disappointment for Ada Sterling and for Virginia. For one thing, both women were in need financially, though Sterling at times believed that her professional life was on the line as well. On February 21, 1905, she wrote Virginia that she had nothing to report on the financial question, "not having received one penny from the publishers nor a report to the present from them."[31] On March 13, 1905, Sterling wrote that she had received the publisher's statement showing that "3005 copies have been sold only. (I had heard prophecies, once upon a time, that 100,000 copies would be easily sold if the book were once on the market!!)" The royalty check she received was $761, which, she wrote, she was not cashing until her lawyer had contacted the publisher for verification.[32] Sterling's disillusionment with the publisher was total and that in turn was transferred to *Belle.* She wrote to Mrs. Humes (but not to Virginia) in September of 1905 that "the mere name of "A Belle" etc. had been enough, for months, to depress me horribly."[33] *Belle* was not a unique case of dashed hopes and expectations. According to Ishbel Ross, Varina Davis's biographer, *Jefferson Davis, A Memoir by His Wife* (1891) "never found its audience," and the money Varina needed so badly never materialized.[34] And Ada Sterling had found copies of *Reminiscences of Peace and War* remaindered at fifty cents a copy because, as she learned from a bookseller, the book was a failure.[35]

The vagaries of the American publishing and reading world of the 1890s and early 1900s are beyond the purview of this introduction, but a few words about literary reviews might be relevant. One assumes that, roughly speaking, the number of reviews as well as the consensus of the reviewers will affect the success of a book. If that is indeed the case, then *A Diary from Dixie* must have fared better than *Belle* in the marketplace. The *Book Review Digest,* volume 1, 1905, cites seven reviews for *Diary* and none for *Belle.*[36] The *Nation* had reviewed *Belle* in the December 1, 1904, issue by an anonymous reviewer (identified elsewhere as G. A. Thayer) in a two-paragraph piece, much of which consisted of a hostile analysis of the antebellum Southern culture. In the reviewer's opinion, "The portions of the book which deal with the period before secession are largely recollections of showy festivities at which gallant men showered compliments upon lovely and beautiful women." When he comes to the "more interesting" final section of *Belle,* however, he admitted that Davis and Clay "were victims of the fierce and somewhat unreasoning resentment which followed Lincoln's death."[37] *A Diary from Dixie* commanded a longer review in the *Nation* (June 15, 1905), but the judgments again are ambivalent. On the one hand, according to the reviewer, "among the ten or fifteen somewhat similar books written by Confederate women this one shows least of the typical Southern spirit of self-sacrifice, and contains more vain chatter about looks and flirtations and love-making than all the others together." On the other hand, the reviewer also described Mrs. Chesnut as open minded and candid, and he grudgingly conceded that "scattered here and there are many vivid descriptions, both interesting and historically valuable."[38] Nevertheless, a bias against the South, women, or both led the reviewer to trivialize everything he or she touched.

The long review that appeared in the September 18, 1904, edition of the *New York Times* should have given *Belle,* which had just been published, a head start, but it apparently failed to do so. The review is worth noting, however, as an instance of a warm reception of a Southern woman's book, in contrast to that in the *Nation.* The review began on a positive note: "Excellent reading and rich in anecdote is the book entitled 'A Belle of the Fifties,' issued yesterday." Much of the review consisted of passages from the book that were well used to support the reviewer's claim that the book "will throw new light upon events, men, and measures of the days immediately following the close of our civil war."[39]

The final mention of royalty money in the Sterling letters occurred in a letter from Sterling to Virginia dated June 15, 1907: "I have had nothing from the D. P.'s [Doubleday and Page] since they sent $56 in Feb. of which you know." In the same letter she notified Virginia that she was shipping back to Huntsville all of the letters that she had gotten from Virginia to use in the preparation of *Belle.*[40] At one time Sterling had contemplated editing the Clay correspondence for publication; unfortunately, she was too discouraged to begin such a project. But Sterling had invested "money . . . as well as time, labor, literary reputation etc." as she put it in a letter to Mrs. Humes,[41] which has already been alluded to, and she could risk nothing further. By 1907 she was working on a translation of the *Autobiography of George Sand,* and she mentioned other projects in a letter to Virginia dated June 15, 1907, none of which "will have D. P. complications."[42]

In her subsequent career Ada Sterling wrote poetry and verse dramas as well as nonfiction prose, including a book titled *The Jew and Civilization*. A dinner in her honor took place at the Ritz Carlton on February 7, 1924, and she received tributes by letter and speech from such notable figures as Nicholas Murray Butler, president of Columbia University, and Adolph Ochs, publisher of the *New York Times*. She died September 1, 1939, and ironically enough, her obituary in the *New York Times* two days later cited *Belle of the Fifties* as her first book (with no mention of Virginia Clay) and mistakenly labeled it as a work of fiction.[43]

Virginia had moved on to other things as well, including leadership in the Alabama women's suffrage movement, evidence of her own ability to transcend tradition and popular opinion, which in Alabama was strongly against giving women the vote. In fact, Alabama never ratified the Nineteenth Amendment to the Constitution. Yet Virginia continued to enjoy strong community appreciation, and her ninetieth birthday, January 16, 1915, "was a great occasion in Huntsville . . . celebrated . . . with a great reception given by her friend, Mrs. Milton Humes."[44] Six months later, on June 23, 1915, Virginia Clay-Clopton died, leaving as a lasting legacy a book about herself; about her husband, his family and community; about Alabama and the South; and about her country. "My memory seems a Herculaneum," she wrote in a passage in her book, "in which let but a spade of thought be sunk, and some long hidden treasure is unearthed."[45] *A Belle of the Fifties* is not diminished by thinking of Ada Sterling as that "blade of thought" and giving due credit to a Northern coauthor. Nor is the work accomplished by Ada Sterling diminished by some errors that still remained in the book even after all her efforts. She was, after all, writing about one of the most turbulent times in American history. In this edition, we have added extensive annotations that both correct these errors and illuminate the text for the modern-day reader.[46]

*A Belle of the Fifties* has been out of print for almost thirty years, which is surprising given the interest in women's history and in the history of that period. With this reprint, the reader has the opportunity to understand another dimension of the southern woman—the belle, if you will. As an admirer of Virginia wrote to her on the death of Clay, "Truly your life, with its opposite poles in Washington and Alabama, has been a varied one!" And, we might add, a most interesting one, indeed, for both the scholar and the general reader.

## NOTES

1. Ulrich Bonnell Phillips, *A History of Transportation of the Eastern Cotton Belt to 1860* (New York: Columbia University Press, 1908), 395. This excellent monograph was dedicated to "The Dominant Class of the South."

2. Central to the genealogical literature are Whit Tunstall, *The First Tunstalls in Virginia and Some of Their Descendants* (San Antonio, Tex.: n.p., 1950); Herbert Bemerton Battle and Lois Yelverton, *The Battle Book: A Genealogy of the Battle Family in America* (Montgomery, Ala.: Paragon Press, 1930); and Claiborne Thweatt Smith Jr. and J. Byron Hilliard, "Arrington of North Carolina," in *Southside Virginia Families,* edited by John Bennett Boddie (Redwood City, Calif.: Pacific Coast, 1955), 2: 1–20. See also Thomas Perkins Abernethy, "Henry Watkins Collier," in *Dictionary of American Biography,* edited by Allen Johnson and Dumas Malone (New York: C. Scribner's Sons, 1928–1936), 4: 302–303; and, for Collier and Alfred Battle, respectively, Thomas McAdory Owen, *History of Alabama and Dictionary of Alabama Biography* (1921; reprint, Spartanburg, S.C.: Reprint Company, 1978), 3: 112–115, 380.

3. *Marmion,* canto 6, stanza 24, line 8; it is repeated in stanza 26, line 19, with mention of "stainless Tunstall's banner." In note 92 Scott explains that "Sir Brian Tunstall, called in the romantic language of the time, Tunstall the Undefiled, was one of the few Englishmen of rank slain at Flodden." The epithet may have been "derived . . . from

his white armour and banner, the latter bearing a white cock, about to crow, as well as from his unstained loyalty and knightly faith."

4. For studies of the Clay family, see Frank Lawrence Owsley, "The Clays in Early Alabama History," *Alabama Review* 2 (October 1949): 243–268, and Ruth Ketring Nuermberger, *The Clays of Alabama: A Planter-Lawyer-Politician Family* (Lexington, Ky.: University of Kentucky Press, 1958).

5. Nuermberger, *Clays of Alabama*, 84. The two best essays on Virginia Clay are Carol Bleser and Frederick M. Heath, "The Clays of Alabama: The Impact of the Civil War on a Southern Marriage," in *In Joy and in Sorrow: Women, Family, and Marriage in the Victorian South, 1830–1900*, edited by Carol Bleser (New York: Oxford University Press, 1991) and a chapter biography, "Virginia Tunstall Clay—Alabama Belle," in Bell Irvin Wiley, *Confederate Women: Contributions in American History*, no. 38 (Westport, Conn.: Greenwood Press, 1975). Their interpretations of Virginia Clay are somewhat different. Bleser and Heath have a more favorable view of Virginia and bring to their analysis a more modern and feminist perspective.

6. Virginia Clay-Clopton, *A Belle of the Fifties: Memoirs of Mrs. Clay of Alabama* (New York: Doubleday, Page and Co., 1905), 10.

7. *Belle*, 11.

8. Benjamin Shillaber (1814–1890) was a humorist, newspaperman, and poet. Mrs. Malaprop, famous for her misapplications of words, was a character created by British dramatist Richard Brinsley Sheridan (1751–1816) in his comedy *The Rivals* (1775).

9. *Belle*, 136 n. Sarah Siddons (1755–1831) was the most famous of all English actresses.

10. C. Vann Woodward, ed., *Mary Chesnut's Civil War* (New Haven: Yale University Press, 1981), 553.

11. On her death in 1915, Virginia left all her papers and the old Clay plantation home, which she called Wildwood, to a cousin, Bettie V. Adams, who lived with her and cared for her during her declining years. Mrs. Adams sold Virginia's family papers to Duke University in 1930. This collection, called the Clement Claiborne Clay Papers, contains 8,545 items. There is also a small collection of Clay papers in the Heritage Room of the Huntsville Public Library, Huntsville, Ala-

bama, and in the Alabama Department of Archives and History, Montgomery, Alabama. See "Huntsville Biography, Clay," typed manuscript, Clay Collection, Huntsville Public Library, and Nuermberger, *Clays of Alabama*, 325. Letters written by Ada Sterling relating to the making of *Belle* are to be found in two collections: the Ada Sterling Manuscripts in the Special Collections Library of Duke University and a much smaller collection in the Huntsville Public Library. In subsequent notes, these sources will be indicated as Duke or Huntsville.

12. Ada Sterling to Virginia Clay (whom she actually addressed as "Dear Mrs. Clopton"), August 22, 1902, Huntsville.

13. Ada Sterling to Mrs. Humes, October 22, 1902, Huntsville.

14. Sterling to Clay, July 31, 1902, Huntsville.

15. Sterling to Clay, July 14, 1903, Duke.

16. Sterling to Clay, February 21, 1905, Duke.

17. Sterling to Humes, July 19, 1902, Huntsville.

18. Sterling to Clay, July 31, 1902, Huntsville.

19. Sterling to Clay, June 24, 1903, Duke.

20. Sterling to Clay, January 17, 1904, Duke.

21. Sterling to Clay, March 9, 1904, and March 28, 1904, Duke.

22. Mrs. Roger A. Pryor [Sara Rice Pryor], *Reminiscences of Peace and War* (New York: Macmillan, 1904), 71.

23. Edmund Wilson, *Patriotic Gore: Studies in the Literature of the American Civil War* (New York: W. W. Norton, 1944), ix.

24. Already known in Washington and Richmond as a political journalist and for a successful mission to Greece, Roger Atkinson Pryor (1828–1919) succeeded to Goode's Virginia congressional seat and served from 1859 to 1861. Later he was a Confederate brigadier general and—much later—a justice of the New York Supreme Court.

25. Pryor, *Reminiscences*, 81.

26. Sterling to Clay, November 9, 1904, Huntsville.

27. Sterling to Clay, ca. March 25, 1905, Duke. Note that the actual title of the book was *A Diary from Dixie*.

28. Elisabeth Muhlenfeld, *Mary Boykin Chesnut* (Baton Rouge: Louisiana State University Press, 1981), 246. In Washington the Chesnuts joined the Clays' "mess" along with other distinguished company. Vir-

ginia referred to Mary Chesnut in *Belle* as "our well-loved Mrs. Chesnut" (50).

29. In many passages in her diary, Mary Chesnut condemns the slave trade, regards slavery as an evil, and says that if she could choose for herself, she would never own slaves. For one example of such opinions, see Woodward, *Mary Chesnut's Civil War,* 726. Virginia Clay, on the other hand, concludes chapter 16 of *Belle* with a lament for the Old South, including an account of happy slaves who were better off then than in the postemancipation world.

30. Mary Chesnut wrote Virginia a poignant letter from the Mulberry plantation shortly after the war's end that expresses her sense of loss: "There are nights here with the moonlight, cold & ghastly, & the whippoorwills, & the screech owls alone disturbing the silence when I could tear my hair & cry aloud for all that is past and gone." See Muhlenfeld, *Mary Boykin Chesnut,* 133.

31. Sterling to Clay, February 21, 1905, Duke.

32. Sterling to Clay, March 13, 1905, Duke.

33. Sterling to Humes, September 10, 1905, Duke.

34. Ishbel Ross, *First Lady of the South: The Life of Mrs. Jefferson Davis* (New York: Harper and Brothers, 1958), 375.

35. Sterling to Clay and Humes, November 14, 1905, Duke. The practice of remaindering books seems to have been a discovery for Sterling. She confessed in this letter that she was too cowardly to inquire about *Belle's* fate.

36. These reviews of Chesnut's *Diary from Dixie* were favorable. The critics (and readers) did not know that Mrs. Chesnut had carefully and extensively reworked her wartime diary, as can be illustrated by this unsuspecting critic: "Her diary could not have been more entertainingly written if she had intended it for publication." Jeannette Gilder, *Critic* 46 (June 1905): 507.

37. *Nation,* December 1, 1904, 446.

38. *Nation,* June 15, 1905, 485, 486.

39. Martha Young, "New Anecdotes and Piquant Tales from 'A Belle of the Fifties,'" *New York Times,* September 18, 1904, sec. 4, p. 2.

40. Sterling to Clay, June 15, 1907, Duke.

41. Sterling to Humes, September 10, 1905, Duke.

42. Sterling to Clay, June 15, 1907, Duke.

43. *New York Times,* September 3, 1939, 19. Another error is her age, which is given as seventy-six in the obituary. Other sources, however, including the *Union Catalogue,* give her birth date as 1870.

44. Nuermberger, *Clays of Alabama,* 318.

45. *Belle,* 119.

46. In a copy of *Belle* that Sterling originally autographed for a friend and that is now in the Huntsville Library, the second sentence on page viii of the preface is scored in the right margin ("I often found myself spellbound by the descriptive powers" and so on) with this handwritten note at the bottom of the page: "It is only fair to say that these powers, at the age of 83 led to the most extravagant departures from the truth; so much so that her nephew, Mr. William Clay, warned me that 'Auntie couldn't speak the truth if she tried.' I have therefore retained her spirit only in writing this book, drawing my facts from several thousand letters, written during the war, and relying upon no human memory for them."

A Belle of the Fifties

# PREFACE

THE memoirs of "Mrs. Clay, of Alabama," by which title Mrs. Clement C. Clay, Jr. (now Mrs. Clay-Clopton), was known during the period comprised by 1850–87, begin in the middle of the second decade of the nineteenth century, the scenes being laid among the affluent plantations of North Carolina and Alabama, and, continuing through two brilliant administrations at the national capital, close, as she emerges from the distresses which overtook her and her husband after the never-to-be-forgotten tragedy that plunged a nation into mourning—the death of Mr. Lincoln.

In the researches made in order to obviate all possible inaccuracies in these memoirs (a precaution always necessary where one's life has been long and experiences so varied), I have come upon no record of any other woman of her time who has filled so powerful a place politically, whose belleship has been so long sustained, or whose magnetism and compelling fascinations have swayed others so universally as have those of Mrs. Clay-Clopton. In the unrestful days at the capital which preceded the Civil War her winning personality was such as to cause even those whom she esteemed the enemies of her section, in those days when "sections" were, to be covetous of her smiles. At no period of her long career have her unique courage, her beautiful optimism, her inspiring buoyancy been more accentuated than during the making of the present book. The recalling of incident after incident, step by step, of so great a procession of memories as are here set down is a task from which many persons of twoscore years might shrink. At the ripe age of almost eight decades Mrs. Clay-Clopton entered into the work with a heart as light as a girl's and a sustained energy and enthusiasm that have been as remarkable as they are unparalleled. While preparing these pages I enjoyed a daily intercourse with her extending over eight months, during which time I often found myself spellbound by the descriptive powers which nearly a half century ago compelled the admiration of leading men and women of that day.

"My wife was amazed at your eloquence," wrote Attorney-General Jeremiah Black in 1866, and in succeeding letters urged Mrs. Clay to put her experiences with Messrs. Johnson, Holt and Stanton into book form. To these and urgings as powerful from many quarters, reiterated during the past forty years, until the present work was undertaken, Mrs. Clay-Clopton has remained indifferent. Her recollections of a long life are now gathered in response to a wide and insistently expressed desire to see them preserved in a concrete form ere the crowding years shall have made impossible the valuable testimony she is able to bear to ante-bellum and bellum conditions in her dearly loved South land. To that end many friends of Mrs. Clay-Clopton have lent an eager aid, and it is an acknowledgment due to them that their names be linked here with the work they have so lovingly fostered.

The inception of the work as now presented is primarily due to Mrs. Milton Humes, of Abingdon Place, Huntsville, Alabama, a daughter of the late Governor Chapman, of that State, and the friend from her childhood of Mrs. Clay-Clopton. For many years Mrs. Humes has ardently urged upon our heroine the necessity for preserving her rich memories as a legacy, not alone to the South, but to all lovers of the romantic and eventful in our national history, to whatsoever quarter of the country they may claim a particular allegiance. Through Mrs. Humes Mrs. Clay-Clopton and I met; through her unintermitting energy obstacles that at first threatened to postpone the beginning of the work were removed, and from these initial steps she has brought a very Minerva-like wisdom and kindness to aid the work to its completion. At the instance of Mrs. Humes General Joseph Wheeler lent me a valuable sympathy; through the courtesy of General Wheeler General James H. Wilson, to whom Clement C. Clay, Jr., surrendered in 1865, kindly gave his consideration to the chapters of the memoirs in which he personally is mentioned, correcting one or two minor inaccuracies, such as misapplied military titles. Through the continued forethought of Mrs. Humes and General Wheeler Colonel Henry Watterson's attention was directed to the work, and he, too, generously scanned the manuscript then ready, at a considerable expense of time, guiding my pen, all untutored in political phrases, from some misleading slips. I owe a large debt of gratitude to Colonel Robert Barnwell Rhett, who, though an invalid while I was a guest of Mr. and Mrs. Humes in Huntsville, gave his unsparing counsels to me, enlightening me as to personages and events appertaining to the formation of the Confederate Government, which would have been unobtainable from any books at present known to me. For the acquaintance with Colonel Rhett I am, on behalf of the memoirs and for my personal pleasure, again the debtor of Mrs. Humes.

The aid of Mrs. Paul Hammond, formerly of Beech Island, South Carolina, but now residing in Jacksonville, Florida, has been peculiarly valuable. Possessed of a fine literary taste, a keen observer, and retaining a vivid recollection of the personages she encountered when a *debutante* under Mrs. Clay's chaperonage in 1857–'58 in

# PREFACE

Washington, the six or seven weeks over which our intercourse extended were a continual striking of rare lodes of incident, which lay almost forgotten in the memory of her kinswoman, Mrs. Clay-Clopton, but which have contributed greatly to the interest of certain chapters dealing with Washington life in antebellum days.

Thanks are due to Mrs. Bettie Adams for her unsparing efforts to facilitate the getting together of the necessary manuscripts to support, and, in some instances, to authenticate and amplify the remembrances carried by our heroine of the crucial times of the great internecine war; to Miss Jennie Clay, who in her editorial pursuits discovered special dates and records and placed them at my disposal in order that the repetition of certain commonly accepted errors might be avoided; and to Mrs. Frederick Myers of Savannah, daughter of Mrs. Philip Phillips, who sent for my perusal (thereby giving me valuable sidelights on the times of '61–62), her mother's letters from Ship Island, together with the latter's journal, kept during her imprisonment by General Benjamin F. Butler.

The letters of Judge John A. Campbell, contributed by his daughter, Mrs. Henrietta Lay, have been so well prized that they have become part of the structure of her friend's memoirs; to Mrs. Lay, therefore, also to Mrs. Myra Knox Semmes, of New Orleans, Mrs. Cora Semmes Ives, of Alexandria, Virginia; Mrs. Corinne Goodman, of Memphis, Tennessee; Mrs. Mary Glenn Brickell, of Huntsville, Alabama; Mrs. George Collins Levey, of England, and Judge John V. Wright, of Washington, D.C., thanks are hereby given for incidents recalled and for suggestive letters received since the work on the memoirs began.

ADA STERLING.

NEW YORK CITY, September 15, 1904.

xxxvi

# CONTENTS

# CONTENTS—*Continued*

# CONTENTS—*Continued*

# CONTENTS—*Continued*

# CONTENTS—*Continued*

xli

# CONTENTS—*Continued*

xliii

# CONTENTS—*Continued*

# CONTENTS—*Continued*

xlv

# CONTENTS—*Concluded*

# LIST OF ILLUSTRATIONS

# A BELLE OF THE FIFTIES

# A BELLE OF THE FIFTIES

## CHAPTER I

### CHILDHOOD, GIRLHOOD, MARRIAGE

MY infant days were spent in North Carolina among the kinsmen of my mother. I do not remember her, save that she was young and fair, being but twenty when she died. She was the twenty-fifth child of the family united under her father's roof, which remarkable circumstance may be explained as follows:

My grandfather, General William Arrington, who won his title in the Revolutionary War, having been left a widower with twelve children, wearying of his solitude, mounted his horse and rode over to visit the comely widow Battle, whose children also numbered twelve. The two plantations lay near together in the old "Tar Heel" State. My gallant ancestor was a successful wooer, and Mrs. Battle, *née* Williams, soon became Mrs. Arrington. Thus it happened that the little Anne—my mother—the one daughter of this union, entered the world and simultaneously into the affections of one dozen half-brothers and sisters Arrington, and as many of the Battle blood. This was a fortunate prevision for me, for, though orphaned at the outset of my earthly pilgrimage—I was but three years old when my girl-mother passed away—I found myself by no means alone, though my dear father, Dr. Peyton Randolph Tunstall, grief-stricken and sorrowful, left my native State at the death of his wife, and I was a half-grown girl ere we met again and learned to know each other.

My recollections of those early days are necessarily few; yet, were I a painter, I might limn one awful figure that lingers in my memory. She was a mulatto, to whose care for some time I was nightly confided. This crafty maid, Pleasant by name, though 'twas a misnomer, anxious to join in the diversions of the other domestics among the outlying cabins on the plantation, would no sooner tuck me into bed than she would begin to unfold to me bloodcurdling stories of "sperrits an' ghoses," and of "old blue eyes an' bloody bones" who would be sure to come out of the plum orchard and carry me to the graveyard if I did not go quickly to sleep. Fortunately, old Major Drake, of whose family I was then a member, chanced one evening to overhear this soothing lullaby, and put an end to her stories ere serious harm had been done; yet so wonderful is the retentive power of the human mind that though seventy and more momentous years have passed since I, a little fearsome child, huddled under the coverings breathless in my dread of the "bogie man," I still recall my heartless, or perhaps my thoughtless, nurse vividly.

At the age of six I was carried to Tuscaloosa, then the capital of the young State of Alabama, where I was placed in the care of my aunt, whose husband, Henry W. Collier, then a young lawyer, afterward became Chief Justice of the Supreme Court of his State, and its Governor. That first journey stretches out in my memory as an interminable pilgrimage. Mr. Fort, of Mississippi, his wife, my mother's sister, and their two children, Mary and Martha, accompanied by a large following of Negroes, being en route for their plantation in Mississippi territory, I was given into their care for delivery to my kin in Tuscaloosa. No palace-car of later days has ever eclipsed the wonders of the cavalcade our company made as we passed along through towns and villages and the occasional Indian settlements that here and there dotted the untilled lands of those early nineteenth-century days!

My uncle drove in his gig at the head of the procession, while my aunt and the children made the journey in a big pudding-shaped carriage in charge of a trusty driver, beside whom my aunt's maid sat. The carriage was built with windows at the sides, and adjustable steps, which were let down when we halted and secured in place by our Negro attendants. These followed behind the vehicles and were at hand to serve us when need arose.

Our cortege included several "Dearborns," similar in shape to the ambulances of the present, in which the old and ailing Negroes were carried, and numerous wagons containing our household goods and provisions followed behind. At night, tents were pitched, in which my aunt and the children slept, unless by chance a storm arose, when the shelter of some hostelry or farmhouse was sought. The preparations for camping were altogether exciting, the erection of tents, the kindling of fires, the unharnessing and watering and feeding of the stock, and the eager industry of the cooks and their assistants in the midst of the array of shining utensils all combining to stamp the scene upon the mind of an impressionable child.

However, in the course of time the slow rolling of our carriage became monotonous to the restive children of the caravan, and the novelty of standing at the windows and gazing over the lifting hills soon wore off. My aunt felt the fatigue less, we thought, for she was a famous soliloquist, and often talked to herself as we rode, sometimes laughing aloud at her own good company. I think we children regarded her as deranged, if harmless, until one day she proved her sanity to our complete satisfaction. In a moment of insupportable tedium we conceived the idea of dropping the little tin cups, with which each was provided, in order to see if the wheels would run over them. One after another the vessels were lowered, and each, to our intense delight, was smashed flat as the proverbial pancake. When my aunt discovered our mischief, being a gentle soul, she merely reprimanded us, and at the next settlement purchased others; but when these and yet others followed the fate of the first, she became less indulgent. Switches were cut from the forest trees, three pairs of pink palms tingled with the punishment then and there administered, and the remembrance thereof restrained my cousins' and my own destructiveness for the remainder of the journey.

Arrived at Tuscaloosa, I spent four years in the shelter of the motherly affection of my aunt, Mrs. Collier, when, her health failing, I was placed in the home of my mother's brother, Alfred Battle, a wealthy planter, residing a day's journey from the little capital. My recollections of that early Alabama life centre themselves about a great white house set in widening grounds, in the midst of which was a wondrous sloe-tree, white with blooms. Many times I and my cousins played under it by moonlight, watching the shadows of the branches as they trembled on the white-sanded earth below, wondering at them, and not sure whether they were fairies' or angels' or witches' shapes. Around that tree, too, we played "Chickamy, Chickamy, Craney Crow," and, at the climax, "What o'clock, Old Witch?" would scamper wildly to elude the pursuit of the imaginary old witch. Here, a healthy and happy child, I pursued my studies. My uncle's wife, a woman of marked domestic tastes, taught me to sew and knit and to make a buttonhole, and I made progress in books under the guidance of a visiting teacher; but, my task ended, I flew to the meadows and orchards and to the full-flowering clover-field, or to the plantation nursery to see the old mammies feed the babies with "clabber," with bread well crumbed in it, or *cush*, made of bread soaked in gravy and softly mashed.

It was during this bucolic period of my life that the stars fell. I did not witness these celestial phenomena, being sound asleep as a child should be; but, for years afterward, time was marked from that great event. I remember perfectly my aunt's description of it. People ran from their houses weeping and falling on their knees, praying for mercy and forgiveness. Everywhere the terrifying belief spread that the Day of Judgment was at hand; and nights were made vocal with the exhortations of the black preachers who now became numerous upon the plantation. To very recent days old Negroes have dated their calendar from "de year when de stars fell."

Ah, me! how long ago that time of childhood's terrors and delights in that young open country! Of all my early playmates, but one, my cousin William Battle, remains, a twin relic of antiquity! From the first we were cronies; yet we had a memorable disagreement upon one occasion which caused a slight breach between us. We were both intensely fond of my aunt's piano, but my cousin was compelled to satisfy his affection for music in secret; for Uncle Battle, who heartily encouraged my efforts, was positive in his disapproval of those of my cousin. He thought piano-playing in a man to be little short of a crime, and was quite resolved his son should not be guilty of it. My cousin and I, therefore, connived to arrange our practice in such a way as would allow him to finish his practice at the instrument before my uncle's return from the day's duties.

Upon the fatal occasion of our disagreement, however, I refused, upon my cousin's appearance, to yield my seat, whereupon, losing his temper, he gave me a tap on the cheek. In a moment the struggle was on! Our

tussle was at its height, I on top and pummelling with all
my might, when, the door opening suddenly, a
startled cousin appeared.

"La!" she exclaimed in terror, "Cousin Will and
Virginia are fighting!"

"No, we're not!" I replied stoutly. "We're just
playing;" and I retired with tufts of reddish hair in both
hands, but leaving redder spots on the face of my cousinly
antagonist. He, thoroughly satisfied to be released, no
longer desired to play the piano, nor *with me*. His head
has long been innocent of hair, an hereditary development, but he has always asserted that his baldness is
attributable to "My cousin, Mrs. Clay, who, in our
youthful gambols, scalped me."

During my twelfth year, my uncle removed to Tuscaloosa, where my real school days began. It was the good
fortune of the young State at that time to have in the
neighbourhood of its capital many excellent teachers,
among whom was my instructress at the school in Tuscaloosa to which I now was sent. I cannot refrain from
telling a strange incident in her altogether remarkable
life. From the beginning it was full of unusual vicissitudes. By birth an English gentlewoman, her mother
had died while she was yet an infant. In the care of a
young aunt, the child was sent to America to be brought
up by family connections residing here. On the long
sailing voyage the infant sickened and, to all appearances,
died. The ship was in midocean, and the young guardian,
blaming her own inexperience, wept bitterly as preparations went on for the burial. At last, all else being ready,
the captain himself came forward to sew the little body
in the sack, which when weighted would sink the hapless
baby into the sea. He bent over the little form, arranging
it, when by some strange fortune a bottle of whisky,
which he carried in his pocket, was spilled and the contents began to flow upon the child's face. Before an

exclamation could be made the little one opened its eyes and gave so many evidences of life that restoratives were applied promptly. The infant recovered and grew to womanhood. She became, when widowed, the mistress of a school in our little capital, and her descendants, in many instances, have risen to places of distinction in public life.

An instructress of that period to whom the women of early Alabama owed much was Maria Brewster Brooks, who, as Mrs. Stafford, the wife of Professor Samuel M. Stafford, became celebrated, and fills a page of conspicuous value in the educational history of the State. She was born on the banks of the Merrimac and came to Tuscaloosa in her freshest womanhood. First her pupil, and afterward her friend, our mutual affection, begun in the early thirties, continued until her demise in the eighties. Many of her wards became in after years notable figures in the social life of the national capital, among them Mrs. Hilary Herbert.

In Tuscaloosa there resided, besides my Aunt Collier, few of my father's and mother's kin, and by a natural affinity I fell under the guardianship of my father's brother, Thomas B. Tunstall, Secretary of State of Alabama. He was a bachelor; but all that I lacked in my separation from my father my uncle supplied, feeding the finer sides of my nature, and inspiring in me a love of things literary even at an age when I had scarce handled a book. My uncle's influence began with my earliest days in Alabama. My aunt, Mrs. Collier, was delicate, Mrs. Battle domestic; Uncle Battle was a famous business man; and Uncle Collier was immersed in law and increasing political interests; but my memory crowds with pictures of my Uncle Tom, walking slowly up and down, playing his violin, and interspersing his numbers with some wise counsel to the child beside him. He taught me orally of poetry, and music, of letters and philosophy, and of the great world's great interests. He early instilled in me a pride of family, while reading to me Scott's fine tribute to Brian Tunstall, "the stainless knight," or, as he rehearsed stories of Sir Cuthbert Tunstall, Knight of the Garter, and Bishop of London in the time of gentle Queen Anne; and it was in good uncle Tom's and my father's company that the fascinations of the drama were first revealed to me.

While I was yet a school-girl, and so green that, had I not been protected by these two loving guardians, I would have been eaten up by the cows on the Mobile meadows, I was taken to see "The Gamester," in which Charles Kean and Ellen Tree were playing. It was a remarkable and ever-remembered experience. As the play proceeded, I became so absorbed in the story, so real and so thrillingly portrayed, that from silent weeping I took to sniffling and from sniffling to ill-repressed sobbing. I leaned forward in my seat tensely, keeping my eyes upon the stage, and equally oblivious of my father and uncle and the strangers who were gazing at me on every side. Now and then, as I sopped the briny outflow of my grief, realising in some mechanical manner that my handkerchief was wet, I would take it by two corners and wave it back and forth in an effort to dry it; but all the while the tears gushed from my eyes in rivulets. My guardians saw little of the play that night, for the amusement I afforded these experienced theatre-goers altogether exceeded in interest the mimic tragedy that so enthralled me.

When the curtain fell upon the death-scene I was exhausted; but another and counteracting experience awaited me, for the after-piece was "Robert Macaire," and now, heartily as I had wept before, I became convulsed with laughter as I saw the deft pickpocket (impersonated by Crisp, the comedian), courtly as a king, bowing in the dance, while removing from the unsuspecting ladies and gentlemen about him their brooches and jewels! My absorption in the performance was so great that I scarce heard the admonitions of my father and uncle, who begged me, in whispers, to control myself. Nor did I realise there was another person in the house but the performers on the stage and myself.

Years afterward, while travelling with my husband, he recognised in a fellow traveller a former friend from southern Alabama, a Mr. Montague, and brought him to me to present him. To my chagrin, he had scarcely taken my hand when he burst into immoderate and inexplicable laughter.

"Never," said he to Mr. Clay, "shall I forget the time when I first saw your wife! We went to see Tree; but, sir, not half the house knew what was going on on the stage for watching the little girl in the auditorium! Never till then had I imagined the full power of the drama! Her delight, her tears and laughter, I am sure, were remembered by the Mobilians long after the 'stars' acting was forgotten."

That visit to Mobile was my first flight into the beautiful world that lay beyond the horizon of my school life. In the enjoyments devised for me by my father in those few charmed days, I saw, if not clearly, at least prophetically, what of beauty and joy life might hold for me. Upon our arrival in the lovely little Bay city, my father, learning of a ball for which preparations were on foot, determined I should attend it. Guided perhaps in his choice of colour by the tints of health that lay in his little daughter's cheeks, he selected for me a gown of peach-blossom silk, which all my life I have remembered as the most beautiful of dresses, and one which transformed me, heretofore confined to brown holland gowns by my prudent aunt, Mrs. Battle, as truly as Cinderella was changed into a princess.

Upon the evening of that never-to-be-forgotten Boat Club Ball, blushing and happy, eager, with delightful anticipations, yet timorous, too, for my guardians, the Battles, had disapproved of dancing and had rigorously excluded this and other worldly pleasures from their ward's accomplishments, I was conducted by my father to the ball.  In my heart lay the fear that I would be, after all, a mere looker-on, or appear awkward if I should venture to dance as did the others; but neither of these misgivings proved to have been well founded.

My father led me at once to Mme. Le Vert, then the reigning queen of every gathering at which she appeared, and in her safe hands every fear vanished.  I had heard my elders speak frequently of her beauty, and somehow had imagined her tall.  She was less so than I had pictured, but so winning and cordial to me, a timid child, that I at once capitulated before the charm she cast over everyone who came into conversation with her.  I thought her face the sweetest I had ever seen.  She had a grace and frankness which made everyone with whom she talked feel that he or she alone commanded her attention.  I do not recall her making a single *bon mot*, but she was vivacious and smiling.  Her charm, it seemed to me, lay in her lovely manners and person and her permeating intellectuality.

I remember Mme. Le Vert's appearance on that occasion distinctly, though to describe it now seems garish.  To see her then was bewildering, and all her colour was harmony.  She wore a gown of golden satin, and on her hair a wreath of coral flowers, which her morocco shoes matched in hue.  In the dance she moved like a bird on the wing.  I can see her now in her shining robe, as she swayed and glided, holding the shimmering gown aside as she floated through the "ladies' chain."  The first dance of my life was a quadrille, *viz-à-vis* with this renowned beauty, who took me under her protection and encouraged me from time to time.

"Don't be afraid, my dear," she would sweetly say,

"Do just as I do," and I glided after my wonderful instructress like one enchanted, with never a mishap.

Mme. Le Vert, who in years to come became internationally celebrated, was a kinswoman of Clement Claiborne Clay, and in after times, when I became his wife, I often met her, but throughout my long life I have remembered that first meeting in Mobile, and her charm and grace have remained a prized picture in my memory.   It was of this exquisite belle that Washington Irving remarked: "But one such woman is born in the course of an empire."

It was to my Uncle Tom that I owed the one love sorrow of my life.   It was an affair of the greatest intensity while it endured, and was attended by the utmost anguish for some twelve or fourteen hours.   During that space of time I endured all the hopes and fears, the yearnings and despairs to which the human heart is victim.

I was nearing the age of fifteen when my uncle one evening bade me put on my prettiest frock and accompany him to the home of a friend, where a dance was to be given.   I was dressed with all the alacrity my old mammy was capable of summoning, and was soon ensconced in the carriage and on my way to the hospitable scene.   En route we stopped at the hotel, where my uncle alighted, reappearing in a moment with a very handsome young man, who entered the carriage with him and drove with us to the house, where he, too, was to be a guest.

Never had my eyes beheld so pleasing a masculine wonder!   He was the personification of manly beauty! His head was shapely as Tasso's (in after life I often heard the comparison made), and in his eyes there burned a romantic fire that enslaved me from the moment their gaze rested upon me.   At their warmth all the ardour, all the ideals upon which a romantic heart had fed rose in recognition of their realisation in him.   During the evening he paid me some pretty compliments, remarking upon my hazel eyes and the gleam of gold in my hair, and he touched my curls admiringly, as if they were revered by him.

My head swam! Lohengrin never dazzled Elsa more completely than did this knight of the poet's head charm the maiden that was I! We danced together frequently throughout the evening, and my hero rendered me every attention a kind man may offer to the little daughter of a valued friend. When at last we stepped into the carriage and turned homeward, the whole world was changed for me.

My first apprehension of approaching sorrow came as we neared the hotel. To my surprise, the knight was willing, nay, desired to be set down there. A dark suspicion crept into my mind that perhaps, after all, my hero might be less gallant than I had supposed, else why did he not seek this opportunity of riding home with me? If this wonderful emotion that possessed me also had actuated him—and how could I doubt it after his devotion throughout the evening?—how could he bear to part from me in this way without a single word or look of tenderness?

As the door closed behind him I leaned back in the darkest corner of the carriage and thought hard, though not hardly of him. After a little my uncle roused me by saying, "Did my little daughter enjoy this evening?"

I responded enthusiastically.

"And was I not kind to provide you with such a gallant cavalier? Isn't Colonel Jere Clemens a handsome man?"

Ah, was he not? My full heart sang out his praises with an unmistakable note. My uncle listened sympathetically. Then he continued, "Yes, he's a fine fellow! A fine fellow, Virginia, and he has a nice little wife and baby!"

No thunderbolt ever fell more crushingly upon the unsuspecting than did these awful words from the lips of my uncle! I know not how I reached my room, but once there I wept passionately throughout the night and much of the following morning.  Within my own heart I accused my erstwhile hero of the rankest perfidy; of villainy of every imaginable quality; and in this recoil of injured pride perished my first love dream, vanished the heroic wrappings of my quondam knight !

Having finished the curriculum of the institute presided over by Miss Brooks, I was sent to the "Female Academy" at Nashville, Tennessee, to perfect my studies in music and literature, whence I returned to Tuscaloosa all but betrothed to Alexander Keith McClung, already a famous duellist.  I met him during a visit to my Uncle Fort's home, in Columbus, Mississippi, and the Colonel's devotion to me for many months was the talk of two States.  He was the gallantest lover that ever knelt at a lady's feet ! Many a winsome girl admired him, and my sweet cousin, Martha Fort, was wont to say she would "rather marry Colonel McClung than any man alive"; but I—I loved him madly while with him, but feared him when away from him; for he was a man of fitful, uncertain moods and given to periods of the deepest melancholy.  At such times he would mount his horse "Rob Roy," wild and untamable as himself, and dash to the cemetery, where he would throw himself down on a convenient grave and stare like a madman into the sky for hours.  A man of reckless bravery, in after years he was the first to mount the ramparts of Monterey shouting victory.  As he ran, carrying his country's flag in his right hand, a shot whizzing by took off two fingers of his left.

I was thrown much in the company of Colonel McClung while at my uncle's home, but resisted his pleading for a binding engagement, telling him with a strange courage and frankness, ere I left Columbus, my reason for this persistent indecision.  Before leaving for the academy at Nashville, I had met, at my Uncle Collier's, in Tuscaloosa, the young legislator, Clement C. Clay, Jr., and had then had a premonition that if we should meet when I returned from school I would marry him. At that time I was an unformed girl, and he, Mr. Clay, was devoted to a young lady of the capital; but this, as I knew, was a matter of the past. I would surely meet him again at Uncle Collier's (I told Mr. McClung), and, if the attraction continued, I felt sure I would marry him. If not, I would marry him, Colonel McClung. So we parted, and, though at that time the Colonel did not doubt but that mine was a dreaming girl's talk, my premonitions were promptly realised.

Upon my return to our provincial little capital, then a community of six thousand souls, I found it thronging with gallants from every county in the State. The belles of the town, in preparation for the gayety of the legislative "season" of two months, were resplendent in fresh and fashionable toilettes. Escritoires were stocked with stationery suitable for the *billet-doux* that were sure to be required; and there, too, were the little boxes of glazed mottoed wafers, then all the fashion, with which to seal the pretty missives. All the swains of that day wrote in verse to the ladies they admired, and each tender rhyme required a suitably presented acknowledgment. I remember, though I have preserved none save those my husband wrote me, several creditable effusions by Colonel McClung, one of which began:

"Fearful and green your breathless poet stands," etc.

Shortly after my return from Columbus, I attended a ball where I danced with William L. Yancey, even then recognised for the splendour of his intellectual powers and his eloquence in the forum. I had heard him speak, and thought his address superb, and I told him so.

"Ah," he answered gayly, "if it had not been for one pair of hazel eyes I should have been submerged in a mere sea of rhetoric!"

On the night of my dance with him I wore a white

feather in my hair, and on the morrow a messenger from Mr. Yancey bore me some charming verses, addressed " To the lady with the snow-white plume ! "

I have said my strange premonitions regarding Mr. Clay were realised. Ten days after we met we were affianced. There was a hastily gathered trousseau selected in part by Mme. LeVert in Mobile, and hurried on to my aunt's home. A month later, and our marriage was celebrated with all the *éclat* our little city could provide, and the congratulations of a circle of friends that included half the inhabitants. It is sixty years since that wonderful wedding day, and of the maidens who attended me—there were six—and the happy company that thronged Judge Collier's home on that crisp February morning when I crossed the Rubicon of life, all—even the bridegroom—have passed long since into the shadowy company of memory and the dead.

That marriage feast in the morn of my life was beautiful; the low, spacious house of primitive architecture was white with hyacinths, and foliage decorated every available space. The legislature came in a body, solons of the State, and young aspirants for fame; the president and faculty of the State University, of which Mr. Clay was a favoured son; Dr. Capers, afterward Bishop of South Carolina, officiated, and, in that glorious company of old Alabamians, my identity as Virginia Tunstall was merged forever with that of the rising young statesman, Clement C. Clay, Jr.

A week of festivity followed the ceremony, and then my husband took me to my future home, among his people, in the northern part of the State. There being no railroad connection between Tuscaloosa and Huntsville in those days (the early forties), we made the journey from the capital in a big four-wheeled stage-coach. The stretch of country now comprised in the active city of Birmingham, the southern Pittsburg, was then a rugged place of rocks and boulders over which our vehicle pitched perilously. Stone Mountain reached, we were obliged to descend and pick our way on foot, the roughness of the road making the passage of the coach a very dangerous one. But these difficulties only lent a charm to us, for the whole world was enwrapped in the glamour of our youthful joys. The sunsets, blazing crimson on the horizon, seemed gloriously to proclaim the sunrise of our life.

We arrived in Huntsville on the evening of the second day of our journey. Our driver, enthusiastically proud of his part in the home-bringing of the bride, touched up the spirited horses as we crossed the Public Square and blew a bugle blast as we wheeled round the corner; when, fairly dashing down Clinton Street, he pulled up in masterly style in front of "Clay Castle." It was wide and low and spacious, as were all the affluent homes of that day, and now was ablaze with candles to welcome the travellers. All along the streets friendly hands and kerchiefs had waved a welcome to us. Here, within, awaited a great gathering of family and friends eager to see the chosen bride of a well-loved son. This was my home-coming to Huntsville, thereafter to be my haven for all time, though called in a few years by my husband's growing reputation to take my place beside him in Congressional circles at Washington.

# CHAPTER II

## Washington Personages in the Fifties

When my husband's parents were members of the Congressional circle in Washington—1829-'35—the journey to the capital from their home in northern Alabama was no light undertaking. In those early days Congressman (afterward Governor, and United States Senator) and Mrs. C. C. Clay, Sr., travelled by coach to the Federal City, accompanied by their coloured coachman, Toney (who, because of his expert driving, soon became notable in Washington), and a maid-servant, Milly, who were necessary to their comfort and station. Many days were consumed in these journeys, that lay through Tennessee, the Carolinas and Virginia, during which the travellers were exposed to all the dangers common to a young and often unsettled forest country. The tangled woods of the South land, odorous with the cedar or blossoming with dogwood, mimosa or magnolias, were often Arcadias of beauty. The land of the sky, now the object of pilgrimages for the wealthy and become the site of palaces built by kings of commerce, was then still more beautiful with primeval freshness. Far as the eye could see, as hills were scaled and valleys crossed, were verdured slopes and wooded mountain crests. The Palisades of the Tennessee, as yet scarcely penetrated by Northern tourists, were then the wonder as they still are the pride of the traveller from the South.

In 1853, my husband was elected a United States Senator, to take the seat of a former college friend, Jere Clemens, whose term had just expired, and succeeding his father C. C. Clay, Sr., after eleven years. In December of the same year, we began our trip to the capital under comparatively modern conditions. My several visits to Vermont and New Jersey Hydropathic Cures, then the fashionable sanitariums, had already inured me to long journeys. By this time steam railways had been established, and, though not so systematically connected as to make possible the taking of long trips over great distances without devious and tiresome changes, they had lessened the time spent upon the road between Alabama and Washington very appreciably; but, while in comparison with those in common use to-day, the cars were primitive, nevertheless they were marvels of comfort and speed to the travellers of the fifties. Sleeping cars were not yet invented, but the double-action seat-backs of the regular coaches, not then, as now, screwed down inexorably, made it a simple matter to convert two seats into a kind of couch, on which, with the aid of a pillow, one managed very well to secure a half repose as the cars moved soberly along.

Our train on that first official journey to Washington proved to be a kind of inchoative "Congressional Limited." We found many of our fellow passengers to be native Alabamians, the majority being on government business bent. Among them were my husband's confrère from southern Alabama, Senator Fitzpatrick and his wife, and a friendship was then and there begun among us, which lasted uninterruptedly until death detached some of the parties to it; also Congressman Dowdell, "dear old Dowdell," as my husband and everyone in the House shortly learned to call him, and James L. Orr of South Carolina, who afterward became Speaker of the House of Representatives, and Minister to Russia under President Grant. Mr. Orr, late in 1860, was one of the three commissioners sent by South Carolina to President Buchanan to arbitrate on the question of the withdrawal of United States troops from Forts Sumter and Moultrie, in Charleston Harbour.

Nor should I omit to name the most conspicuous man on that memorable north-bound train, Congressman W. R. W. Cobb, who called himself the "maker of Senators," and whom people called the most successful vote-poller in the State of Alabama. Mr. Cobb resorted to all sorts of tricks to catch the popular votes, such as the rattling of tinware and crockery—he had introduced bills to secure indigent whites from a seizure for debt that would engulf all their possessions, and in them had minutely defined all articles that were to be thus exempt, not scorning to enumerate the smallest items of the kitchen—, and he delighted in the singing of homely songs composed for stump purposes. One of these which he was wont to introduce at the end of a speech, and which always seemed to be especially his own, was called "The Homestead Bill." Of this remarkable composition there were a score of verses, at least, that covered every possible possession which the heart of the poor man might crave, ranging from land and mules to household furniture. The song began,

"Uncle Sam is rich enough to give us all a farm!" and Mr. Cobb would sing it in stentorian tones, winking, as he did so, to first one and then another of his admiring listeners, and punctuating his phrases by chewing, with great gusto, a piece of onion and the coarsest of corn "pone." These evidences of his democracy gave huge delight to the masses, though it aroused in me, a young wife, great indignation, that, in the exigencies of a public career my husband should be compelled to enter a contest with such a man. To me it was the meeting of a Damascus blade and a meat-axe, and in my soul I resented it.

In 1849 this stump-favourite had defeated the brilliant Jere Clemens, then a candidate for Congress, but immediately thereafter Mr. Clemens was named for the higher office of U. S. Senator and elected. In 1853 an exactly similar conjunction of circumstances resulted in the election of Mr. Clay. I accompanied my husband during the canvass in which he was defeated, and thereby became, though altogether innocently, the one obstacle to Mr. Cobb's usually unanimous election.

It happened that during the campaign Mr. Clay and I stopped at a little hostelry, that lay in the very centre of one of Mr. Cobb's strongest counties. It was little more than a flower-embowered cottage, kept by "Aunt Hannah," a kindly soul, whose greatest treasure was a fresh-faced, pretty daughter, then entering her "teens." I returned to our room after a short absence, just in time to see this village beauty before my mirror, arrayed in all the glory of a beautiful and picturesque hat which I had left upon the bed during my absence. It was a lovely thing of the period, which I had but recently brought back from the North, having purchased it while *en route* for Doctor Wesselhœft's Hydropathic Institute in Brattleboro, Vermont.

The little rustic girl of Alabama looked very winsome and blossomy in the pretty gew-gaw, and I asked her impulsively if she liked it. Her confusion was sufficient answer, and I promptly presented it to her, on condition that she would give me her sunbonnet in return.

The exchange was quickly made, and when Mr. Clay and I departed I wore a pea-green cambric bonnet, lined with pink and stiffened with pasteboard slats. I little dreamed that this exchange of millinery, so unpremeditated, and certainly uncalculating, was a political master-stroke; but, so it proved. It undermined Mr. Cobb's Gibraltar; for at the election that followed, the vote in that county was practically solid for Mr. Clay, where formerly Mr. Cobb had swept it clean.

When, upon the train *en route* for the capital in the winter of '53, Senator Fitzpatrick insisted upon presenting the erstwhile triumphant politician, I took the long, flail-like hand he offered me with no accentuated cordiality; my reserve, however, seemed not to disturb Mr. Cobb's proverbial complacency.

"I've got a crow to pick with you, Mrs. Clay," he began, "for that pink bonnet trick at old Aunt Hannah's!"

"And I have a buzzard to pick with you!" I responded promptly, "for defeating my husband!"

"You ought to feel obliged to me," retorted the Congressman, continuing "For I made your husband a Senator!"

"Well," I rejoined, "I'll promise not to repeat the bonnet business, if you'll give me your word never again to sing against my husband! That's unfair, for you know *he* can't sing!" which, amid the laughter of our fellow-passengers, Mr. Cobb promised.

Our entrance into the Federal City was not without its humorous side. We arrived in the early morning, about two o'clock, driving up to the National Hotel, where, owing to a mistake on the part of the night-clerk, an incident occurred with which for many a day I twitted my husband and our male companions on that eventful occasion.

At that period it was the almost universal custom for Southern gentlemen to wear soft felt hats, and the fashion was invariable when travelling. In winter, too, long-distance voyagers as commonly wrapped themselves in the blanket shawl, which was thrown around the shoulders in picturesque fashion and was certainly comfortable, if not strictly *à la mode*. My husband and the other gentlemen of our party were so provided on our journey northward, and upon our arrival, it must be admitted, none in that travel-stained and weary company would have been mistaken for a Washington exquisite of the period.

As our carriage stopped in front of the hotel door, Mr. Dowdell, muffled to the ears, his soft-brimmed hat well down over his face (for the wind was keen), stepped out quickly to arrange for our accommodation. The night was bitterly cold, and the others of our company were glad to remain under cover until our spokesman returned.

This he did in a moment or two. He appeared crest-fallen, and quite at a loss.

"Nothing here, Clay!" he said to my husband. "Man says they have no rooms!"

"Nonsense, Dowdell!" was Senator Clay's response. "You must be mistaken. Here, step inside while I inquire!" He, muffled as mysteriously, and in no whit more trust-inspiring than the dejected Mr. Dowdell, strode confidently in. Not many minutes elapsed ere he, too, returned.

"Well!" he said. "I don't understand it, but Dowdell's right! They say they have no rooms for us!"

At this we were dismayed, and a chorus of exclamations went up from men and women alike. What were we to do? In a moment, I had resolved.

"There's some mistake! I don't believe it," I said. "I'll go and see;" and, notwithstanding my husband's remonstrances, I hurried out of the carriage and into the hotel. Stepping to the desk I said to the clerk in charge: "Is it possible you have no rooms for our party in this large hostelry? Is it possible, Sir, that at this season, when Congress is convening, you have reserved no rooms for Congressional guests?" He stammered out some confused reply, but I hurried on.

"I am Mrs. Clay, of Alabama. You have refused my husband, Senator Clay, and his friend, Representative Dowdell. What does it mean?"

"Why, certainly, Madam," he hastened to say, "I have rooms for *those*." And forthwith ordered the porters to go for our luggage. Then, reaching hurriedly for various keys, he added, "I beg your pardon, Madam! I did not know you were those!"

What he did believe us to be, piloted as we were by two such brigand-like gentlemen as Senator Clay and Mr. Dowdell, we never knew; enough that our tired party were soon installed in comfortable apartments. It was by reason of this significant episode that I first realized the potency in Washington of conventional apparel and Congressional titles.

My husband being duly sworn in on the 14th of December, 1853, in a few days our "mess" was established at the home of Mr. Charles Gardner, at Thirteenth and G Streets. Here my first season in Washington was spent. Besides Senator Clay and myself, our party was composed of Senator and Mrs. Fitzpatrick, and Representatives Dowdell and Orr, and to this little nucleus of congenial spirits were afterward added in our later residences at historic old Brown's Hotel and the Ebbitt House, many whose names are known to the nation.

Though a sad winter for me, for in it I bore and buried my only child, yet my recollections of that season, as its echoes reached our quiet parlours, are those of boundless entertainment and bewildering ceremony. The season was made notable in the fashionable world by the great *fête champêtre* given by the British Minister, Mr. Crampton, and the pompous obsequies of Baron Bodisco, for many years resident Minister from Russia; but of these I learned only through my ever kind friend, Mrs. Fitzpatrick, who for months was my one medium of communication with the fashionable outside world. She was a beautiful woman, with superb carriage and rare and rich colouring, and possessed, besides, a voice of great sweetness, with which, during that winter of seclusion, she often made our simple evenings a delight. While shortly she became a leader in matters social, Mrs. Fitzpatrick was still more exalted in our own little circle for her singing of such charming songs as "Roy's Wife of Aldivalloch," and other quaint Scotch ditties. Nor was Mrs. Fitzpatrick the one musician of our "mess," for Mr. Dowdell had a goodly voice and sang with lusty enjoyment the simpler ballads of the day, to say nothing of many melodious Methodist hymns.

My experiences as an active member of Washington society, therefore, began in the autumn of 1854 and the succeeding spring, when, notwithstanding an air of gravity and reserve that was perceptible at that social pivot, the White House, the gaiety of the capital was gaining an impetus in what later appeared to me to be a veritable "merry madness."

It is true that it did not even then require the insight of a keen observer to detect in social, as in political gatherings, the constantly widening division between the Northern and Southern elements gathered in the Government City. For myself, I knew little of politics, notwithstanding the fact that from my childhood I had called myself "a pronounced Jeffersonian Democrat." Naturally, I was an hereditary believer in States' Rights, the real question, which, in an attempt to settle it, culminated in our Civil War; and I had been bred among the law-makers of the sturdy young State of Alabama, many of whom had served at the State and National capitals with marked distinction; but from my earliest girlhood three lessons had been taught me religiously, viz.: to be proud alike of my name and blood and section; to read my Bible; and, last, to know my "Richmond Enquirer." Often, as an aid to the performance of this last duty, have I read aloud its full contents, from the rates of advertisement down, until my dear uncle Tom Tunstall has fallen asleep over my childish efforts. It is not, then, remarkable that, upon my arrival, I was at once cognisant of the feeling which was so thinly concealed between the strenuous parties established in the capital.

MRS. BENJAMIN FITZPATRICK
of Alabama

During the first half of the Pierce administration, however, though feeling ran high in the Senate and the House, the surface of social life was smiling and peaceful. The President had every reason to feel kindly toward the people of the South who had so unanimously supported him, and he was as indiscriminating and impartial in his attitude to the opposing parties as even the most critical could desire; but, gradually, by a mutual instinct of repulsion that resolved itself into a general consent, the representatives of the two antagonistic sections seldom met save at promiscuous assemblages to which the exigencies of public life compelled them. To be sure, courtesies were exchanged between the wives of some of the Northern and Southern Senators, and formal calls were paid on Cabinet days, as etiquette demanded, upon the ladies of the Cabinet circle; but, by a tacit understanding, even at the entertainments given at the foreign legations, and at the houses of famous Washington citizens, this opposition of parties was carefully considered in the sending out of invitations, in order that no unfortunate *rencontre* might occur between uncongenial guests.

The White House, as I have said, was scarcely a place of gaiety. Mrs. Pierce's first appearance in public occurred at the Presidential levee, late in 1853. An invalid for several years, she had recently received a shock, which was still a subject of pitying conversation throughout the country. It had left a terrible impress upon Mrs. Pierce's spirits. While travelling from her home in New Hampshire to Washington to witness her husband's exaltation as the President of the United States, an accident, occurring at Norwalk, Connecticut, suddenly deprived her of her little son, the last surviving of her several children. At her first public appearance at the White House, clad in black velvet and diamonds, her natural pallor being thereby greatly accentuated, a universal sympathy was awakened for her. To us who knew her, the stricken heart was none the less apparent because hidden under such brave and jewelled apparel, which she had donned, the better to go through the ordeal exacted by "the dear people."

I had made the acquaintance of General and Mrs. Pierce during the preceding year while on a visit to the New England States; my husband's father had been the President's confrère in the Senate early in the forties; and my brother-in-law, Colonel Hugh Lawson Clay, had fought beside the New Hampshire General in the Mexican War. The occupants of the Executive Mansion therefore were no strangers to us; yet Mrs. Pierce's sweet graciousness and adaptability came freshly to me as I saw her assume her place as the social head of the nation. Her sympathetic nature and very kind heart, qualities not always to be perceived through the formalities of governmental etiquette, were demonstrated to me on many occasions. My own ill-health proved to be a bond between us, and, while custom forbade the paying of calls by the wife of the Chief Magistrate upon the wives of Senators, I was indebted to Mrs. Pierce for many acts of friendliness, not the least of which were occasional drives with her in the Presidential equipage.

A favourite drive in those days was throughout the length of Pennsylvania Avenue, then but sparsely and irregularly built up. The greatest contrasts in architecture existed, hovels often all but touching the mansions of the rich. The great boulevard was a perfect romping ground for the winds. Chevy Chase and Georgetown were popular objective points, and the banks of the Potomac, in shad-seining season, were alive with gay sightseers. The markets of Washington have always excelled, affording every luxury of earth and sea, and that at a price which gives to the owner of even a moderate purse a leaning toward epicureanism. In the houses of the rich the serving of dinners became a fine art.

On the first occasion of my dining at the President's table, I was struck with the spaciousness of the White House, and the air of simplicity which everywhere pervaded. Very elaborate alterations were made in the mansion for Mr. Pierce's successor, but in the day of President and Mrs. Pierce it remained practically as unimposing as in the time of President Monroe.

The most remarkable features in all the mansion, to my then unaccustomed eyes, were the gold spoons which were used invariably at all State dinners. They were said to have been brought from Paris by President Monroe, who had been roundly criticised for introducing into the White House a table accessory so undemocratic! Besides these extraordinary golden implements, there were as remarkable bouquets, made at the government greenhouses. They were stiff and formal things, as big round as a breakfast plate, and invariably composed of a half-dozen wired japonicas ornamented with a pretentious cape of marvellously wrought lace-paper. At every plate, at every State dinner, lay one of these memorable rigid bouquets. This fashion, originating at the White House, was taken up by all Washington. For an entire season the japonica was the only flower seen at the houses of the fashionable or mixing in the toilettes of the belles.

But if, for that, my first winter in Washington, the White House itself was sober, the houses of the rich Senators and citizens of Washington, of the brilliant diplomatic corps, and of some of the Cabinet Ministers, made ample amends for it. In the fifties American hospitality acquired a reputation, and that of the capital was synonymous with an unceasing, an augmenting round of dinners and dances, receptions and balls. A hundred hostesses renowned for their beauty and wit and vivacity vied with each other in evolving novel social relaxations. Notable among these were Mrs. Slidell, Mrs. Jacob

Thompson, Miss Belle Cass, and the daughters of Secretary Guthrie; Mrs. Senator Toombs and Mrs. Ogle Tayloe, the Riggses, the Countess de Sartiges and Mrs. Cobb, wife of that jolly Falstaff of President Buchanan's Cabinet, Howell Cobb. Mrs. Cobb was of the celebrated Lamar family, so famous for its brilliant and brave men, and lovely women. Highly cultured, modest as a wild wood-violet, inclined, moreover, to reserve, she was nevertheless capable of engrossing the attention of the most cultivated minds in the capital, and a conversation with her was ever a thing to be remembered. No more hospitable home was known in Washington than that of the Cobbs. The Secretary was a *bon vivant*, and his home the rendezvous of the epicurean as well as the witty and the intellectual.

Probably the most brilliant of all the embassies, until the coming of Lord and Lady Napier, was that of France. The Countess de Sartiges, who presided over it, was an unsurpassed hostess, besides being a woman of much *manner* and personal beauty; and, as did many others of the suite, she entertained on a lavish scale.

Mrs. Slidell, wife of the Senator from Louisiana, whose daughter Mathilde is now the wife of the Parisian banker, Baron Erlanger, became famous in the fifties for her matinée dances at which all the beauties and beaux of Washington thronged. Previous to her marriage with Senator Slidell she was Mlle. des Londes of New Orleans. A leader in all things fashionable, she was also one of the most devout worshippers at St. Aloysius's church. I remember with what astonishment and admiration I watched her devotions one Sunday morning when, as the guest of Senator Mallory, himself a strict Romanist, I attended that church for the purpose of hearing a mass sung.

I knew Mrs. Slidell as the devotée of fashion, the wearer of unapproachable Parisian gowns, the giver of unsurpassed entertainments, the smiling, tireless hostess; but that Sunday morning as I saw her enter a pew just ahead of Senator Mallory and myself, sink upon her knees, and, with her eyes fixed upon the cross, repeating her prayers with a concentration that proved the sincerity of them, I felt as if another and greater side of her nature were being revealed to me. I never met her thereafter without a remembrance of that morning flitting through my mind.

During the early spring of 1854 I heard much of the imposing ceremonials attending the funeral of Baron Alexandre de Bodisco, Minister from Russia since 1838, the days of Van Buren. His young wife, a native of Georgetown, was one of the first to draw the attention of foreigners to the beauty of American women. The romantic old diplomat had learned to admire his future wife when, as a little girl, upon her daily return from school, he carried her books for her. Her beauty developed with her growth, and, before she was really of an age to appear in society, though already spoken of as the most beautiful woman in Georgetown, Harriet Williams became the Baroness de Bodisco, and was carried abroad for presentation at the Russian Court. Her appearance in that critical circle created a *furore*, echoes of which preceded her return to America. I have heard it said that this young bride was the first woman to whom was given the title, "the American Rose."

I remember an amusing incident in which this lovely Baroness, unconsciously to herself, played the part of instructress to me. It was at one of my earliest dinners at the White House, ere I had thoroughly familiarised myself with the gastronomic novelties devised by the Gautiers (then the leading restaurateurs and confectioners of the capital), and the other foreign *chefs* who vied with them. Scarcely a dinner of consequence but saw some surprise in the way of a heretofore unknown dish. Many a time I have seen some one distinguished for his *aplomb*

look about helplessly as the feast progressed, and gaze
questioningly at the preparation before him, as if uncertain as to how it should be manipulated. Whenever
I was in doubt as to the proper thing to do at these dignified dinners, I turned, as was natural, to those whose
longer experience in the gay world was calculated to
establish them as exemplars to the novice.

On the evening of which I write, the courses had proceeded without the appearance of unusual or alarm-
inspiring dishes until we had neared the end of the *menu*,
when I saw a waiter approaching with a large salver on
which were dozens of mysterious parallelograms of paper,
each of which was about five inches long and three broad,
and appeared to be full of some novel conserve.
Beside them lay a silver trowel. The packages were folded
daintily, the gilt edges of their wrapping glittering at-
tractively. What they contained I could not guess, nor
could I imagine what we were supposed to do with them.

However, while still struggling to read the mystery
of the salver, my eye fell upon Mme. de Bodisco, my
*vis-à-vis*. She was a mountain of lace and jewels, of
blonde beauty and composure, for even at this early period
her proportions were larger than those which by common
consent are accredited to the sylph. I could have no
better instructress than this lady of international renown.
I watched her; saw her take up the little trowel,
deftly remove one of the packages from the salver to her
plate, and composedly proceed to empty the paper
receptacle of its contents—a delicious glacé. My suspense was at an end. I followed her example, very well
satisfied with my good fortune in escaping a pitfall which
a moment ago I felt sure yawned before me, for this
method of serving creams and ices was the latest
of culinary novelties.

I wondered if there were others at the great board who
were equally uncertain as to what to do with the care-

fully concealed dainties. Looking down to the other side of the table, I saw our friend Mr. Blank, of Virginia, hesitatingly regarding the pile of paper which the waiter was holding toward him. Presently, as if resigned to his fate, he took up the trowel and began to devote considerable energy to an attempt to dig out the contents of the package nearest him, when, as I glanced toward him, he looked up, full of self-consciousness, and turned his gaze directly upon me. His expression told plainly of growing consternation.

I shook my head in withering pseudo-rebuke and swiftly indicated to him "to take a whole one." Fortunately, he was quick-witted and caught my meaning, and, taking the hint, took likewise the cream without further mishap. After dinner we retired to the green-room, where, as was the custom, coffee and liqueurs were served. Here Mr. Blank approached, and, shaking my hand most gratefully, he whispered, "God bless my soul, Mrs. Clay! You're the sweetest woman in the world! But for your goodness, heaven only knows what would have happened! Perhaps," and he sipped his liqueur contemplatively, "perhaps I might have been struggling with that, *that problem* yet!"

I met Mme. de Bodisco many times during her widowhood, and was present at old St. John's when her second marriage, with Captain Scott of Her British Majesty's Life Guards, was celebrated. It was early in the Buchanan administration, and the bride was given away by the President. While St. John's, I may add, was often referred to as a fashionable centre, yet much of genuine piety throve there, too.

Mme. de Bodisco, who, during her widowhood, had continued her belleship and had received, it was said, many offers of marriage from distinguished men, capitulated at last to the young guardsman just named. Great therefore was the interest in the second nuptials of so popular a beauty.  Old St. John's was crowded with the most distinguished personages in the capital.  The aisles of the old edifice are narrow, and the march of the bride and the President to the altar was memorable, not only because of the distinction, but also by reason of the imposing proportions of both principals in it.  In fact, the plumpness of the stately bride and the President's ample figure, made the walk, side by side, an almost impossible feat.  The difficulty was overcome, however, by the tactfulness of the President, who led the lady slightly in advance of himself until the chancel was reached.  Here the slender young groom, garbed in the scarlet and gold uniform of his rank, stepped forward to claim her, and, though it was seen that he stood upon a hassock in order to lessen the difference in height between himself and his bride, it was everywhere admitted that Captain Scott was a handsome and gallant groom, and worthy the prize he had won.

This was Mme. de Bodisco's last appearance in Washington.  With her husband she went to India, where, it was said, the climate soon made havoc of her health and beauty; but her fame lingered long on the lips of her hosts of admirers in Washington.  Nor did the name of de Bodisco disappear from the social list, for, though his sons were sent to Russia, there to be educated, Waldemar de Bodisco, nephew of the late Minister, long continued to be the most popular leader of the German in Washington.

Throughout the fifties, and indeed for several preceding decades, the foreign representatives and their suites formed a very important element in society in the capital.  In some degree their members, the majority of whom were travelled and accomplished, and many representative of the highest culture in Europe, were our critics, if not our mentors.  The standard of education was higher in Europe fifty years ago than in our own land, and to be a favourite at the foreign legations was equivalent to a certificate of accomplishment and social charms. An acquaintance with the languages necessarily was not the least of these. The celebrated Octavia Walton, afterward famous as Mme. Le Vert, won her first social distinction in Washington, where, chaperoned by Mrs. C. C. Clay, Sr., a recognition of her grace and beauty, her intellectuality and charming manner was instantaneous. At a time when a knowledge of the foreign tongues was seldom acquired by American women, Miss Walton, who spoke French, Spanish and Italian with ease, speedily became the favourite of the Legations, and thence began her fame which afterward became international.

During my early residence in Washington, Addie Cutts (who became first the wife of Stephen A. Douglas and some years after his death married General Williams) was the admired of all foreigners. Miss Cutts was the niece of Mrs. Greenhow, a wealthy and brilliant woman of the capital, and, when she became Mrs. Douglas, held a remarkable sway for years. As a linguist Miss Cutts was reputed to be greatly gifted. If she spoke the many languages of which she was said to be mistress but half so eloquently as she uttered her own when, in 1865, she appealed to President Johnson on behalf of "her loved friend" my husband, the explanation of her remarkable nightly levees of the late fifties is readily found.

Though never, strictly speaking, a member of our "mess," Mrs. Douglas and I were always firm friends. While she was still Miss Cutts, and feeling keenly the deprivations that fall to the lot of the beautiful daughter of a poor department clerk, * she once complained to me poutingly of the cost of gloves.

* Apropos of this reference to Mrs. Douglas, Col. Henry Watterson said to me: "Her passport into Washington society was her relationship to Mistress Dolly Madison, who was her grandaunt. It is true, Mr. James Madison Cutts, Mrs. Douglas's father, was a department clerk, but he was the nephew of the former mistress of the White

"Nonsense," I answered. "Were I Addie Cutts, with hands that might have been chiselled by Phidias, I would never disguise them in gloves, whatever the fashion!"

Miss Cutts entered into the enjoyment of the wealth and position which her marriage with Stephen A. Douglas gave her, with the regal manner of a princess. Her toilettes were of the richest and at all times were models of taste and picturesqueness. The effect she produced upon strangers was invariably one of instant admiration. Writing to me in 1863, my cousin, Mrs. Paul Hammond (who, before her marriage, had spent a winter with me at Washington), thus recalled her meeting with the noted beauty:

"Yesterday, with its green leaves and pearl-white flowers, called to my memory how Mrs. Douglas looked when I first saw her. She was receiving at her own house in a crêpe dress looped with pearls, and her hair was ornamented with green leaves and lilies. She was a beautiful picture!"

I had the pleasure, on one occasion, of bringing together Mrs. Douglas and Miss Betty Beirne, the tallest and the shortest belles of their time. They had long desired to meet, and each viewed the other with astonishment and pleasure. Miss Beirne, who afterward became the wife of Porcher Miles of South Carolina, was one of the tiniest of women, as Mrs. Douglas was one of the queenliest, and both were toasted continually in the capital.

During the incumbency of Mr. Crampton, he being a bachelor, few functions were given at the British Embassy which ladies attended. Not that the Minister and his

House. Mrs. Douglas was very beautiful," Colonel Watterson continued. "I remember stepping into the Douglas library one morning, and coming upon her unexpectedly as she was dusting some bit of precious bric-à-brac, over which she extended a personal care. She was *en negligée*, and, as the colour mounted her cheek, upon my unexpected appearance, I thought I had never seen so beautiful, so rosy a girl. I told Douglas so!" A. S.

suite were eremites.   On the contrary, Mr. Crampton was exceedingly fond of "cutting a figure."   His traps were especially conspicuous on the Washington avenues. Always his own reinsman, the Minister's fast tandem driving and the stiffly upright "tiger" behind him, for several years were one of the sights of the city.   In social life the British Embassy was admirably represented by Mr. Lumley, Chargé d'Affaires, an affable young man who entered frankly into the life of the city and won the friendly feeling of all who met him.   He was one of the four young men who took each the novel part of the elephant's leg at a most amusing impromptu affair given by Mrs. George Riggs in honour of the girl *prima donna*, Adelina Patti.   It was, I think, the evening of the latter's début in "la Traviata."   Her appearance was the occasion of one of the most brilliant audiences ever seen in Washington.   Everyone of note was present, and the glistening of silk and the flash of jewels no doubt contributed their quota of stimulus to the youthful star.

Within a day of the performance, Senator Clay and I received a note from Mrs. Riggs, inviting us informally, not to say secretly, to an after-the-opera supper, to meet the new diva and her supporting artists.   We responded cordially and drove to the Riggs residence shortly after the close of the performance.

There, upon our arrival, we found representatives from all the foreign legations, Patti's entire troupe, and perhaps a dozen others, exclusive of the family of our hostess. The *prima donna* soon came in, a lovely little maiden in evening dress, with a manner as winsome as was her appearance.   The entertainment now began by graceful compliment from all present to the new opera queen, after which Mr. Riggs led her to the dining-room where the sumptuous supper was spread.

The table was almost as wide as that of the White House.   Its dazzling silver and gold and crystal vessels, and viands well worthy these receptacles, made a brilliant centre around which the decorated foreigners seemed appropriately to cluster. The little cantatrice's undisguised pleasure was good to see. She had worked hard during the performance of the opera, and her appetite was keen. She did ample justice, therefore, to Mrs. Riggs's good cheer, and goblets were kept brimming for quite two hours.

This important part of the programme over, a young Englishman, by name Mr. Palmer, who, as the Chevalier Bertinatti (the Sardinian Minister) whispered to me, had been asked "to make some leetle fun for leetle Mees Patti," opened the evening's merriment by an amusing exhibition of legerdemain. Mr. Palmer, at that time a favourite music-teacher, who spent his time between Washington and Baltimore, Philadelphia and New York, having in each city numerous fashionable pupils, afterward became known to the world as the great prestidigitator, Heller.

On the evening of the Riggses' supper the young magician was in his best form. Handkerchiefs and trinkets disappeared mysteriously, only to come to light again in the most unexpected places, until the company became almost silent with wonder. Mr. Palmer's last trick required a pack of cards, which were promptly forthcoming. Selecting the queen of hearts, he said, looking archly in the direction of the diminutive Patti: "This is also a queen; but she is a naughty girl and we will not have her!" saying which, with a whiff and a toss, he threw the card into the air, where it vanished!

Everyone was mystified; but Baron de Staeckl, the Russian Minister, incontinently broke the spell Mr. Palmer was weaving around us by picking up a card and pronouncing the same formula. Then, as all waited to see what he was about to do, in a most serio-comic manner he deftly and deliberately crammed it down

ADELINA PATTI
Aged Sixteen

Mr. Palmer's collar! Amid peals of laughter from all present, the young man gave place to other and more general entertainment, in which the most dignified ambassadors indulged with the hilarity of schoolboys.

From the foregoing incident it will be seen that Baron de Staeckl was the buffo of the evening. He was a large man of inspiring, not to say portly figure, and his lapels glittered with the insignia of honours that had been conferred upon him. Like his predecessor, the late Baron de Bodisco, he had allied himself with our country by marrying an American girl, a native of New Haven, whose family name I have now forgotten. She was a lovely and amiable hostess, whose unassuming manner never lost a certain pleasing modesty, notwithstanding the compliments she, too, invariably evoked. Her table was remarkable for its napery—Russian linen for the larger part, with embroidered monograms of unusual size and perfection of workmanship, which were said to be the handiwork of Slav needlewomen. Although I had enjoyed their hospitality and had met the de Staeckles frequently elsewhere, until this evening at the Riggses' home I had never suspected the genial Baron's full capacity for the enjoyment of pure nonsense.

There were many amateur musicians among the guests, first among them being the Sicilian Minister, Massoni. He was a finished vocalist, with a full operatic repertory at his easy command. His son Lorenzo was as fine a pianist, and accompanied his father with a sympathy that was most rare. That evening the Massonis responded again and again to the eager urgings of the other guests, but at last the Minister, doubtless desiring to "cut it short," broke into the "Anvil Chorus." Instantly he was joined by the entire company.

At the opening strain, the jolly Baron de Staeckl disappeared for a second, but ere we had finished, his glittering form was seen to re-enter the door, with a stride like Vulcan's and an air as mighty. In one hand he held a pair of Mrs. Riggs's glowing brass tongs, in the other a poker, with which, in faultless rhythm, he was beating time to his own deep-bellowing basso. He stalked to the centre of the room with all the pomposity of a genuine king of *opera bouffe*, a sly twinkle in his eye being the only hint to the beholders that he was conscious of his own ludicrous appearance.

Meantime, Mlle. Patti had mounted a chair, where her liquid notes in alt joined the deep ones of the baron. As he stopped in the centre of the room, however, the little diva's amusement reached a climax. She clapped her hands and fairly shouted with glee. Her mirth was infectious and quite upset the solemnity of the basso. Breaking into a sonorous roar of laughter, he made as hasty an exit as his cumbrous form would allow. I think a walrus would have succeeded as gracefully.

We were about to withdraw from this gay scene when the Chevalier Bertinatti, with the utmost enthusiasm, begged us to stay. "You must!" he cried. "Ze elephant is coming! I assure you zere ees not hees equal for ze fun!" A moment more and we fully agreed with him. Even as he spoke, the doors opened and Mr. Palmer bounded in, a gorgeously got-up ring-master. I saw my own crimson opera cloak about his shoulders and a turban formed of many coloured *rebozos* of other guests twisted together in truly artistic manner.

"Ladies and gentlemen!" he began grandiloquently, "I have the honour to present to your astonished eyes the grand elephant, Hannibal, costing to import twenty thousand dollars, and weighing six thousand pounds! An elephant, ladies and gentlemen, whose average cost is three and one-half dollars a pound! He is a marvellous animal, ladies and gentlemen, warranted to be as intrepid as his namesake! He has been called a vicious creature, but in the present company I intend to prove him as docile as — the ladies themselves! Advance, Hannibal!"

He threw himself prone upon the floor as the wide doors opened and "Hannibal " lumbered in, deliberately wagging his trunk from side to side, in a manner that was startlingly lifelike.

Arrived at the prostrate ring-master, he put out one shapeless leg (at the bottom of which a handsomely shod man's foot appeared) and touched the prostrate one lightly, as if fearful of hurting him; he advanced and retreated several times, wagging his trunk the while; until, at last, at the urgings of the recumbent hero, the animal stepped cleanly over him. Now, with a motion of triumph, Mr. Palmer sprang up and, crossing his arms proudly over his bosom, cried, "Ladies and gentlemen! I *live!*" and awaited the applause which rang out merrily. Then, leaping lightly upon his docile pet's back, the latter galloped madly around the room and made for the door amid screams and shouts of laughter.

In the mad exit, however, the mystery of the elephant was revealed; for his hide, the rubber cover of Mrs. Riggs's grand piano, slipped from the shoulders of the hilarious young men who supported it, and "Hannibal" disappeared in a confusion of brilliant opera cloaks, black coats, fleeing patent-leathers, and trailing piano cover!

This climax was a fitting close to our evening's fun-making. As our host accompanied us to the door, he said slyly to my husband, "Not a word of this, Clay! To-night must be as secret as a Democratic caucus, or we shall all be tabooed."

# CHAPTER III

## A Historic Congressional "Mess"

Our "mess" at Brown's Hotel shortly became so well-known, because of the interest attaching to so many of its members, that the enterprising proprietress of (what afterward became known as) the Ebbitt House, Mrs. Smith, came in person, with tempting terms to lure us to her newer establishment.

Heretofore our quarters in the historic old hostelry had been altogether satisfactory. It was the rendezvous of Southern Congressmen, and therefore was "very agreeable and advantageous," as my husband wrote of it. For thirty-five years Brown's Hotel had been the gathering-place for distinguished people. So long ago as 1820, Thomas Hart Benton met there the representatives of the rich fur-trader, John Jacob Astor, who had been sent to the capital to induce Congressional indorsement in perfecting a great scheme that should secure to us the trade of Asia as well as the occupation of the Columbia River. Within its lobbies, many a portentous conference had taken place. Indeed, the foundations of its good reputation were laid while it was yet the Indian Queen's Tavern, renowned for its juleps and bitters. It was an unimposing structure even for Pennsylvania Avenue, then but a ragged thoroughfare, and, as I have said, notable for the great gaps between houses; but the cuisine of Brown's Hotel, as, until a few years ago, this famous house continued to be known, was excellent.

In my days there, the presence of good Mrs. Brown,

the hostess, and her sweet daughter Rose (who married Mr. Wallach, one of Washington's rich citizens, and afterward entertained in the mansion that became famous as the residence of Mrs. Stephen A. Douglas) added much to the attractions of the old house. Nevertheless, those of the new also tempted us. Thither we went in a body, and there we spent one or two gay winters; but, the Ebbitt becoming more and more heterogeneous, and therefore less congenial to our strictly legislative circles, we retraced our ways, our forces still intact, to good old Brown's.

In the interim, our continually enlarging numbers found the new quarters convenient and in many respects even desirable. "Our 'mess,' so far from being willing to separate," I wrote to my husband's father, late in '57, "has insisted upon becoming enlarged. We are located in a delightful part of the city, on F Street, near the Treasury Buildings, the Court end as well as the convenient end; for all the Departments as well as the White House are in a stone's throw. Old Guthrie's is opposite, and we have, within two blocks, some true-line Senators, among them Bell, Slidell, Weller, Brodhead, Thomson, of New Jersey, who are married and housekeeping, to say naught of Butler, Benjamin, Mason and Goode in a 'mess' near us. Our 'mess' is a very pleasant one. Orr, Shorter, Dowdell, Sandidge and Taylor, of Louisiana, with the young Senator Pugh and his bride, Governor Fitzpatrick and wife, and ourselves compose the party. Taylor is a true Democrat, and Pugh is as strongly Anti-Free-soil as we. We keep Free-soilers, Black Republicans and Bloomers on the other side of the street. They are afraid even to inquire for board at this house."

To the choice list then recorded were added shortly Congressmen L. Q. C. and Mrs. Lamar, David Clopton, Jabez L. M. Curry and Mrs. Curry, and General and Mrs. Chestnut. Our circle included representatives from several States. Messrs. Fitzpatrick, Shorter, Dowdell, David Clopton and Jabez L. M. Curry were fellow-Alabamians, and had been the long-time friends of my husband and his father, ex-Governor Clay, and of my uncle, Governor Collier; Congressmen Lamar and Sandidge were from Mississippi and Louisiana, respectively; Congressmen Orr and Chestnut represented South Carolina, and Senator Pugh was from Ohio. It was a distinguished company. Scarcely a male member of it but had won or was destined to win a conspicuous position in the Nation's affairs; scarcely a woman in the circle who was not acknowledged to be a wit or beauty.

When Mrs. Pugh joined us, her precedence over the belles of the capital was already established, for, as Thérèse Chalfant, her reign had begun a year or two previous to her marriage to the brilliant young Senator from Ohio; Miss Cutts, afterward Mrs. Douglas, and Mrs. Pendleton and the beautiful *brune*, Mrs. Roger A. Pryor, being estimated as next in order of beauty. Like Mrs. Chestnut, also a renowned belle, Mrs. Pugh was something more than a woman of great personal loveliness. She was intellectual, and remarked as such even in Washington, where wits gathered. Both of these prized associates remained unspoiled by the adulation which is the common tribute to such unusual feminine comeliness.

I was not present when the Austrian Minister, the Chevalier Hulseman, paid his great compliment (now a classic in the capital) to Miss Chalfant; but it was soon thereafter repeated to me. It was at a ball at which pretty women thronged. As the Minister's gaze rested upon Miss Chalfant, his eyes expanded with admiration. Approaching, he knelt suddenly before her, exclaiming, "Madame! I have from my Empress a piece of precious lace " (and he fumbled, but, alas! vainly, in his pockets as he spoke) "which her Majesty has commanded me

MRS. ROGER A. PRYOR
of Virginia

to present to the most beautiful woman in Washington. You—you are more, the most beautiful in the world! I have not with me the lace, but I will send it if you will permit me!" And he kept his word. We were glad to welcome to our "mess" so lovely and famous a bride. Mrs. Pugh's beauty was of so exquisite a type, the bodily so permeated by the spiritual, that she shone preëminent wherever she appeared, and this wholly independent of showy attire. Though always presenting an appearance of elegance, Mrs. Pugh's gowns were invariably of the simplest. Our "mess" soon became aware that our beautiful favourite was primarily a lovely woman, and no mere gay butterfly. Her nature was grave rather than vivacious, the maternal in her being exceedingly strong.

I recall the reply she gave me on the afternoon of a certain Cabinet day. It was the custom on this weekly recurring occasion for several of the ladies of our "mess" to make their calls together, thus obviating the need for more than one carriage. As my parlours were the only ones that boasted a pier-glass, and, besides, had the advantage of being on the drawing-room floor of the hotel, it became a custom for the women composing our circle to come to my rooms before going out, in order to see how their dresses hung. Those were the days of hoop-skirts, and the set of the outer skirt must needs be adjusted before beginning a round of calls. As we gathered there, it was no uncommon thing for one of us to remark: "Here comes Pugh, simply dressed, but superb, as usual. She would eclipse us all were she in calico!" On the occasion alluded to, I commented to Mrs. Pugh upon the beauty and style of her bonnet.

"My own make," she answered sweetly. "I can't afford French bonnets for every-day use when I have 'tockies and shoes to buy for my little fellows!"

My friendship for Mrs. Pugh is a dear memory of that

life of perpetual gaiety ere the face of Washington society was marred by war and scarred by the moral pestilences that followed in its train; nor can I resist the desire to quote her own remembrance of our association as she wrote it in a letter to Senator Clay late in '64, when the glories of those earlier days had passed away, and the faces of erstwhile friends from the North were hidden by the smoke of cannon and a barrier of the slain.

"Your dear wife," she wrote, "was the first and best friend of my early married life; and, when I was ushered into a strange and trying world, she at once took me into her heart and counsel and made me a better woman and wife than I would have been alone. No one in this world ever treated me with the same love outside of my own family. When I cease to remember either of you accordingly, it will be when I forget all things!"

Strangely enough, there comes before my mind a picture of Mrs. Pugh in affliction that overshadows all the memories of the homage I have seen paid to her. It was late in the spring of 1859; Congress had adjourned and many of our "mess" had gone their several ways, to mountain or seashore, bent on rest or recreation, when the little daughter of Senator and Mrs. Pugh was suddenly taken ill. For weeks the distracted mother hovered over the sick-bed of the child, until her haggard appearance was pitiful to see. My husband and I could not bear to leave her, and often I shared her vigils, watching hours beside the dying little Alice.

On an occasion like this (it was evening), my cousin Miss Hilliard, her cheeks glowing and eyes shining with all the mysterious glow of expectant youth, came into the sick-room for a few moments on her way to some social gathering. She was dressed in a pale green, filmy gown, which lent to her appearance a flower-like semblance that was very fresh and lovely. As Miss Hilliard entered, Mrs. Pugh lifted her burning eyes from the

MRS. GEORGE E. PUGH (THÉRÈSE CHALFANT)
of Ohio
" The most beautiful woman in Washington "

couch where the rapidly declining little one lay, and gazed at her visitor like one in a dream. We were all silent for a moment. Then the worn mother spoke.

"So radiant! So beautiful!" she said in a voice of indescribable pathos, "And to think you, too, may come to this!"

I have spoken of Mrs. Pryor, the beautiful wife of the young diplomat, who had won general public approbation for his success in conducting a mission to Greece. Not of our especial mess, Mrs. Pryor frequently mingled with us, being the friend of Mrs. Douglas and Mrs. Pugh. They were, in truth, a very harmonious trio, Mrs. Pugh being a perfect brunette, Mrs. Douglas a blonde, and Mrs. Pryor a lighter brunette with soft-brown hair and eyes. She wore a distinctive coiffure, and carried her head charmingly. Even at that time Mrs. Pryor was notable for the intellectuality which has since uttered itself in several charming books.

Though not members of our resident circle, my memories of dear old Brown's would scarcely be complete without a mention of little Henry Watterson, with whose parents our "mess" continually exchanged visits for years. Henry, their only child, was then an invalid, debarred from the usual recreations of other boys, by weak eyes that made the light unbearable and reading all but impossible; yet at fifteen the boy was a born politician and eager for every item of news from the Senate or House.

"What bills were introduced to-day? Who spoke? Please tell me what took place to-day?" were among the questions (in substance) with which the lad was wont to greet the ladies of our "mess," when he knew them to be returning from a few hours spent in the Senate gallery; and, though none foresaw the later distinction which awaited the invalid boy, no one of us was ever so hurried and impatient that she could not and did not take time to answer his earnest inquiries.

It is safe to say that no member of our pleasant circle was more generally valued than that most lovable of men, Lucius Q. C. Lamar, "Moody Lamar," as he was sometimes called; for he was then, as he always continued to be, full of dreams and ideals and big, warm impulses, with a capacity for the most enduring and strongest of friendships, and a tenderness rarely displayed by men so strong as was he.*    Mr. Lamar was full of quaint and caressing ways even with his fellow-men, which frank utterance of his own feelings was irresistibly engaging. I have seen him walk softly up behind Mr. Clay, when the latter was deep in thought, touch him lightly on the shoulder, and, as my husband turned quickly to see what was wanted, "Lushe" or "big Lushe," as all called him, would kiss him suddenly and lightly on the forehead.

Yes! Mr. Lamar and his sparkling, bright-souled wife, Jennie Longstreet, were beloved members of that memorable "mess" in ante-bellum Washington.

Next to Congressman Lamar, I suppose it may safely be said no man was more affectionately held than another of our mess-mates, Congressman Dowdell, "old Dowdell," "dear old Dowdell," and sometimes "poor, dear old Dowdell" being among the forms by which he was continually designated.    Mr. Dowdell had a large and loose frame, and walked about with a countryman's easy

---

* Writing to Mrs. Clay from the Department of the Interior, late in 1885, E. V. D. Miller said of Mr. Lamar, then Secretary of the Interior: "Those nearest in his labours only understand and have compassion for him, to try to save him all we can.    He would take us *all* in his arms, and confer the greatest benefits on us if he could; and a more tender, appreciative, industrious, kind-hearted man I have never been associated with, to say nothing of his giant intellect and cultivated brain and taste.    I never knew him until I came to this office with him and saw him in all these entangling relations.    I used to get angry and avoid him because I thought he neglected my requests and was so indifferent that there seemed to be a lack of respect; but a closer knowledge of the demands upon him have disarmed me entirely, and I fight him no longer."    A. S.

indifference to appearances. A born wag, he some-times took a quiet delight in accentuating this seeming guilelessness.

One evening he came strolling in to dinner, prepared for a comfortable chat over the table, though all the rest of our little coterie were even then dressing for attend-ance at a grand concert. It was an event of great impor-tance, for Gottschalk, the young Créole musician, of whom all the country was talking, was to be heard in his own compositions.

"What!" I exclaimed as I saw Mr. Dowdell's every-day attire, "You don't mean to tell me you're not going to the concert! I can't allow it, brother Dowdell! Go right out and get your ticket and attend that concert with all the rest of the world, or I'll tell your constituents what sort of a country representative they've sent to the capital!"

My laughing threat had its effect, and he hurried off in quest of the ticket, which, after some difficulty, was procured.

The concert was a memorable one. During the eve-ning I saw Mr. Dowdell across the hall, scanning the per-formers with an enigmatical expression. At that time Gottschalk's popularity was at its height. Every con-cert programme contained, and every ambitious amateur included in her repertory, the young composer's "Last Hope." At his appearance, therefore, slender, agile and Gallic to a degree, enthusiasm ran so high that we forgot to hunt up our friend in the short interval between each brilliant number.

When Mr. Dowdell appeared at the breakfast table the following morning, I asked him how he had enjoyed the evening. The Congressman's response came less enthusi-astically than I had hoped.

"Well," he began, drawing his words out slowly and a bit quizzically, "I went out and got my ticket; did the

right thing and got a seat as near Harriet Lane's box as
I could; even invested in new white gloves, so I felt all
right; but I can't say the music struck me exactly! Mr.
Gottschalk played mighty pretty; hopped up on the
black keys and then down on the white ones" (and the
Congressman illustrated by spanning the table rapidly in
a most ludicrous manner). "He played slow and then
fast, and never seemed to get his hands tangled up once.
But for all that I can't say I was struck by his music!
He played mighty pretty, but he didn't play nary *tchune!*"

Two interesting members of our "mess" were General
and Mrs. Chestnut. The General, a member from South
Carolina, who became afterward one of the staff of Jefferson Davis, was among the princes in wealth in the South
in the fifties. Approximately one thousand slaves owned
by him were manumitted by Mr. Lincoln's proclamation
in 1863, when, childless, property-less, our well-loved
Mrs. Chestnut suffered a terrible eclipse after her brilliant
youth and middle age. She was the only daughter of
Governor Miller, of South Carolina, and having been
educated abroad, was an accomplished linguist and
ranked high among the cultured women of the capital.

Moreover, Mrs. Chestnut was continually the recipient
of toilette elegancies, for which the bazaars of Paris were
ransacked, and in this way the curiosity of the emulative
stay-at-home fashionables was constantly piqued. Her
part in that brilliant world was not a small one, for, in
addition to her superior personal charms, Mrs. Chestnut
chaperoned the lovely Preston girls of South Carolina,
belles, all, and the fashionable Miss Stevens, of Stevens
Castle, who married Muscoe Garnett of Virginia. Indeed,
the zest for social pleasures among our circle was often
increased by the coming of guests from other cities.
Among others whom I particularly recall was my cousin
Miss Collier, daughter of Governor Collier of Alabama,
and who married the nephew of William Rufus King, vice-

President of the United States under Mr. Pierce; and our cousins Loula Comer, Hattie Withers, and Miss Hilliard. The latter's wedding with Mr. Hamilton Glentworth of New York was one of the social events of the winter of 1859.

Nor should I forget to mention the presence, at the Ebbitt House and at Brown's Hotel, of another much admired South Carolinian, Mrs. General McQueen, who was a Miss Pickens, of the famous family of that name. My remembrance of Mrs. McQueen is always associated with that of the sudden death of Preston Brooks, our neighbour at Brown's Hotel.  At the time of this fatality, Dr. May, the eminent surgeon, was in the building in attendance upon Mrs. McQueen's little boy, who was suffering from some throat trouble.

Mr. Brooks had been indisposed for several days, and, being absent from his seat in the House, it was the custom for one or the other of his confrères to drop into his room each afternoon, to give him news of the proceedings. On that fatal day, Colonel Orr ("Larry," as his friends affectionately designated him) had called upon the invalid and was in the midst of narrating the day's doings, when Mr. Brooks clutched suddenly at his throat and cried out huskily, "Air! Orr, air!"

Mr. Orr hastily threw open the window and began to fan the sufferer, but became bewildered at the alarming continuation of his struggles.  Had the Congressman but known it, even as he tried to relieve his friend, Dr. May passed the door of Mr. Brooks's room, on his way out of the house, his surgical case in hand; but the suddenness of the attack, and a total absence of suspicion as to its gravity, coupled with the swiftness with which it acted, confused the watcher, and, ere assistance could be obtained, the handsome young Southern member had passed away!

Congressman Orr, as has been said, was one of our

original "mess" in the capital. From the first he was
a conspicuous figure, nature having made him so. He
was of gigantic stature, weighing then somewhat over
two hundred pounds. His voice was of bugle-like clear-
ness, and when, in 1857, he became speaker of the House
of Representatives, it was a source of remark how wonderfully his words penetrated to the farthermost corner
of the hall. He was extremely tender-hearted and
devoted to his family, around the members of which his
affections were closely bound.

Just previous to our arrival in the capital, Mr. Orr had
lost a little daughter, and often, ere he brought his family
to the Federal City, in a quiet hour he would come to our
parlours and ask me to sing to him. He dearly loved
simple ballads, his favourite song being "Lilly Dale," the
singing of which invariably stirred him greatly. Often
I have turned from the piano to find his eyes gushing with
tears at the memories that pathetic old-fashioned ditty
had awakened. Mr. Orr was a famous flatterer, too,
who ranked my simple singing as greater than that of
the piquant Patti; and I question the success of any one
who would have debated with him the respective merits
of that great *artiste* and my modest self.

When Mr. Orr became Speaker of the House, Mrs.
Orr and his children having joined him, the family
resided in the famous Stockton Mansion for a
season or two. Here brilliant receptions were held, and
Mrs. Orr, a *distinguée* woman, made her entrée into
Washington society, often being assisted in receiving by
the members of the mess of which, for so long, Mr. Orr
had formed a part. Mrs. Orr was tall and lithe in figure,
of a Spanish type of face. She soon became a
great favourite in the capital, where one daughter, now
a widow, Mrs. Earle, still lives.

It was at the Stockton Mansion that Daniel E. and
Mrs. Sickles lived when the tragedy of which they formed

two of the principals took place. Here, too, was run the American career of another much-talked-of lady, which, for meteoric brilliancy and brevity, perhaps outshines any other episode in the chronicles of social life in Washington.

The lady's husband was a statesman of prominence, celebrated for his scholarly tastes and the fineness of his mental qualities. The arrival of the lady, after a marked absence abroad, during which some curious gossip had reached American ears, was attended by great *éclat;* and not a little conjecture was current as to how she would be received. For her home-coming, however, the Stockton Mansion was fitted up in hitherto undreamed-of magnificence, works of art and of *vertu*, which were the envy of local connoisseurs, being imported to grace it, regardless of cost. So far, so good!

The report of these domiciliary wonders left no doubt but that entertaining on a large scale was being projected. The world was slow in declaring its intentions in its own behalf; for, notwithstanding her rumoured delinquencies, the lady's husband was high in the councils of the nation, and as such was a figure of dignity. Shortly after her arrival our "mess" held a conclave, in which we discussed the propriety of calling upon the new-comer, but a conclusion seeming impossible (opinions being so widely divergent), it was decided to submit the important question to our husbands.

This was done duly, and Senator Clay's counsel to me was coincided in generally.

"By all means, call," said he. "You have nothing to do with the lady's private life, and, as a mark of esteem to a statesman of her husband's prominence, it will be better to call."

Upon a certain day, therefore, it was agreed that we should pay a "mess" call, going in a body. We drove accordingly, in dignity and in state, and, truth to tell, in soberness and ceremony, to the mansion aforenamed. It was the lady's reception day. We entered the drawing-room with great circumspection, tempering our usually cordial manner with a fine prudence; we paid our devoirs to the hostess and retired. But now a curious retribution overtook us, social faint-hearts that we were; for, though we heard much gossip of the regality and originality of one or more dinners given to the several diplomatic corps (the lady especially affected the French Legation), I never heard of a gathering of Washingtonians at her home, nor of invitations extended to them, nor, indeed, anything more of her until two months had flown. Then, Arab-like, the lady rose in the night, "silently folded her tent and stole away" (to meet a handsome German officer, it was said), leaving our calls unanswered, save by the sending of her card, and her silver and china and crystal, her paintings, and hangings, and furniture to be auctioned off to the highest bidder!

Everyone in Washington now thronged to see the beautiful things, and many purchased specimens from among them, among others Mrs. Davis. By a curious turn of fate, the majority of these treasures were acquired by Mrs. Senator Yulee, who was so devoutly religious that her piety caused her friends to speak of her as "the Madonna of the Wickliffe sisters!" The superb furniture of the whilom hostess was carried to "Homosassa," the romantic home of the Yulees in Florida, where in later years it was reduced to ashes.

Of the Wickliffe sisters there were three, all notably good as well as handsome women, with whom I enjoyed a life-time friendship. One became the wife of Judge Merrick, and another, who dearly loved Senator Clay and me, married Joseph Holt, who rose high in Federal honours after the breaking out of the war, having sold his Southern birthright for a mess of Northern pottage.

For several years before her death, Mrs. Holt was an

invalid and a recluse, yet she was no inconspicuous figure in Washington, where the beauty of the "three graces" (as the sisters of Governor Wickliffe were always designated) was long a criterion by which other belles were judged. Mrs. Mallory, the wife of Senator Yulee's confrère from Florida, was particularly a favourite in the capital. The Mallorys were the owners of great orange groves in that lovely State, and were wont from time to time to distribute among their friends boxes of choicest fruit.

Of our "mess," Congressman and Mrs. Curry were least frequently to be met with in social gatherings. Mrs. Curry, who was a Miss Bowie, devoted her time wholly to her children, apparently feeling no interest in the gay world about her, being as gentle and retiring as her doughty relative (the inventor of the Bowie knife) was war-like. Mr. Curry was an uncommonly handsome man, who, in the fifties and early sixties, was an ambitious and strenuous politician. He died early in 1903, full of years and honours, while still acting as the General Agent of the Peabody fund.

Nor should I fail to recall the lovely Mrs. Clopton, wife of one of Senator Clay's most trusted friends, Congressman David Clopton. She joined our "mess" late in the fifties, and at once added to its fame by her charm and beauty. She was a sister of Governor Ligon of Alabama. One of her daughters married the poet, Clifford Lanier, and another became the wife of Judge William L. Chambers, who for several exciting years represented our Government at Samoa.

But my oldest and dearest mess-mate during nearly a decade in the capital was, as I have said elsewhere, Mrs. Fitzpatrick, whose husband, Senator Benjamin Fitzpatrick, was President of the Senate for four consecutive sessions. Senator Fitzpatrick was very many years older than his wife, having, indeed, held office in

1818, when Alabama was a territory, and when few of his Alabamian associates in Congress had been ushered upon the stage of life. Between Mrs. Fitzpatrick and me there was an undeviating attachment which was a source of wonder, as it doubtless was rare, among women in fashionable life. As confrères in the Senate, our husbands, despite the disparity in their years, were fully in accord; and a more congenial quartette it would have been hard to find.

I think of all the harmonious couples I have known, Senator and Mrs. Fitzpatrick easily led, though near to them I must place General and Mrs. McQueen. It was a standing topic in Brown's Hotel, the devotion of the two middle-aged gentlemen—Messrs. Fitzpatrick and McQueen—to their young wives and to their boys, *enfants terribles*, both of them of a most emphatic type. "The Heavenly Twins" as a title had not yet been evolved, or these two young autocrats of the hostelry would surely have won it from the sarcastic.

Benny Fitzpatrick was at once the idol of his parents and the terror of the hotel; and, as Mrs. Fitzpatrick and I were cordially united in other interests of life, so we shared the maternal duties as became two devoted sisters, "Our boy Benny" receiving the motherly oversight of whichsoever of us happened to be near him when occasion arose for aid or admonition. "Mrs. Fitz" delivered her rebukes with "Oh, Benny dear! How could you!" but I, his foster-mother, was constrained to resort betimes to a certain old-fashioned punishment usually administered with the broadside of a slipper, or, what shortly became as efficacious, a threat to do so.

Benny, like George Washington, was the possessor of a little hatchet, with which he worked a dreadful havoc. He chopped at the rosewood furniture of his mother's drawing-room, while his proud parents, amazed at his precocity, not to say prowess, stood by awestruck, and—

paid the bill! The child was plump and healthy, and boys will be boys! Thus were we all become his subjects; thus he overran Hannah, his coloured nurse, until one day Pat came—, Pat Dolan.

Pat had been a page at the Senate, and in some forgotten way he and little Benny had become inseparable friends. Thereafter, Benny was taken by his fond guardian, into whose hands his three anxious parents consented to consign him, to see the varying sights and the various quarters of the city. As his experiences multiplied, so his reputation for precocity increased in exact ratio.

One day Hannah's excitement ran high. "Lor! Miss 'Relia," she burst out impetuously to Mrs. Fitzpatrick, "Pat Dolan done carried Benny to the Cath'lic church an' got him sprinkled, 'n den he brung him to communion, an' first thing Pat knowed, Benny he drunk up all the holy water an' eat up the whole wafer!"

# CHAPTER IV

## The Cabinet Circles of the Pierce and Buchanan Administrations

Writing to my father-in-law, ex-Governor Clay, on Christmas night, 1856, of the deep inward excitement of the times, I said: "We feel a little as Fanny Fern says Eugénie felt when she espoused Louis Napoleon, as if we are 'dancing over a powder magazine!' Everything is excitement and confusion. I tell you Fusion reigns in truth, and Southern blood is at boiling temperature all over the city, and with good cause, too. Old Giddings, Thurlow Weed, Sumner, Seward, Chase (who is here for a few days prior to his inauguration*) are daily taunting and insulting all whom they dare. There is no more prospect of a Speaker now than there was at first; indeed, less, and our men have despaired of Christmas holidays at home. Desertion of their post would mean death to their party and themselves, and they know and appreciate it, and, so far, stand firm as a Roman phalanx. Should there prove one deserter, the 'game is up,' for there is a Black Republican at every corner of our political fence, and if ever the gap is down we are gone. I wish you could be here to witness the scenes daily enacted in the halls of Congress, to hear the hot taunts of defiance hurled into the very teeth of the Northerners by our goaded but spirited patriots. I expect any day to hear of bloodshed and death, and would not be surprised at any time to witness (repeated here) the Civil War of Kansas! We still hope for Orr, though *he* is not sanguine.

* As Governor of Ohio.

The President still holds his message, fearing to give it to the press, and it is thought it will go to Congress in manuscript. He, poor fellow, is worn and weary, and his wife in extremely delicate health."

President Pierce was, in fact, a very harassed man, as none knew better than did Senator Clay. My husband's friendship was unwearying toward all to whom his reserved nature yielded it, and his devotion to Mr. Pierce was unswerving. Though twelve years the President's junior, from the first my husband was known as one of the President's counsellors, and none of those who surrounded the Nation's executive head more sacredly preserved his confidence. Senator Clay believed unequivocally that our President was "not in the roll of common men."

Bold and dauntless where a principle was involved, Mr. Pierce's message of '55 fell like a bombshell on the Black Republican party. Its bold pro-slaveryism startled even his friends; for, never had a predecessor, while in the Executive Chair, talked so strongly or so harshly to sectionalists and fanatics. To this stand, so bravely taken, his defeat at the next Presidential election was doubtless at least partially attributable. Meantime, the South owed him much, and none of its representatives was more staunchly devoted to President Pierce than was the Senator from northern Alabama. How fully Mr. Pierce relied upon Senator Clay's discretion may be illustrated by an incident which lives still very vividly in my memory.

My husband and I were seated one evening before a blazing fire in our parlour at the Ebbitt House, in the first enjoyment of an evening at home (a rare luxury to public folk in the capital), when we heard a low and unusual knock at the door. My trim maid, Emily, hastened to open it, when there entered hastily a tall figure, wrapped in a long storm-cloak on which the snow-flakes still lay thickly. The new-comer was muffled to the eyes. He glanced quickly about the rooms, making a motion to us, as he did so, to remain silent. My husband rose inquiringly, failing, as did I, to recognise our mysterious visitor. In a second more, however, perceiving that we were alone, he threw off his outer coat and soft hat, when, to our astonishment, our unceremonious and unexpected guest stood revealed as the President!

"Lock that door, Clay!" he said, almost pathetically, "and don't let a soul know I'm here!" Then, turning, he handed me a small package which he had carried under his coat.

"For you, Mrs. Clay," he said. "It is my picture. I hope you will care to take it with you to Alabama, and sometimes remember me!"

I thanked him delightedly as I untied the package and saw within a handsome photograph superbly framed. Then, as he wearily sat down before our crackling fire, I hastened to assist Emily in her preparation of a friendly egg-nog.

"Ah, my dear friends!" said Mr. Pierce, leaning forward in his arm-chair and warming his hands as he spoke; "I am so tired of the shackles of Presidential life that I can scarcely endure it! I long for quiet— for—" and he looked around our restful parlours—"for this! Oh! for relaxation and privacy once more, and a chance for home!"

His voice and every action betrayed the weary man. We were deeply moved, and my husband uttered such sympathetic words as only a wise man may. The egg-nog prepared, I soon had the pleasure of seeing the President and Mr. Clay in all the comfort of a friendly chat. Primarily, the object of his visit was to discuss an affair of national moment which was to be brought before the Senate the next day; but the outlook of the times which also fell naturally under discussion formed no small part in the topics thus intimately scanned. Both

FRANKLIN PIERCE
President of the United States, 1853-57

were men to whom the horrid sounds of coming combat were audible, and both were patriots seeking how they might do their part to avert it. It was midnight ere Mr. Pierce rose to go. Then, fortified by another of Emily's incomparable egg-nogs, he was again, incognito, on his way to the White House.

My remembrances of that secret visit have ever remained most keen. Often, when I think of the lonely grave on the quiet hillside at Concord, I recall the night when weariness of body and State formalities impelled the President to our cozy fireside, though he beat his way to it through snow and winds, stealing from the trammels of his position for the mere pleasure of walking the streets unimpeded and free as any other citizen.

President Pierce entered the White House in 1853, full as a youth of leaping life. A year before his inauguration I had seen him bound up the stairs with the elasticity and lightness of a schoolboy. He went out after four years a staid and grave man, on whom the stamp of care and illness was ineradicably impressed.

I often contrasted the pale, worn, haggard man whose "wine of life was drawn, and the mere lees left i' the vault," ere his term (so coveted by many) was spent, with the buoyant person I first met on the breezy New Hampshire hills!

Especially a lovable man in his private character, President Pierce was a man of whom our nation might well be proud to have at its head. Graced with an unusually fine presence, he was most courtly and polished in manner. Fair rather than dark, of graceful carriage,* he was also an eloquent speaker, and, though reserved to a degree, was very winning in manner. He was still in middle life when elected to the

* "President Pierce was one of the handsomest men I have ever seen!" was the remark of Colonel Watterson to me, while dwelling on those ante-bellum personages. A. S.

Presidency, being less than forty-nine years of age when inaugurated.

Taken all in all, the Cabinet circle formed by Mr. Pierce was one of the most interesting bodies that has ever surrounded an American Chief Magistrate. Selected wisely, the ministerial body remained unchanged throughout the entire Administration, and this at a time of unceasing and general contention. But three such instances are recorded in the histories of the twenty-six Presidents of the United States, the others occurring in the terms of J. Q. Adams and James A. Garfield. The tie which bound President Pierce and his Cabinet so inalienably was one of mutual confidence and personal friendship. Perhaps the closest ally of the President's was his Secretary of State, William L. Marcy. That great Secretary was a man whose unusual poise and uniform complacency were often as much a source of envy to his friends as of confusion to his enemies. I commented upon it to my husband on one occasion, wondering interrogatively at his composure, whereupon Senator Clay told me the following story:

Some one as curious as I once asked the Secretary how he preserved his unvarying calmness. "Well," he answered, confidentially, "I'll tell you. I have given my secretary orders that whenever he sees an article eulogistic of me, praising my 'astuteness,' my 'far-seeing diplomacy,' my 'incomparable statesmanship,' etc., he is to cut it out and place it conspicuously on my desk where I can see it first thing in the morning; everything to the contrary he is to cut out and up and consign to the waste-basket. By this means, hearing nothing but good of myself, I have come naturally to regard myself as a pretty good fellow! Who wouldn't be serene under such circumstances?"

To add to his contentment thus philosophically assured, the Secretary's home surroundings were peculiarly

MRS. WILLIAM L. MARCY
of New York

satisfactory to him. Mrs. Marcy was a demure and retiring woman, taking little part in the gayer happenings of the city, but on Cabinet days her welcome was always diplomatically cordial and her full parlours gave evidence of her personal popularity. A charming member of her family, Nellie, daughter of General R. B. Marcy, became the wife of General McClellan, whose son, named for that military hero, at this writing is Mayor of America's metropolis. Between President and Mrs. Pierce and Secretary and Mrs. Marcy a firm friendship existed. It was to the home of the Secretary that President and Mrs. Pierce retired while the White House was being rehabilitated for the occupancy of Mr. Buchanan, who had just returned from his residence abroad, where, as Mr. Pierce's appointee, he served as Minister to the Court of St. James.

On the day of Mr. Buchanan's inauguration a curious oversight occurred which demonstrated in marked manner how eagerly a populace hastens to shout "The king is dead! Long live the King!" The procession of carriages had already formed and the moment for beginning the march to the Capitol had almost arrived ere it was observed that the vehicle set apart for President Pierce was unoccupied. Inquiry was hastily instituted, when it was discovered that, owing to some omission on the part of the Master of Ceremonies, his Excellency had not been sent for! The horses' heads were turned in a trice, and they were driven furiously to the Marcy residence, where the quiet gentleman who was still the President of the United States awaited them.

Late in the afternoon my husband called upon Mr. Pierce, and, during the conversation that followed, Mr. Clay referred indignantly to the unfortunate affair.

"Ah, Clay!" said Mr. Pierce, smiling quietly. "Have you lived so long without knowing that all the homage is given to the rising sun, never to the setting, however resplendent its noonday?"

Of Secretaries Campbell and McClelland, the gay, and especially the Southern world, saw but little; nor did Caleb Cushing, the Attorney-General, for whom every Southerner must ever feel a thrill of admiration for his spirited speech on their behalf in Faneuil Hall, mingle much with the lighter element. He was a silent man, a bachelor, who entertained not at all, though paying dutifully such formal calls as seemed obligatory; and Senator Clay, whose delicate health and naturally studious mind made continual attendance upon society an onerous and often shirked duty, had much in common with and greatly esteemed Mr. Cushing, at that time regarded as one of the most earnest statesmen in the capital.

In later life, one who had been a conspicuous Senator from Mississippi in ante-bellum days, appraised him differently, for in 1872 he wrote to my husband in this wise: "I had no confidence in Cushing beyond that of a follower to a quicker intellect and a braver heart  He could appreciate the gallantry and fidelity of Pierce, so he followed him. Like the chameleon, he was green, or blue, or brown, according to what he rested upon."

An affable young man, Mr. Spofford, member of Mr. Cushing's household, and serving as that gentleman's secretary, was no inconsiderable figure in Washington. He became a great favourite in all the notable drawing-rooms, especially with young ladies, and the names of a half-dozen belles were given who had fallen in love with him; but he remained invulnerable to the flashing eyes and bright spirits about him, and married a clever authoress, whose writings, as Harriet Prescott Spofford, have become familiar to a large class of American readers.

My personal favourite of all the Cabinet Ministers was the Secretary of the Navy, J. C. Dobbin. He was a North Carolinian, and the children of my native State were always dear to me. Being a widower, Mr. Dobbin's home was also closed from formal entertainment, but the Secretary was seen now and then in society, where he was much sought after (though not always found) by the leading hostesses, whenever he consented to mingle with it. In his parlours, which now and then he opened to his most favoured friends, he kept on exhibition for years, sealed under a glass case, the suit in which Dr. Kane, the Arctic explorer, had lived during his sojourn among the icy seas.

Secretary Dobbin was a small man; in truth, a duodecimo edition of his sex, and exquisitely presented—a fact which was as freely yielded by his confrères as by his gentler admirers. A man of conspicuous intellectuality and firmness in the administration of his department, his heart was also very tender. Of this he once gave me an especially treasured demonstration.

My friend, Emily Spicer, wife of Lieutenant William F. Spicer, afterward Commander of the Boston Navy Yard, at a very critical time, was suddenly obliged, by the exigencies of the Naval Service, to see her husband prepare for what promised to be a long, and, it might prove, a final separation. Tenderly attached to each other, the young husband at last literally tore himself from his wife, leaving her in an unconscious state, from which she did not recover for many hours. Grave fears were entertained as to the disastrous effect the parting would have upon the young matron.

Having witnessed the sad scene, I went at once to Secretary Dobbin and told him of it. His eyes lighted up most sympathetically, even while he explained to me the necessity for adhering strictly to the rules of the Service, but, even as he marshalled the obstacles to my plea, by intuition I knew his heart was stirred, and when I parted from him, he said, "Comfort her, dear Mrs. Clay, with this assurance: If Spicer is on the high seas he shall be ordered home; if he has arrived in Italy" (for which coast the Lieutenant's ship was booked) "he shall remain there and his wife may join him." I went away grateful for his sympathy for my stricken friend, and hastened to soothe her.

The Secretary kept his word. In a few passing weeks the young couple were reunited on the coast of Italy. "God bless you, my dear Madame," wrote Lieutenant Spicer, thereupon. "I am forever thankfully yours!" And they kept a promise I had exacted, and named the baby, which proved to be a boy, after my dear husband! Long after his distinguished namesake had vanished from the world's stage, a bearded man of thirty came across the ocean and a continent to greet me, his "second mother," as he had been taught to think of me by my grateful friend, his mother, Mrs. Spicer.

Once more I called upon Secretary Dobbin, on behalf of a young naval officer, but this time with a less pathetic request. Our young friend Lieutenant ——, having returned from a long cruise (which, while it lasted, had seemed to be all but unbearable because of its many social deprivations), upon his arrival was so swiftly enthralled by the attractions of a certain young lady (who shall be as nameless as is he) that in his augmenting fervour he proposed to her at once.

The lady accepted. She was very young, very beautiful, very romantic, and, alas! very poor! He was scarcely older, fully as romantic, and also, alas! was, if anything, poorer than she—a fact of which his swashing and naval display of gold-plated buttons and braid gave no hint.

The romance lasted about two weeks, with waning enthusiasm on the youth's side, when, in great distress, he came to see me. He made a clean breast of the dilemma into which he had plunged.

"I beg you will rescue me, Mrs. Clay," he said. "Get me transferred, or sent out anywhere! I've made a fool of myself. I can't marry her," he declared. "I haven't income enough to buy my own clothes, and, as for providing for a girl of her tastes, I don't know whether I shall ever be able to do so."

"But," I remonstrated, "how can I help you? You've only just returned, and in the ordinary course of events you would remain on shore at least six weeks. That isn't long. Try to bear it a while!"

"Long enough for a marriage in naval life," he declared, ruefully. "And I can't break it off without your assistance Help me, Mrs. Clay! If you don't—" He looked sheepish, but dogged. "I'll do what the Irishman did in Charleston!"

"What was that?" I asked.

"Well! he was in exactly the same pickle I am in, so he hired a man and a wheel-barrow, and lying down, face up in it, had himself rolled past the lady's house at a time when he knew she was at home. Then, as the barrow arrived at this point, he had his man stop for a few moments to wipe the sweat of honest toil from his forehead, and, incidentally, to give the lookers-on an opportunity for complete identification. . . . Only difficulty with that is, how would it affect me in the service?" And the Lieutenant became dubious and I thoughtful.

"If I knew on what grounds to approach Secretary Dobbin," I began.

"There aren't any," the Lieutenant answered eagerly. "But there are two ships just fitting out, and lots of men on them would be glad to get off from a three-years' cruise. I would ship for six years, nine—anything that would get me out of this fix!"

On this desperate statement I applied to the Secretary. Within ten days my gallant "friend" was on the sea, and one of Washington's beautiful maidens in tears. Glancing over my letters, I see that at the end of ten years the young Naval officer was still unwed, though not altogether scarless as to intervening love affairs; but the lady was now the happy wife of a member of one of the oldest and wealthiest families in the United States!

Secretary Dobbin was my escort on my first (a most memorable) visit to Fort Monroe. The occasion was a brilliant one, for the President and his Cabinet had come in a body to review the troops. Jefferson Davis, then Secretary of War, and but recently the hero of the battle of Buena Vista, directed the manœuvres, his spirited figure, superb horsemanship, and warlike bearing attracting general attention. An entire day was given up to this holiday-making, and the scene was one of splendid excitement. At night the Fort and the waters beyond were lit up by a pyrotechnic display of great gorgeousness, and enthusiasm rose to its highest when, amid the booming of cannon and the plaudits of happy people, an especially ingenious device blazed across the night sky the names of Franklin Pierce and Jefferson Davis!

Always a man of distinguished appearance, Secretary Davis at that time was exceedingly slender, but his step was springy, and he carried himself with such an air of conscious strength and ease and purpose as often to cause a stranger to turn and look at him. His voice was very rich and sonorous, his enunciation most pleasing. In public speech he was eloquent and magnetic, but, curiously enough, he was a poor reader, often "mouthing" his phrases in a way that would have aroused Hamlet's scorn. Though spoken of as cold and haughty, in private his friends found him refreshingly informal and frank. From their first meeting, Secretary Davis was the intimate friend of my husband, whose loyalty to Mr. Davis in the momentous closing days of the Confederacy reacted so unfortunately upon his own liberty and welfare.

Neither the Secretary of War nor his wife appeared frequently in society in the earlier days of his appointment, the attention of Mr. Davis being concentrated upon the duties of his office, and a young family engaging that of his wife. I have heard it said that so wonderful was Mr. Davis's oversight of the Department of War while under his charge, that it would have been impossible for the Government to have been cheated out of the value of a brass button! So proud was his adopted State of him, that at the close of Mr. Pierce's administration, Mississippi promptly returned Mr. Davis to Washington as Senator. Almost immediately thereafter he became the victim of a serious illness, which lasted many weeks, and a complication of troubles set in which culminated in the loss of sight in one eye. During that period my husband gave up many nights to the nursing of the invalid, who was tortured by neuralgic pains and nervous tension. Senator Clay's solicitude for Mr. Davis was ever of the deepest, as his efforts to sustain and defend him to the last were of the most unselfish.

Aaron V. Brown, who became Postmaster-General in 1857, was at once one of the kindest-hearted and simplest of men, loving his home and being especially indifferent to all things that savoured of the merely fashionable and superficial. He occupied a house which by long association with distinguished people had become prominently known. Not infrequently the Brown residence was alluded to as the "Cabinet Mansion." Here, among other celebrities, had lived Attorney-General Wirt, and in it Mrs. Wirt had compiled the first "Flora's Dictionary." The hospitality of Mr. and Mrs. Brown, being boundless, served to accentuate its reputation, for, unlike her husband, Mrs. Brown was socially most industrious, and, being exceedingly well-to-do, was full of enterprise in the invention of novel surprises for her guests. Mrs. Brown, who was the sister of the afterward distinguished Major-General Pillow, of the Confederate Army, was the first hostess in Washington, I think, to introduce orchestral music at dinner, and her daughter, Narcissa Sanders,

with as pronounced a spirit of innovation,* sent out
enormous cards of invitation in her own name, inviting
the distinguished folk of the capital to the house of the
Postmaster-General to meet—herself!

I remember a dinner at this luxurious home of Mr.
Brown, at which my host, who took me in, amused me
immensely at the expense of the elaborate feast before
us, and at some of his wife's kindly, if costly, foibles.
Behind a barrier of plants a band played softly; around
us were the obsequious waiters from Gautier's.

"All from Gautier's!" sighed the Postmaster-General,
in mock despair. "My wife's napery is the best to be
had, but she will have Gautier's! Our silver is—certainly not the plainest in the city, but Mrs. Brown must
have Gautier's! We have an incomparable *chef*, but
nothing will please my wife but these"; and he scanned
the mysterious *menu* with its tier after tier of unknown
French names. Then he turned suddenly and asked me,
pointing to a line, "My child, what's this? Don't know,
eh? Well, neither do I, but let's try it, anyway. I don't
suppose it will kill us," and so on, the good old gentleman keeping me in a continual bubble of smothered
laughter to the end of the dinner.

A member of Mr. Pierce's Cabinet, whose house was
as conspicuous for its large and lavish entertaining as
was Mr. Brown's, was the Secretary of the Treasury,
Guthrie, the wealthy Kentuckian. Mr. Guthrie was no
society lover (it was a time when statesmen had need to
be absorbed in weightier things), but he entertained, I
always thought, as a part of his public duty. His was a
big, square-shouldered and angular figure, and his appear-

* "I remember," said General Joseph Wheeler, "hearing of those
innovations, and that the guests entered the dining-room two by two,
and left it in the same order, to the music of the orchestra. They
introduced the custom of announcing the arrival of each guest at
receptions, by having a functionary call the name, aloud, a novelty
against which a good many rebelled." A. S.

ance, it was obvious, at receptions was perfunctory rather
than a pleasure. A widower, his home was presided over
by his two daughters, Mrs. Polk and Mrs. Coke, both
also widowed. I often thought Secretary Guthrie's
capacious ballroom suggestive, in its proportions, of a
public hall.

Here, one evening, I had my never-to-be-forgotten
*rencontre* with Chevalier Bertinatti, the Sardinian Minister. Dear old Bertinatti! In all the diplomatic circle
of the Pierce and Buchanan administrations there was
not to be found a personage at once more dignified and
genial. Serious, yet enthusiastic, his naturally kind
heart adding warmth to the gallantry for which foreigners are famous, the Chevalier was a typical ambassador
of the Latin people. He was a learned man, especially
in matters American, and knew our Constitution better
than did many of our native representatives in Washington. He encountered bravely, though not always successfully, the difficulties of the English language, and his
defeats in this field (such is the irony of fate) have served
to keep him longer in the minds of many than have his
successes.

Upon the occasion to which I have referred, a soirée
was held at Secretary Guthrie's house, at which half the
world was present. I wore that evening a gown of foreign
silk, the colour of the pomegranate blossom, and with it
a Sardinian head-dress and ornaments which had been
sent me by a Consular friend. Seeing me at some distance, the Chevalier failed to recognise me and asked
one of the hostesses, with whom he was conversing,
"Who is zat lady wis my kontree-woman's ornaments?"

Upon learning my identity he came forward quickly
and, gazing admiringly at me, he threw himself on his
knee before me (kissing my hand as he did so, with
ardent gallantry) as he exclaimed: "Madame, you are
charming wis zat head-dress like my kontree-women!

Madame! I assure you, you have conquest me behind and now you conquest me before!" and he bowed profoundly.

This remarkable compliment was long remembered and recounted wherever the name of the kind-hearted diplomat was mentioned. A great many ties bound Monsieur Bertinatti to Washington society, not the least of which was his marriage to Mrs. Bass of Mississippi, an admired member of the Southern and predominating element in the capital. Her daughter, who returned to die in her native land (she was buried from the Cathedral in Memphis, Tennessee), became the Marquise Incisa di Camerana.

When, after decades of political strife, the crucial time of separation came between the North and the South, and we of the South were preparing to leave the Federal City, I could not conceal my sorrow; and tears, ever a blessed boon to women, frequently blinded me as I bade first one and then another of our associates what was to be a long good-bye. At such an expression of my grief the Chevalier Bertinatti was much troubled.

"Don't weep," he said. "Don't weep, my dear Mrs. Clay. You have had sixty years of uninterrupted peace! This is but a revolution, and all countries must suffer from them at times! Look at my poor country! I was born in revolution, and reared in revolution, and I expect to die in revolution!" And with this offering of philosophic consolation we parted.

# CHAPTER V

## Solons of the Capital

THE classes of Washington society in the fifties were peculiarly distinct. They were not unlike its topography, which is made up of many small circles and triangles, into each of which run tributary streets and avenues. In the social life, each division in the Congressional body was as a magnetic circle, attracting to itself by way of defined radii those whose tastes or political interests were in sympathy with it. Not less prominent than the Cabinet circle (outranking it, in fact), and fully as interesting by reason of its undisguised preference for things solid, scientific and intellectual, was the Judiciary or Supreme Court set. The several Justices that composed this august body, together with their wives and daughters, formed a charmed circle into which the merely light-minded would scarcely have ventured. Here one met the wittiest and the weightiest minds of the capital, and here, perhaps more than in any other coterie, the newcomer was impressed with what Messrs. Nicolay and Hay describe as "the singular charm of Washington life." In the Supreme Court circle, the conditions attending Congressional life in those strenuous times forced themselves less boldly upon one. Here one discussed philosophies, inventions, history, perhaps, and the arts; seldom the fashions, and as seldom the *on dits*.

The Nestor of that circle in the fifties was quaint old Roger B. Taney (pronounced Tawney), who, after various political disappointments, including a refusal by the Senate to confirm his appointment as a member of the

Cabinet, had received his appointment to the Supreme Court bench in 1836. Upon the death of Chief Justice Marshall, Judge Taney became the head of the Supreme Court body; thus, for more than thirty years, he had been a prominent personage in the country's legal circles and a conspicuous resident in Washington. He was an extremely plain-looking man, with frail body, which once rose tall and erect, but now was so bent that one always thought of him as small, and with a head which made me think of a withered nut. Swarthy of skin, but grey-haired, Judge Taney was a veritable skeleton, "all mind and no body"; yet his opinion settled questions that agitated the nation, and his contemporaries agreed he was the ablest man who had ever sat upon the Supreme Court bench. Judge Taney's daughters, gifted and brilliant women, were seldom seen in society, but from choice or necessity chose bread-winning careers. They were great draughtswomen and made coloured maps, for which, in those days of expanding territory, there was a great and constant need.

Of Chief Justice Taney's associates, Judges Catron and John A. Campbell became best known to Senator Clay and myself. These, and other statesmen equally distinguished and later to be mentioned, having been the friends of ex-Governor (then Senator) C. C. Clay, Sr., my husband had been known to them from the days when, as a school-boy, he had visited his parents in the Federal City. Mrs. Judge Catron, whom I met soon after my arrival in Washington, was a woman of great elegance of manner and dress, and always brought to my mind the thought of a dowager Duchess. An associate of my husband's mother, and a native of gay Nashville, Mrs. Catron had been a social queen in Washington in the late thirties, and her position of interest was still preserved in 1855.

Judge and Mrs. Campbell, being rich beyond many others, their home was widely known for sumptuous entertaining as well as for its intellectual atmosphere. Sharing to an extent the public favour, Judge Campbell, Reverdy Johnson, and Robt. J. Walker were the three legal giants of their day. Judge Campbell's clients were among the weathiest in the country, and his fees were said to be enormous. Had not the war ensued, undoubtedly he would have been appointed to the Chief Justiceship, as was commonly predicted for him. He was a man of great penetration and erudition, and was held in high esteem by everyone in the capital. In 1861 he cast his lot with the people of the South, among whom he was born, and went out of the Federal City to meet whatsoever fate the future held. Judge Campbell became the earnest adviser of Mr. Davis, and was a Commissioner of the Confederate Government, together with Alexander H. Stephens and R. M. T. Hunter, when the three conferred with Mr. Seward, acting as delegate from the Northern President, Lincoln. Nor did the ensuing years diminish the great regard of great men for our beloved Southern scholar.* Writing to Judge Campbell from Washington on December 10, 1884, Thomas F. Bayard thus reveals the exalted regard which the former sustained to the close of a long life:

"Mr. Lamar, now Associate Judge of the Supreme Court, concurs with me," he wrote, "in considering it highly important that your counsel and opinions should be freely given to Mr. Cleveland at this important juncture, and respectfully and earnestly I trust you will concur in our judgment in the matter. Mr. Cleveland will resign from his present office early in January, but

* Wrote the Assistant Attorney-General, William A. Maury, in 1885, to Judge Campbell: "I called on the President in company with Judge Gilbert and Mr. Corcoran, and, a most fitting opportunity having occurred in the course of our talk, I pleased the President greatly by telling him you said he was the biggest man who had been in the White House since you were a child! Which Mr. Corcoran supplemented by saying, 'And Judge Campbell is a man who means what he says!'"

can easily and conveniently receive you for the purpose suggested in the interview."*

In those days of Washington's splendour, Mrs. Campbell and her daughter Henrietta were no less distinguished for their culture, intellectuality, and exclusiveness. Mrs. Campbell was the first Southern woman to adopt the English custom of designating her coloured servant as "my man." At the home of the Campbells one met not only the legal lights of Washington, but scientists and travellers, as if law and the sciences were drawn near to each other by natural selection. Professor Henry, of the Smithsonian Institution, was a frequent visitor at this home, as was also Professor Maury, the grand road-master of the ocean, who, by the distribution of his buoys, made a track in the billows of the Atlantic for the safe passing of ships.

I remember an amusing visit paid by a party from our mess to the observatory of Professor Maury. It was an occasion of special interest. Jupiter was displaying his brilliancy in a marvellous way. For no particular reason, in so far as I could see, the Professor's great telescope seemed to require adjusting for the benefit of each of the bevy present. I noticed Professor Maury's eye twinkling as he went on with this necessary (?) preliminary, asking, betimes: "What do you see? Nothing clearly? Well, permit me!" And after several experiments he would secure, at last, the right focus. When all of his guests had been treated to a satisfactory view of the wonders of the sky, Professor Maury delivered himself somewhat as follows:

"Now, ladies, whilst you have been studying the heavenly bodies, I have been studying you!" and the quizzical expression deepened in his eye.

"Go on," we assented.

* Held between Messrs. Cleveland, President-elect, and Bayard in the official residence, which is segregated from the Capitol.

"Well," said the Professor, "I have a bill before Congress," (mentioning its nature) "and if you ladies don't influence your husbands to vote for it, I intend *to publish the ages of each and every one of you to the whole of Washington!*"

Remembering the mutability of political life, it was and remains a source of astonishment to me that in the Government circles of the fifties were comprised so many distinguished men who had retained their positions in the political foreground for so many years; years, moreover, in which an expanding territory was causing the envy for office to spread, infecting the ignorant as well as the wise, and causing contestants to multiply in number and their passions to increase in violence at each election.

When Senator Clay and I took up our residence in the Federal City, there were at least a dozen great statesmen who had dwelt almost continuously in Washington for nearly twoscore years.    Writing of these to Governor Clay, in 1858, my husband said "Mr. Buchanan looks as ruddy as ever; General Cass as young and vigorous as in 1844, and Mr. Dickens * appears as he did in 1834, when with you I was at his home at an evening party!" Thomas Hart Benton, the great Missourian, who for seven long years struggled against such allied competitors as Senators Henry Clay, Calhoun, and Webster, in his fight against the Bank of the United States, probably out-ranked all others in length of public service; but, besides Mr. Benton, there were Chief Justice Taney and his associates, Judges Catron, James M. Wayne, and John McLean, of Ohio; Senator Crittenden, of Kentucky, and General George Wallace Jones—all men who had entered political life when the century was young.

Among my pleasantest memories of Washington are

* Asbury Dickens, Clerk of the Senate.

the evenings spent at the home of Mr. Benton. His household, but recently bereft of its mistress, who had been a long-time invalid, was presided over by his daughters, Mrs. General Frémont, Mrs. Thomas Benton Jones, and Mme. Boileau. The last-named shared, with the Misses Bayard and Maury, a reputation for superior elegance among the young women of the capital. The daughters of Mr.. Benton had been splendidly educated, it was said, by their distinguished father, and they repaid his care of them by a lifelong adoration. A handsome man in ordinary attire, the great old author and statesman was yet a more striking figure when mounted. He rode with a stately dignity, quite unlike the pace indulged in by some other equestrians of that city and day; a day, it may be said in passing, when equestrianism was common. Mr. Benton's appearance and the slow gait of his horse impressed me as powerful and even majestic, and often (as I remarked to him at dinner one evening) there flashed through my mind, as I saw him, a remembrance of Byron's Moorish King as he rode benignly through the streets of Granada. He seemed gratified at my comparison.

"I'm glad you approve of my pace," he said. "I ride slowly because I do not wish to be confounded with post-boys and messengers sent in haste for the surgeon. They may gallop if they will, but not Senators."

At his own table Mr. Benton was an oracle to whom everyone listened eagerly. I have seen twenty guests held spellbound as he recited, with thrilling realism, a history of the Clay-Randolph duel, with the details of which he was so familiarly acquainted. I never heard him allude to his great fight in the Senate, when, the galleries crowded with men inimical to him, his wife and General Jones sent out for arms to protect the fearless Senator from the onslaught which seemed impending; nor to his nearly thirty years' strife for the removal of the onerous Salt Tax; but the dinners before which his guests sat down were flavoured with the finest of Attic salt, of which he was a connoisseur, which served to sting into increased eagerness our interest in his rich store of recollections.

Wherever Mr. Benton was seen he was a marked personage. There was something of distinction in the very manner in which he wore his cravat, and when he spoke, men listened instinctively. Of his daughters, Mrs. Frémont was probably the most gifted, and Mme. Boileau the most devoted to fashionable society. Mme. Boileau was the wife of a French attaché, and was remarked as she drove about in the streets with a be-ribboned spaniel upon the front seat of her calash. Many years after my acquaintance in Washington with Mr. Benton's family (it was during the Cleveland Administration), I was present at a reception given by Mrs. Endicott when I observed among the guests a very busy little woman, in simple black apparel, whose face was familiar to me, but whom I found myself unable to place; yet everyone seemed to know her. I heard her address several foreigners, in each case employing the language of his country, and, my curiosity increasing, I asked at last, "Who is that small lady in black?"

To my surprise, she proved to be Mrs. Frémont!

I soon made my way to her. She seemed almost impatient as I said, "Mrs. Frémont, I can never forget you, nor the charming evenings at your father's house, though you, I am sure, have forgotten me!" She looked at me searchingly and then spoke, impetuously:

"Yes! yes! I remember your face perfectly, but your name—Tell me who you are, quick. Don't keep me waiting!" I promptly gratified her, and in the conversation that followed, I added some reference to her father's great book, "Thirty Years' View," which, until the destruction of my home during the Civil War, had formed two of our most valued volumes.

"Ah!" cried Mrs. Frémont. "You are a woman of penetration! I have always said my father's book is the Political Bible of America. I know it will not perish!"

I have referred to General George Wallace Jones. No memory of ante-bellum Washington and its moving personages would be complete were he, the pet of women and the idol of men, left out. He was born in 1804, when the Union was young; and adventure and patriotism, then sweeping over our country, were blended in him. As a child he came out of the young West, still a wilderness, to be educated in Kentucky. He had been a sergeant of the body-guard of General Jackson, and to the Marquis de la Fayette upon the latter's last visit to the United States in 1824. Thereafter he figured in the Black Hawk War as aid to General Dodge. His life was a continual panorama of strange events. In the Great Indian War he became a Major-General; then a County Judge; and appeared at the capital as delegate from the Territory of Michigan early in 1835. General Jones's personal activity becoming known to the Government, he was made Surveyor-General of the Northwest. It was about this time that he, being on the Senate floor, sprang to the side of Mr. Benton while the gallery hummed ominously with the angry threats of the friends of the Bank defenders, and personal violence seemed unavoidable. I never knew how many of the Western States were laid out by General Jones, but they were numerous. In his work of surveying he was accompanied by young military men, many of whom played conspicuous parts in the history of the country, at that time but half of its present size. Among these was Jefferson Davis, then a civil engineer.

General Jones was indefatigable in his attendance at social gatherings, and continued to out-dance young men, even when threescore rich years were his. He had been a great favourite with my husband's parents during their Congressional life, so great indeed that father's message of introduction spoke of him as "My son!" and his fraternal offices to us are among the brightest memories I hold of life at the capital. The General was a small, wiry man, renowned for his long black hair, glossy and well-kept as was any belle's, and which seemed even to a very late period to defy time to change it. In society he was sprightly as a kitten, and at seventy-five would poke his glistening black head at me, declaring as he did so, "I'll give you anything you ask, from a horse to a kiss, if you can find one grey hair among the black!"

General Jones died in the West, just before the close of the nineteenth century, but to the end he was gay and brave, and elastic in body and mind. So indomitable was his spirit even in those closing days, that he revived a memory of the war days in the following spirited letter written in 1894, just after the celebration of his ninetieth birthday. At this time he was made King of the Carnival, was complimented by the Governor of Iowa, "the two branches of the General Assembly, and by the Supreme Court, they, too, being Republicans and total strangers to me save one Republican Senator and one Democratic representative from this County," as his gay account of the episode ran.

"I told several times," he added, "of how you and dear Mrs. Bouligny prevented me from killing Seward. It was the day you stopped me, as you sat in your carriage in front of Corcoran & Riggs's bank, and I was about to pass you. I would certainly have killed Seward with my sword-cane but that you stopped me. I was about to follow the Secretary as he passed the bank door, between his son Frederick and some other men. I would have run my sword through him and immediately have been cut into mince-meat by the hundreds of negro guards who stood all round. Do you recollect that fearful incident? God sent two guardian angels to save my life. How can I feel otherwise than grateful to you for saving me that day!"

The recalling of this pioneer-surveyor of the great Western wilderness revives, too, the name of as notable a character in the Southwest, and one who will always be identified with the introduction of cotton in the Southern States, and the land-grants of the territory of Louisiana. I never met Daniel Clarke, but very early in my married life, and some years before I went to the capital to reside, I became acquainted with that remarkable woman, his daughter, Mrs. Myra Clarke Gaines.

I had accompanied my husband to New Orleans, where we stopped at the St. Charles Hotel, then two steps or more above the ground level, though it settled, as all New Orleans buildings do sooner or later, owing to the moist soil.

The evening of our arrival we were seated in the dining-room when my attention was attracted by the entrance of a very unusual couple. The man was well-advanced in years, but bore himself with a dignified and military air that made him at once conspicuous. There was a marked disparity between this tall, commanding soldier and the very small young woman who hung upon his arm "like a reticule or a knitting-pocket," as I remarked *sotto voce* to Mr. Clay. Her hair was bright, glistening chestnut, her colour very fresh and rich, and her golden-hazel eyes glowed like young suns. These orbs were singularly searching, and seemed to gauge every-one at a glance. Mr. Clay, having already an acquaintance with General Gaines, in a few moments I was presented to the (even then) much-talked-of daughter of General Clarke.

Never did woman exhibit more wifely solicitude,

From the beginning of that dinner Mrs. Gaines became the General's guardian. She arranged his napkin, tucking it carefully into the V of his waistcoat, read the menu and selected his food, waiting upon him as each course arrived, and herself preparing the dressing for his salad. All was done in so matter-of-fact and quiet a manner that the flow of General Gaines's discourse was not once interrupted. Though I met this interesting woman a number of times in later years, in Washington and elsewhere, that first picture of Mrs. Gaines, probably the bravest woman, morally, of her time, has remained most vividly. When, as a widow, accompanied by her daughter, Mrs. Gaines visited Washington, she was the cynosure of all eyes in every assemblage in which she was seen. Her fearless pleading in the Supreme Court was the theme of conversation the country over. People thronged to see a woman whose courage was so indomitable, and none but were surprised at the diminutive and modest heroine.

Senator Crittenden, of Kentucky, was already a Solon in the counsels of the Nation, when, in 1841, Senator C. C. Clay, Sr., left the Senate. A major in the army in 1812, Mr. Crittenden had made his appearance in Congress in 1817, and thereafter continued prominent in Washington life, as Senator or Cabinet member (in the Cabinets of Presidents Harrison and Fillmore), so that for thirty or more years his name had been associated with the names of our great law-makers, especially with those of the second quarter of the century. When I met Senator Crittenden in the middle fifties, he was a carefully preserved gentleman of courtly and genial manners. Besides the brilliancy that attached to his long career in Congressional life, he was distinguished as the husband of a still charming woman, whose proud boast it was that she was perfectly happy. This declaration alone was enough to make any woman in society remarkable; yet, to judge from her serene and smiling appearance, Mrs. Crittenden did not exaggerate her felicity. She was a sweet type of the elderly fashionable woman, her face reflecting the utmost kindness, her corsage and silvery hair gleaming with brilliants, her silken petticoats rustling musically, and, over the lustrous folds of her rich and by no means sombre costumes, priceless lace fell prodigally.

Nor were there lacking notes and even whole gowns of warm colour significant of the lady's persistent cheeriness. I remember my cousin, Miss Comer, a débutante of seventeen at that time, remarking upon Mrs. Crittenden's dress one evening at a ball.

"It's exactly like mine, cousin!" she said, not without a pout of disappointment. And so, in truth, it was, both being of bright, cherry corded silk, the only difference between them being that the modest round-necked bodice of my little cousin by no means could compete with the noble *décolleté* of the older lady. But, in justice to the most estimable Mrs. Crittenden, it must be added that her neck and shoulders were superbly moulded, and, even in middle age, excited the envy of her less fortunate sisters.

"Lady" Crittenden, as she was often called, accounted for her contentment in this wise: "I have been married three times, and in each alliance I have got just what I wanted. My first marriage was for love, and it was mine as fully as I could wish; my second for money, and Heaven was as good to me in this instance; my third was for position, and that, too, is mine. What more could I ask?"

What more, indeed!

One met dear old Mrs. Crittenden everywhere. She was of the most social disposition, a fact which sometimes aroused the good-natured irony of her distinguished husband. I remember an instance in which this was

MRS. J. J. CRITTENDEN
of Kentucky

demonstrated, at the White House, which greatly amused me at the time. It was at a dinner party, and Senator Crittenden, who boasted that he had eaten at the White House table with every President since the days of Monroe, assumed the *blasé* air which everyone who knew him recognised as a conscious affectation.

"Now there's 'Lady' Crittenden," he began, nodding in the direction of that smiling personage, "in all the glory of a new and becoming gown, and perfectly happy in the glamour of this." And he waved his hand about the room with an air of fatigue and, at the same time, a comprehensiveness that swept in every member, grave or giddy, in the large assemblage. "If I had my way," and he sighed as he said it, "nothing would give me greater pleasure than to hie me back to the wilds of dear old Kentucky! Ah! to don my buckskins once more, shoulder a rifle, and wander through life a free man, away from all this flummery!"

He sighed again (for the tangled woods?) as he detected a speck upon his faultless sleeve and fastidiously brushed it off!

"Pshaw! Stuff and nonsense, Senator!" I retorted, rallying him heartlessly. "Fancy your being condemned to that! You wouldn't stand it two days, unless an election were in progress and there were country constituents to interview. Everyone knows you are as fond of fat plums and plump capons, both real and metaphorical, as any man in the capital! As for society being disagreeable to you, with a good dinner in view and pretty women about you—Fie, Senator! I don't believe you!" Whereat our Solon laughed guiltily, like one whose pet pretense has been discovered, and entered forthwith into the evening's pleasures as heartily as did his spouse, the perfectly happy "Lady" Crittenden.

# CHAPTER VI

## Fashions of the Fifties

To estimate at anything like their value ante-bellum days at the capital, it must be borne in mind that the period was one of general prosperity and competitive expenditure. While a life-and-death struggle raged between political parties, and oratorical battles of ominous import were fought daily in Senate Chamber and House, a very reckless gaiety was everywhere apparent in social circles. Especially was this to be observed in the predominant and hospitable Southern division in the capital; for predominant Southern society was, as even such deliberately partisan historians as Messrs. Nicolay and Hay admit; and, what these gentlemen designate as "the blandishments of Southern hospitality," lent a charm to life in the Government circles of that day which lifted the capital to the very apex of its social glory. Writing of these phases of life in the capital, in a letter dated March, 1858, I said to Governor Clay: "People are mad with rivalry and vanity. It is said that Gwin is spending money at the rate of $75,000 a year, and Brown and Thompson quite the same. Mrs. Thompson (of Mississippi) is a great favourite here. Mrs. Toombs, who is sober, and has but one daughter, Sally, who is quite a belle, says *they* spend $1,800 per month, or $21,000 per annum."

The four years' war, which began in '61, changed these social conditions. As the result of that strife poverty spread both North and South. The social world at Washington, which but an administration before had been scarcely less fascinating and brilliant than the Court of Louis Napoleon, underwent a radical change; and the White House itself, within a month after it went into the hands of the new Black Republican party, became degraded to a point where even Northern men recoiled at the sight of the metamorphosed conditions.*

In the days of Presidents Pierce and Buchanan, Washington was a city of statesmen, and in the foreground, relieving the solemnity of their deliberations in that decade which preceded the Nation's great disaster, were fashion and mirth, beauty and wit. It was then, as the government city of a Republic must ever be, a place of continuous novelty, of perpetual changes, of new faces. The fashionable world comes and goes in the Federal City with each Presidential term of four and Senatorial term of six years, and its longer or shorter stays of the army and navy contingent, and always it gathers its personnel from as many points as there are States in the Union, and as many parts of the world as those to which our diplomatic relations extend.

In the fifties, when the number of States was but two dozen, the list of representatives gathering at the capital was proportionately smaller than in the present day, and society was correspondingly select. Moreover, political distinction and offices not infrequently continued in many families through several generations, sons often succeeding their fathers in Congress, inheriting, in some degree, their ancestors' friends, until a social security had been established which greatly assisted to give

* In a letter dated New York, April 6, 1861, a correspondent, the intimate associate of James Gordon Bennett, wrote as follows: "I have been in Washington twice since I had the pleasure of seeing you, and I can say truthfully, that . . . the *ensemble* of the personnel of the White House has sadly changed, more befitting a restaurant than the House of the President. They tell me many droll stories of them, and all are deservedly rich. 'Old Abe' tells stories and Mrs. Lincoln simpers. They keep a household of those horrid . . . people with them all the time, *mais assez!*"

charm and prestige to the fashionable coteries of the Federal centre. For example, for forty years previous to my husband's election to the Senate, the two branches of the Clay family had been prominent in the life of the capital. In the late twenties, C. C. Clay, Sr., had been active in the House, while the great Henry Clay was stirring the country through his speeches in the Senate; in the fifties, Mr. James B. Clay, son of the great Kentuckian, was a Congressman when the scholarly statesmanship of Senator C. C. Clay, Jr., of Alabama, was attracting the admiration and praise of North and South alike. It is a pathetic coincidence that to my husband, during his sojourn in Canada, fell the sad privilege of ministering at the death-bed of Mr. Clay, of Kentucky, who died in that alien land without the solacing presence of wife or children. Shortly before the end came, he presented to Senator Clay the cane which for years had been carried by the great orator, Henry Clay.*

The fashions of the times were graceful, rich and picturesque. Those of the next decade, conspicuous for huge *chignons*, false hair, and distorting bustles, rose like an ugly barrier between the lovely costuming of the fifties and the dressing of to-day. A half-century ago, the beauties of the capital wore their hair *à la Grecque*, with flowers wreathed over it, or a simple golden dagger or arrow to secure it. Their gowns were festooned with blossoms that trailed over bodice and skirt until not seldom they became, by reason of their graceful orna-

---

* Some time after Clement C. Clay's return to the Confederate States, this cane was purloined by some unknown person. Years passed; one day Mr. Clay received an inquiry as to whether he had ever owned a cane on which his name appeared below that of the Kentucky Senator's; the writer explained that he wished to know its history and to return the cane to its rightful owner. Eager for the recovery of his valued souvenir, Mr. Clay responded; but his unknown correspondent, having gained the information he sought, lapsed into silence. Said Mrs. Clay, in relating this incident, "And we never heard more of the cane!" A. S.

ments, veritable Perditas. These delicate fashions continued until nearly the end of the decade, when they were superseded by more complicated coiffures and a general adoption of heavy materials and styles.

In 1858–'59 the hair was arranged on the top of the head in heavy braids wound like a coronet over the head, and the coiffure was varied now and then with a tiara of velvet and pearls, or jet or coral. Ruffled dresses gave place to panelled skirts in which two materials, a plain and embossed or brocaded fabric, were combined, and basques with postillion backs became the order of the day. The low-coiled hair and brow free from frizzes and bangs (*à l'idiote*, as our satirical friends, the French, describe them) was the style adopted by such preëminent beauties as Mrs. Senator Pugh, who was regarded by Baron Hulseman as without a peer, and Mrs. Senator Pendleton, who, in Lord Napier's opinion, had the most classic head he had seen in America.

Low necks and lace berthas, made fashionable because of their adoption by Miss Lane, were worn almost universally, either with open sleeves revealing inner ones of filmy lace, or sleeves of the shortest possible form, allowing the rounded length of a pretty arm to be seen in its perfection. Evening gloves were half-length only, or as often reaching only half-way to the elbow. They were of kid or silk with backs embroidered in delicate silks, with now and then a jewel sparkling among the colours. Jewels, indeed, were conspicuous even in men's dressing, and gentlemen of fashion were rare who did not have varieties of sparkling studs and cravat-pins to add to the brightness of their vari-coloured vests. The latter not infrequently were of richest satin and velvet, brocaded and embroidered. They lent a desirable note of colour, by no means inconspicuous, to the swallow-tailed evening dress of that time, a note, by-the-bye, which was supplemented by a tie of bright soft silk, and of ample proportions. President Buchanan was remarkable for his undeviating choice of pure white cravats. Fashion was not then arbitrary in the matter of gentlemen's neckwear, and high or low collars were worn, as best suited the taste of the individual.

To the attire of the women of the Government City in that day our home manufacturers contributed but little. In fact, the industries of our country yielded but a common grade of materials designed for wearing apparel, and were altogether unequal to the demands of a capital in which the wealthy vied with their own class in foreign cities in the acquisition of all that goes to make up the moods and character of fashion. Our gloves and fans and handkerchiefs, our bonnets and the larger part of our dress accessories, as well as such beautiful gown patterns as were purchased ready to be made up by a New York or Washington dressmaker, were all imported directly from foreign houses, and the services of our travelling and consular friends were in constant requisition for the selection of fine laces, shawls, flounces, under-sleeves and the other fashionable garnitures. Scarcely a steamer but brought to the capital dainty boxes of Parisian flowers, bonnets and other foreign novelties, despatched by such interested deputies.

It was astonishing how astute even our bachelor representatives abroad became in the selection of these articles for the wives of their Senatorial indorsers in Washington. I was frequently indebted for such friendly remembrances to my cousin, Tom Tait Tunstall, Consul at Cadiz, and to Mrs. Leese, wife of the Consul at Spezia and sister of Rose Kierulf and Mrs. Spicer. Thanks to the acumen of these thoughtful friends, my laces, especially, and a velvet gown, the material of which was woven to order at Genoa, were the particular envy of my less fortunate "mess-mates."

I remember with much pleasure the many courtesies

of William Thomson, Consul at Southampton, England, who was one of the many from whom the war afterward separated us. From the time of his appointment in 1857 his expressions of friendliness were frequent toward Miss Lane, Mrs. Fitzpatrick, myself, and, I doubt not, toward many other fortunate ones of the capital.

To the first named he sent a remarkable toy-terrier, so small that "it might be put under a quart bowl," as he wrote to me. The little stranger was a nine-days' curiosity at the White House, where it was exhibited to all who were on visiting terms with Miss Lane. That I was not the recipient of a similar midget was due to the death of "Nettle," the animal selected for me.

"Please ask Miss Lane," he wrote, "to show you her terrier, and you will be sure it is the identical 'Nettle.' I shall succeed in time in finding a good specimen for you!"

But Mr. Thomson's efforts and discrimination were by no means directed solely toward the selection of canine rarities. In truth, he showed himself in every way fitted to become a most satisfactory Benedick (which I sincerely hope was his fate in the course of time), for, besides picking up now and then odd and choice bits of quaint jewelry, such as may please a woman's fancy, and many an interesting legend about which to gossip, he discovered a power of discernment in regard to the wearing apparel of my sex, which was as refreshing in its epistolary revelations as it was rare among his sex.

"I did think of sending you and Mrs. Fitzpatrick one of the new style petticoats," he wrote in March, 1858, "so novel, it seems, at the seat of government; but, upon inquiry for the material, my bachelor wits were quite outdone, for I could not even guess what size might suit both you ladies! Since sending a few lines to you, I have spent a day at Brighton, which is in my district, and I saw quite a new style and decided improvement on the petticoat. A reversible crimson and black striped linsey-wolsey under a white cambric skirt, with five, seven, or nine tucks of handsome work, not less than ten or twelve inches deep. This style of new garment is very *distingué* to my feeble bachelor eye, and would attract amazingly in Washington just now."

Among the first to introduce in the capital the fashion of holding up the skirt to show these ravishing petticoats were the lovely sisters of Thomas F. Bayard, afterward Secretary of State and Minister to England under President Cleveland, and the Misses Maury, daughters of the ex-Mayor of Washington, all of whom were conspicuous for their Parisian daintiness. None of this bevy but looked as if she might have stepped directly from the rue St. Germain.

The bewildering description by Mr. Thomson had scarcely arrived, ere fashion was busy evolving other petticoat novelties and adjuncts. A quaint dress accessory at this time, and one which remained very much in vogue for carriage, walking, and dancing dresses, consisted of several little metal hands, which, depending from fine chains attached at the waist, held up the skirt artistically at a sufficient height to show the flounces beneath. The handkerchiefs of the time, which were appreciably larger than those in use to-day, and very often of costly point-lace, were drawn through a small ring that hung from a six-inch gold or silver chain, on the other end of which was a circlet which just fitted over the little finger.

I have spoken of our Washington dressmakers; how incomplete would be my memories of the capital did I fail to mention here Mrs. Rich, the favourite mantua-maker of those days, within whose power it lay to transform provincial newcomers, often already over-stocked with ill-made costumes and absurdly trimmed bonnets, into women of fashion! Mrs. Rich was the only Reconstructionist, I think I may safely say, on whom Southern ladies looked with unqualified approval. A Reconstructionist? She was more; she was a physician who cured many ills for the women of the Congressional circles, ills of a kind that could never be reached by our favourite physician, Dr. Johnston, though he had turned surgeon and competed in a contest of stitches; for, to the care of the wives of our statesmen each season, came pretty heiresses from far-off States, to see the gay Government City, under their experienced guardianship, and to meet its celebrities. These, often mere buds of girls, were wont to come to the capital supplied with costly brocade and heavy velvet gowns, fit in quality for the stateliest dame; with hats weighty with plumes that might only be worn appropriately in the helmet of a prince or a Gainsborough duchess, and with diamonds enough to please the heart of a matron. To strip these slim maidens of such untoward finery, often of antediluvian, not to say outlandish, cut and fashion, and to reapparel them in such soft fabrics as became their youth and station, was no small or easy task for her who had undertaken to chaperone them.

Nor were these sartorial *faux pas* confined to the girl novices and their far-off kind, and usually lavish parents. Many a charming matron came to the capital as innocent of any knowledge of the demands of fashionable life as a schoolgirl. There was the wife of a distinguished legislator who afterward presided over an American embassy abroad, a sweet little nun of a woman, who arrived in Washington with a wardrobe that doubtless had caused her country neighbours many a pang of envy. It comprised garments made of the costliest fabrics, but, alas! which had been cut up so ridiculously by the local seamstress that the innocent wearer's first appearance in the gay world of the capital was the signal for irrepressible smiles of amusement and simpers of derision from the more heartless.

Because of a friendship between our husbands, our little nun fell into my hands, and I promptly convoyed her to the crucible of Mrs. Rich, that dauntless spirit, and my unfailing resource, sure of her ability to work the necessary transmutation. Alas! as we were about to step out of our carriage, I was startled by the appearance, above a shapely enough foot, of a bright, yes! a brilliant indigo-blue stocking! Not even Mr. Shillaber's heroine from Beanville could boast a trapping more blatantly blue! I held my breath in alarm! What if the eye of any of the more scornful fashionables should detect its mate? I hurried my charge back into the vehicle at once and summoned our good friend Mrs. Rich to the door; and our errand that morning was accomplished by the aid of a trim apprentice, who brought to our calash boxes of samples and fashion-plates for our scanning.

Many, indeed, were the debtors to Mrs. Rich in those days, for the taste and despatch with which she performed her incomparable miracles. And I would not refrain from acknowledging an act of kindness at her hands in darker days; for, when I returned to Washington in 1865 to plead with the President for my husband's release from Fortress Monroe, she generously refused payment for the making of the modest dress I ordered, declaring that she longed to serve one who had directed so many clients to her in former days!

But there were occasions when a pressure upon the time of Mrs. Rich necessitated the seeking of other assistance, and a hasty journey was made to Mlle. Rountree, of Philadelphia, or even to New York, where the fashionable dressmakers were capable of marvellous expedition in filling one's order completely, even to the furnishing of handkerchiefs and hosiery and slippers to

MRS. CHESTNUT
of South Carolina

suit a special gown. I remember the arrival of some wonderful "creations" made in the metropolis for Miss Stevens, of Stevens Castle, who was spending the season with my "mess-mate," Mrs. Chestnut, and boxes of gowns as admirable, and from the same source, for the lovely Marian Ramsey, who became Mrs. Brockholst Cutting, of New York. Miss Ramsey, who was an especially admired belle in Washington, was the daughter of that delightfully irascible old Admiral, who, it was said, was such a disciplinarian that he never entered port without having one or more of his crew in irons.

Brilliant as was the social life in Washington at this time, and remarkable for its numbers of handsome men and lovely women, I remember no exquisites of the Beau Brummel or Disraeli type, though there were many who were distinguished as men of fashion, of social graces and talent.

Foremost among the popular men of the capital were Philip Barton Key (brother of the classic Mrs. Pendleton, Mrs. Howard of Baltimore, and of Mrs. Blount, who attained a reputation among her contemporaries upon the stage), Preston Brooks, and Laurence Keitt, members of Congress from South Carolina, the last named of whom married the wealthy Miss Sparks. For a long time previous to that alliance, Mr. Keitt and his colleague from North Carolina, Mr. Clingman, were looked upon as rival suitors for the hand of Miss Lane. Mr. Keitt was the friend of Preston Brooks, who was one of the most magnetic and widely admired men in the capital. Were half of the compliments here repeated which the name alone of Mr. Brooks at that time elicited, they must serve to modify the disfavour into which this spirited young legislator from South Carolina fell after his historic assault upon Mr. Sumner in the Senate. When, a few months after that unfortunate affair, the body of Mr. Brooks lay on view in the Federal City, mourning for him became general, and his obsequies were remarkable for the crowds that hastened to pay their last tribute to him.

I recall an amusing incident by which I offended (happily, only momentarily) our good friends Congressman and Mrs. Keitt, owing to a tendency I possessed to indulge in nonsense whenever furnished with the slightest pretext for it. When the former arrived at the capital, he was commonly addressed and alluded to as "Kitt," a wholly unwarrantable mispronunciation of his name, but one which had become current in the vernacular of his State, and which, from sheer force of habit, continued in use in the Federal City. To the retention of this nickname, however, his bride strongly objected, and so persistently did she correct all who miss-called the name, that the Congressman's old friends, though publicly conforming to the lady's wishes, smiled in private, and among themselves clung fondly to the old pronunciation.

This little contention was still in operation when an interesting event took place in the Keitt household. On the evening of the happy day, meeting Senator Hammond at dinner, he asked me casually, "What's the news?"

"Why! haven't you heard?" I replied. "Kitt has a kitten!"

My poor joke, so unexpected, exploded Senator Hammond's gravity immediately. So well did the sally please him, that it speedily became an *on dit*, alas! to the passing annoyance of the happy young pair. Mrs. Keitt was one of Washington's most admired young matrons, a graceful hostess, and famous for her social enterprise. It was she who introduced in the capital the fashion of sending out birth-cards to announce the arrival of infants.

I have spoken of Barton Key. He was a widower during my acquaintance with him, and I recall him as the handsomest man in all Washington society. In appearance an Apollo, he was a prominent figure at all the principal fashionable functions; a graceful dancer, he was a favourite with every hostess of the day. Clever at repartee, a generous and pleasing man, who was even more popular with other men than with women, his death at the hands of Daniel E. Sickles in February, 1859, stirred Washington to its centre.

I remember very vividly how, one Sunday morning, as I was putting the finishing touches to my toilette for attendance at St. John's, Senator Clay burst into the room, his face pale and awe-stricken, exclaiming: "A horrible, horrible thing has happened, Virginia! Sickles, who for a year or more has forced his wife into Barton's company, has killed Key; killed him most brutally, while he was unarmed!"

This untimely death of a man allied to a famous family, and himself so generally admired, caused a remarkable and long depression in society. Yet, so strenuous were the political needs of the time, and so tragic and compelling the demands of national strife now centred in Washington, that the horrible calamity entailed no punishment upon its author.

Only the Thursday before the tragedy, in company with Mrs. Pugh and Miss Acklin, I called upon the unfortunate cause of the tragedy. She was so young and fair, at most not more than twenty-two years of age, and so naïve, that none of the party of which I was one was willing to harbour a belief in the rumours which were then in circulation. On that, Mrs. Sickles' last "at home," her parlours were thronged, one-half of the hundred or more guests present being men. The girl hostess was even more lovely than usual. Of an Italian type in feature and colouring (she was the daughter of a famous musician, Baggioli, of New York), Mrs. Sickles was dressed in a painted muslin gown, filmy and graceful, on which the outlines of the crocus might be traced. A broad sash of brocaded ribbon girdled her slender waist, and in her dark hair were yellow crocus blooms. I never saw her again, but the picture of which she formed the centre was so fair and innocent, it fixed itself permanently upon my mind.

When my husband first entered the United States Senate, in 1853, there were not more than four men in that body who wore moustaches. Indeed, the prejudice against them was great. I remember a moustached gallant who called upon me on one occasion, to whom my aunt greatly objected, for, she said, referring to the growth upon his upper lip, "No one but Tennessee hog-drivers and brigands dress like that!" When Mr. Clay withdrew from the Senate, in January, 1861, there were scarcely as many without them. Side and chin whiskers were worn, if any, though the front of the chin was seldom covered. Many of the most distinguished statesmen wore their faces as smoothly shaven as the Romans of old. Until late in the fifties, men, particularly legislators, wore their hair rather long, a fashion which has been followed more or less continuously among statesmen and scholars since wigs were abandoned.

This decade was also notable as that in which the first radical efforts of women were made toward suffrage, and the "Bloomer" costume became conspicuous in the capital. "Bloomers are 'most as plenty as blackberries,'" I wrote home late in '56, "and generally are followed by a long train of little boys and ditto 'niggers'!"

Nor were there lacking figures among the "stronger" sex as eccentric as those of our women innovators. Of these, none was more remarkable than "old Sam Houston." Whether in the street or in his seat in the Senate, he was sure to arrest the attention of everyone. He wore a leopard-skin vest, with a voluminous scarlet neck-tie, and over his bushy grey locks rested an immense sombrero. This remarkable headgear was made, it was said, from an individual block to which the General reserved the exclusive right. It was of grey felt, with a brim seven or eight inches wide. Wrapped around his broad shoulders he wore a gaily coloured Mexican *serape*, in which scarlet predominated. So arrayed, his huge form, which, notwithstanding this remarkable garb, was distinguished by a kind of inborn grandeur, towered above the heads of ordinary pedestrians, and the appearance of the old warrior, whether viewed from the front or the rear, was altogether unique. Strangers stared at him, and street urchins covertly grinned, but the Senatorial Hercules received all such attentions from the public with extreme composure, not to say gratification, as a recognition to which he was entitled.

In the Senate, General Houston was an indefatigable whittler. A seemingly inexhaustible supply of soft wood was always kept in his desk and out of it he whittled stars and hearts and other fanciful shapes, while he cogitated, his brows pleated in deep vertical folds, over the grave arguments of his confrères. A great many conjectures were made as to the ultimate use of these curious devices. I can, however, explain the fate of one.

As our party entered the gallery of the Senate on one occasion, we caught the eye of the whittling Senator, who, with completest *sang-froid*, suspended his occupation and blew us a kiss; then with a plainly perceptible twinkle in his eye, he resumed his usual occupation. A little while afterward one of the Senate pages came up and handed me a most pretentious envelope. It was capacious enough to have contained a package of government bonds. I began to open the wrappings; they were mysteriously manifold. When at last I had removed them all, I found within a tiny, shiny, freshly whittled wooden heart, on which the roguish old hero had inscribed, "Lady! I send thee my heart! Sam Houston."

This remarkable veteran was seldom to be seen at social gatherings, and I do not remember ever to have met him at a dinner, but he called sometimes upon me on my weekly reception days, and always in the remarkable costume I have described. He had acquired, besides the Mexican-Spanish *patois*, a number of Indian dialects, and nothing amused him more than to reduce to a confused silence those who surrounded him, by suddenly addressing them in all sorts of unknown words in these tongues. My own spirit was not so to be crushed, and, besides, I had a lurking doubt as to the linguistic value of the sounds he uttered. They bore many of the indicia of the newly invented, and I did not hesitate upon one occasion to enter upon a verbal contest of gibberish on my side, and possibly on his, running the gamut of emphasis throughout it; and, notwithstanding General Houston's deprecations (in *Indian dialect*), sustained my part so seriously that the tall hero at last yielded the floor and, wrapping his scarlet *serape* about him, made his exit, laughing hilariously at his own defeat.

# CHAPTER VII

## The Relaxations of Congressional Folk

In that period of social activity it was no uncommon thing for society women to find themselves completely exhausted ere bedtime arrived. Often so tired was I that I have declared I couldn't have wiggled an antennae had I numbered anything so absurd and minute among my members! For my quicker recuperation, after a day spent in the making of calls, or in entertainment, with, it may be, an hour or two in the Senate gallery, in preparation for the evening's pleasure, my invaluable maid, Emily (for whom my husband paid $1,600), was wont to get out my "shocking-box" (for so she termed the electrical apparatus upon which I often depended), and, to a full charge of the magical current and a half-hour's nap before dinner, I was indebted for many a happy evening.

Amid the round of dinners, and dances, and receptions, to which Congressional circles are necessarily compelled, the pleasures of the theatre were only occasionally to be enjoyed. Nor were the great artists of that day always to be heard at the capital, and resident theatre and music-lovers not infrequently made excursions to Baltimore, Philadelphia, or New York, in order to hear to advantage some particularly noted star. Before our advent in the capital it had been my good fortune, while travelling in the North, to hear Grisi and Mario, the lovely Bozio, and Jenny Lind, the incomparable Swede, whose concerts at Castle Garden were such epoch-marking events to music-lovers in America. I remember that one estimate of the audience present on the occasion of my hearing the last-named cantatrice was placed at ten thousand. Whether or not this number was approximately correct I do not know, but seats and aisles in the great hall were densely packed, and gentlemen in evening dress came with camp-stools under their arms, in the hope of finding an opportunity to place them, during a lull in the programme, where they might rest for a moment.

The wild enthusiasm of the vast crowds, the simplicity of the singer who elicited it, have been recorded by many an abler pen. Suffice to say that none have borne, I think, for a longer time, a clearer remembrance of that triumphant evening. When, at the end of the programme the fair, modest songstress came out, music in hand, to win her crowning triumph in the rendering of a familiar melody, the beauty of her marvellous art rose superior to the amusement which her broken English might have aroused, and men and women wept freely and unashamed as she sang.

> "Mid bleasures and balaces,
> Do we may roam," etc.

It was by way of a flight from the capital that Senator Clay and I and a few congenial friends were enabled to hear Parepa Rosa and Forrest; and Julia Dean, in "Ingomar," drew us to the metropolis, as did Agnes Robertson, who set the town wild in the "Siege of Sebastopol."

I remember very well my first impression of Broadway, which designation seemed to me a downright misnomer; for its narrowness, after the great width of Pennsylvania Avenue, was at once striking and absurd to the visitor from the capital. Upon one of my visits to New York my attention was caught by a most unusual sight. It was an immense equipage, glowing and gaudy under the sun as one of Mrs. Jarley's vans. It was drawn by six prancing steeds, all gaily caparisoned, while in the huge

JENNY LIND
From a photograph made about 1851

structure (a young house, "all but"——) were women in gaudy costumes.  A band of musicians were concealed within, and these gave out some lively melodies as the vehicle dashed gaily by the Astor House (then the popular *up-town* hotel), attracting general attention as it passed. Thinking a circus had come to town, I made inquiry, when I learned to my amusement that the gorgeous cavalcade was but an ingenious advertisement of the new Sewing Machine!

Charlotte Cushman, giving her unapproachable "Meg Merrilies" in Washington, stirred the city to its depths. Her histrionism was splendid, and her conversation in private proved no less remarkable and delightful.  "I could listen to her all day," wrote a friend in a brief note. "I envy her her genius, and would willingly take her ugliness for it!  What is beauty compared with such genius!"

A most amusing metrical farce, "Pocahontas," was given during the winter of '57–58, which set all Washington a-laughing.   In the cast were Mrs. Gilbert, and Brougham, the comedian and author.  Two of the ridiculous couplets come back to me, and, as if it were yesterday, revive the amusing scenes in which they were spoken.

Mrs. Gilbert's rôle was that of a Yankee schoolma'am, whose continual effort it was to make her naughty young Indian charges behave themselves.   "Young ladies!" she cried, with that inimitable austerity behind which one always feels the actress's consciousness of the "fun of the thing" which she is dissembling,

"Young Ladies!   Stand with your feet right square!
Miss Pocahontas! just *look* at your hair!"

and as she wandered off, a top-knot of feathers waving over her head, her wand, with which she had been drilling her dusky maidens, held firmly in hand, she cut a pigeonwing that brought forth a perfect shout of laughter from the audience.

This troupe appeared just after the Brooks-Sumner encounter, of which the capital talked still excitedly, and the comedian did not hesitate to introduce a mild local allusion which was generally understood.  Breaking in upon her as Pocahontas wept, between ear-splitting cries of woe at the bier of Captain Smith, he called out impatiently,

"What's all this noise?  Be done!  Be done!
D'you think you are in Washington?"

Mr. Thackeray's lecture on poetry was a red-letter occasion, and the simplicity of that great man of letters as he recited "Lord Lovel" and "Barbara Allen" was long afterward a criterion by which others were judged. Notable soloists now and then appeared at the capital, among them Ap Thomas, the great Welsh harpist, and Bochsa, as great a performer, whose concerts gained so much in interest by the singing of the romantic French woman, Mme. Anna Bishop.  Her rendering of "On the Banks of the Gaudalquiver" made her a great favourite and gave the song a vogue.  That musical prodigy, Blind Tom, also made his appearance in ante-bellum Washington, and I was one of several ladies of the capital invited by Miss Lane to hear him play at the White House. Among the guests on that occasion were Miss Phillips of Alabama and her cousin Miss Cohen of South Carolina, who were brilliant amateur players with a local reputation. They were the daughter and niece, respectively, of Mrs. Eugenia Phillips, who, less than two years afterward, was imprisoned by the Federal authorities for alleged assistance to the newly formed Confederate Government.

At the invitation of Miss Lane, the Misses Phillips and Cohen took their places at the piano and performed a brilliant and intricate duet, during which Blind Tom's face twitched with what, it must be confessed, were horrible grimaces.  He was evidently greatly excited by the music he was listening to, and was eager to reproduce it.  As the piece was concluded, he shuffled about nervously.  Seeing his excitement, one of the pianistes volunteered to play with him and took her seat at the instrument.  Desiring to test him, however, in the second rendering, the lady cleverly, as she supposed, elided a page of the composition; when, drawing himself back angrily, this remarkable idiot exclaimed indignantly, "You cheat me!  You cheat me!"

While a visit to the dentist, be he never so famous, may hardly be regarded as among the recreations of Congressional folk, yet a trip to Dr. Maynard, the fashionable operator of that day, was certainly among the luxuries of the time; as costly, for example, as a trip to New York, to hear sweet Jenny Lind.  Dr. Maynard was distinctively one of Washington's famous characters.  He was not only the expert dentist of his day, being as great an element in life at the capital as was Dr. Evans in Paris, but he was also the inventor of the world-renowned three-barrelled rifle known as the Maynard.  His office was like an arsenal, every inch of wall-space being taken up with glittering arms.

A peculiarity of Dr. Maynard was his dislike for the odour of the geranium, from which he shrank as from some deadly poison.  Upon the occasion of one necessary visit to him, unaware of this eccentricity, I wore a sprig of that blossom upon my corsage.  As I entered the office the doctor detected it.

"Pardon me, Mrs. Clay," he said at once, "I must ask you to remove that geranium!"  I was astonished, but of course the offending flower was at once detached and discarded; but so sensitive were the olfactories of the doctor, that before he could begin his operating, I was obliged to bury the spot on which the blossom had lain under several folds of napkin.

Dr. Maynard was exceedingly fond of sleight of hand, and on one occasion bought for his children an outfit which Heller had owned. In after years the Czar of Russia made tempting offers to this celebrated dentist, with a view to inducing him to take up his residence in St. Petersburg, but his Imperial allurements were unavailing, and Dr. Maynard returned again to his own orbit.

A feature of weekly recurrence, and one to which all Washington and every visitor thronged, was the concert of the Marine Band, given within the White House grounds on the green slope back of the Executive Mansion overlooking the Potomac. Strolling among the multitude, I remember often to have seen Miss Cutts, in the simplest of white muslin gowns, but conspicuous for her beauty wherever she passed. Here military uniforms glistened or glowed, as the case might be, among a crowd of black-coated sight-seers, and one was likely to meet with the President or his Cabinet, mingling democratically with the crowd of smiling citizens.

At one of these concerts a provincial visitor was observed to linger in the vicinity of the President, whom it was obvious he recognised. Presently, in an accession of sudden courage, he approached Mr. Pierce, and, uncovering his head respectfully, said, "Mr. President, can't I go through your fine house? I've heard so much about it that I'd give a great deal to see it."

"Why, my dear sir!" responded the President, kindly, "that is not my house. It's the people's house. You shall certainly go through it if you wish!" and, calling an attendant, he instructed him to take the grateful stranger through the White House

The recounting of that episode revives the recollection of another which took place in the time of President Buchanan, and which was the subject of discussion for full many a day after its occurrence. It was on the occasion of an annual visit of the redmen, always a rather exciting event in the capital.

The delegations which came to Washington in the winters of '54–58 numbered several hundred. They camped in a square in the Barracks, where, with almost naked bodies, scalps at belt and tomahawks in hand, they were viewed daily by crowds of curious folk as they beat their monotonous drums, danced, or threw their tomahawks dexterously in air. Here and there one redskin, more fortunate than the rest, was wrapped in a gaudy blanket, and many were decked out with large earrings and huge feather-duster head-dresses. A single chain only separated the savages from the assembled spectators, who were often thrown into somewhat of a panic by the sullen or belligerent behaviour of the former. When in this mood, the surest means of conciliating the Indians was to pass over the barrier (which some spectator was sure to do) some whisky, whereupon their sullenness immediately would give place to an amiable desire to display their prowess by twirling the tomahawk, or in the dance.

To see the copper-hued sons of the Far West, clad in buckskin and moccasins, paint and feathers, stalking about the East Room of the White House at any time was a spectacle not easily to be forgotten; but, upon the occasion of which I write, and at which I was present, a scene took place, the character of which became so spirited that many of the ladies became frightened and rose hurriedly to withdraw. A number of chiefs were present, accompanied by their interpreter, Mr. Garrett, of Alabama, and many of them had expressed their pleasure at seeing the President. They desired peace and goodwill to be continued; they wished for agricultural implements for the advancement of husbandry among their tribes; and grist mills, that their squaws no longer need grind their corn between stones to make "sofky" (and the spokesman illustrated the process by a circular motion of the hand). In fact, they wished to smoke the Calumet pipe of peace with their white brothers.

Thus far their discourse was most comfortable and pleasing to our white man's *amour propre;* but, ere the last warrior had ceased his placating speech, the dusky form of a younger redskin sprang from the floor, where, with the others of the delegation, he had been squatting. He was lithe and graceful as Longfellow's dream of Hiawatha. The muscles of his upper body, bare of all drapery, glistened like burnished metal. His gesticulations were fierce and imperative, his voice strangely thrilling.

"These walls and these halls belong to the redmen!" he cried. "The very ground on which they stand is ours! You have stolen it from us and I am for war, that the wrongs of my people may be righted!"

Here his motions became so violent and threatening that many of the ladies, alarmed, rose up instinctively, as I have said, as if they would fly the room; but our dear old Mr. Buchanan, with admirable diplomacy, replied in most kindly manner, bidding the interpreter assure the spirited young brave that the White House was his possession in common with all the people of the Great Spirit, and that he did but welcome his red brothers to their own on behalf of the country. This was the gist of his speech, which calmed the excitement of the savage, and relieved the apprehension of the ladies about.

A conspicuous member of the delegation of '54–55 was the old chief Apothleohola, who was brought to see me by the interpreter Garrett. His accumulated wealth was said to be $80,000, and he had a farm in the West, it was added, which was worked entirely by negroes. Apothleohola was a patriarch of his tribe, some eighty years of age, but erect and powerful still. His face on

JAMES BUCHANAN
President of the United States, 1857-61

the occasion of his afternoon visit to me was gaudy with paint, and he was wrapped in a brilliant red blanket, around which was a black border; but despite his gay attire there was about him an air of weariness and even sadness.

While I was still a child I had seen this now aged warrior. At that time, five thousand Cherokees and Choctaws, passing west to their new reservations beyond the Mississippi, had rested in Tuscaloosa, where they camped for several weeks. The occasion was a notable one. All the city turned out to see the Indian youths dash through the streets on their ponies. They were superb horsemen and their animals were as remarkable. Many of the latter, for a consideration, were left in the hands of the emulous white youth of the town. Along the river banks, too, carriages stood, crowded with sight-seers watching the squaws as they tossed their young children into the stream that they might learn to swim. Very picturesque were the roomy vehicles of that day as they grouped themselves along the leafy shore of the Black Warrior, their capacity tested to the fullest by the belles of the little city, arrayed in dainty muslins, and bonneted in the sweet fashions of the time.

During that encampment a redman was set upon by some quarrelsome rowdies, and in the altercation was killed. Fearing the vengeance of the allied tribes about them, the miscreants disembowelled their victim, and, filling the cavity with rocks, sank the body in the river. The Indians, missing their companion, and suspecting some evil had befallen him, appealed to Governor C. C. Clay, who immediately uttered a proclamation for the recovery of the body. In a few days the crime and its perpetrators were discovered, and justice was meted out to them. By this prompt act Governor Clay, to whose wisdom is accredited by historians the repression of the

Indian troubles in Alabama in 1835–'37, won the good-will of the savages, among whom was the great warrior, Apothleohola.

It was at ex-Governor Clay's request I sent for the now aged brave. He gravely inclined his head when I asked him whether he remembered the Governor. I told him my father wished to know whether the chief Nea Mathla still lived and if the brave Apothleohola was happy in his western home. His sadness deepened as he answered, slowly, "Me happy, some!"

Before the close of his visit, Mr. Garrett, the interpreter, asked me if I would not talk Indian to his charge. "You must know some!" he urged, "having been brought up in an Indian country!"

I knew three or four words, as it happened, and these I pronounced, to the great chief's amusement; for, pointing his finger at me he said, with a half-smile, "She talk Creek!"

A few days after this memorable call, I happened into the house of Harper & Mitchell, then a famous dry-goods emporium in the capital, just as the old warrior was beginning to bargain, and I had the pleasure and entertainment of assisting him to select two crêpe shawls which he purchased for his daughters at one hundred dollars apiece!

It was my good fortune to witness the arrival of the Japanese Embassy, which was the outcome of Commodore Perry's expedition to the Orient. The horticulturist of the party, Dr. Morrow, of South Carolina, was a frequent visitor to my parlours, and upon his return from the East regaled me with many amusing stories of his Eastern experiences. A special object of his visit to Japan was to obtain, if possible, some specimens of the world-famous rice of that country, with which to experiment in the United States. Until that period our native rice was inferior; but, despite every effort made and inducement offered, our Government had been unable to obtain even a kernel of the unhusked rice which would germinate.

During his stay in the Orient, Dr. Morrow made numberless futile attempts to supply himself with even a stealthy pocketful of the precious grain, and in one instance, he told us, remembering how Professor Henry had introduced millet seed by planting so little as a single seed that fell from the wrappings of a mummy,* he had offered a purse of gold to a native for a single grain; but the Japanese only shook his head, declining the proposition, and drew his finger significantly across his throat to indicate his probable fate if he were to become party to such commerce.

On the arrival of the Japanese embassy in Washington, to the doctor's delight, it was found that among the presents sent by the picturesque Emperor of Japan to the President of the United States was a hogshead of rice. Alas! the doctor's hopes were again dashed when the case was opened, for the wily donors had carefully sifted their gift, and, though minutely examined, there was not in all the myriad grains a single kernel in which the germinal vesicle was still intact!

The arrival of the browned Asiatics was made a gala occasion in the capital. Half the town repaired to the Barracks to witness the debarkation of the strange and gorgeously apparelled voyagers from the gaily decorated vessel. Their usually yellow skins, now, after a long sea-trip, were burned to the colour of copper; and not stranger to our eyes would have been the sight of Paul du Chaillu's newly discovered gorillas, than were these Orientals as they descended the flag-bedecked gang-planks and passed out through a corridor formed of eager people, crowding curiously to gaze at them. Some

---

* This story, though quite commonly repeated, has been rather effectually disproved by scientists. It obtained currency for many years, however. A. S.

of the Japanese had acquired a little English during the journey to America, and, as friendly shouts of "Welcome to America" greeted them, they nodded cordially to the people, shaking hands here and there as they passed along, and saying, to our great amusement, "How de ¡ "

Dr. Morrow had brought a gift to me from the East, a scarf of crêpe, delicate as the blossom of the mountain laurel, the texture being very similar to that of the petals of that bloom, and, to do honour to the occasion, I wore it conspicuously draped over my corsage.  Observing this drapery, one of the strangers, his oily face wreathed in smiles, his well-pomatumed top knot meantime giving out under the heat of a scorching sun a peculiar and never-to-be-forgotten odour, advanced toward me as our party called their welcome, and, pointing to my beautiful trophy, said, "Me lakee! me lakee!" Then, parting his silken robe over his breast, he pulled out a bit of an undergarment (the character of which it required no shrewdness to surmise) which proved identical in weave with my lovely scarf!  Holding the bit of crêpe out toward us, the Oriental smiled complacently, as if in this discovery we had established a kind of preliminary international *entente cordiale !*

This same pomatum upon which I have remarked was a source of great chagrin to the proprietor of Willard's Hotel, who, after the departure of his Oriental visitors, found several coats of paint and a general repapering to be necessary ere the pristine purity of atmosphere which had characterised that hostelry could again be depended upon not to offend the delicate olfactories of American guests.

During the stay of this embassy, its members attracted universal attention as they strolled about the streets or drawing-rooms which opened for their entertainment. Their garments were marvellously rich and massed with elaborate ornamentation in glistening silks and gold thread. They carried innumerable paper handkerchiefs tucked away somewhere in their capacious sleeves, the chief purpose of these filmy things seeming to be the removal of superfluous oil from the foreheads of their yellow owners. A happy circumstance; for, having once so served, the little squares were dropped forthwith wherever the Oriental happened to be standing, whether in street or parlour, and the Asiatic dignitary passed on innocently, ignorant alike of his social and hygienic shortcoming.

It was no uncommon thing during the sojourn of these strangers at the capital, to see some distinguished Senator or Cabinet Minister stoop at the sight of one of these gauzy trifles (looking quite like the *mouchoir* of some fastidious woman) and pick it up, only to throw it from him in disgust a moment later. He was fortunate when his error passed unseen by his confrères; for the Japanese handkerchief joke went the round of the capital, and the victim of such misplaced gallantry was sure to be the laughing-stock of his fellows if caught in the act.

The most popular member of this notable commission was an Oriental who was nicknamed "Tommy." He had scarce arrived when he capitulated to the charms of the American lady; in fact, he became so devoted to them that, it was said, he had no sooner returned to Japan than he paid the price of his devotion by the forfeit of his head in a basket!

# CHAPTER VIII

## The Brilliant Buchanan Administration

THE advent of Lord and Lady Napier was practically coincident with the installation of Miss Harriet Lane at the White House, and, in each instance, the *entrée* of Miss Lane and Lady Napier had its share in quickening the pace at which society was so merrily going, and in accentuating its allurements. Miss Lane's reign at the White House was one of completest charm. Nature, education and experience were combined in the President's niece in such manner as eminently to qualify her to meet the responsibilities that for four years were to be hers. Miss Lane possessed great tact, and a perfect knowledge of Mr. Buchanan's wishes. Her education had been largely directed and her mind formed under his careful guardianship; she had presided for several years over her uncle's household while Mr. Buchanan served as Minister to England. The charms of young womanhood still lingered about her, but to these was added an *aplomb* rare in a woman of fifty, so that, during her residence in it, White House functions rose to their highest degree of elegance; to a standard, indeed, that has not since been approached save during the occupancy of the beautiful bride of President Cleveland.

Miss Lane's entrance into life at the American capital, at a trying time, served to keep the surface of society in Washington serene and smiling, though the fires of a volcano raged in the under-political world, and the vibrations of Congressional strife spread to the furthermost ends of the country the knowledge that the Govern-

**MISS HARRIET LANE**
Mistress of the White House, 1857-61

ment was tottering. The young Lady of the White House came to her new honours with the prestige of Queen Victoria's favour. In her conquest of statesmen, and, it was added, even in feature, she was said to resemble the Queen in her younger days. Miss Lane was a little above the medium height, and both in colour and physique was of an English rather than an American type—a characteristic which was also marked in the President. The latter's complexion was of the rosiest and freshest, and his presence exceedingly fine, notwithstanding a slight infirmity which caused him to hold his head to one side, and gave him a quizzical expression that was, however, pleasing rather than the contrary.

In figure, Miss Lane was full; her complexion was clear and brilliant. In her cheeks there was always a rich, pretty colour, and her hair, a bright chestnut, had a glow approaching gold upon it. She had a columnar, full neck, upon which her head was set superbly. I thought her not beautiful so much as handsome and healthful and good to look upon. I told her once she was like a poet's ideal of an English dairymaid, who fed upon blush roses and the milk of her charges; but a lifting of the head and a heightening of the pretty colour in her cheeks told me my bucolic simile had not pleased her.

Of the Napiers it may be said that no ministerial representatives from a foreign power ever more completely won the hearts of Washingtonians than did that delightful Scotch couple. In appearance, Lady Napier was fair and distinctly a patrician. She was perhaps thirty years of age when she began her two-years' residence in the American capital. Her manner was unaffected and simple; her retinue small. During the Napiers' occupancy, the British Embassy was conspicuous for its complete absence of ostentation and its generous hospitality. Their equipages were of the handsomest, but in no instance showy, and this at a period when Washington streets thronged with the conspicuous vehicles affected by the foreign Legations. Indeed, at that time the foreigner was as distinguished for his elaborate carriages as was the Southerner for his blooded horses.*

Lady Napier's avoidance of display extended to her gowning, which was of the quietest, except when some great public function demanded more elaborate preparation. On such occasions her laces—heirlooms for centuries—were called into requisition, and coiffure and corsage blazed with diamonds and emeralds. Her cozy at-homes were remarkable for their informality and the ease which seemed to emanate from the hostess and communicate itself to her guests. A quartette of handsome boys comprised the Napier family, and often these princely little fellows, clad in velvet costumes, assisted their mother at her afternoons, competing with each other for the privilege of passing refreshments. At such times it was no infrequent thing to hear Lady Napier compared with "Cornelia and her Jewels."

Lord Napier was especially fond of music, and I recall an evening dinner given at this embassy to Miss Emily Schaumberg, of Philadelphia, in which that lady's singing roused the host to a high pitch of enthusiasm. Miss Schaumberg was a great beauty, as well as a finished singer, and was most admired in the capital, though she stayed but a very short time there.

A ball or formal dinner at the British Embassy (and

* A notable vehicle of this sort was purchased in Philadelphia by Mrs. Clay, at a cost of $1,600, and was carried to Alabama, where, among the foliaged avenues of beautiful Huntsville, it attracted universal attention. It was a capacious and splendid equipage, lined with amber satin, and was drawn by the high-bred horses, "Polk" and "Dallas." From Mrs. Clay's possession this gorgeous landau passed into that of Governor Reuben Chapman, and, in the course of years, by various transfers, into the hands of a station hackman, of colour! A. S.

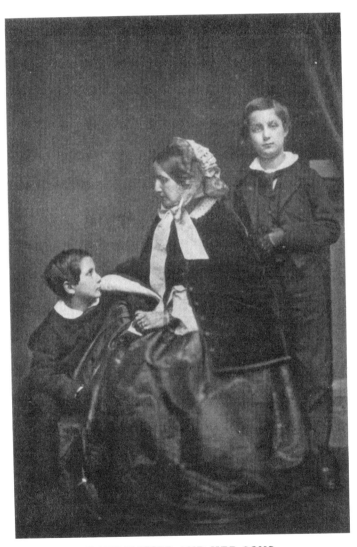

LADY NAPIER AND HER SONS

these were not infrequent) was always a memorable event. One met there the talented and distinguished; heard good music; listened to the flow of wholesome wit; and enjoyed delectable repasts. Early in 1859 the Napiers gave a large ball to the young Lords Cavendish and Ashley, to which all the resident and visiting belles were invited; and, I doubt not, both lords and ladies were mutually delighted. Miss Corinne Acklin, who was under my wing that season (she was a true beauty and thoroughly enjoyed her belleship), was escorted to supper by Lord Cavendish, and, indeed, had the lion's share of the attentions of both of the visiting noblemen, until our dear, ubiquitous Mrs. Crittenden appeared. That good lady was arrayed, as usual, with remarkable splendour and frankly décolleté gown. She approached Miss Acklin as the latter, glowing with her triumphs, stood chatting vivaciously with her lordly admirers. "Lady" Crittenden smilingly interrupted the trio by whispering in the young lady's ear, though by no means *sotto voce:* "Present me to Lord Ashley, my dear. Ashley was my second husband's name, you know, and maybe they were kin!"

"I thought her so silly," said the pouting beauty afterward. "She must be almost sixty!" But Mrs. Crittenden's kindly inquiry was not an unnatural one, for, as the rich widow Ashley, whose husband's family connections in some branches were known to be foreign, she had been renowned from Florida to Maine for years before she became Mrs. Crittenden.

At the home of the Napiers one frequently met Mr. Bayard, between whom and the English Ambassador there existed a close intimacy. Mr. Bayard was the most unobtrusive of men, modesty being his dominant social characteristic. When I visited England in 1885, I had a signal testimony to Lord Napier's long-continued regard for the great Delaware statesman. During my

stay in London, the former Minister constituted himself
cicerone to our party, and, upon one memorable afternoon,
he insisted upon drinking a toast with us.

"Oh, no!" I demurred. "Toasts are obsolete!"

"Very well, then," Lord Napier declared. "If you
won't, I will. Here's to your President, Mr. Cleveland!
But," he continued with a suddenly added depth, "Were
it your Chevalier Bayard, I would drink it on my knee!"

Upon my return to America I had the pleasure of
shouting to Mr. Bayard, then Secretary of State, a
recital of this great tribute. He had now grown very
deaf, but my words reached him at last, and he smiled
in a most happy way as he asked, almost shyly, but
with a warm glance in the eye, despite his effort to remain
composed, "Did Napier really say that?"

A feeling of universal regret spread over the capital
when it became known that the Napiers were to return
to England; and the admiration of the citizens for the
popular diplomat expressed itself in the getting-up of a
farewell ball, which, in point of size, was one of the most
prodigious entertainments ever given in Washington.
One group of that great assemblage is vividly before me.
In it the young James Gordon Bennett, whom I had seen
in earlier days at a fashionable water-cure (and whose
general naughtiness as a little boy defies description by
my feeble pen), danced *vis-à-vis*, a handsome, courtly
youth, with his mother and Daniel E. Sickles.

During the Pierce administration the old-fashioned
quadrilles and cotillions, with an occasional waltz number,
were danced to the exclusion of all other Terpsichorean
forms; but in the term of his successor, the German was
introduced, when Miss Josephine Ward, of New York,
afterward Mrs. John R. Thomson, of New Jersey,
became prominent as a leader.

When I review those brilliant scenes in which passed
and smiled, and danced and chatted, the vast multitude

of those who called me "friend," the army of those now numbered with the dead—I am lost in wonder!  My memory seems a Herculaneum, in which, let but a spade of thought be sunk, and some long-hidden treasure is unearthed.    I have referred to the citizens of Washington. The term unrolls a scroll in which are listed men and women renowned in those days as hostesses and entertainers.  They were a rich and exclusive, and, at the same time, a numerous class, that gave body to the social life of the Federal City.    Conspicuous among these were Mrs. A. S. Parker and Mrs. Ogle Tayloe.    The home of the former was especially the rendezvous of the young.    In the late fifties and sixties it was a palatial residence, famous for its fine conservatories, its spacious parlours, and glistening dancing floors.    To-day, so greatly has the city changed, that what is left of that once luxurious home has been converted into small tenements which are rented out for a trifle to the very poor.    At the marriage of Mrs. Parker's daughter, Mary E., in 1860, to Congressman J. E. Bouligny, of Louisiana, crowds thronged in these now forgotten parlours.    The President himself was present to give the pretty bride away, and half of Congress came to wish Godspeed to their fellow-member.

The home of Mr. and Mrs. Ogle Tayloe was a museum of things rare and beautiful, vying in this respect with the Corcoran Mansion and the homes of the several members of the Riggs family.    One of its treasured mementos was a cane that had been used by Napoleon Bonaparte. Mrs. Tayloe belonged to a New York family; the Tayloes to Virginia.    She was a woman of fine taste and broad views, a very gracious hostess, who shrank from the coarse or vulgar wherever she detected it.    When Washington became metamorphosed by the strangers who poured into its precincts following the inauguration of Mr. Lincoln in 1861, the Tayloe Mansion was shrouded, its pictures were covered, and its chandeliers wound with protective wrappings. Entertaining there ceased for years. "Nor have I," said Mrs. Tayloe to me in 1866, "crossed the threshold of the White House since Harriet Lane went out."

At the Tayloe home I often exchanged a smile and a greeting with Lilly Price, my hostess's niece, who, when she reached womanhood, was distinguished first as Mrs. Hamersley, and afterward as Lillian, Duchess of Marlborough. At that time she was a fairy-like little slip of a schoolgirl, who, in the intervals between Fridays and Mondays, was permitted to have a peep at the gay gatherings in her aunt's home. Many years afterward, being a passenger on an outgoing steamer, I learned that Mrs. Hamersley, too, was on board; but before I could make my presence known to her, as had been my intention, she had discovered me and came seeking her "old friend, Mrs. Clay," and I found that there lingered in the manner of the brilliant society leader, Mrs. Hamersley, much of the same bright charm that had distinguished the little Lilly Price as she smiled down at me from her coign of vantage at the top of the stairway of the Tayloe residence.

But the prince of entertainers, whether citizen or official, who was also a prince among men, the father of unnumbered benefactions and patron of the arts, was dear Mr. Corcoran. When my thoughts turn back to him they invariably resolve themselves into

"And, lo! Ben Adhem's name led all the rest"

Throughout our long acquaintance Mr. Corcoran proved himself to be what he wrote himself down, "one of the dearest friends of my dear husband." He was already a widower when, shortly after our arrival in Washington, I met him; and, though many a well-known beauty would have been willing to assume his distinguished name, my own conviction is that Mr. Corcoran never thought of marriage with any woman after he committed to the grave the body of his well-beloved wife, Louise Morris, daughter of the brave Commodore.

Mr. Corcoran was a tall and handsome man, even in his old age. In his younger days his expression was the most benignant I have ever seen, though in repose it was tinged with a peculiar mournfulness. The banker's weekly dinners were an institution in Washington life. During each session he dined half of Congress, to say nothing of the foreign representatives and the families of his fellow-citizens.

Evening dances were also of frequent occurrence at the Corcoran Mansion, the giving of which always seemed to me proof of the host's large and great nature; for Louise Corcoran, his daughter, afterward Mrs. Eustis, was a delicate girl, who, owing to some weakness of the heart, was debarred from taking part in the pleasures of the dance. Nevertheless, Mr. Corcoran opened his home to the young daughters of other men, and took pleasure in the happiness he thus gave them. The "Greek Slave," now a principal object of interest in the Corcoran Art Gallery, was then an ornament to the banker's home, and stood in an alcove allotted to it, protected by a gilded chain.

The hospitality of Mr. Corcoran's home, which Senator Clay and I often enjoyed, was a synonym for "good cheer" of the most generous and epicurean sort. I remember an amusing meeting which my husband and I had one evening with Secretary Cobb. It took place on the Treasury pavement. Recognising us as we approached, the bland good humour which was habitual to the Secretary deepened into a broad smile.

"Ah, Clay!" he said to my husband, pulling down his vest with a look of completest satisfaction, "Been to Corcoran's. Johannisberg and *tar*repin, sir! I wish," and he gave his waistcoat another pull, glancing up significantly at the tall stone pile before us, "I wish the Treasury were as full as I!"

Mr. Corcoran was famous for his Johannisberg, and I recall a dinner at his home when, being escorted to the table by the Danish Minister, who had somewhat the reputation of a connoisseur, our host and my companion immediately began a discussion on the merits of this favourite wine, which the Minister declared was of prime quality, and which, if I remember rightly, Mr. Corcoran said was all made on the estate of the Prince de Metternich. When the Minister announced his approval, our host turned quietly to me and said, *sotto voce,* "I hoped it was pure. I paid fifteen dollars for it!"

I wish it might be said that all the lavish hospitality of that incomparable gentleman had been appreciated with never a record to the contrary to mar the pleasure he gave; but it must be confessed that the host at the capital whose reputation for liberality extends so widely as did Mr. Corcoran's runs the risk of entertaining some others than angels unaware. The receptions at the Corcoran residence, as at the White House and other famous homes, were occasionally, necessarily, somewhat promiscuous. During the sessions of Congress the city thronged with visitors, many of them constituents of Senators and Congressmen, who came to Washington expecting to receive, as they usually did receive, social courtesies at the hands of their Representatives. Many kindly hosts, aware of these continually arising emergencies, gave latitude to Congressional folk in their invitations sufficient to meet them.

At the Corcoran receptions, a feature of the decorations was the elaborate festooning and grouping of growing plants, which were distributed in profusion about the banker's great parlours. Upon one occasion, in addition to these natural flowers, there was displayed a handsome *épergne,* in which was placed a most realistic bunch of

artificial blooms. These proved irresistibly tempting
to an unidentified woman visitor; for, in the course of
the afternoon, Mr. Corcoran, moving quietly among his
guests, saw the stranger take hold of a bunch of these
curious ornaments and twist it violently in an effort to
detach it from the rest. At this surprising sight Mr.
Corcoran stepped to the lady's side, and said with a
gentle dignity: "I would not do that, Madam. Please
desist. The blossoms are not real. They are rare,
however, and have been brought from Europe only by
the exercise of the greatest care!"

"Well! If they have? What's that to you?" snapped
the lady defiantly.

"Nothing, Madam!" he responded, quietly. "Except
that I am Mr. Corcoran!"

Fortunately, not all strangers who were so entertained
were of this unpleasant sort. Sometimes the amusement
the more provincial afforded quite out-balanced the
trouble their entertainment cost our resident representatives. I remember an occasion on which I, acting
for my husband, was called upon to show a young woman
the sights of the capital. She was the daughter of an
important constituent. One morning, as I was about to
step into the calash of a friend who had called to take
me for a drive, a note was handed to me. It read:
"My dear Mrs. Clay: I hope you will recall my name
and, in your generosity of heart, will do me a favour.
My daughter is passing through Washington and will be
at the ——— Hotel for one day," naming that very day!
"She is very unsophisticated and will be most grateful
for anything you can do toward showing her the sights
of the capital," etc., etc.

As I knew I might command the services of my escort
for the morning (he was a Mr. Parrish, recently from the
mines of Africa, and in Washington for the purpose of
securing our Government's aid in pressing certain of his

claims against a foreign power), I proposed that we proceed at once to the ———— Hotel and take the young woman with us on our drive. To this a kind consent was given, and in a short time I had sent my card to the young stranger. I found her a typical, somewhat callow schoolgirl, over-dressed and self-conscious, who answered every question in the most agitated manner, and who volunteered nothing in the way of a remark upon any subject whatsoever, though she assented gaspingly to all my questions, and went with a nervous alacrity to put on her hat when I invited her to accompany us upon our drive.

We began our tour by taking her directly to the Capitol. We mounted to the dome to view the wonderful plan of the Government City; thence to the House and the Senate Chamber, and into such rooms of state as we might enter; and on to the Government greenhouses, with their horticultural wonders. We paused from time to time in our walk to give the young lady an opportunity to admire and to consider the rare things before her—to remark upon them, if she would; but all our inviting enthusiasm was received in dull silence.

Failing to arouse her interest in the gardens, we next directed our steps to the Smithsonian Institution, where corridor after corridor was explored, in which were specimens from the obscurest corners of the earth, monsters of the deep, and tiny denizens of the air, purchased at fabulous sums of money, but now spread freely before the gaze of whomsoever might desire to look upon them. The Smithsonian Institution, at that time still a novelty even to Washingtonians, has ever been to me a marvellous example of man's humanity to man. I hoped it would so reveal itself to my whilom protégée.

Alas for my hopes! Her apathy seemed to increase. We arrived presently at the Ornithological Department. A multitude of specimens of the feathered tribes were here, together with their nests and eggs; still nothing appeared to interest my guest or lessen what I was rapidly beginning to regard as a case of hebetude, pure and simple. I was perplexed; Mr. Parrish, it was plain, was bored when, arriving almost at the end of the cases, to my relief the girl's attention seemed arrested. More, she stood literally transfixed before the nest of the great Auk, and uttered her first comment of the day:

"Lor'!" she said, in a tone of awestruck amazement, "What a big egg!"

# CHAPTER IX

## A Celebrated Social Event

EARLY in the season of 1857–'58, our friend Mrs. Senator Gwin announced her intention of giving a ball which should eclipse every gathering of the kind that had ever been seen in Washington. Just what its character was to be was not yet decided; but, after numerous conferences with her friends in which many and various suggestions were weighed, the advocates for the fancy ball prevailed over those in favour of a masquerade, to which, indeed, Senator Gwin himself was averse, and these carried the day.

Surely no hostess ever more happily realised her ambitions! When the function was formally announced, all Washington was agog. For the ensuing weeks men as well as women were busy consulting costumers, ransacking the private collections in the capital, and conning precious volumes of coloured engravings in a zealous search for original and accurate costuming. Only the Senators who were to be present were exempt from this anticipatory excitement, for Senator Gwin, declaring that nothing was more dignified for members of this body than their usual garb, refused to appear in an assumed one, and so set the example for his colleagues.

As the time approached, expectation ran high. Those who were to attend were busy rehearsing their characters and urging the dressmakers and costumers to the perfect completion of their tasks, while those who were debarred deplored their misfortune. I recall a pathetic lament from my friend Lieutenant Henry Myers, who was obliged to leave on the United States ship *Marion* on the fourth of April (the ball was to occur on the ninth), in which he bemoaned the deprivations of a naval officer's life, and especially his inability to attend the coming entertainment.

When the evening of the ball arrived there was a flutter in every boudoir in Washington, in which preparation for the great event was accelerated by the pleasurable nervousness of maid and mistress.    Mrs. Gwin's costume, and those of other leading Washingtonians, it was known, had been selected in New York, and rumours were rife on the elegant surprises that were to be sprung upon the eventful occasion.

With Senator Clay and me that winter were three charming cousins, the Misses Comer, Hilliard and Withers. They impersonated, respectively, a gypsy fortune-teller, a Constantinople girl, and "Titania"; and, to begin at the last (as a woman may do if she will), a wonderful "Titania" the tiny Miss Withers was, robed in innumerable spangled tulle petticoats that floated as she danced, her gauze wings quivering like those of a butterfly, and her unusually small feet glistening no less brilliantly with spangles.

"Miss Withers, yon tiny fairy," wrote Major de Havilland, who in his "Metrical Glance at the Fancy Ball" immortalised the evening, "as 'Titania' caused many a Midsummer Night's Dream." Miss Hilliard, whose beauty was well set off in a costly and picturesque costume of the East, owed her triumph of the evening to the kindness of Mrs. Joseph Holt, who had bought the costume (which she generously placed at my cousin's disposal) during a tour of the Orient.    So attractive was my cousin's charming array, and so correct in all its details, that as she entered Mrs. Gwin's ballroom, a party of Turkish onlookers, seeing the familiar garb, broke into applause.

Miss Comer, in a brilliant gown that was plentifully covered with playing-cards, carried also a convenient pack of the same, with which she told fortunes in a mystifying manner, for I had coached her carefully in all the secrets of the day. I must admit she proved a clever pupil, for she used her knowledge well whenever an opportunity presented, to the confusion of many whose private weaknesses she most tormentingly exposed.

My chosen character was an unusual one, being none other than that remarkable figure created by Mr. Shillaber, Aunt Ruthy Partington. It was the one character assumed during that memorable evening, by one of my sex, in which age and personal attractions were sacrificed ruthlessly for its more complete delineation.

I was not the only one anxious to impersonate the quaint lady from Beanville, over whose grammatical *faux pas* all America was amusing itself. Ben Perley Poore no sooner heard of my selection of this character than he begged me to yield to him, but I was not to be deterred, having committed to heart the whole of Mrs. Partington's homely wit. Moreover, I had already, the previous summer, experimented with the character while at Red Sweet Springs, where a fancy ball had been given with much success, and I was resolved to repeat the amusing experience at Mrs. Gwin's ball.

Finding me inexorable, Mr. Poore at last desisted and chose another character, that of Major Jack Downing. He made a dashing figure, too, and we an amusing pair, as, at the "heel of the morning," we galoped wildly over Mrs. Gwin's wonderfully waxed floors. The galop, I may add in passing, was but just introduced in Washington, and its popularity was wonderful.

If I dwell on that evening with particular satisfaction, the onus of such egotism must be laid at the door of my flattering friends; for even now, when nearly twoscore years and ten have passed, those who remain of that merry assemblage of long ago recall it with a smile and a tender recollection. "I can see you now, in my mind's eye," wrote General George Wallace Jones, in 1894; "how you vexed and tortured dear old President Buchanan at Doctor and Mrs. Gwin's famous fancy party! You were that night the observed of all observers!" And still more recently another, recalling the scene, said, "The orchestra stopped, for the dancers lagged, laughing convulsively at dear Aunt Ruthy!"

Nor would I seem to undervalue by omitting the tribute in verse paid me by the musical Major de Havilland:

> "Mark how the grace that gilds an honoured name,
> Gives a strange zest to that loquacious dame
> Whose ready tongue and easy blundering wit
> Provoke fresh uproar at each happy hit!
> Note how her humour into strange grimace
> Tempts the smooth meekness of yon Quaker's face.*
>
> .    .    .    .    .    .    .
> But—denser grows the crowd round Partington;
> 'T'were vain to try to name them one by one." †

It was not without some trepidation of spirit that I surrendered myself into the hands of a professional maker-up of theatrical folk and saw him lay in the shadows and wrinkles necessary to the character, and adjust my front-piece of grey hair into position; and, as my conception of the quaint Mrs. Partington was that

* A reference to Mrs. Emory, a notably attractive member of Washington society.

† Nevertheless, the chronicler named in rapid succession as among Mrs. Clay's attendants, Lord Napier, Sir William Gore Ouseley, K.C.B., and many prominent figures in the capital. "Mrs. Senator Clay," he added in prose, "with knitting in hand, snuff-box in pocket, and 'Ike the Inevitable' by her side, acted out her difficult character so as to win the unanimous verdict that her personation of the loquacious *malapropos* dame was the leading feature of the evening's entertainment. Go where she would through the spacious halls, a crowd of eager listeners followed her footsteps, drinking in her instant repartees, which were really superior in wit and appositeness, and, indeed, in the vein of the famous dame's cacoëthes, even to the original contribution of Shillaber to the nonsensical literature of the day." A. S.

of a kindly soul, I counselled the attendant—a Hungarian attaché of the local theatre—to make good-natured vertical wrinkles over my brow, and not horizontal ones, which indicate the cynical and harsh character.

My disguise was soon so perfect that my friend Mrs. L. Q. C. Lamar, who came in shortly after the ordeal of making-up was over, utterly failed to recognise me in the country woman before her. She looked about the room with a slight reserve aroused by finding herself thus in the presence of a stranger, and asked of Emily, "Where is Mrs. Clay?" At this my cousins burst into merry laughter, in which Mrs. Lamar joined when assured of my identity.

Thus convinced of the success of my costume, I was glad to comply with a request that came by messenger from Miss Lane, for our party to go to the White House on our way to Mrs. Gwin's, to show her our "pretty dresses," a point of etiquette intervening to prevent the Lady of the White House from attending the great ball of a private citizen. Forthwith we drove to the Executive Mansion, where we were carried *sans cérémonie* to Miss Lane's apartments. Here Mrs. Partington found herself in the presence of her first audience. Miss Lane and the President apparently were much amused at her verdancy, and, after a few initiative malapropisms, some pirouettes by "Titania" and our maid from the Orient, done to the shuffling of our little fortune-teller's cards, we departed, our zest stimulated, for the Gwin residence.

My very first conquest as Mrs. Partington, as I recall it now, was of Mrs. Representative Pendleton, whom I met on the stairs. She was radiantly beautiful as the "Star-Spangled Banner," symbolising the poem by which her father, Francis Scott Key, immortalised himself. As we met, her face broke into a smile of delicious surprise.

"How inimitable!" she cried. "Who is it? No! you shan't pass till you tell me!" And when I laughingly informed her in Aunt Ruthy's own vernacular, she exclaimed: "What! Mrs. Clay? Why! there isn't a vestige of my friend left!"

My costume was ingeniously devised. It consisted of a plain black alpaca dress and black satin apron; stockings as blue as a certain pair of indigos I have previously described, and large, loose-fitting buskin shoes. Over my soft grey front piece I wore a high-crowned cap, which, finished with a prim ruff, set closely around the face. On the top was a diminutive bow of narrowest ribbon, while ties of similarly economical width secured it under the chin. My disguise was further completed by a pair of stone-cutter's glasses with nickel rims, which entirely concealed my eyes. A white kerchief was drawn primly over my shoulders, and was secured by a huge medallion pin, in which was encased the likeness, as large as the palm of my hand, of "my poor Paul."

On my arm I carried a reticule in which were various herbs, elecampane and catnip, and other homely remedies, and a handkerchief in brilliant colours on which was printed with fearless and emphatic type the Declaration of Independence. This bit of "stage property" was used ostentatiously betimes, especially when Aunt Ruthy's tears were called forth by some sad allusion to her lost "Paul." In my apron pocket was an antique snuff-box which had been presented to me, as I afterward told Senator Seward, by the Governor of Rhode Island, "a lover of the Kawnstitution, Sir."

But, that nothing might be lacking, behind me trotted my boy "Ike," dear little "Jimmy" Sandidge (son of the member from Louisiana), aged ten, who for days, in the secrecy of my parlour, I had drilled in the aid he was to lend me. He was a wonderful little second, and the

fidelity to truth in his make-up was so amusing that I
came near to losing him at the very outset.   His ostentatiously darned stockings and patched breeches, long
since outgrown, were a surprising sight in the great
parlours of our host, and Senator Gwin, seeing the little
urchin who, he thought, had strayed in from the street,
took him by the shoulder and was about to lead him out
when some one called to him, "Look out, Senator!
You'll be getting yourself into trouble!  That's Aunt
Ruthy's boy, Ike!"

Mrs. Partington was not the only Yankee character
among that throng of princes and queens, and dames
of high degree, for Mr. Eugene Baylor, of Louisiana,
impersonated a figure as amusing—that of "Hezekiah
Swipes," of Vermont.   He entered into his part with a
zest as great as my own, and kept "a-whittlin' and
a-whittlin' jes' as if he was ter hum!"   For myself, I
enjoyed a peculiar exhilaration in the thought that,
despite my amusing dress, the belles of the capital
(and many were radiant beauties, too) gave way before
Aunt Ruthy and her nonsense.   As I observed this my
zeal increased, and not even Senator Clay, who feared
my gay spirits would react and cause me to become
exhausted, could prevail upon me to yield a serious word
or one out of my character throughout the festal night.
If I paid for it, as I did, by several days' retirement, I
did not regret it, since the evening itself went off so
happily.

Mrs. Gwin, as the Queen of Louis Quatorze, a regal
lady, stood receiving her guests with President Buchanan
beside her as Aunt Ruthy entered, knitting industriously,
but stopping ever and anon to pick up a stitch which the
glory of her surroundings caused her to drop.   Approaching my hostess and her companion, I first made my
greetings to Mrs. Gwin, with comments on her "invite,"
and wondered, looking up at the windows, if she "had

énough venerators to take off the execrations of that large assemblage"; but, when she presented Mrs. Partington to the President, "Lor!" exclaimed that lady, "Air you ralely 'Old Buck'?   I've often heern tell o' Old Buck up in Beanville, but I don't see no horns!"

"No, Madam," gravely responded the President, assuming for the nonce the cynic, "I'm not a married man!"

It was at this memorable function that Lord Napier (who appeared in the character of Mr. Hammond, the first British Minister to the United States) paid his great tribute to Mrs. Pendleton.   Her appearance on that occasion was lovely.   She was robed in a white satin gown made dancing length, over which were rare lace flounces.   A golden eagle with wings outstretched covered her corsage, and from her left shoulder floated a long tricolour sash on which, in silver letters, were the words "*E Pluribus Unum.*"   A crown of thirteen flashing stars was set upon her well-poised head, and a more charming interpretation in dress of the national emblem could scarcely have been devised.

Ah! but that was a remarkable throng!   My memory, as I recall that night, seems like a long chain, of which, if I strike but a single link, the entire length rattles! Beautiful Thérèse Chalfant Pugh as "Night"—what a vision she was, and what a companion picture Mrs. Douglas, who, as "Aurora," was radiant in the pale tints of the morning!   There were mimic Marchionesses, and Kings of England and France and Prussia; White Ladies of Avenel and Dukes of Buckingham, Maids of Athens and Saragossa, gypsies and fairies, milkmaids, and even a buxom barmaid; Antipholus himself and the Priestess Norma, Pierrots and Follies, peasants and Highland chiefs moving in heterogeneous fashion in the great ballrooms.

Barton Key, as an English hunter, clad in white satin

breeks, cherry-velvet jacket, and jaunty cap, with lemon-coloured high-top boots, and a silver bugle (upon which he blew from time to time) hung across his breast, was a conspicuous figure in that splendid happy assemblage, and Mlle. de Montillon was a picture in the Polish character costume in which her mother had appeared when she danced in a Polonaise before the Empress at the Tuilleries.

Sir William Gore Ouseley, the "Knight of the Mysterious Mission," attracted general attention in his character of Knight Commander of the Bath. The Baroness de Staeckl and Miss Cass were models of elegance as French Court beauties, and Mrs. Jefferson Davis as Mme. de Staël dealt in caustic repartee as became her part, delivered now in French and again in broken English, to the annihilation of all who had the temerity to cross swords with her.

Among the guests "our furrin relations" were numerously represented, and I remember well the burst of laughter which greeted Mrs. Partington when she asked Lady Napier, with a confidential and sympathetic air, "whether the Queen had got safely over her last encroachment." Incidentally she added some good advice on the bringing up of children, illustrating its efficacy by pointing to Ike, whom *she* "was teaching religiously both the lethargy and the cataplasm!"

My memories of Mrs. Gwin's ball would be incomplete did I not mention two or more of Aunt Ruthy's escapades during the evening. The rumour of my intended impersonation had aroused in the breast of a certain Baltimorean youth the determination to disturb, "to break up Mrs. Clay's composure." I heard of the young man's intention through some friend early in the evening, and my mother-wit, keyed as it was to a pitch of alertness, promptly aided me to the overthrow of the venturesome hero. He came garbed as a newsboy, and, nature having provided him with lusty lungs, he made amusing an-

**MRS. JEFFERSON DAVIS**
of Mississippi

nouncements as to the attractions of his wares, at the most unexpected moments. Under his arm he carried a bundle of papers which he hawked about in a most professional manner. At an unfortunate moment he walked hurriedly by as if on his rounds, and stopping beside me he called out confidently, "*Baltimore Sun!* Have a '*Sun*,' Madam?"

"Tut, tut! Man!" said Mrs. Partington, horrified. "How dare you ask such a question of a virtuous female w dow woman?" Then bursting into sobs and covering her eyes with the broad text of the "Declaration of Independence," she cried, "What would my poor Paul think of that?" To the hilarious laughter of those who had gathered about us, the routed hero retreated hastily, and, for the remainder of the evening, restrained by a wholesome caution, he gave Aunt Ruthy a wide berth.

Such kind greetings as came to this unsophisticated visitor to the ball! "You're the sweetest-looking old thing!" exclaimed "Lushe" Lamar before he had penetrated my disguise. "I'd just like to buss you!"

I had an amusing *recontre* with Senator Seward that evening. That this pronounced Northerner had made numerous efforts in the past to meet me I was well aware; but my Southern sentiments were wholly disapproving of him, and I had resisted even my kinder-hearted husband's plea, and had steadily refused to permit him to be introduced to me. "Not even to save the Nation could I be induced to eat his bread, to drink his wine, to enter his domicile, to *speak* to him!" I once impetuously declared, when the question came up in private of attending some function which the Northern Senator was projecting.

At Mrs. Gwin's ball, however, I noticed Mr. Seward hovering in my neighbourhood, and I was not surprised when he, "who could scrape any angle to attain an end," as my cousin Miss Comer said so aptly, finding none brave enough to present him, took advantage of my temporary merging into Mr. Shillaber's character, and presented himself to "Mrs. Partington." He was very courteous, if a little uncertain of his welcome, as he approached me, and said, "Aunt Ruthy, can't I, too, have the pleasure of welcoming you to the Federal City? May I have a pinch of snuff with you?" It was here that Mrs. Partington reminded him that the donor of her snuff-box "loved the Kawnstitewtion." I gave him the snuff and with it a number of Partingtonian shots about his opinions concerning "Slave Oligawky," which were fearless even if "funny," as the Senator seemed to find them, and I passed on. This was my first and only meeting with Mr. Seward.*

I was so exhilarated at the success of my rôle that I had scarce seen our cousins during the evening (I am sure they thought me an ideal chaperone), though I caught an occasional glimpse of the gauzy-winged "Titania," and once I saw the equally tiny Miss Comer go whirling down the room in a wild galop with the tall Lieutenant Scarlett, of Her Majesty's Guards, who was conspicuous in a uniform as rubescent as his patronymic. And I recall seeing an amusing little bit of human nature in connection with our hostess, which showed how even the giving of this superb entertainment could not disturb Mrs. Gwin's perfect oversight of her household.

The "wee sma' hours" had come, and I had just finished complimenting my hostess on her "cold hash and *cider*," when the butler stepped up to her and, in discreet pantomime, announced that the wine had given out.

---

* While this playful exchange of ideas was going on, Senator Clay stood near his Northern confrère, with whom his relations were always courteous and kindly. At Mrs. Clay's parting sally, Senator Seward turned to the lady's husband and remarked, "Clay, she's superb!" "Yes," replied Senator Clay; "when she married me America lost its Siddons!" A. S.

Then she, Queen for the nonce of the most magnificent of the Bourbons, did step aside and, lifting her stiff moiré skirt and its costly train of cherry satin (quilled with white, it was), did extract from some secret pocket the key to the wine cellar, and pass it right royally to her menial. This functionary shortly afterward returned and rendered it again to her, when, by the same deft manipulation of her rich petticoats, the implement was replaced in its repository, and the Queen once more emerged to look upon her merrymakers.

For years Mrs. Gwin's fancy ball has remained one of the most brilliant episodes in the annals of ante-bellum days in the capital. For weeks after its occurrence the local photograph and daguerreotype galleries were thronged with patrons who wished to be portrayed in the costumes they had worn upon the great occasion; and a few days after the ball, supposing I would be among that number, Mr. Shillaber sent me a request for my likeness, adding that he "would immortalise me." But, flushed with my own success, and grown daring by reason of it, I replied that, being *hors de combat*, I could not respond as he wished. I thanked him for his proffer, however, and reminded him that the public had anticipated him, and that by their verdict I had already immortalised myself!

# CHAPTER X

In the winter of '59 and '60 it became obvious to everyone that gaiety at the capital was waning. Aside from public receptions, now become palpably perfunctory, only an occasional wedding served to give social zest to the rapidly sobering Congressional circles. Ordinary "at-homes" were slighted. Women went daily to the Senate gallery to listen to the angry debates on the floor below. When belles met they no longer discussed furbelows and flounces, but talked of forts and fusillades. The weddings of my cousin, Miss Hilliard, in 1859, and of Miss Parker, in 1860, already described, were the most notable matrimonial events of those closing days of Washington's splendour.

To Miss Hilliard's marriage to Mr. Hamilton Glentworth, of New York, which occurred at mid-day at old St. John's, and to the reception that followed, came many of the Senatorial body and dignitaries of the capital. A procession of carriages drawn by white horses accompanied the bridal party to the church, where the celebrated Bishop Doane, of New Jersey, performed the ceremony. The bride's gown and that of one of the bridesmaids were "gophered," this being the first appearance of the new French style of trimming in the capital. One of the bridesmaids, I remember, was gowned in pink crêpe, which was looped back with coral, then a most fashionable garniture; the costume of another was of embroidered tulle caught up with bunches of grapes; and each of the accompanying ushers—such were the fashions of the day—wore inner vests of satin, embroidered in colour to match the gown of the bridesmaid alloted to his charge.

Notable artists appeared in the capital, among them Charlotte Cushman, and there were stately, not to say stiff and formal, dinners at the British Embassy, now presided over by Lord Lyons. This Minister's arrival was looked upon as a great event. Much gossip had preceded it, and all the world was agog to know if it were true that feminine-kind was debarred from his menage. It was said that his personally chartered vessel had conveyed to our shores not only the personages comprising his household, but also his domestics and skilful gardeners, and even the growing plants for his conservatory. It was whispered that when his Lordship entertained ladies his dinner-service was to be of solid gold; that when gentlemen were his guests they were to dine from the costliest of silver plate. Moreover, the gossips at once set about predicting that the newcomer would capitulate to the charms of some American woman, and speculation was already rife as to who would be the probable bride.

Lord Lyons began his American career by entertaining at dinner the Diplomatic Corps, and afterward the officials of our country, in the established order of precedence, the Supreme Court, the Cabinet, and Senate circles leading, according to custom. His Lordship's invitations being sent out alphabetically, Senator Clay and I received a foreign and formidable card to the first Senatorial dinner given by the newly arrived diplomat. My husband's appearance at this function, I remember, was particularly distinguished. He was clad in conventional black, and wore with it a cream-coloured vest of brocaded velvet; yet, notwithstanding my wifely pride in him, we had what almost amounted to a disagreement on our way to the famous feast. We drove to Lord Lyons's domicile with Senator and Mrs. Crittenden, and my perturbation furnished them with much amusement. For some reason or for lack of one I was obsessed by a suspicion that the new Minister, probably being unaware of the state of feeling which continually manifested itself between Northern and Southern people in the capital, might assign to me, as my escort to table, some pronounced Republican.

"What would you do in that event?" asked Senator Clay.

"Do?" I asked, hotly and promptly. "I would refuse to accept him!"

My husband's voice was grave as he said, "I hope there will be no need!"

Arriving at the Embassy, I soon discovered that, as had been rumoured, the maid ordinarily at hand to assist women guests had been replaced by a fair young English serving-man, who took charge of my wraps, and knelt to remove my overshoes with all the deftness of a practised *femme de chambre.* These preliminaries over, I rejoined my husband in the corridor, and together we proceeded to our host, and, having greeted him, turned aside to speak to other friends.

Presently Senator Brown, Mr. Davis's confrère from Mississippi, made his way to me. Senator Brown was one of the brightest men in Congress. As he approached, my misgivings vanished and I smiled as I said, "Ah! you are to be my gallant this evening!"

"Not so," replied he. "I'm to go in with Mme. ———, and shall be compelled to smell 'camphired' cleaned gloves for hours!"

He left my side. Presently he was replaced by Mr. Eames, ex-Minister to Venezuela. Again I conjectured him to be the man who was destined to escort me; but, after the exchange of a few words, he, too, excused

**LORD LYONS**
British Ambassador to the United States

himself, and I saw him take his place at the side of his rightful partner.  In this way several others came and went, and still I stood alone.  I wondered what it all meant, and gave a despairing look at my husband, who, I knew, was rapidly becoming as perturbed as was I. Presently the massive doors slid apart, and a voice proclaimed, "Dinner, my Lord!"  Now my consternation gave way to overwhelming surprise and confusion, for our host, glancing inquiringly around the circle, stepped to my side, and, bowing profoundly, offered his arm with, "I have the honour, Madam!"  Once at the table, I quickly regained my composure, assisted, perhaps, to this desirable state, by a feeling of triumph as I caught from across the table the amused glance of my erstwhile companion, Mrs. Crittenden.

Lord Lyons's manner was so unconstrained and easy that I soon became emboldened to the point of suggesting to him the possibility of some lovely American consenting to become "Lyonised."  His Lordship's prompt rejoinder and quizzical look quite abashed me, and brought me swiftly to the conclusion that I would best let this old lion alone; for he said, "Ah, Madam! do you remember what Uncle Toby said to his nephew when he informed him of his intended marriage?"  Then, without waiting for my assent, he added, "Alas! alas! quoth my Uncle Toby, you will never sleep slantindicularly in your bed more!"

I had an adventure at a ball in 1859, which, though unimportant in itself, turns a pleasing side-light upon one of the more courteous of our political opponents.  A dance had been announced, the music had begun, and the dancers had already taken their places, when my partner was called aside suddenly.  Something occurred to detain him longer than he had expected, and the time for us to lead having arrived, there was a call for the missing gallant, who was nowhere to be seen.  I looked about helplessly, wondering what I was to do, when Anson Burlingame, who was standing near, seeing my dilemma, stepped promptly forward, and, taking my hand in most courtly manner, he said, "Pardon me, Madam!" and led me, bewildered, through the first steps of the dance!

Lost in amazement at his courtesy, I had no time to demur, and, when we returned to my place, the delinquent had reappeared. Bowing politely, Mr. Burlingame withdrew. The circumstance caused quite a ripple among those who witnessed it. Those who knew me best were amused at my docility in allowing myself thus to be led through the dance by a rank Abolitionist; but many were the comments made upon "Mr. Burlingame's audacity in daring to speak to Mrs. Clement Clay!"

Such were the scenes, both grave and gay, that preceded what was surely the saddest day of my life—January 21, 1861—when, after years of augmenting dissension between the Sections, I saw my husband take his portfolio under his arm and leave the United States Senate Chamber in company with other no less earnest Southern Senators. For weeks the pretense of amity between parties had ceased, and social formalities no longer concealed the gaping chasm that divided them. When the members of each met, save for a glare of defiance or contempt, each ignored the other, or, if they spoke, it was by way of a taunt or a challenge. Every sentence uttered in Senate or House was full of hot feeling born of many wrongs and long-sustained struggle. For weeks, men would not leave their seats by day or by night, lest they might lose their votes on the vital questions of the times. At the elbows of Senators, drowsy with long vigils, pages stood, ready to waken them at the calling of the roll.

Not a Southern woman but felt, with her husband, the stress of that session, the sting of the wrongs the Southern faction of that great body was struggling to right. For forty years the North and the South had striven for the balance of power, and the admission of each new State was become the subject of bitter contention. There was, on the part of the North, a palpable envy of the hold the South had retained so long upon the Federal City, whether in politics or society, and the resolution to quell us, by physical force, was everywhere obvious. The face of the city was lowering, and some of the North agreed with us of the South that a nation's suicide was about to be precipitated.

Senator Clay, than whom the South has borne no more self-sacrificing son, nor the Nation a truer patriot, was an ill man as that "winter of national agony and shame" (*vide* the Northern witness, Judge Hoar) progressed. The incertitude of President Buchanan was alarming; but the courage of our people to enter upon what they knew must be a defense of everything they held dear in State and family institution rose higher and higher to meet each advancing danger. The seizure by South Carolina of United States forts that lay, a menace, within her very doorway, acted like a spur upon the courage of the South.

"We have been hard at work all day," wrote a defender of our cause from Morris Island, January 17, 1861, "helping to make, with our own hands, a battery, and moving into place some of the biggest guns you ever saw, and all immediately under the guns of old Anderson.* He fired a shell down the Bay this afternoon to let us know what he could do. But he had a little idea what *we* can do from his observation of our firing the other morning,† at the '*Star of the West*,' all of which he saw, and he thought we had ruined the ship, as Lieutenant Hall represented in the city that morning. . . . We learn to-day that in Washington they are trying to

* Major Anderson, in command at Fort Sumter.
† January 9, 1861.

procrastinate. That does not stop our most earnest preparation, for we are going to work all night to receive from the steamboat three more enormous guns and place them ready to batter down Fort Sumter, and we can do it. We hope the other points are as forward in their preparations as we are. If so, we can *smoke him out* in a week. We are nearest to him, and he may fire on us to-night, but if he were to kill everybody in the State, and only one woman was left, and she should bear a child, that child would be a secessionist. Our women are even more spirited than we are, though, bless the dear creatures, I have not seen one in a long time."

Yet, despite these buoyant preparations for defense, there was a lingering sentiment among us that caused us to deplore the necessity that urged our men to arms. My husband was exceedingly depressed at the futility of the Peace Commission, for he foresaw that the impending conflict would be bloody and ruinous. One incident that followed the dissolution of that body impressed itself ineradicably upon my mind. Just after its close ex-President Tyler came to our home. He was now an old man and very attenuated. He was completely undone at the failure of the Peace men, and tears trickled down his cheeks as he said to Senator Clay, with indescribable sadness, "Clay, the end has come!"

In those days men eyed each other warily and spoke guardedly, save to the most tried and proved friend. One evening early in 1861, Commander Semmes, U. S. N., called upon us, and happened to arrive just as another naval officer, whose name I have now forgotten, was announced. The surprise that spread over the faces of our visitors when they beheld each other was great, but Senator Clay's and my own was greater, as hour after hour was consumed in obvious constraint. Neither of the officers appeared to be at ease, yet for hours neither seemed to desire to relieve the situation by taking his departure. Midnight had arrived ere our now forgotten guest rose and bade us "good night." Then Commander Semmes hastened to unbosom himself. He had resolved to out-sit the other gentleman if it took all night.

"As my Senator, Mr. Clay," he said, "I want to report to you my decision on an important matter. I have resolved to hand in my resignation to the United States Government, and tender my services to that of the Confederate States. I don't know what the intention of my brother officer is, but I could take no risk with him," he added. Many a scene as secret, as grave, and as "treasonable," took place in those last lowering weeks.

I have often mused upon the impression held by the younger generation of those who were adverse to the South, viz.: that she "was prepared for the war" into which we were precipitated practically by the admission of Kansas; that our men, with treasonable foresight, had armed themselves individually and collectively for resistance to our guileless and unsuspicious oppressors. Had this been true, the result of that terrible civil strife would surely have been two nations where now we have one. To the last, alas! too few of our people realised that war was inevitable. Even our provisional Secretary of War for the Confederate States,* early in '61, publicly prophesied that, should fighting actually begin, it would be over in three months! It must be apparent to thinkers that such gay dreamers do not form deep or "deadly plots."

Personally I knew of but one man whose ferocity led him to collect and secrete weapons of warfare. He was Edmund Ruffin, of Virginia, with whom I entered into collusion. For months my parlour was made an arsenal for the storing of a dozen lengthy spears. They were handsome weapons, made, I suspect, for some decorative purpose, but I never knew their origin nor learned of

* General L. Pope Walker.

their destination. On them were engraved these revolutionary words:

"Out of this nettle, danger, we pluck the flower of safety."

As Senator Clay's unequivocal position as a Southern man was everywhere understood, our parlours were frequently the gathering-place of statesmen from our own section and such others as were friendly to our people and believed in our right to defend the principles we had maintained since the administration of the first President of the United States. Among the last mentioned were Senators Pendleton and Pugh, and the ardent member of Congress from Ohio, Mr. Vallandigham. Often the "dread arms" deposited by Mr. Ruffin proved a subject of conjecture and mirth, with which closed some weightier conversation. As the day drew near, however, for the agreed upon withdrawal of our Senators, the tension under which all laboured made jests impossible, and keyed every heart to the utmost solemnity. Monday, January 21st, was the day privately agreed upon by a number of Senators for their public declaration of secession; but, as an example of the uncertainty which hobbled our men, until within a day or two of the appointed time several still awaited the instructions from their States by which their final act must be governed. Early on Sunday morning, January 20th, my husband received from a distinguished colleague the following letter:

"WASHINGTON, Saturday night, January 19, 1861.

"*My Dear Clay:* By telegraph I am informed that the copy of the ordinance of secession of my State was sent by mail *to-day*, one to each of two branches of representation, and that *my* immediate presence at —— is required. It thus appears that —— was expected to present the paper in the Senate and some one of the members to do so in the House. All have gone save me, I, alone, and I am called away. *We have piped and they would not dance, and now the devil may care.*

"I am grieved to hear that you are sick, the more so that I cannot go to you. God grant your attack may be slight."

And now the morning dawned of what all knew would be a day of awful import. I accompanied my husband to the Senate, and everywhere the greeting or gaze of absorbed, unrecognising men and women was serious and full of trouble. The galleries of the Senate, which hold, it is estimated, one thousand people, were packed densely, principally with women, who, trembling with excitement, awaited the denouement of the day. As, one by one, Senators David Yulee, Stephen K. Mallory, Clement C. Clay, Benjamin Fitzpatrick, and Jefferson Davis rose, the emotion of their brother Senators and of us in the galleries increased; and, when I heard the voice of my husband, steady and clear, notwithstanding his illness, declare in that Council Chamber:

"Mr. President, I rise to announce that the people of Alabama have adopted an ordinance whereby they withdraw from the Union, formed under a compact styled the United States, resume the powers delegated to it, and assume their separate station as a sovereign and independent people," it seemed as if the blood within me congealed.

As each Senator, speaking for his State, concluded his solemn renunciation of allegiance to the United States, women grew hysterical and waved their handkerchiefs, encouraging them with cries of sympathy and admiration. Men wept and embraced each other mournfully. At times the murmurs among the onlookers grew so deep that the Sergeant-at-Arms was ordered to clear the galleries; and, as each speaker took up his portfolio and gravely left the Senate Chamber, sympathetic shouts rang from the assemblage above. Scarcely a member of that Senatorial body but was pale with the terrible significance of the hour. There was everywhere a feeling of suspense, as if, visibly, the pillars of the temple were being withdrawn and the great Government structure was tottering; nor was there a patriot on either side who did not deplore and whiten before the evil that brooded so low over the nation,

When Senator Clay concluded his speech, many of his colleagues, among them several from Republican ranks, came forward to shake hands with him. For months his illness had been a theme of public regret and apprehension among our friends. "A painful rumour reached me this morning," wrote Joseph Holt to me late in 1860, "in relation to the health of your excellent husband. . . . While I hope sincerely this is an exaggeration, yet the apprehensions awakened are so distressing, that I cannot resist the impulse of my heart to write you in the trust that your reply will relieve me from all anxiety. It is my earnest prayer that a life adorned by so many graces may be long spared to yourself, so worthy of its devotion, and to our country, whose councils so need its genius and patriotism. . . . Believe me most sincerely your friend, Joseph Holt."

In fact, the news of Senator Clay's physical sufferings had been telegraphed far and near, and, merged with the fear for our country, there was, in my own heart, great anxiety and sadness for him. Our mail was full of inquiries as to his welfare, many from kindly strangers and even from States that were bitterly inimical to our cause. One of these came from the far North, from one who signed himself, "A plain New Hampshire minister, Henry E. Parker." Nor can I refrain from quoting a portion of his letter, which bears the never-to-be-forgotten date of January 21st, 1861. He wrote as follows:

"I am utterly appalled at this projected dissolution of our Government. To lose, to throw away our place and name among the nations of the earth, seems not merely like the madness of suicide, but the very blackness of annihilation. If this thing shall be accomplished, it will be, to

**CLEMENT C. CLAY, JR.**
United States Senator, 1853-61

my view, the crime of the nineteenth century; the partition of Poland will be nothing in comparison.  . . .

"Born and educated as we are at the North, sensible men at the South cannot wonder at the views we entertain, nor do sensible men at the North think it strange that, born and educated as the Southerner is, he should feel very differently from the Northerner in some things; but why should not all these difficulties sink before our common love for our common country?"

Why, indeed! Yet the cry of "disunion" had been heard for forty years* and still our Southern men had forborne, until the party belligerents, whose encroachments had now, at last, become unbearable, had begun to look upon our protests as it were a mere cry of "wolf." Of those crucial times, and of that dramatic scene in the United States Senate, no Southern pen has written in permanent words; and such Northern historians as Messrs. Nicolay and Hay elide, as if their purpose were to obscure, the deliberate and public withdrawal of those representatives, our martyrs to their convictions, their institutions and their children's heritages; and would so bury them under the sweeping charges of "conspiracy" and "treason" that the casual reader of the future is not likely to realise with what candour to their opponents, with what dignity to themselves, out of what loyalty to their States, and yet again with what grief for the nation and sacrifice of life-time associations, the various seceding Senators went out at last from that august body!

For months the struggle of decades had been swiftly approximating to its bloody culmination. Our physical prosperity, no less than the social security we enjoyed, had caused us to become objects of envy to the rough ele-

* "Talk of disunion, threats of disunion, accusations of intentions of disunion lie scattered plentifully through the political literature of the country from the very formation of the Government," say Messrs. Nicolay and Hay.  See vol. II, page 296, of "Abraham Lincoln."  Also, "Benton's Thirty Years' View."   Vol. II, page 786.

ments in the new settlements, especially of the North-west.* So inimical was the North to us that though the South was the treasury of the nation; though she had contributed from her territory the very land upon which the Federal City was built; though her sons ranked among the most brilliant of whom the young Republic could boast—it was impossible for the South to get an appropriation of even a few hundred thousand dollars, to provide for the building of a lighthouse on that most dangerous portion of the Atlantic coast, the shore of North Carolina!

An era of discovery and expansion preceded the outbreak of the war. By means of costly embassies to the Eastern countries, new avenues of commerce had been opened. The acquisition of Cuba and of the Mexican States became an ambition on the part of Mr. Buchanan, who was anxious to repeat during his Administration the successes of his predecessors, Presidents Fillmore and Pierce. So long ago as '55, the question of the purchase of the island of St. Thomas from the Danish Government was a subject that called for earnest diplomacy on the part of Mr. Raasloff, the Danish Minister; and the gold fever which made Northern adventurers mad carried many to rifle the distant Pacific coast of its treasures. By this time the cotton gin had demonstrated its great worth, and the greed of acquisition saw in our cotton fields a new source of envy, for we had no need to dig or to delve—we shook our cotton plants and golden dollars dropped from them. Had the gathering of riches been our object in life, men of the South had it in their power to have rivalled the wealth of the fabled Midas; but, as was early observed by a statesman who never was partisan, the " Southern statesmen went for the honours and the Northern for the benefits." In consequence, wrote Mr. Benton (1839),

* This fact is emphasised by Messrs. Nicolay and Hay. See vol. I, page 142, "Abraham Lincoln."

"the North has become rich upon the benefits of the Government; the South has grown lean upon its honours."

From the hour of this exodus of Senators from the official body, all Washington seemed to change. Imagination can scarcely conjure up an atmosphere at once so ominous and so sad. Each step preparatory to our departure was a pang. Carriages and messengers dashed through the streets excitedly. Farewells were to be spoken, and many, we knew, would be final. Vehicles lumbered on their way to wharf or station filled with the baggage of departing Senators and Members. The brows of hotel-keepers darkened with misgivings, for the disappearance from the Federal City of the families of Congressional representatives from the fifteen slave-holding States made a terrible thinning out of its population; and, in the strange persons of the politicians, already beginning to press into the capital, there was little indication that these might prove satisfactory substitutes for us who were withdrawing.

"How shall I commence my letter to you?" wrote the wife of Colonel Philip Phillips to me a month or two after we had left Washington. "What can I tell you, but of despair, of broken hearts, of ruined fortunes, the sobs of women, and sighs of men! . . . I am still in this *horrible city* . . . but, distracted as I am at the idea of being forced to remain, we feel the hard necessity of keeping quiet. . . . For days I saw nothing but despairing women leaving [Washington] suddenly, their husbands having resigned and sacrificed their all for their beloved States. You would not know this God-forsaken city, our beautiful capital, with all its artistic wealth, desecrated, disgraced with Lincoln's low soldiery. The respectable part [of the soldiers] view it also in the same spirit, for one of the Seventh Regiment told me that never in his life had he seen such ruin going on as is now enacted in the halls of our once honoured Capitol! I cannot but think that the presentiment that the South would wish to keep Washington must have induced this desecration of all that should have been respected by the mob in power. . . . The Gwins are the only ones left of our intimates, and Mrs. G—— is packed up ready to leave. Poor thing! her eyes are never without tears. . . . There are 30,000 troops here. Think of it! They go about the avenue insulting women and taking property without paying for it. . . . Such are the men waged to subjugate us of the South. . . . We hear constantly from Montgomery. Everything betokens a deep, abiding faith in the cause.

"I was told that those *giant* intellects, the Blairs, who are acting under the idea of being second Jacksons, wishing to get a good officer to do some of their dirty work (destroying public property), wished Colonel Lee sent for. 'Why, he has resigned!' 'Then tell Magruder!' 'He has resigned, too.' 'General Joe Johnston, then!'— 'He, too, has gone out!' 'Smith Lee?' Ditto!

"'Good God!' said Blair. 'Have all our good officers left us?'

"I hear these Blairs are at the bottom of all this war policy. Old Blair's country place was threatened, and his family, including the fanatical Mrs. Lee, had to fly into the city. This lady was the one who said to me that 'she wished the North to be deluged with the blood of the South ere Lincoln should yield one iota!'

"Do not believe all you hear about the Northern sympathy for Lincoln. The Democrats still feel for the South. If Congress does not denounce Lincoln for his unlawful and unconstitutional proceedings, I shall begin to think we have no country!"

# CHAPTER XI

## War Is Proclaimed

UPON leaving the Federal capital we proceeded to the home of Senator Clay's cousin, Doctor Thomas Withers, at Petersburg, Va. My husband's health, already feeble, had suffered greatly from the months of strife which culminated in the scenes through which we had just passed, and we had scarcely arrived in Petersburg when a serious collapse occurred. Mr. Clay now became so weakened that fears were reiterated by all who saw him that he could not survive. I was urged to take him at once to Minnesota, the attending physicians all agreeing that this was the one experiment in which lay a chance for prolonging his life. In those days the air of that far western State was supposed to have a phenomenally curative effect upon the victims of asthma, from which for years Mr. Clay had suffered an almost "daily death." In the present acute attack, his body sick and his heart sore from our late ordeals, fearful of the danger of delay, I at once put into execution plans for the northward trip in which lay even a slender hope for his recovery. No one who had witnessed my husband's dignified withdrawal from the Senate, who had heard his firm utterance of what was at once a challenge to arms and a warning that Alabama would defend her decision to stand alone, would have recognised the invalid now struggling for his life against the dread disease. He was extremely emaciated.

"When I last saw you," wrote John T. Morgan * from

* Now United States Senator from Alabama.

camp, some months later, "your health scarcely justified the hope that you would become one of the first Senators in a new Confederacy. I was grieved that when we came to meet the great struggle in Alabama you were not permitted to aid us further than by your counsels and recorded opinions. I rejoice that you are again our representative in a Senate where the South is not to be defended against foes within her own bosom, but to reap the advantage of the wisdom and experience of her own statesmen."

My brother-in-law, Hugh Lawson Clay, afterward Colonel on the staff of our friend, General E. Kirby Smith, hurried, therefore, from Alabama to accompany us upon the slow journey made necessary by Mr. Clay's extreme weakness.

In due time we arrived at the International Hotel, St. Paul. Here, though our stay was short, we had an unpleasant experience, a single one, due to sectional feeling. Having safely bestowed Mr. Clay in his room, our brother made his way to the drug-store, which, as we entered, we had observed was below the hotel, to purchase a necessary restorative for my husband. While waiting there for the wrapping of the medicine, two young men entering met, and one exclaimed to the other:

"Here's a good chance! Clay, the fire-eating Senator from Alabama, is in this house. Let's mob him!"

My brother, both indignant and surprised, was also fearful lest they should carry out their threat and thereby work incalculable evil to our invalid. He turned promptly and addressed them:

"Mr. Clay, of whom you speak," he said, "is my brother, and, it may be, a hopeless invalid. He is here seeking health. You can molest him only through me!"

But now a second surprise met him, for the two youths began a very duet of apology, declaring they "had only been joking." They meant no offense, they said, and, in fact, themselves were democrats. Feeling, they continued, was at high tide, and it was the fashion of the times to denounce the South. Upon this frank acknowledgment the trio shook hands and parted, nor did Senator Clay and I hear of the altercation until the next day, when it was repeated to us by a kind friend, Mr. George Culver, at whose home, in St. Paul, we lingered for several weeks. Here the wonderful climate appreciably restored the invalid, and Mr. Clay was soon able to move about, and added to his weight almost visibly.

In the meantime, the news of the gathering together of armies, both North and South, came more and more frequently. Everywhere around us preparations were making for conflict. The news from the seceding States was inspiring. My husband's impatience to return to Alabama increased daily, stimulated, as it was, by the ardour of our many correspondents from Montgomery and Huntsville, civil and military.

"I was improving continuously and rapidly," he wrote to our friend E. D. Tracy, "when Lincoln's proclamation and that of the Governor of Minnesota reached me, and I think I should have been entirely restored to health in a month or two had I remained there with an easy conscience and a quiet mind. But after those bulletins, the demonstrations against the "Rebels" were so offensive as to become intolerable. So we left on the 22d [April], much to the regret of the few real friends we found or made. Many, with exceeding frankness, expressed their deep sorrow at our departure, since I was improving so rapidly; but, while appreciating their solicitude for me, I told them I preferred dying in my own country to living among her enemies."

Shortly after the breaking up of the ice in Lake Minnetonka, we bade farewell to the good Samaritans at St. Paul and took passage on the *Grey Eagle.* She was a celebrated boat of that day, and annually took the prize for being the first to cut through the frozen waters. I have never forgotten the wonders and beauties of that trip, beginning in the still partially ice-locked lake, and progressing gradually until the emerald glories of late April met us in the South! It was on this journey that we caught the first real echoes of the booming guns of Fort Sumter. The passengers on board the *Grey Eagle* discussed the outlook with gravity. To a friendly lady, whose sympathies were aroused on behalf of my husband, still pale and obviously an invalid, I remember expressing my sorrows and fears. I think I wept, for it was a time to start the tears; but her reply checked my complainings.

"Ah, Mrs. Clay!" she said, "think how my heart is riven! I was born in New Orleans and live in New York. One of my sons is in the Seventh New York Regiment, and another in the New Orleans Zouaves!"

At Cairo, already a great centre of military activity for the Federals, we caught a first gleam of the muskets of United States soldiery. A company was drawn up in line on the river bank, for what purpose we did not know, but we heard a rumour that it had to do with the presence on the boat of the Southern Senator Clay, and I remember I was requested by an officer of the *Grey Eagle* to place in my trunk my husband's fine Maynard rifle, which had been much admired by our fellow passengers, and which once had been shot off during the trip, to show its wonderful carrying power. Needless to say, the possibly offending firearm was promptly put away. After a short colloquy between the captain of the vessel and the military officer, who appeared to catechise him, the *Grey Eagle* again swung out on the broad, muddy river, and turned her nose toward Memphis. Now, as we proceeded down the important water-course, at many a point were multiplying evidences that the fratricidal war had begun.

Memphis, at which we soon arrived, and which was destined within a year to be taken and held by our enemy, was now beautiful with blossoms. Spirea and bridal wreaths whitened the bushes, and roses everywhere shaking their fragrance to the breezes made the world appear to smile. My heart was filled with gratitude and joy to find myself once more among the witchery and wonders of my "ain countree"; where again I might hear the delightful mockery of that "Yorick of the Glade," whose bubbling melody is only to be heard in the South land! It was a wonderful home-coming for our invalid, too eager by much to assume his share of the responsibilities that now rested upon the shoulders of our men of the South. A period of complete physical weakness followed our arrival in Mr. Clay's native city, a busy political and military centre in those early days.

We spent our summer in "Cosy Cot," our mountain home, set upon the crest of Monte Sano, which overlooks the town of Huntsville below, distant about three miles; nor, save in the making of comparatively short trips, did we again leave this vicinity until Mr. Clay, his health improved, was called to take his seat in the Senate of the new Confederate Government, at Richmond, late in the following autumn. In the meantime Senator Clay had declined the office of Secretary of War in Mr. Davis's Cabinet, privately proffered, believing his physical condition to be such as to render his assumption of the duties of that department an impossibility. In his stead he had urged the appointment of Leroy Pope Walker, our fellow-townsman and long-time friend, though often a legal and political opponent of my husband.

Now, at the time of our return, Secretary Walker was at the side of our Executive head, deep in the problems of the military control of our forces. Communications between Huntsville and Montgomery, where the provisional Government temporarily was established, were frequent. A special session of Congress was sitting, and every one identified with our newly formed Legislature at the little capital was alert and eager in perfecting our plans for defense. We were given a side glimpse of our President's personal activity in the following letter received a few days after our return to Alabama:

"MONTGOMERY, Alabama, May 10, 1861.

". . . Mr. Davis seems just now only conscious of things left undone, and to ignore the much which has been achieved. Consequently, his time seems all taken up with the Cabinet, planning (I presume) future operations. . . . Sometimes the Cabinet depart surreptitiously, one at a time, and Mr. Davis, while making things as plain as did the preacher the virtues of the baptismal, finds his demonstrations made to one weak, weary man, who has no vim to contend. To make a long story short, he overworks himself and all the rest of mankind, but is so far quite well, though not fleshily inclined.

" There is a good deal of talk here of his going to Richmond as commander of the forces. I hope it may be done, for to him military command is a perfect system of hygiene. . . . There have been some here who thought, with a view to the sanitary condition, that the Government had better be moved to Richmond, and also that it would strengthen the weak-fleshed but willing-spirited border States. . . . This is a very pretty place, and, were not the climate as warm as is the temperament of the people, it would be pleasant; but nearly all my patriotism oozes out, not unlike Bob Acres' courage, at the pores, and I have come to the conclusion that Roman matrons performed their patriotism and such like duties in the winter. I wish your health would suffice for you to come and see the Congress. They are the finest-looking set of men I have ever seen collected together—grave, quiet and thoughtful-looking men, with an air of refinement which makes my mind's picture gallery a gratifying pendant to Hamlin, Durkee, Doolittle, Chandler, etc. . . .

"The market is forlorn, but then we give our best and a warm welcome. If you are able to come and make us a visit, we will have the concordances of Washington and Montgomery. . . . Mrs. Mallory is in town on a short visit, Mrs. Fitzpatrick and the Governor, Mrs. Memminger, Constitution Brown and his wife, Mr. and Mrs. Toombs (the latter is the only person who has a house). I could gossip on *ad infinitum.* . . ."

In Huntsville a feeling of diligence in preparation was everywhere evident. Our historic little town was not only in the direct line of travel between larger cities, and therefore a natural stopping place for travellers; but, by reason of the many legal and political lights residing there, and because of its being the county seat of one of the most affluent counties in northern Alabama, was, and is, a town of general interest throughout the State. Almost in an unbroken line, the United States Senators of northern Alabama have been citizens of my husband's native town.

Situate among the low hills that separate the higher points of the Cumberland range, Huntsville smiles up at the sky from a rare amphitheatre, hollowed in the cedar-covered mountains. It is in the heart of one of the most fertile portions of the Tennessee Valley. Within an hour's swift ride, the Tennessee flood rolls on its romantic way, and as near in another direction is the forked Flint River, every bend along its leafy edges a place of beauty. Up hill and down dale, ride wherever one will, may be seen the hazy tops of mountains, disappearing in the blue ether, and intervening valleys yellow with corn or white with cotton, or green with the just risen grain. In the summer the sweetness of magnolia and jasmine, of honeysuckle and mimosa, scents the shady avenues along which are seen, beyond gardens and magnolia trees, the commodious town houses of the prosperous planters. Among these affluent surroundings a high public spirit had been nourished. Here the first State Legislature of Alabama was convened and that body met which formed the State Constitution. The simple structure in which those early statesmen gathered (being, in general, representatives from the families of

Virginia and the Carolinas) stood yet intact in the early part of 1903. The first newspaper printed in Alabama, except the *Madison Gazette*, was published in Huntsville, and Green Academy (taking its name from the rich sward that surrounded it), a renowned institution of learning, was long a famous feature of Twickenham Town, by which name Huntsville was once known.

In the early days of the township's existence, a hot contest continued for years to wage between the followers of two of its richest settlers as to the future appellation of the pretty place. The friends of Colonel Pope, who had contributed from the very centre of his plantation the square upon which was built the County Court House, for a time overbore the opposing parties and named the town in honour of the birthplace of the immortal poet; but, though this choice was ratified by legislative act, the adherents of the pioneer, John Hunt, refused to yield their wishes. Mr. Hunt had discovered the site of the town while still the valley was part of the Territory of Mississippi. Lured by the deer he was stalking, he had come upon the big spring, gushing with limpid waters. Here he pitched his tent, and, gathering others about him, he fostered the building of the town which, until the contest that arose with the aristocratic Colonel Pope, was known as Huntsville. For two years, until the original name was restored by a second act of Legislature, the little city was known as "Twickingham Town," and to many of its old families this name remains so dear that among themselves it still continues to be affectionately applied.

Half the youth of Alabama in that early day delved in the classics under the guidance of the studious professors of Green Academy. It was situated in a large plot of ground which commanded a view of the mountain. Its site was given to the town by Judge William Smith (the warm friend of Andrew Jackson) on the condition that it should be used only for a building for educational purposes forever. This distinguished judge was, I think, the only man until Roscoe Conkling to refuse a seat on the Supreme Court Bench of the United States.*

The charms and fascinations and general winsomeness of the girls of the lovely vale, even in that early period, in a measure may be imagined from the references to them in the following letter, written to Clement C. Clay, Jr., by this time entered at the State University at Tuscaloosa:

"FEBRUARY 2, 1833.

"*My Dear Clement:* Richard Peete, Jere Clemens, Richard Perkins, Withers Clay, John E. Moore† and myself are in a class reading Horace and *Graeca Majora.* Clio is nearly broken up, and I fear it will never be revived, as the members do nothing but walk with the girls, nor do they appear to think of anything else. The girls in this town are the most jealous little vixens that ever breathed. I would advise you as a friend (for I have gone through the fiery ordeal, and should know something of the character of woman) to keep a respectful distance from the fair ones; for, if you mingle with them at all, you will be persuaded to mingle with them more and more. How much I would give if they would never harass me more!"

The roll of Huntsville's prominent men includes a peculiarly large number of names that have been potent in State and National capitals, in civil and in military life. Scarcely a stone in its picturesque "God's Acre" but bears a name familiar to the Southern ear. From under the low hill on which the columned Court House and historic National Bank building stand, the Big Spring gushes, which has had its part in swelling the city's

---

* Judge Smith was the grandfather of Mrs. Meredith Calhoun, who, with her husband, played a brilliant part in Paris society when Eugénie's triumphs were at their height. A. S.

† John E. Moore became celebrated on the bench. He declined the office of territorial judge, offered him by President Pierce, but was serving as judge in a military court when he died, in 1864. He was a brother of Colonel Sydenham Moore, who fell at the battle of Seven Pines. A. S.

fame. Where its source lies none can say, though
myths are plenty that tell of subterranean caves through
which it passes, and which gleam with stalactite glories.
Trickling freely from the sides of the mountain beyond
are numerous medicinal springs, and silver streams
thread their way among the valleys; but nowhere within
the Tennessee region exists a flow that at all may
be compared with Huntsville's "Big Spring." If Hygeia
still exercises her functions, her modern home is surely
here. The flow of clear limestone water as it issues from
the rocks is wonderfully full and seemingly boundless.
Since the founding of the town the spring has supplied
all the needs of the residents, and that of armies camped
about it. So late as 1898 its splendid daily yield of
twenty-four million gallons influenced the present Government to locate in and about the pretty city, while
awaiting the development of the Cuban War, an army
of twenty thousand men.

In the sixties the spring was already famous. From
time immemorial the pool below it had served the same
purpose for the negroes about as did the River Jordan
for the earlier Christians, and a baptism at the Big
Spring, both impressive and ludicrous, was a sight never
to be forgotten. The negroes came down the hill,
marching with solemn steps to weird strains of their own
composing, until they reached the edge of the stream
that forms below the spring. Here the eager candidates
for immersion were led into the water, when, doused for
a moment, they would come up again shrieking shrilly
a fervent Hallelujah! As a rule, two companions were
stationed near to seize the person of the baptised
one as it rose, lest in a paroxysm of religious fervour he
should harm himself or others. As the baptisms, always
numerous, continued, the ardour of the crowd of participants and onlookers was sure to augment, until a mani-
acal mingling of voices followed, that verged toward

pandemonium. The ceremony was as strange and blood-curdling as any rite that might be imagined in the interior of the Dark Continent.

Once, upon the occasion of a visit of two New York friends, one candidate for baptism, a black man, a veritable Goliath, broke loose from those who tried to hold him and ran up the hill in his ecstasy, bellowing like a wounded buffalo. The sounds were enough to excite unmixed horror in the unaccustomed listener, but the appearance of the enthusiast to me was more comical than terrifying; for, being in his stockings, and these conspicuous by reason of their enormous holes, his heels, revealed at every step, appeared as they flashed up the acclivity like the spots on a bull-bat's wings. When this sable son of Anak took the field, the spectators scattering right and left, my friends turned toward me as if panic-stricken. They paused but a brief moment, then, "standing not upon the order of their going," they, too, fled from the possible charge of the half-crazed enthusiast. It was no uncommon thing at such baptisms for the candidates to suffer from an attack of "Jerks," a kind of spasm which resulted from their excited imaginations. I have seen the strength of four stout men tested to its utmost to hold down one seemingly delicate negress, who, fired by the "glory in her soul," was now become its victim, jerking and screaming in a manner altogether horrible to witness.

Above the spring and about the picturesque Square and Court House, in the spring and early summer of '61, the gay-hearted youth of Madison County, thronging to the county seat, met in companies to drill and prepare themselves for service in the war now upon us. Already, by the early part of June, Alabama had "contributed to the Confederacy about 20,000 muskets and rifles," though she retained of these, "for her own immediate protection and defense, only four thousand! I hope," wrote Governor A. B. Moore, in sending this information to Mr. Clay, "that volunteer companies throughout the State will put the rifles and double-barrelled shot-guns in order, and drill them until called into actual service."

The youths and men of Madison County needed small urging. They were heart and soul for the conflict that at last must be waged to preserve the homes of their fathers, the heritages that were to be theirs, and their right to independent government. These were the incentives of our soldiers, allied to each other, regiment by regiment, by blood and long association. There was no need for alien hirelings to swell our ranks. The questions at issue were vital, and every Southern man who could bear arms sprang eagerly to assume them.

Upon our arrival in Huntsville we found the city alive with preparations for defense, our mail heavy with reports from every quarter of the South, of friends and kinsmen who had entered the army, and many exhilarated by the battles already won. An idea may be gathered of the confluent interests that bound together our Southern army, by a mention, as an example, by no means unique, of the ramifications of the two families represented by Senator Clay and myself. My husband's uncle, General Withers, was already in command at Mobile; his brother, Hugh Lawson Clay, was in Lynchburg, recruiting; his cousin, Eli S. Shorter, was enrolled as Colonel in the C. S. A., besides whom there were enlisted numerous cousins of the Withers, Comer, and Clayton families. Thirty-nine cousins of my own, bearing the name of Williams, were in the field at one time, and innumerable Arlingtons, Drakes and Boddies, Hilliards, Tunstalls and Battles served the beloved cause in various capacities in civil and military life.

These conditions knit neighbourhoods as well as regiments very closely together, and largely go to furnish an explanation of our long struggle against the numerically

L. Q. C. LAMAR
1862

superior armies of our invaders. Our victories in those early days were great, though the blood spilled to gain them was precious; but the sound of mourning was stilled before the greater need for encouragement to the living. "Beauregard and Johnston have given the fanatics something to meditate upon," wrote a cousin in July of '61. "A despatch says that our loss was three thousand, theirs seven thousand. Steady Beauregard and brave Johnston ! We owe them our gratitude !"

Yes! we owed them gratitude and we gave it to them and to every man in the ranks. The women at home knitted and sewed, sacrificed and prayed, and wept, too, especially the aged, as they packed away the socks and underwear and such comforts for the young men in the field as might be pressed into a soldier's knapsack. "I met Mr. Lamar's mother," wrote my sister from Macon, late in May, "and spoke to her of her son's having gone to Montgomery. She had not heard of it before and burst into tears ! This is her fourth and last son gone to the war !"

From Huntsville had gone out the gallant E. D. Tracy, who, now at Harper's Ferry, wrote back most thrilling accounts of military proceedings in that important section of our Confederate States:

"I continue entirely well," began a letter dated from Camp, near Harper's Ferry, June 8, 1861: "And, while I perfectly agree with, since conversing with, General Smith, in regard to our situation, am in good spirits. I trust I am ready to die *when my hour comes*, as becomes a Christian soldier and gentleman; until that hour, I am proof against shell and shot. If the enemy attacks us 'we'll memorise another Golgotha' and achieve a victory, or martyrdom. Our men believe the post to be impregnable and are anxious for fight; if they were better informed, I have no idea that their courage would be in the least abated.

"From the arrival of troops during the last few days, I conclude that it is the purpose of Government to hold Harper's Ferry. At one time I think that point was undecided, and am glad to believe that it is now settled as stated. The moral effect of an evacuation of a place believed to be a Gibraltar would be terribly disastrous to our cause; it would encourage our enemies, depress our troops, and disappoint the expectation of the world. Better that we perish in making a gallant defense than that such consequences should be risked."

My sister, Mrs. Hugh Lawson Clay, who had joined her husband in Lynchburg, wrote buoyantly, yet gravely, from that troubled centre: "I wrote you a long, long letter last Saturday," begins one epistle from her, "but Mr. Clay would not let me send it, because, he said, I told too much. He was afraid it might be read by other eyes than yours. . . . I look hourly to hear the result of an awful battle. I cannot but fear, for we cannot hope to gain such victories often as the one at Bethel Church. . . . Here we hear everything, for there are persons passing all the time to and from Winchester and Manassas Junction. So many men from this place are stationed there that mothers and sisters manage to hear every day. Mr. Tracy wrote in his last that he fully expected to be in a big battle. His men were eager for the fight, and he would be sure to write as to the result, if it did not result in a termination of his life's candle!"

As the time drew near for the opening of Congress in Richmond, Mr. Clay's health, spurred to a better state by an eager patriotism, eager to express itself in the forum if debarred from the field, became appreciably restored, and preparations were begun for an absence of a few months from Huntsville. Anxious as everyone was throughout the South, and feeling the strain even of victory, now flowing toward us and again ebbing to our

MRS. PHILIP PHILLIPS
of Washington, D. C.

enemies, my husband and I had few misgivings concerning the safety of the home we were leaving. A hundred greater dangers surrounded Richmond (as it was thought), that lay so near to the Federal lines and was the prize above all others which we looked to see grappled for. Yet our field lay there, and, in anticipation, it seemed a pleasant and an active one, for already it was peopled with throngs of our former friends.

"I almost imagined myself in Washington," wrote Mrs. Philip Phillips, now returning from the Federal capital, where for months she had been a prisoner. "There are so many dear, old friends [in Richmond]— Mrs. Mallory, Mrs. Joe Johnston, and others—awaited us at the Spottswood Hotel. I spent an evening with Mrs. Davis, who received me with great feeling. . . . We have a terrible struggle before us. The resources of Lincoln's army are great, and a defensive war will prove our greatest safeguard, but, it is presumption in speaking thus; only, having come so recently from the seat of war, my ideas, founded upon practical knowledge of what is going on at the North, may derive some value. I brought on from Washington, sewed in my corsets, a programme of the war sent to me by a Federal officer, many of whom are disaffected. The capitalists of the North demand a decisive blow, else they will not back the Government."

# CHAPTER XII

## RICHMOND AS A NATIONAL CAPITAL

RICHMOND, as seen from the hill, with the James River flowing by, its broad, level streets, full foliaged trees, and spacious homes, is a beautiful city. Rich in historic association, never did it appear more attractive to Southern eyes than when, arriving in the late autumn of '61, we found our Confederate Government established there, and the air full of activity. To accommodate the influx of Congressional and military folk, the houses of the patriotic residents were thrown open, until the capacity of every residence, hotel and lodging-house was tested to the fullest. By the time Senator Clay and I arrived, there was scarcely an extra bed to be had in the city, and though everywhere it was apparent that an unsettled feeling existed, there was nothing either indeterminate or volatile in the zeal with which the dense community was fired. As the new-comers, for the greater part, represented families which a season before had been conspicuous in Washington, society was in the most buoyant of spirits. Our courage was high, for our army had won glorious battles against remarkable odds, and, though gallant men had fallen, as occasion demanded them, new heroes sprang to meet it.

For a few months we revelled in canvas-backs and green-backs, undisturbed by forewarnings of coming draw-backs. To furnish the tables of Richmond nearly all the ducks in Chesapeake Bay fell victims. We feasted on oysters and terrapin of the finest, and unmeasured hospitality was the order of the day on every side.  Never had I looked upon so great an activity, whether military, political, or social.  I had demurred when, as we were about to start for the capital, my maid packed an evening dress or two.

"We are going to war, Emily," I said; "we shall have no need for velvet or jewels.  We are going to nurse the sick; not to dress and dance."  But Emily's ardour on my behalf led her to rebel.

"There's bound to be somethin' goin' on, Miss 'Ginie,'" she declared, "an' I ain't goin' to let my Mistis be outshined by Mis' —— an' dem other ladies!"  And, despite my protests, the gowns were duly packed.  There were many occasions afterward when I blessed the thoughtfulness of my little gingerbread-tinted maid; for there were heroes to dine and to cheer in Richmond, both civil and military, and sombre garments are a sorry garb in which to greet or brighten the thoughts of men tired with the strain of building or fighting for a government.

A sororal spirit actuated our women, and while our greatest entertainment missed some of the mere display which had marked the social events in the Federal City, they were happier gatherings, for we were a people united in interest and in heart.  Some of the brightest memories I carry of that first session are of informal evenings where neighbours gathered *sans cérémonie*.  I recall one such spent at the home of the Mallorys, the occasion being a dinner given to Brigadier General John H. Morgan, who did the Confederacy such gallant service, and was rewarded while in Richmond by the hand of one of its prettiest daughters, Miss Reedy, who had been a favourite in Washington society.  A daughter of Mr. Reedy, M.C., from Tennessee, she was the first girl of her day in Washington to wear a curl upon her forehead, which coquettish item of coiffure was soon imitated by a hundred others.

The family of Mr. Mallory was a model one, every member seeming to have his or her share in rounding out the general attractiveness. An informal meal taken with that family was an experience long to be remembered, for the little children took each his turn in asking the blessing, which was never omitted, and which was especially impressive in those days, in which the shadows of growing privations soon grew to be recognised if not openly discussed or admitted. Our Secretary of the Navy, Mr. Mallory, was the merriest of hosts, with a wit as sudden and as brilliant as sheet-lightning, and a power of summing up, when he chose to exert it, both events and people, in the most amusing manner. A picture remains clearly in my mind of the evening devoted to General Morgan. Ruby Mallory, then about thirteen years of age, recited for us Holmes's "The Punch-bowl," while our host, in hearty enjoyment of the verses,

> "Stirred the posset with his ladle,"

to the rhythm of his little daughter's speech.

During our first winter in Richmond my husband and I made our home with Mrs. Du Val, near to the Exchange Hotel, a terrifically over-crowded hostelry at all Confederate times, and within a short walk of the Seddon home, now the Executive Mansion. It was a commodious and stately structure, in which our President, now domiciled, lived with an admirable disdain of display. Statesmen passing through the halls on their way to the discussion of weighty things were likely to hear the ringing laughter of the care-free and happy Davis children issuing from somewhere above stairs or the gardens. The circle at Mrs. Du Val's, our headquarters, as it came and went for three eventful years, comprised some of our former Washington mess-mates, and others newly called into public service. Among the favourites was General J. E. B. Stuart, a rollicking fellow, who loved music, and himself could sing a most pleasing ballad. He was wont to dash up to the gate on his horse, his plumes waving, and he appearing to our hopeful eyes a veritable Murat. He was a gallant soldier, what might be termed delightful company, and one of the most daring cavalry officers our service boasted. Twice, with comparatively but a handful of men, he circled McClellan's big, unwieldly force as it lay massed, for months at a time, contemplating the possibility of closing in upon our capital. It may be said that upon his return to Richmond after his first brilliant feat, General Stuart was the idol of the hour. When the exigencies of the service brought him again and again to the capital, he entered heartily into its social relaxations. Two years passed. He was conspicuous one night in charades, and the next they brought him in, dying from a ghastly wound received upon the battle-field.

I have said we were in gay spirits during that first session of the Confederate Congress; but this condition was resolved upon rather than the spontaneous expression of our real mood, though hope was strong and we were armed with a conviction of right upon our side, and with the assurance of the courage of our soldiers, which filled us with a fine feminine scorn of the mere might of our assailants. Our editors, filled with patriotism and alert, kept us informed of the stirring events of the field and of the great victories which, until the loss of Fort Donelson and the fall of Nashville, so often stood to our credit. Scarcely a triumph, nevertheless, in which was not borne down some friend who was dear to us, so that all news of victory gained might be matched with the story of fearful loss. However, such was our loyalty to the cause, that the stimulus of our victories overbore the sorrow for our losses, sustaining our courage on every side. Before that first session of Congress adjourned, we had buried an army of brave men, among them Generals

Zollicoffer and Albert Sidney Johnston. Our coast was closed by the blockading fleets of the Federal Government. We had lost New Orleans, and the Tennessee Valley was slipping from us. Huntsville, which lay directly in the path of the invading army, itself threatened, was now become a hospital for the wounded from abandoned Nashville. By the early spring the news from our family was ominous of deeper disaster to our beloved town.

"The public stores have been sent on from Nashville," wrote mother, early in March of '62, from Huntsville, "and from four to ten thousand men are said to be here or expected. . . . Yesterday the excitement was greater than I have known. Men were seen walking or riding quickly, and martial music told the tale of danger. . . . There are said to be a thousand sick and wounded here. They have no bedding but a blanket, and are placed in houses through which the wind blows. Rain spurts over the sick men's couches, cooling their fever and making their blood congeal, so that death interposes for their relief! It is rumoured that the President will be here to-night. People were up (last night) till two o'clock, waiting to see him. . . .

General Pillow is at the hotel, but told Dr. Slaughter he would not bring Mrs. Pillow here, as General Buell intends to make this place his headquarters! . . . I have no time to speculate on the future, but try to encourage others to have courage and faith, and not to discourage our soldiers by permitting their fears to be known; but to stimulate them by letting them see the firmness and calm trustfulness with which we commit more than our lives to their keeping!"

The news of Huntsville's danger was our private anxiety in Richmond, where each Senator and Congressman carried the burden of apprehension for his own kin and family possessions well concealed; for at the capital the nation's losses and gains loomed large and obscured the lesser ones of individuals.   Moreover, always before us was the stimulus of the presence of fearless men and the unceasing energy of our President.

I remember on one occasion seeing President Davis passing down the street, beside him, on the left, General Buckner; on the right, General Breckenridge—three stalwart and gallant men as ever walked abreast; and as I watched them the thought came involuntarily, "Can a cause fail with such men at the head?"

Throughout the life of Richmond as a capital, the streets were peopled with soldiers on their way to or from the several headquarters.   There was an unintermitting beating of drums, too often muffled, and the singing of merry bugles.   With the knowledge that we were in the city which, more than any other, invited and defied the attacks of the enemy, a sense of danger spurred our spirits. Though the boom of guns was often not a distant sound, and the solemn carrying in of our wounded became increasingly frequent, few gave way to apprehensions or doubts;   for, as I have said, there were heroes in Richmond to cheer, and our women, putting away from their minds the remembrance of the wounds they had dressed in the morning visit to the hospitals, smiled and devised entertainments well calculated to lift the burden of responsibility, at least for the time being, from the minds and hearts of our leaders, legislative and military. Among the most active hostesses were Mrs. Randolph, wife of one of the members of President Davis's Cabinet, and Mrs. Ives, who put on some charming private theatricals in their parlours; there were the Lees and Harrimans; the Ritchies and Pegrams and Welfords; the Masons and Warwicks, MacFarlanes, Seldens, Leighs (near relatives, these, of Patrick Henry);   besides the

Branders, West Robinsons, Walkers, Scotts, Coxes, Cabells, Semmes, Ives, and other hostesses of renown and long pedigree, whose homes dispensed the friendliest hospitality.

"Do you not remember?" wrote Mrs. Semmes, of New Orleans, to whom I put some queries concerning an episode of that life in Richmond, "do you not remember Mrs. Stannard, who had such a charming house and gave such delicious teas, alluring such men as Soulé, Commodore Barrow, Henry Marshall, of Louisiana, Butler King, and last, though not least, our dear old Vice-President Stephens? She boasted that she never read a book, and yet all these distinguished gentlemen gathered around her board and ate those hot muffins and broiled chicken with gusto!"

These, and unnumbered other faces, rise before me as I recall the great amateur performance of "The Rivals," which made that first winter in Richmond memorable and our hostess, Mrs. Ives, famous. In that performance Constance Cary, a beauty of the Fairfax family, captured all hearts as the languishing Lydia, among them that of our President's Secretary, Colonel Burton Harrison, whose wife she afterward became.

Recalling that interesting evening, Mrs. Harrison wrote very recently, "It seems an aeon since that time, but I have a very vivid recollection of the fun we had and of how prettily Mrs. Ives did everything, spite of grim-visaged war! How I wish I could do anything now with the same zest and rapture with which I put on Lydia's paduasoy and patches! Brother Clarence, then a very youthful midshipman, was the Fag, and my hero, Captain Absolute, was Mr. Lee Tucker, who has vanished, for me, into the mists of time! I have not heard his name in years!"

The fame of that entertainment, the excitement which the preparation for it caused, spread far beyond the picket lines, and we heard afterward that a daring officer of McClellan's army had planned to don the Confederate uniform and cross the lines to take a peep at the much-talked-of performance. "There was a galaxy of talent and beauty in that fairest city of the South," writes my friend, Mrs. Ives, recalling, in 1903, those scenes of the early sixties, "from which I was able to select a strong cast which pre-assured us a brilliant performance. Miss Cary was bewitching, her fair beauty accentuated by the rich costumes she donned for the occasion and which had been worn by her distinguished ancestors in the days of the Old Dominion's glory! Your sister-in-law, Mrs. H. L. Clay, was so fascinating as Lucy that she captivated her husband anew, as he afterward told me; and then, besides, there was pretty Miss Herndon, who tortured her Falkland into jealousy."*

As that historic evening's pleasures crown all other recollections of social life in the Confederate capital, so soon to be in the eclipse of sorrow and undreamed-of privations, I cannot refrain from recording some incidents of it. Those who took part in the performance (or their descendants) are now scattered in every State of the Union, and it is only by the coöperation of some who remember, among them Mrs. Cora Semmes Ives, of Alexandria, Va., Mrs. Myra Knox Semmes, of New Orleans, and Mrs. Burton Harrison, of New York, that I am enabled to gather together again the names of the cast which charmed Richmond's three hundred during the first session of the C. S. A. Congress. They were:

* Of Mrs. Clay herself, renowned for her histrionic talent, Mrs. Ives wrote: "It was the hope of having you take the part of Mrs. Malaprop that encouraged me to undertake the amateur production of Sheridan's play. I felt sure that if all others failed, your acting would redeem all deficiencies. You carried the audience by storm. . . . I can see you yet, in imagination, in your rich brocaded gown, antique laces and jewels, high puffed and curled hair, with nodding plumes which seemed to add expression to your amusing utterances!" A. S.

Sir Anthony Absolute....Mr. Randolph, of Richmond
Captain Absolute......................Mr. Lee Tucker
Sir Lucius O'Trigger (and he had an unapproachable brogue)
                         Robert W. Brown, N. Carolina
Fag.........................Midshipman Clarence Cary
David.....................Mr. Robinson, of Richmond
Lydia Languish............Miss Constance Cary, Virginia
Julia .......................... Miss Herndon, Virginia
Lucy, maid to Lydia......Mrs. Hugh Lawson Clay, Alabama
Mrs. Malaprop .......... Mrs. Clement C. Clay, Alabama
            Harpist, Mrs. Semmes Fitzgerald
            Pianist, Miss Robinson.

For this great occasion no efforts were spared in the rehearsing of our cast, nor in the preparation of our wardrobe. Mrs. Drew, being at that time engaged in playing a precarious engagement at the local theatre (the price of seats not exceeding seventy-five cents, as befitted the times), was invited to a private consultation and criticism of the parts, and it gives me some pleasure, even at this day, to remember her approval of my interpretation of the difficult rôle I had had the hardihood to assume. Our Sir Lucius acquired for the occasion a brogue so rich that almost as much time (and trouble) were necessary to eradicate it from his speech in the weeks that followed as had been spent in attaining it.

The defection of one of the cast for the after-piece (Bombastes Furioso) caused our hostess to display a genuine ability for stage management. Unacquainted with the part she was herself compelled to assume, Mrs. Ives resolved to bring her audience to a state of leniency for any possible shortcomings by dazzling them with the beauty of her apparel. A picture hat from Paris had just run the blockade and arrived safely to the hands of little Miss Ruby Mallory, for whom it had been destined. It was a Leghorn, trimmed with azure velvet and plumes of the same shade. It was an especially appropriate headgear for a character given to dreaming "that all the pots and pans had turned to gold," and an appeal made to the owner brought it swiftly into the possession of Mrs. Ives. Her success was instantaneous. "I declare," she said when the play was over, "nothing but that Paris hat saved me from an attack of stage fright !"

The home of Lieutenant Ives on this occasion was crowded to its utmost capacity, the guests comprising President and Mrs. Davis, the Cabinet and Congressional members, together with prominent generals, numbering in all three hundred. The stage, erected under the supervision of our host, an expert engineer, was a wonderful demonstration of his ingenuity. Placed at one end of the long Colonial parlours, it commanded the eye of every visitor. The performance gave the utmost delight to our audience, and Secretary Mallory, who had seen "The Rivals" (so he told me) in every large city of the United States, and on the boards at Drury Lane, declared it had never been given by a cast at once so brilliant and so able ! Be that as it may, the remembrance of that performance for forty years has remained as the most ambitious social event in the Confederate States' capital.

# CHAPTER XIII

## GLIMPSES OF OUR BELEAGUERED SOUTH LAND

WHILE few, I think, perceived it clearly at that early day, yet in the spring of '62 the fortunes of the Confederacy were declining. Many of our wisest men were already doubtful of the issue even where belief in the justice of our cause never wavered. Looking back upon the prophecies of ultimate defeat that were uttered in those days, by men accustomed to sound the security of governments, I am thrilled at the flood of patriotic feeling on which our men and women were borne to continue in arms against such overwhelming forces and conditions as were brought against them. For months before that first Congress adjourned, from every part of our federated States, eager petitioning, complaints and ominous news reached us. Gold, that universal talisman, was scarce, and Confederate currency began to be looked upon with a doubtful eye. So far-seeing a man as Judge John A. Campbell, writing to Mrs. Campbell from New Orleans early in April, 1862, said: "In the event of the restoration of Northern rule, Confederate money may be worthless. I proceed on that assumption. It will certainly depreciate more and more. Hence, your expenditures should be Confederate money, and, in any event, the bank-notes of Georgia, Virginia and Louisiana are preferable to Confederate bills. If the war should last another year, the embarrassments of everyone will be increased tenfold!"

Within a few months the face of our capital had changed. McClellan's ever-swelling army in the peninsula became more and more menacing. The shadow of coming battles fell over the city, and timid ones hastened away to points that promised more security.   Some went to the mountain resorts "to escape the hot term" in Richmond, but many of the wives and daughters of non-householders, even among those known to possess a cool courage, moved on to the Carolinas or returned to their native States.   As the close of the Congressional session drew near, there was a continual round of good-byes and hand-shakings, and even an attempt now and then at a gaiety which no one actually felt.

Our markets grew suddenly poor, and following quickly upon the heels of a seeming prosperity, a stringency in every department of life in the city was felt.   The cost of living was doubled, and if, indeed, any epicures remained, they were glad to put aside their fastidiousness.   Within a year our vermicelli, when we had it at all, would have warranted an anglicising of its first two syllables, and our rice, beans, and peas, as well as our store of grains and meal, began to discover a lively interest in their war-time surroundings.   We heard tales of a sudden demand for green persimmons, since a soldier, feeding upon one of these, could feel his stomach draw up and at once forget that he was "hawngry."   I remember hearing the story of a certain superficial lady who spoke disdainfully, in the hearing of Mrs. Roger A. Pryor, of a barrel of sorghum which some friend had sent her from a distance.   Full of contempt, she ordered the offending gift to be taken away. "Horrid stuff!" she said.

"Horrid?" asked Mrs. Pryor, gently.   "Why! in these days, with our country in peril, I am grateful when I am able to get a pitcher of sorghum, and I teach my children to thank God for it!"

Our mail, from many quarters, was now become a Pandora's box, from which escaped, as we opened it, myriad apprehensions, dissatisfactions or distresses. "Pray," wrote a friend from New Orleans, "when you see the President, beg him to give some attention to the dis-loyal element in the cities, and particularly in *this city*, which is filled with strangers who appear and disappear in the most mysterious manner, go to private boarding-houses, examine the defenses, etc., etc."

"I am thus far on my way home," wrote William L. Yancey, from the same city, in a letter dated March 14, 1862, "having left Havana on the 26th ultimo on a small schooner, and arrived at Sabine Pass on the 6th. Two of Lincoln's vessels had been anchored in the channel of that harbour for a week and only left twenty-four hours before my arrival. . . . This city is almost in a state of revolution," he added. "Fifteen hundred of its weathiest and most respectable citizens and good Southerners have organised an association and resolved to assume executive and judicial functions to arrest, try, imprison, banish or hang! . . . There is un-doubtedly a deep-seated feeling of wrong done them and of anxiety for the city's safety at the bottom of all this, and this association should not be treated as a mere lawless mob. Their success, however, would be the knell of our cause in England, and perhaps on the Continent. I am doing all I can to throw oil on the troubled waters, and I hope with some effect."

Shortly after his arrival in Richmond, Mr. Yancey, whom my husband greatly admired, spent a morning in our chamber—space was too costly at this time to admit of our having a private parlour—in conference with Mr. Clay, and a more hopeless and unhappy statesman I never saw. The people in England, he declared, were for, but Parliament opposed to us, and his mission, therefore, had been fruitless. Every action and each word he uttered demonstrated that he knew and felt the ultimate downfall of the Confederacy.

By a singular coincidence, almost under the same circumstances but some months later, a similar conference took place in our rooms, but Mr. Lamar was now the returned diplomat. But recently home from an unfinished mission to Russia, our long-time friend talked, as had Mr. Yancey, with a conviction that our cause was hopeless. Mr. Lamar had proceeded only so far as London and Paris, when, observing the drift of public feeling abroad, he took ship again, arriving, as did many of our returned foreign emissaries, on the top of a friendly wave. The sea was peculiarly inimical to the cause of the Confederate States, sinking many of the merchant ships we succeeded in sending through the blockading fleets that beset our coast, and wrecking our ambassadors wherever it could grapple them, even on our very shores.

By the time Congress closed in the spring of '62, the news from the Tennessee Valley was distracting. The enemy had succeeded in reaching our home, and Huntsville was now become the headquarters of General O. M. Mitchell. If that gentleman had taken delight in anything besides the vigorous exercise of an unwelcome authority, he might have found there an ideal spot for the prosecution of his astronomical researches. The span that rests upon the opposite apices of Monte Sano and Lookout Mountain is one of gorgeous beauty. Upon a clear night the planets glow benignly upon the valley, the little stars laugh and leap and go shooting down great distances in a manner unparalleled in more northerly latitudes. Though generally loyal to the cause of the Confederacy, the people of Huntsville were not indisposed to look upon the author-soldier with considerate eyes, had that General adopted a humane course toward them. Unfortunately, his career in our valley from beginning to end was that of a martinet bent upon the subjugation of the old and helpless and the very young, our youths and strong men being away in the field.

The accounts that reached us by letter and by eyewitnesses of the scenes in the Clay home were alarming.

Everything belonging to the Clays, it was rumoured, was to be confiscated. "Judge Scruggs told Stanley," wrote mother, "that the Clays are to be stript of all." Father's negroes, and most of our own, were conducting themselves in an insolent manner, taking to the mountains when there was work to be done, or wandering in the train of straggling Union soldiers, but returning when hungry to feed upon their master's rapidly diminishing stores. In some instances, relying upon the protection of the soldiers, the negroes of the town would take possession of the home of an absent master, revelling in an opportunity to sleep in his bed or to eat from the family silver and china.

A dozen times a day, and at unreasonable hours, if the invading soldiery saw fit, they entered the houses of the citizens in what was often merely a pretended search for some concealed Confederate, or to demand food or drink or horses. They were constantly on the lookout for the possible visits, to their families, of the distinguished citizens in temporary banishment from Huntsville. The presence of General Pope Walker being suspected (though no longer Secretary of War, he would have been a desirable prize to take, since he had issued orders for the firing of the first gun at Fort Sumter), for months the home of our friend ex-Governor Chapman, in which the family of General Walker had taken refuge, was searched daily, the vigilants being so scrupulous in their investigations that even the leaves of a dictionary were parted, lest the wily late Secretary should spirit himself away between its covers.*

"The enemy came demanding food or horses," wrote

* I asked Mrs. Milton Humes, daughter of ex-Governor Chapman, concerning these war-time search-parties. "I remember distinctly," she answered, "seeing them look into preserve jars and *cut-glass decanters*, until my mother's risibles no longer could be repressed. 'You don't expect to find General Walker in that brandy bottle, do you?' she asked." A. S.

mother, "taking all they could of breadstuffs, meat stock, and all the able-bodied negroes, whether willing or not. Our men hid, but they took the horses and mules, and promised to return in a week and take everything!"

Alas, poor little mother! Those were but the beginning of bitterer days and yet sterner deprivations! For months the only hope of our beleagured neighbours in Huntsville lay in the prayed-for advance of General Bragg, though their prayers, too, were interdicted when made in the church; and, upon the investment of the town, our pastor, Doctor Bannister, * was quickly instructed as to the limited petitions with which he might address his God on behalf of his people.

In the meanwhile, the courage of our citizens was kept alive by General Roddy, who lay over the crest of Monte Sano. The forays of his men were a perpetual worry to the Federals in the valley. So audacious, indeed, did they become that the Federal general razed the houses on "The Hill" and threw up breastworks, behind which he built a stout fort, the better to resist the possible attacks from the mountain side by brave General Roddy and his merry men.

During General Mitchell's investment of Huntsville he was accompanied by his daughters, who, in the ransacking of our home, fell heiresses to certain coveted and "confiscated" articles of my own, but the possession of which could scarcely have been an unmixed pleasure. I heard of my losses first through a letter written late in August. "Mr. Hammond," began the epistle, "says in Atlanta he saw a lady just from Nashville who told him that Miss Mitchell rode out in *your green habit on your mare!* This part of the story," continued my witty sister, "may be true, but there is another: that the other Miss Mitchell

† Dr. J. M. Bannister, at the ripe age of eighty-six, still continues in active pastoral charge of the Church of the Nativity in Huntsville. A. S.

rode in my habit on *my* mare! I'm glad I had no mare, and am sorry for poor 'Jenny Lind'!"

Months afterward I heard (and any who asks may still hear the story in the town, for it has become one of Huntsville's war-time annals) an account of Miss Mitchell's outings in my now celebrated green habit. Her path, it seems, as she trotted my pretty mare about the streets, was not strewn with roses; for, though absent from our beloved little city, I was not forgotten. One day the horsewoman, passing proudly on her way, saw, looking over the garden gate of a pretty cottage, the laughing face of sweet Alice Spence, a right loyal admirer of my undeserving self. Alice looked up at the passing apparition, and, full of daring, half mischievously, half indignantly, cried out after it, "Hey! Git off 'Ginie Clay's mare! Git—off—'Ginie Clay's ma—are!"

At the sound of these words Miss Mitchell galloped away in great anger. While Alice was still regaling her mother with a jubilant account of her championship of my property, a proof reached her of General Mitchell's implacability. That afternoon her brother was ordered into arrest, and for months thereafter was kept in custody as a guarantee for his sister's good behaviour!

When, later, Mr. Clay and I were enabled to visit Huntsville (the Federals having been beaten back for a time), I heard of an amusing encounter which took place at the home of the Spences between Mrs. Spence and John A. Logan. A swarthy stripling in appearance, the young officer stood carelessly about, whilst several soldiers of his command were engaged in a search of the premises. As Mrs. Spence entered the room in which the officer stood, she eyed him with genuine curiosity.

"Whose boy are you?" she asked at last. Her daughter, who was beside her, caught her mother's arm in alarm.

"Why, ma!" she gasped. "That's General Logan!"

"General Logan!" repeated her mother, contemptuously. "I tell you he's nothing of the kind! He's black!"

It was already early summer when we left the troubled capital, where everyone was keyed to a high pitch of excitement by the manœuvrings of the enemy, now so near that the reverberating sound of distant cannon was plainly audible. Our way was southward. Though withdrawing, as I supposed, for a change of scene during the Congressional recess only, in reality my refugee days had now begun; for, notwithstanding I made several later stays of varying duration at Richmond, the greater part of the two succeeding years was spent at the homes of hospitable kin far away from that centre of anxiety and deprivation. Upon leaving Richmond, in May of '62, Senator Clay and I, stopping *en route* at the home of my uncle, Buxton Williams, in Warrenton, North Carolina, proceeded by easy stages to Augusta, Macon and Columbus, where many of our kinfolks and friends resided, and to which cities I often returned, when, from time to time, the exigencies of the war compelled my husband and me to separate. Georgia, save when Sherman's men marched through it, two years later, was the safest and most affluent State in the Confederacy; but in the summer of '62 there were few localities which did not retain, here and there at least, an affluent estate or two. Until almost the end of hostilities the home of my uncle Williams in Warrenton continued to be with us in Richmond the synonym for plenty. When I had starved in the capital, I dropped down to "Buxton Place," whence I was sure to return laden with hampers of sweets and meats and bread made of the finest "Number One" flour, which proved a fine relief to the "seconds" to which the bread-eaters of the Confederate capital were now reduced. In the course of a year molasses and "seconds" (brown flour with the bran still in it) came to be regarded as luxuries by many who but a short time ago had feasted capriciously upon the dainties of a limitless market.

My uncle Williams was an astute man, and when he was assured that war had become a settled fact, instead of hoarding his means for the benefit of invading soldiers, he retired to his country home, bought out the contents of a local store, which he transferred to his own cupboards and pantry, and made "Buxton Place" to "kith and kin" the most generous and hospitable of asylums. It was a peaceful, happy place, set among ample grounds, with noble trees rising about, in which birds carolled as they coquetted among the foliage and squirrels gambolled at their will through the long, lazy days. No chicory and sugar, adopting the *alias* of coffee, found place on that sumptuous board in those first years, but only the *bona fide* stuff! We had sugar in abundance, and pyramids of the richest butter, bowls of thick cream, and a marvellous plenitude of incomparable "clabber."

Once, during our wandering that autumn, we slipped over to "Millbrook," the home of my cousins the Hilliards, and thence to Shocco Springs, long a famous North Carolina resort, where, to the music of a negro band, the feet of a merry little company went flying over the polished floor as if the world were still a happy place, despite its wars and wounds and graves and weeping women.

Life at dear old "Millbrook," rich with a thousand associations of my childhood and family, still ran serenely on. The loudest sound one heard was the hum of the bee on the wing as it rushed to riot in the amber honey sacs of the flowers. But whether at "Millbrook" or "Buxton Place," whether we outwardly smiled or joined in the mirth about us, inwardly my husband and I were tortured with fears born of an intimate knowledge of our national situation. We watched eagerly for our despatches, and, when they came, trembled as we opened them.   Some of our communications rang with triumph, others with an overwhelming sadness.

A thrilling letter from Richmond reached us after the terrible "Battle of Seven Pines."   A mere mention of that deadly conflict for years was enough to start the tears in Southern eyes, and sons and daughters, as they grew up, were taken back to look upon the bloody field as to a sacred mausoleum.   The letter was written by Robert Brown, our erstwhile Sir Lucius, of Mrs. Ives's famous performance, and now serving as aide-de-camp to General Winder.

"I have been beholding scenes of carnage," he wrote on the 10th of June.   "On the afternoon of the 31st ult. Winder and myself rode down to the battle-field.   The reports of the cannon were distinctly heard here, and as we approached the field, the firing became terrific !   We met wounded and dying men, borne upon litters and supported by solicitous friends.   The scene was revolting to me, but, singular to say, in a very short time I became accustomed to this sight of horror, and the nearer we approached the line of battle, the nearer we wished to get; but we were quite satisfied to get so near the line (proper) as the headquarters of General Longstreet, which was under a fine old oak tree on a slight elevation.   The General was there, sitting most complacently upon a fine horse, surrounded by his staff, who were riding away at intervals bearing his orders to the line and returning.   We were about a quarter of a mile from the engagement, and we could distinctly hear the shouts of victory of our gallant troops, literally driving the enemy before them. Entrenchment and battery after battery were wrested from the Yankees by our splendid troops, old North Carolina leading them !

"Imagine the powder burnt !   I tell you, the firing was awful, but glorious !   Near the headquarters of Longstreet were regiments of splendid, eager troops drawn up in line as a reserve. Amid the heavy firing, the glorious cheering of our troops, squad after squad of Yankee prisoners were brought up to Longstreet under guards buoyant with victory; and, as each reached headquarters, I tell you that the reserve force would send up a *yell* of delight that split the air and made old earth tremble! One little brave band of fifty-five South Carolinians brought in one hundred and sixty-six live Yankees and a Captain whom *they had taken!* The excitement was intense! The firing ceased at seven o'clock. I remained in the field until the last gun was fired. Our troops occupied the enemy's camp that night and all the next day; and Monday our military talent thought it prudent and best to fall back and give the enemy the vantage ground we had gained!

"General Johnston was wounded, but not seriously, it is said. Smith's horse was shot in two places, on the shoulder and just back of the saddle; the General's coat-tail, they say, was *seriously* injured. Lieutenant-Colonel Sydenham Moore was wounded; the ball struck his watch, literally shattering it! General Pettigrew was *not* killed, but seriously wounded, and fell into the hands of the enemy. *They*, thank God, lost two brigadier generals and one seriously wounded. Our total loss, killed and wounded, was thirty-five hundred. The enemy acknowledge eight hundred killed and four thousand wounded. It was a fearful fight!

"We have good news every day from Jackson! To-day brings us the news of his having 'completely routed the enemy, taking six pieces of artillery!' Old Stonewall is certainly the Hero of the War, and unless our Generals Beauregard and Johnston look sharp, he will entirely take the wind out of their sails and leave them in the *Lee*-ward!"

"The city is filled with the wounded and dead," echoed our cousin John Withers. "It is fortunate you are away and saved the necessity of beholding the horrible sights which are now so common here! Great numbers of Alabamians are killed and wounded. . . ." And he added in a letter, written in an interval of the awful Seven Days Battles: "For four days I have been awaiting some decisive move on the part of our forces, but nothing has been done yet to settle affairs. McClellan has not been routed, but his army is, no doubt, demoralised to such an extent as to render any other demonstration against Richmond out of the question for many weeks. . . . The President has come up from the battle-field, and I hear that a courier from the French and British Consuls is to leave here for Washington to-night or in the morning. We will secure between thirty and forty thousand small arms by our late operations; many of them much injured by being bent. The enemy have a position now which we cannot well assail successfully. They are under their gunboats and have gotten reinforcements. . . . There is a report to-night that Magruder has captured eight hundred Yankees to-day, but I place no reliance upon any rumour until it is confirmed as truth. General Beauregard has made a most successful retreat to Baldwin, thirty-five miles south of Corinth, on the Mobile and Ohio Railroad. The move was necessary, and I have no doubt will be a great blow to the enemy. He carried all his heavy guns, tents, and so on. General Lee is in command of the army hereabouts, and I am sure we will whip McClellan's army when the grand contest shall take place. The rain of last night will forbid any movement for two or three days. When the fight opens again, we will have thousands upon thousands of wounded here!"

Such were the accruing records of woe and of personal and national loss which followed Senator Clay and me throughout those autumn months of '62. The inroad made upon the gallant regiments of our own State were frightful. The ranks of the splendid Fourth Alabama Regiment, picked men of our finest blood, the flower of our hopes, as handsome a body as a State might muster, were terribly thinned. Wherever a call came our Alabamians were found in the front, the envy and admiration of the army, quickening the courage and firing the imaginations of every company that beheld them. But oh! our men had need of a mighty courage, for soon the very seed-corn of our race became a sacrifice. The picture rises before me of a youthful cousin * who fell at Malvern Hill, shot down as he bore aloft the banner which he fondly hoped would lead to victory. His blood-stained cap, marked by a bullet hole, was all that returned of our fair young soldier boy. Another youth,† on whom the love and hope of a dear circle was settled, fell with his heart pierced, and so swift was the passing of his soul that he felt no pain nor sorrow. They say an eager smile was on his face when they found him. For years his loved ones, gazing upon it with weeping eyes, treasured the blood-stained, bullet-torn handkerchief that had lain over the wounded heart of the boy!

The tears start afresh when, looking into my memory, there passes before me that army of the dead and gone. Oh! the sorrow that overcame all who knew him (and the circle was wide as half the South itself) when the news came of the death of Colonel Sydenham Moore, who fell at Seven Pines; and even the enemy spoke solemnly at the passing of our beloved General Tracy, who died so courageously fighting in the battle of Port Gibson, within three-quarters of a year! "I have little active service at this post," he complained from Vicksburg, in March of '63, "and the very fact incapacitates me for the discharge of duties of other kinds. In fact, I am *ennuied* past description!" So, chafing impatiently to

* Harry, son of Buxton Williams.

† James Camp Turner, of Alabama, died at Manassas.

write his name in brave deeds across some page of the Confederate States' history, he sprang to meet the call when it came, and fell, crowned with immortal glory in the hearts of a loving people.

General Tracy's young wife was awaiting him, an infant at her bosom, when we returned late in November of '62 for a brief stay at Huntsville, from which, for a time, the Union soldiers had been beaten back. By this time our valley seemed so safe that families from other threatened districts came to take refuge in it. Colonel Basil Duke, among others, brought his wife to Huntsville. Numerous absentee householders came back; and interest in local enterprises was resumed. When, in December, my husband returned to his duties in the Senate, there was small reason to apprehend an early reappearance, in Huntsville, of the Federals. "North Alabama," General Bragg assured my husband, "is as secure now as it was when I held Murfreesboro!" And on this assurance our spirits rose and we departed again, promising ourselves and our parents we would return within a few months at most.

Mr. Clay proceeded at once to Richmond, beset now with deadly enemies within as well as without. Small-pox and scarlet fever raged there, as in many of our larger cities, and I pleaded in vain to be allowed to accompany him. I turned my way, therefore, in company with others of our kin, toward Macon, where was sojourning our sweet sister, Mrs. Hugh Lawson Clay, at the home of Major Anderson Comer, her father. Thence it was proposed I should proceed with her later to Richmond under the escort of Colonel Clay.

That winter the weather was peculiarly cold, so much so that on the plantations where wheat had been sown, a fear was general lest the grain be killed in the ground. The journey to Macon, therefore, was anything but comfortable, but it had its amusing sides nevertheless.   We were a party of women.

"We arrived safely (self, Kate, Alice and servants)," I wrote in a kaleidoscopic account which I gave my husband of the indications of the times as seen *en route*.   "We rode from Stevenson to Chattanooga on the freight train, the baggage-cars on the passenger-train being unable to receive a single trunk.   Arriving at Chattanooga, we would have been forced to go to the small-pox hotel or remain in the streets but for the gallantry of an acquaintance of ours, an army officer of Washington memory, who gave up his room to us, and furnished some wagons to have our baggage hauled to the depot.   At Atlanta there was a scatteration of our forces.   .   .   . When night came" (being fearful of robbery, for hotels were unsafe) "I stuffed in one stocking all my money, and in the other, mine and Alice's watches, chains, pins, and charms.   I felt not unlike Miss Kilmansegg, of the precious Leg.   We fumigated the room, had a bed brought in for Emily, and retired.   At breakfast Colonel Garner told me that Uncle Jones [Withers] was in the house, and in a few minutes he presented himself.   He got in at three that morning, *en route* for Mobile with thirty days' leave; looked worn, and was sad, I thought. Colonel George Johnson, of Marion, also called, and we had them all and Dr. W., of Macon, to accompany us to the cars.   The guard at the gate said 'Passport, Madam,' but I replied, 'Look at my squad; General Withers, Colonel Garner of Bragg's staff, and a Colonel and Lieutenant in the Confederate service.   I think I'll *pass!*'" And I passed!

# CHAPTER XIV

## REFUGEE DAYS IN GEORGIA

OUR stay in Macon, where it had been my intention to remain but a few weeks, lengthened into months; for, upon his arrival in Richmond, Senator Clay found the conditions such as to render my joining him, if not impracticable, at least inadvisable. The evils of a year agone had multiplied tenfold. Food was growing scarcer; the city's capacity was tested to the uttermost, and lodgings difficult to obtain. The price of board for my husband alone now amounted to more than his income. Feeling in legislative circles was tense, the times engendering a troublesome discontent and strife among eager and anxious politicians. Complaints from the army poured in. Our soldiers were suffering the harshest deprivations. Wearing apparel was scarce. Many of our men marched in ragged and weather-stained garments and tattered shoes, and even these were luxuries that threatened soon to be unattainable. Our treasury was terribly depleted, and our food supply for the army was diminishing at a lamentable rate.

"You will be surprised to know," wrote General Tracy from Vicksburg, in March, 1863, "that in this garrisoned town, upon which the hopes of a whole people are set, and which is liable at any time to be cut off from its interior lines of communication, there is not now subsistence for one week. The meat ration has already been virtually discontinued, the quality being such that the men utterly refuse to eat it, though the contract continues to be worth between one thousand and fifteen hundred dollars per diem."

"A general gloom prevails here because of the scarcity and high price of food," ran a letter from my husband, written in the same month from Richmond. "Our soldiers are on half rations of meat, one-quarter pound of salt, and one-half pound of fresh meat, without vegetables, or fruit, or coffee or sugar! Don't mention this, as it will do harm to let it get abroad. Really there is serious apprehension of having to disband part of the army for want of food. In this city the poor clerks and subaltern military officers are threatened with starvation, as they cannot get board on their pay. God only knows what is to become of us, if we do not soon drive the enemy from Tennessee and Kentucky and get food from their granaries. . . . I dined with the President yesterday at six P. M., *en famille*, on beef soup, beef stew, meat pie, potatoes, coffee and bread. I approved his simple fare and expressed the wish that the army in the field had more to eat and that out of the field less!"

The receipt of this news stirred me to the core. Spring was in its freshest beauty in Macon. Its gardens glowed with brilliant blossoms. A thousand fragrant odours mingled in the air; the voices of myriad birds sang about the foliaged avenues. I thought Aunt Comer's home a terrestrial Paradise. The contrast between the comfort in this pretty city of lower Georgia, a city of beautiful homes and plentiful tables, and our poverty-stricken capital and meagre starving camps, was terrible to picture. I wrote impulsively (and, alas! impotently) in reply to my husband's letter:

"Why does not the President or some proper authority order on from here and other wealthy towns, and immediately at that, the thousands of provisions that fill the land? Monopolists and misers hold enough meat and grain in their clutches to feed our army and Lincoln's!

Put down the screws and make them release it! Talk of disbanding an army at a time like this? No! empty the coffers and graneries and meat houses of every civilian in the land first!"

Many an eager and impatient hour my sister and I spent in those months of waiting for the call from our husbands to join them in the capital. Her sprightly wit and unfailing courage made her a most enjoyable companion, and a great favourite with all who knew her. "Give my love to your sunbeam of a sister," Secretary Mallory wrote me during those dark days. "If not one of the lost Pleiads, at least she is a heavenly body!" And when I quoted this to dear "Lushe" Lamar, he answered from the fulness of his heart: "Mallory's compliments grow languid in their impotence to do justice to that beautiful embodiment of bright thoughts and ideal graces, your sister, Celeste." I found her all this and more in that spring we spent together in Macon, as we daily sat and planned and compared our news of the battle-fields, or discussed the movements of the army. We did a prodigious amount of sewing and knitting for our absent husbands, to whom we sent packages of home-made wearing apparel by whomsoever we could find to carry them. I remember one such which gave us considerable anxiety; for, proving too large to impose upon General Alf. Colquitt, who had undertaken to deliver another to Senator Clay, we sent the bundle by express. The robe which General Colquitt carried was soon in the hands of its future wearer, but not so the express package, which contained a pair of much-needed boots for Colonel Clay. It lingered provokingly along the road until we were filled with apprehension for its safety.

"Won't it break us if all those things are stolen?" I wrote my husband. "A thousand dollars would not buy them now!" And I said truly, for the prices of the commonest materials were enormous. "Men's boots here are from sixty to eighty dollars," wrote Mr. Clay from Richmond; and in Macon all goods were a hundred per cent. higher than they had been in Huntsville. Ordinary fifteen-cent muslin now sold in Georgia at two and a half dollars per yard, and "sold like hot-cakes" at that. My sister and I bought what we could and made our husbands' shirts—knitting the heavier ones—and hemmed their handkerchiefs; and we rose to such a proficiency with the needle that we did not hesitate to undertake the manufacture of vests and trousers of washable stuffs. I made a pair of the last-named for my husband's little god-son, Joe Davis, and sent them to Richmond by Colonel Lamar; but I think the dear child did not live to don them. He died tragically at the Executive home within a year, the waves of the war quickly obscuring from the world about the remembrance of the sweet baby face.

April had arrived when, journeying from Macon to Richmond, I had my first real experience of war-time travel. By this time people were hurrying from place to place in every direction, some to seek refuge, and some to find or to bring back their dead. The country beyond the Georgia boundary was alert, apprehending the approach of the steadily advancing Federals Throughout the spring the feeling had been rife that a crucial period was approaching. My husband wrote cautioning me to prepare to meet it. "During the months of April and May," he said, in a letter dated March 22d, "the result of the war will be decided by at least four of the greatest battles the world has ever witnessed, near Charleston or Savannah, Fredericksburg, Murfreesboro, and Vicksburg or Port Hudson. If they triumph on the Mississippi, the war will continue for years; if they fail there, I cannot think it will last longer than Lincoln's administration, or till March of 1865.* I

* It ended in April, 1865.

regard events there as the most important, because the Northwest will not aid the war much longer if the Mississippi is not opened to their trade. The result of the grand battle to come off at the first opportunity between Bragg and Rosecrans will determine our movements during the recess of Congress, and, it may be, our destiny for life. If we whip the enemy, our home will again be open to us; if he whips us, it will fall under his dominion for many months to come, and nothing will be left to us that he can use or destroy." Almost as Mr. Clay wrote, Huntsville was again invested by Federal soldiery, and we could not, if we had wished, have returned to it.

When my sister and I departed from Georgia, passenger-cars generally were impressed for the use of soldiers, sick or wounded, or for those who were hurrying to the front. I heard of instances in which travellers, unable to find room in the regular cars, and eager to get to some given point, begged for the privilege of squeezing into the car in which express packages were carried.

Having held ourselves for some months in readiness for the journey, we had kept informed as to the presence of possible escorts in Macon. Once we planned to travel under the protection of Captain Harry Flash, a poet who had won some distinction for his affecting lines on the death of General Zollicoffer, and his stirring verses on the Confederate Flag. It fell to our lot, however, to travel with two poets, who in days to come were to be known to a wider world. They were Sidney and Clifford Lanier, young soldiers, then, on their way to Virginia. Sidney's sweetheart lived in the town, and the brothers had stopped at Macon to make their adieux. Upon learning of the objective destination of the young men, my sister and I held out the bribe to them, if they would undertake to escort us, of a fine luncheon *en route;* "broiled partridges, sho' nuf' sugar and sho' nuf' butter, and spring chickens, 'quality size,'" to which allurements, I am glad to say, the youthful poets succumbed with grace and gallantry, and we began our journey.

The aisles of the cars were crowded. At many stations, as we came through North Carolina, women entered the car with baskets of "big blues," the luscious native huckleberries, with full, deep bloom upon them; these and other tempting edibles were brought aboard at almost every station along the way. When our pleasant party separated at Lynchburg, and the youths sat alone in their tents, they recalled in pages truly characteristic the memories of that long journey, in which, like tired children, they had sometimes fallen asleep, Clifford's head upon my sister's shoulder, and Sid's upon mine.

"I will wait no longer," wrote Clifford,* from the camp near Suffolk (Virginia), on April 17th, "but at once, and without *cérémonie*, write the little love letter I have promised, disarming (if men, as some one says of flowers, 'be jealous things') the jealousy of your Lieges, by addressing it to my *Two Dear Friends* and quondam fellow-travellers. What a transition is this—from the spring and peace of Macon, to this muddy and war-distracted country! Going to sleep in the moonlight and soft air of Italy, I seem to have waked imbedded in Lapland snow. Yet, as I would not be an Antony, with a genius bold, and confident in Egypt, but a trembler and white-livered, in presence of Octavius at Rome, I summon all my heroism, doff that which became me when environed by flowers, poetry, music and blooming maidens, and don shield and mail (that's figurative for Kersey), prepared to resist ruder shocks than those of love's arrows. Par *parenthese*, how the Yankees would suffer, if we could do our *devoirs* as bravely and as heartily in the heat and dust and smoke of battle, as in the charmed air of ladies!

* Then in the Mounted Signal Service, Milligan's Battalion, from Georgia, and on the staff of General S. D. French, now of Florida. A.S.

"Enough about us. I wonder what this will find our friends doing? My dear Mrs. Celeste? Embroidering the Senatorial *laticlave* or musing on sweet Macon, sweeter Huntsville? Mrs. Virginia? In whatever mood or occupation, it is agreed you have this advantage of us: you carry your sunshine with you; we men, being but opaque and lunatic bodies, can give light only by reflection. Imagine, then, in what 'Cimmerian darkness' we revolve here. If you would throw a ray through this darkness, show us one glimpse of the blue sky through all this battle-smoke, write to us, directing care General French, Franklin, Virginia. I shall regard, most affectionately, the carrier who brings such intelligence from that office to these headquarters. The huge shell that has just shrieked across the intervening distance from the enemy's trenches to our pickets, and exploding, is not yet done reverberating, reminds me that I might tell you a little of our situation here.

"The reticence of our General forbids all knowledge of his plans and ultimate designs. I can only say that our army, embracing three divisions, closely invests Suffolk on three sides, its water and railroad communications into Norfolk being still complete, except that General French, having possession of one bank of the river, is working hard to get into position guns of sufficient calibre to destroy their gun-boats. That, in the meantime, large foraging parties and immense wagon-trains have been sent out for provisions. So that this of forage may be the grand design after all, and instead of living that we may fight, are fighting that we may live, the latter being a very desperate situation, but the more laudable endeavour of the two, perilling our lives, not only for the vitality of our principles as patriots, but for the very sustenance of our lives as men, seeking corn and bacon as well as the 'bubble reputation at the cannon's mouth.' But I began a love-letter; I fear I am

ending most unetherially.   Starting to wing a flight across
the sea, Icarus-like, my wings have proved to be of wax,
melting with a too near approach to the sun, and I find
myself floundering, and clearing my nose and eyes and
mouth of the enveloping salt water.   Being not even a
swimmer, I escape drowning by ending (Icarus found
nereids and yellow-haired nymphs to assist him), with
much love to your husbands, and an infinite quantity to
yourselves,                    Yours,

"CLIFF LANIER."

"God bless you both.   Write to us!" said Sid., our
dear Orpheus of the South.   "Have you ever, my Two
Good Friends, wandered, in an all-night's dream, through
exquisite flowery mosses, through labyrinthine grottoes,
'full of all sparkling and sparry loveliness,' over mountains of unknown height, by abysses of unfathomable
depth, all beneath skies of an infinite brightness caused
by no sun; strangest of all, wandered about in wonder,
as if you had lived an eternity in the familiar contemplation of such things?

"And when, at morning, you have waked from such
a dream and gone about your commonplace round
of life, have you never stopped suddenly to gaze
at the sun and exclaimed to yourself, 'what a singular
thing it is up there; and these houses, bless me, what
funny institutions, not at all like my grottoes and
bowers, in which I have lived for all eternity; and those
men and women walking about there, uttering strange
gibberish, and cramming horrid messes of stuff in their
mouths, what dear, odd creatures!   What does it all
mean, anyhow, and who did it, and how is one to act,
under the circumstances?'   .   .   .

"If you have dreamed, thought and felt *so*, you can
realise the imbecile stare with which I gaze on all this
life that goes on around me here.   Macon was my two-

weeks' dream. I wake from that into Petersburg, an indefinitely long, real life. . . .

"SID LANIER."

Of the after months of '63, the story of my life is one of continuous change. I migrated between Richmond and our kin at Petersburg, paying an occasional visit to Warrenton, North Carolina, so long as the roads were open, or sometimes visiting our friends, the McDaniels, at Danville; sometimes, accompanied by our sister, I made a visit to the near-by camps, or to the multiplying colonies of the sick and wounded. He was a fortunate soldier in those terrible days, who fell into the hands of private nurses. Patients in the hospitals suffered, even for necessary medicines. Sugar was sold at fifty Confederate dollars a pound. Vegetables and small fruits were exceedingly scarce. My visits to the hospital wards were by no means so constant as those of many of my friends, yet I remember one poor little Arkansas boy in whom I became interested, and went frequently to see, wending my way to his cot through endless wards, where an army of sick men lay, minus an arm, or leg, or with bandaged heads that told of fearful encounters. The drip—drip of the water upon their wounds to prevent the development of a greater evil is one of the most horrible remembrances I carry of those days. I went through the aisles of the sick one morning, to see my little patient, a lad of seventeen, not more. Above the pillow his hat was hung, and a sheet was drawn over the cot —and the tale was told.

In Richmond, Miss Emily Mason (sister of John Y. and James M. Mason), and Mrs. General Lee were indefatigable in their hospital work; and Mrs. Phoebe Pember, sister of Mrs. Philip Phillips, was a prominent member of a regularly organised Hospital Committee, who, afterward, recorded her experiences in an interesting volume, reflecting the gay as well as the grave scenes through which she had passed ; for, happily, in the experiences of these self-sacrificing nurses there was often a mingling of the comical with the serious which had its part in relieving the nerve-tension of our noble women.   On every side the inevitable was plainly creeping toward us.   The turmoil in the governmental body augmented constantly.   The more patriotic recognised that only in increased taxation lay the prolonging of our national life; but, at the mention of such measure, protests poured in from many sides. Our poor, wearied citizens could ill sustain a further drain upon them.   To the credit of my sex, however, we never complained.   No Roman matron, no Spartan mother, ever thrilled more to the task of supporting her warriors, than did we women of the South land! To the end we held it to be a proud privilege to sacrifice where by so doing we might hold up the hands of our heroes in field or forum.

"I pity those who have no country to love or to fight for!" wrote Mrs. Yulee, the "Madonna of the Wickliffe sisters," from her home in Florida.   "It is this very country of yours and mine that induces me to write this letter.   I want you to use your influence (you have much) to induce those law-makers to come up to our necessities.   Tax! tax! tax our people to half we have, if necessary, but let the world know we are paying! Ten victories will not give the Yankees such a blow as this fact.   Now, Mrs. Clay, God has given you many friends.   Stir them up to their duty!   .   .   .   Bragg's defeat fills us all with gloom, yet we are not discouraged. I have never felt a doubt of my country, but dark and painful trials are yet before us, perhaps!"

Alas!  Alas!

# CHAPTER XV

## C. C. Clay, Jr., Departs for Canada

I was in Richmond at my husband's side when Dahlgren's raid was made. Early one morning the cry of danger came. We were still at breakfast, when Senator Henry, of Tennessee, hurried in. "No Senate to-day, Clay!" he cried. "A big force of the enemy is at Lyons's, and every man in the city is needed! Arm yourself, and come on!" and he hastened on his way to warn others. Members of Congress shouldered guns, where they could get them, and mounted guard around the capital. They were an untrained mass, but they came back victors and deliverers of the city.

The armies having gone into winter quarters, as the close of Mr. Clay's Senatorial career in Richmond drew near, he seriously contemplated a period of needed rest from public duties. Bent upon this, he declined a judgeship in the Military Court, which had been pressed upon him by Mr. Davis. We dallied with enticing invitations that reached us from Florida, and planned what was to be a veritable vacation at last, together.

"Mr. Yulee is delighted with the hope of seeing you!" wrote the lovely *chatelaine* of "Homosassa." "He will fish with Mr. Clay, and *we* will do the same! Just think how good oysters will be in these sad times! Do come, dear Mr. and Mrs. Clay, just as soon as Congress adjourns! My dear sister, Mrs. Holt, had a tender and sincere affection for you. . . . "

The prospect of a visit to that lovely retreat, built upon an island, deep in the green glades of Florida and

far away from the political and martial strife of the intervening States, was very tempting to my wearied husband,
a true lover of woods and trees and the sweet solitudes
of a bucolic life; but we were destined not to enjoy it.
Early in the spring of '64, Mr. Clay felt it his duty to
accept the high responsibility of a diplomatic mission to
Canada, with a view to arousing in the public mind of
this near-by British territory a sympathy for our cause
and country that should induce a suspension of hostilities.
Despite the failure of our representatives in European
countries to rouse apathetic kings and dilly-dallying
emperors to come to our aid, it was hard for us to believe
that our courage would not be rewarded at length by
some powerful succour, or yielding.

"I send you my speech," wrote dear Lamar to me
from his sick-bed in Oxford, Georgia, so late as June, '64.
"The views presented in reference to Louis Napoleon may
strike you as at variance with some of the acts, in which
his Imperial Highness has done some very uncivil things
in a very civil way. But his sympathy is with us. It
is his policy to frighten the Yankees into acquiescence in
his Mexican enterprise, and he no doubt would be glad to
give French neutrality in American affairs for Yankee
neutrality in Mexican affairs. In this he will fail, and
he will sooner or later find his policy and inclinations
jump together. After all, the British people are more
friendly to us than all the world besides, outside of the
[question of] Southern Confederacy. This friendship,
like most national friendships, is mixed up with a large
part of alloy, fear of the Yankees forming the base. But
respect for the South and admiration of her position
is the pure metal, and there is enough of it to make their
good-will valuable to us."

So thought many of our noblest statesmen, when, early
in the Spring, Mr. Clay started on his way through our
blockaded coast for Canada. "I earnestly desire that

his services may prove effectual in securing a permanent peace to our bleeding country; that his efforts may be recorded as one of the brightest pages in its history," wrote one; and from every quarter Mr. Clay and his companions were followed by the prayers of a people, wrung from hearts agonised by our long, exhausting strife. When the parting came, the shadow of impending evil fell so blackly upon my soul, I hastened away from disturbed Petersburg, accompanied by my faithful maid, Emily, and her child, determined to act upon Mr. Clay's suggestion and seek my kin in Georgia. Petersburg was in the greatest confusion, guns resounding in every direction. Our dear Aunt Dollie Walker, the saint, whose faith (her Bishop said) had kept Episcopalianism alive in Virginia through those troublous times, told us in after days of having been literally chased up the streets by cannon balls. It was one of the best cities in the Confederacy at that period to get away from.

I began my journey southward, pausing a day or two at Danville; but, fearing each moment to hear news of the appearance of impeding armies, blocking my way through the Carolinas, I hastened on. The news from the capital which reached us while in Petersburg had been of the worst.

"You have no idea of the intense excitement," wrote my sister. "I am so nervous I know not what to write! No one goes to bed here at night. For several nights past no one could have slept for the confusion and noise. The city has been in a perfect uproar for a week. We have heard firing in two directions all the morning, on the Brook Turnpike and at Drewry's Bluff. The wounded are being brought into the city in great numbers. General Walker is wounded! Poor General Stafford's death cast a gloom over the city. I went with Mr. Davis to his funeral, and carried flowers! . . . General Benning is wounded, and Colonel Lamar, our dear L. Q. C.'s brother, also. . . . At the wedding" [of Miss Lyons] "you never saw such disorder in God's house before in your life. Mrs. Davis and Mrs. Mallory and Mrs. Most-everybody-else, stood up in the pews, and you could not hear one word of the service for the noise. Mr. Davis was there—Mrs. Chestnut sat with me. She is going home very *soon*, so the Colonel told me. He said it was impossible for her to remain in Richmond with nothing to eat!"

To my sister's panorama of horrors, our brother, who was stationed in Richmond, added a masculine picture.

"The enemy press us sorely with powerful forces of cavalry and infantry," he wrote. "The former cut off our communications everywhere, hoping to reduce Lee to starvation, and the presence of the latter keeps from him reinforcements that otherwise would be promptly sent. We have lost severely around the city. General Stuart was shot by a Yankee soldier who fired upon him at ten paces as he galloped past him. He died last night, about twenty-eight hours after he received the wound. Brigadier General Gordon, also of the cavalry, had his arm shattered yesterday above the elbow, and 'tis said will probably have to suffer amputation. Mr. Randolph, the 'Sir Anthony Absolute' of your play, was wounded yesterday in the shoulder and thigh, and will lose the limb to-day. All the clerks of the office are in the intrenchments and no work goes on!"

Upon learning of my determination to push on to Georgia, our sister put away her anxiety and grew facetious at my expense. "I am inclined to think you are a great coward," she wrote. "Why did you run from Petersburg? . . . I am almost ashamed of you! You never catch me running from Yankees! Georgia is certainly a *safe* place. . . . When we have killed *all the Yankees* and the city is perfectly quiet, I invite you to come on and see us. . . . I am weary from walking (not *running*) to see the wounded!"

A month or so later and my sweet sister, speeding *to overtake me*, joined me at Macon, in time to accompany me to the home of our friend, Mrs. Winter, in Columbus. Here, to compensate for the tribulations of the past months, we were promised the most care-free of summers. Refugees were flocking to that land of safety and plenty just then, and whether in Macon or Columbus, our time was spent in welcoming late-comers, in visiting and exchanging news or comment of the times, or making little excursions to near-by towns. Once we formed a party and visited the "White Farm" of Augusta Evans, then unmarried. It was a unique place and celebrated for the unsullied whiteness of every bird and beast on the place.

Upon our arrival at our friend's home in Columbus, we found a very active field awaiting us. It was now mid-summer of '64, somewhat after the bloody battle of Atlanta. In anticipation of our coming, Mrs. Winter had prepared her largest and coolest rooms for us. All was ready and we about due to arrive, when an unforeseen incident frustrated our hostess's plans in regard of our intended pleasuring, and put us all to more serious work. It was in the late afternoon when our friend, driving in her calash along the boundaries of the town, came upon a pitiful sight. Near a group of tents a sick man, a soldier, lay writhing upon the ground in a delirium, while near by and watching him stood his alarmed and helpless coloured servant. Mrs. Winter, aroused to pity by the sight, immediately gave orders that the sufferer be carried to her home, where he was placed in the room that had been prepared for me.

When my sister and I arrived, a few hours afterward, our sympathies, too, were at once enlisted for the unfortunate man. He proved to be Captain Octave Vallette, a Creole, who, previous to his enlistment, with his brother, had been a ship-builder at Algiers, Louisiana.

A physician was already in attendance when my sister and I arrived, and an examination of the invalid's wounds was making.

A week had elapsed since the first hasty dressing of the wound, and the blackened flesh now suggested the approach of the dreaded gangrene.

The cleansing of the dreadful wound was a terrible ordeal. For days the patient raved, and to us, just from the camps and hospitals of Virginia, his frenzied words conveyed most vivid pictures of the experiences our men were meeting in the deadly fray.

"God! What a hole for soldiers to be in!" he would cry; and then would mumble on incoherently until, in an accession of fevered strength, he would burst out, "Give them hell, boys!" while his negro man stood by, blinded by tears.

Finally, however, our care was rewarded, and our invalid began slowly to recover. The first day he was able to ebdure it, we took the Captain to drive in Mrs. Winter's calash. He was still weak, and very melancholy; the injured arm was stiff and all but a useless member. We tried to cheer him by merry talk. "Surely," we said at last, as we drove by a new-made cemetery, with its bare little whitewashed head-boards, "weak as you are, isn't this a great deal better than lying out there with a board at your head marked 'O. V.'?" At this he smiled, but grimly.

The ensuing months to me were a time of indecision. My sister departed to rejoin her husband in Richmond, and I, feeling quite cut off from those nearest to me, formed numerous plans for leaving the Confederate States. I wished to go to Mr. Clay in Canada, or to England, where so many dear friends were already installed; and so earnestly did this desire fix itself in my mind that wheels were set in motion for the securing of a passport. My friends in Richmond and in Georgia

urged me to reconsider. Mr. Clay might even then be on
his way home; would I not come to the capital and wait?
But I declined, and kind Secretary Mallory acceded to
my wishes, though cautioning me against our enemies on
the seas. "I only wish I could send you abroad in a
public vessel,"he wrote, as he inclosed Mr. Seddon's passport, "but I have not a blockade runner under my
control.

"You will, of course, avoid Bermuda and Nassau.
The yellow-fever still rages and embraces new-comers at
the very beach; and knowing that nothing on earth
would ever fail to embrace you that had the power of
doing so, and having a painful experience of his warm
and glowing nature, I am anxious that you shall keep
out of his way. . . . Angela and Ruby send their
love. They regret, with me, that your promised visit to
us is not to be paid."

Yet, after all these preparations I remained; for, as
the weeks passed, it seemed clear Mr. Clay was likely to
arrive at any time. His associate, Professor Holcombe,
had already returned, though wrecked off the coast of
Wilmington. Whole ship-loads of cotton, which had
succeeded in running the blockade and which we fondly
hoped would replenish our pocket-books, had gone to
the bottom. On the whole, travel by sea grew less and
less attractive. I concluded to remain on *terra firma*,
but to go on toward Augusta and Beech Island, South
Carolina, that I might be nearer the coast when Mr.
Clay should arrive. Ere I left Columbus I had a ludicrous adventure. Upon coming downstairs one morning, I saw, approaching the outer, wide-open door,
a large, portly figure clad in Macon Mills muslin.
Beyond him, in the street, a wagon stood, or was
passing. It was loaded with watermelons. As I
noted them and the figure approaching, I connected the
two at once, and called back to my hostess, with all the

enthusiasm for which I was ever famous at the near prospect of a "million," "Cousin Victoria! Don't you want some melons? Here's a watermelon man!" To my surprise, as I neared the door a hearty laugh rang out; a cordial hand was extended to me, and I recognised before me genial, jovial General Howell Cobb, who had left his military duties for the moment, in order to welcome me to Georgia. His long beard, which he declared he never would shave until our cause was won, together with the copperas and unbleached suit of muslin, had quite disguised him for the moment.

# CHAPTER XVI

## The Departed Glories of the South Land

My memories would be incomplete were I to fail to include in them a description of plantation life that may be taken as a type of the beautiful homes of the South in that long ago before the Civil War. From Maryland to Louisiana there had reigned, since colonial times, an undisturbed, peaceful, prosperous democracy, based upon an institution beneficial alike to master and servant. It was implanted in the South by the English settlers, approved by the English rulers, and fostered by thrifty merchants of New England, glad to traffic in black men so long as there were black men upon the African coasts who might be had in exchange for a barrel of rum. Generations living under these conditions had evolved a domestic discipline in Southern homes which was of an ideal order. Nothing resembling it had existed in modern times. To paraphrase the nursery rhyme, the planter was in his counting-house counting out his money; his wife was in the parlour eating bread and honey; the man servant was by his master's side, the maid with her mistress, the meat-cook at his spit and the bread-cook at the marble block where the delicious beaten biscuit were made in plenty. The laundress was in the laundry (Chinamen then in China), and in the nursery lived, ever at her post, the sable sentinel of cribs and cradles, the skilful manufacturer of possets and potions. None but a Southerner to the manner born can appreciate or imagine the tie that bound us of that old-time South to our dear black mammy, in whose capacious lap the little ones confided to her care cuddled in innocent slumber.

Fruitful vineyards and gardens furnished our luxuries, and talent and faithful public service were the criterion of social standing. Of those bygone days, Mr. E. Spann Hammond * recently wrote, "To me it seems as if I had been in two worlds, and two existences, the old and the new, and to those knowing only the latter, the old will appear almost like mythology and romance, so thorough has been the upheaval and obliteration of the methods and surroundings of the past."

Yes! the old glories have passed away, but even those who destroyed them, looking back to that time and that Southern civilisation, recognise to-day how enviable were our solidarity as a people, our prosperity and the moral qualities that are characteristic of the South. "I have learned not only to respect, but to love the great qualities which belong to my fellow citizens of the Southern States," said Senator Hoar, recently. "Their love of home, their chivalrous respect for women, their courage, their delicate sense of honour, their constancy, which can abide by an appearance or a purpose or an interest for their States through adversity, and through prosperity, through years and through generations, are things by which the more mercurial people of the North may take a lesson. And there is another thing," he added, "the low temptation of money has not found any place in our Southern politics."

It was my good fortune during the late autumn and winter of 1864 to be invited to take refuge in a spacious and representative plantation home in South Carolina, where the conditions that obtained were so typically those of the Southern home that I could choose no better example for description, were I to scan here the numberless instances of a similar character, known to

* Son of Senator Hammond, of South Carolina.

SENATOR JAMES H. HAMMOND
of South Carolina

me before those unquiet days. "Redcliffe," the home
of Senator Hammond, is still a point of interest to travellers, and a beautiful feature of the landscape in which it
is set. It is built upon a high knoll on Beech Island,
South Carolina, and is visible to the naked eye at a distance
of thirty-five miles. It lies within view of Sand Hill,
where the famous Madame Le Vert spent her declining
years, and is pointed out to the visitor by the residents
of Augusta, Georgia, and the smaller towns about, as an
object of local admiration and pride. In the decades
preceding the war it was owned by Governor, afterward
Senator, James H. Hammond, a wealthy man in his own
right, whose possessions were greatly increased by his
marriage to Miss Catherine Fitzsimmons. Miss Fitzsimmons was a daughter of one of South Carolina's
richest citizens, and brought to Governor Hammond a
splendid dowry. Her sister became the wife of Colonel
Wade Hampton, who had been on General Jackson's
staff at the battle of New Orleans, and whose son,
General and Senator Wade Hampton, served in the same
Congress with Senator Hammond. While in Washington,
the latter, distinguished alike for his reserve and scholarli-
ness, became known as the "Napoleon of the Senate."
He was no lover of public life, however, and the senatorial
office was literally thrust upon him. Especially as the
strenuousness in Congress increased, his desire deepened
to remain among his people and to develop what was, in
fact, one of the most productive plantations in South
Carolina. The estate of "Redcliffe" was stocked with the
finest of Southdowns, with sleek, blooded kine, and
horses, and a full flock of Angora goats. The prolific
"Redcliffe" vineyards yielded unusual varieties of grapes,
planted and cared for by white labourers. Four hundred
slaves or more were owned by Senator Hammond, but
these were set to less skill-demanding duties. For the
planting of this vineyard, forty acres of land, sub-soiled

to a depth of three feet, were set apart, and the clear, straw-coloured wine for which the Senator's cellar was famous came from his own wine-presses.

On the plantation was a large grist-mill, from which every human creature in that vast family was fed. It was a big, heavy timbered building, grey even then with age, and run by water. Here the corn was crushed between the upper and the nether mill-stones, and so skilful was the miller that each could have his hominy ground as coarse or as fine as his fancy dictated, and all the sweetness of the corn left in it besides. The miller could neither read nor write, but he needed no aid to his memory. For years he had known whose meal-bag it was that had the red patch in the corner. He knew each different knot as well as he knew the negros' faces, and if any of the bags presented had holes in it the miller would surely make its owner wait till the last.

Lower down on the same water-course was the saw-mill, which had turned out all the lumber used in the building of "Redcliffe." On one occasion it happened that this mill, needing some repairs, a great difficulty was encountered in the adjustment of the mud-sills, upon which the solidity of the whole superstructure depended. The obstacles to be removed were great, and it cost much time and money to overcome them. While Mr. Hammond was Senator, and in the official chamber was grappling with the problem of labour and capital, his experience with the mud-sills was opportunely recalled, and his application of that name to certain of the labour-ing classes at once added to his reputation for ready wit.

On the "Redcliffe" plantation the blacksmith was to be found at his forge, the wheelwright in his shop, and the stock-minder guarding the welfare of his charges. Measured by the standard that a man has not lived in vain who makes two blades of grass to grow where but one grew before, Senator Hammond might have been crowned King of agricultural enterprise, for his highest producing corn-lands before he rescued them had been impassible swamp-lands. Drained and put under cultivation, their yield was enormous, no less than eighty bushels of corn being the average quantity to the acre. There was scarcely a corner of the old "stake-and-rider fences" in which Mr. Hammond did not cause to be planted a peach or apple or other fruit tree.

Our cousin Miss Comer, who late in the fifties married the son of Senator Hammond, and made her home at "Redcliffe," though accustomed to affluent plantation life, was at once impressed by the splendid system that directed the colony of slaves at Beech Island. Each marriage and birth and death that took place among them was registered with great exactness. The Senator's business ability was remarkable. He knew his every possession to the most minute particular. The Hammond slaves formed an exclusive colony, which was conducted with all the strictness of a little republic. They were a happy, orderly, cleanly, and carefree lot, and Mr. Hammond was wont to say that if the doctrine of transmigration of souls was true, he would like to have his soul come back and inhabit one of his "darkies."

I have said they were an exclusive colony. My pretty little cousin realised this upon her arrival at "Glen Loula," a charming residence named for her, and set apart for the young couple by the owner of "Redcliffe."

"The Hammond negro, as I have found him," she wrote, "has a decided personal vanity, and nothing will offend him more than to have you forget his name. For a long time after coming I felt I was not exactly admitted by the different servants as 'one ob de fambly.' In fact, it was plain I was on trial, being 'weighed in the balance!' How I wished I knew all about diplomacy!

I never saw a more august appearance than Daddy 'Henry,' an old African, who remembers the slave ship on which he was brought over, his foreign name, and, perhaps, many things which he never tells about. He cleans the silver, polishes the floors and windows and the brasses in the fireplaces, and, besides this, claims the boys' guns as his by some divine right.

"In order to hasten an expression of their good-will, I thought one day of making a Sterling exchange with the aid of some Washington finery; and, with a black silk dress to one servant and a morning-robe to another, I have pulled through famously, even with Marm Jane, the cook, who is supreme in her kitchen. I have heard her turn my husband out. But the silk dress brought me a *carte blanche*. 'Come on, Missy, jes w'en you feels like it!' is the way she greets me now.

"I cannot help seeing the wise arrangement of every part of this extensive plantation, especially for the negroes. The house of the overseer is in the midst of a grove of live oaks, and in each street are a certain number of cabins, each in the midst of a little garden with space in which to raise chickens. The hospital is well arranged, and there is a separate house where the children, especially the babies, are left to be fed and cared for while their mothers are at work.

"My poor memory for faces would be my undoing but for Paul, who always tells me as we come upon any of the negroes, 'Now this is Jethro! Be sure to call him distinctly.' I fall in with this righteous deception and it works like a charm. They admire what they think wit, and especially love to memorise some easy little rhyme. Every one makes the same atrocious wish to me:

'God blass you, ma Missie. I wishes you joy
An' every year a gal or a boy.'

"I thought I would die when I heard it first, but I've

gotten over it now. Senator Hammond gives a barbecue to the slaves every Fourth of July and Christmas, and the dances of the negroes are very amusing. There is a tall black man, called Robin, on this plantation, who has originated a dance which he calls the turkey-buzzard dance. He holds his hands under his coat-tails, which he flirts out as he jumps, first to one side, and then to the other, and looks exactly like the ugly bird he imitates."

In the uncertain days of the war, Huntsville being unapproachable, and we having no fixed abode in the intervals between Congressional sessions at Richmond, Senator Clay and I made several enjoyable visits to the sheltered home of Mr. Hammond, even while battles raged and every heart was burdened with apprehension. The hospitality of the owner of "Redcliffe" was well known. It was his custom in those uncertain days, whether guests were known to be coming or not, to send his carriage daily to Augusta to meet the afternoon train, and the unexpected or chance arrival who might be seeking a conference or a refuge at "Redcliffe"; and once a year, like a great feudal landlord, he gave a fête or grand dinner to all the country people about, at which he always contrived to have some distinguished guest present. Senator Clay and I had the good fortune to be visiting Mr. Hammond on such an occasion, when every neighbour, poor or rich, for miles about was present. They made a memorable picture; for the majority were stiff and prim and of the quaint, simple, religious class often to be found in back districts. They seemed ill at ease, if not consciously out of place, in Senator Hammond's parlours, filled as those great rooms were with evidences of a cosmopolitan culture, with paintings and statuary, bronze and marble groups.*

---

\* Many of these possessions are still retained by Messrs. Spann and Harry Hammond.

In their efforts to entertain their guests, our host and hostess's ingenuity had been tested to its utmost, when suddenly Senator Hammond's eye twinkled, and he turned to Senator Clay.

"I remember once seeing you dance at our home in Washington, Mr. Clay," he began, and then proceeded to recall an amusing evening, where, strictly *en famille*, Senator Butler, of South Carolina, together with Secretary and Mrs. Cobb, Senator Clay and myself, had dined, finishing up the hours together by singing our favourite ballads. Upon my playing a merry tune, Secretary Cobb, rotund and jolly, suddenly seized my husband, slender and sedate, and together they whirled madly about the room to the music of the piano, and the great amusement of dear old Senator Butler, who laughed until the tears rolled down his cheeks.

When Mr. Hammond at "Redcliffe" proposed that Mr. Clay repeat his terpsichorean success for the pleasure of the Beach Islanders there gathered, my husband at first (emulating the distinguished artist wherever he is encountered) demurred. He "could not dance without music," he said.

"Well," said our host, "Mrs. Clay can play!"

"But I need a partner!" my husband persisted. At last, however, he yielded to Senator Hammond's persuasion and danced an impromptu Highland fling, abandoning himself completely to the fun of the moment. As the music went on and his spirit of frolic rose, the faces of some of the spectators around us grew longer and longer, and, I am sure, those good people felt themselves to be a little nearer to the burning pit than they had ever been before. Their prim glances at my husband's capers increased the natural sedateness of our hostess, who, seeing the expressions of alarm, plainly was relieved when at last the terrible Bacchanalian outburst was over! I felt sure it would be a difficult task to try to convince my husband's audience that his own religious feelings and convictions were of the deepest and most spiritual quality. For his black dependents, Senator Hammond had built several churches; the favourite one, called St. Catherine's (named for Mrs. Hammond), being nearest the "Redcliffe" residence and most frequently visited by the family. Once a month a white preacher came, and all the slaves gathered to listen to the monthly sermon. Senator Hammond's views for the civilising of the negroes led him to forbid the presence of exciting negro preachers, for the religion of the black man, left to himself, is generally a mixture of hysteria and superstition. The conversion of the negroes under their own spiritual guides was a blood-curdling process in those days, for they screamed to Heaven as if the Indians with their tomahawks were after them, or danced, twisting their bodies in most remarkable manner.* As their emotion increased, as they "got feelin'," and the moment of conversion approached, as a rule they fell all in a heap, though in thus "coming through" the wenches were altogether likely to fall into the arms of the best-looking young brother who happened to be near. By reason of Senator Hammond's wise discipline, such religious excesses were impossible at "Redcliffe," and I can recall no church service at once more thrilling and reverential than that I attended, with Senator Clay, at quaint St. Catherine's on the "Redcliffe" plantation shortly before my husband's departure for Canada.

The negroes, clean, thrifty, strong, all dressed in their best, vied with each other in their deference to Mars'

---

* To overcome these conditions, the Right-Reverend William Capers, distinguished in the Methodist Church, organised a wide system of missionary work among the plantation negroes, whereby preaching and catechising by white ministers took place once a month. Many of the great planters assisted in this good work, Senator R. Barnwell Rhett, Sr., being prominently associated with Bishop Capers. Senator Rhett built a large church, which was attended by the negroes from five plantations, and regularly by his own family. A. S.

Paul's guests, as we entered the church. They listened quietly to the sermon as the service proceeded.

It was a solemn and impressive scene. There was the little company of white people, the flower of centuries of civilisation, among hundreds of blacks, but yesterday in the age of the world, wandering in savagery, now peaceful, contented, respectful and comprehending the worship of God. Within a day's ride, cannon roared, and a hunter, laying his ear to the ground, might have heard the tread of armies, bent upon the blotting out of just such scenes as these. Only God might record our thoughts that morning, as the preacher alluded in prayer and sermon to the issues of the times. At the close of the morning, the hymn "There is rest for the weary" was given out, and when the slaves about us had wailed out the lines

"On the other side of Jordan

. . . . .

Where the tree of life is blooming
There is rest for you!"

my husband, at the signal for prayer, fell upon his knees, relieving his pent-up feelings in tears which he could not restrain. My own commingling emotions were indescribably strange and sad. Would abolitionists, I thought, could they look upon that scene, fail to admit the blessings American "slavery" had brought to the savage black men, thus, within a few generations at most, become at home in a condition of civilisation.

There were many fine voices on the plantation at "Redcliffe," and as they followed their leader down the row "chopping out" cotton, or, when later they worked in gangs at picking it, it was their custom, seeming to act from instinct in the matter, to sing. One voice usually began the song, then another would join him, and then another, until dozens of voices blended in weird and melodious harmonies that floated from the distant cotton fields to the house of the master, and the music of the unseen choristers, a natural and rhythmic song, was of a kind we shall not hear again in these later practical times. Sometimes, one by one, all would drop out of the song, until only the leader's high voice was heard; then, gradually, they would join in again, and often, when all seemed finished, a challenge would come from some distant gang, and a fuller and freer antiphonal song would be heard, answering from field to field.

When I remember that throng of well-fed, plump and happy coloured people, and compare it with the ragged and destitute communities common among the freedmen of to-day, the contrast is a sad one. "What's de reason?" asked an old darky of me during Reconstruction days, "dat de Yankees caint make linsey-wolsey like ole Mistis did in de ole time? 'N dose days one par breeches las me mos a year! I could cut trees, roll logs, burn bresh-heaps an' cut briers an' I couldn't wear dem breeches out! Now when I buys dis shoddy stuff de Yankees done bro't an' sets down on de lawg ter eat ma grub, bress Gawd! when I gits up, I leaves de seat o' my breeches on de lawg! I done got down on my knees an' prayed for God ter send me linsey-wolsey clothes so I won't have rheumatiz an' aint none come. Where's dat mule an' forty acres? When is dey a comin', dat's what I wants ter know!"

# CHAPTER XVII

## Conditions in 1863–'64

By the autumn of 1864 the Southern States found themselves ravaged of everything either edible or wearable. Food was enormously high in cities and in locations which proved tempting to foragers. Delicately bred women were grateful when they were able to secure a pair of rough brogan shoes at one hundred dollars a pair, and coarse cotton cloth from the Macon Mills served to make our gowns. For nearly three years the blockade of our ports and frontier had made the purchase of anything really needful, impracticable. Nor could we utilise the stores in Southern cities once these had fallen into the enemies' clutches. A correspondent, Mrs. Captain du Barry,* who in December, 1863, was permitted to visit Memphis, now in the enemy's possession, wrote, "I deeply regretted not being able to fill your commissions. I put them on my list that I sent in to General Hurlburt, when I requested a passport, but they were refused. All the principal stores were closed and their contents confiscated. There is a perfect reign of terror in Memphis. Not even a spool of cotton can be purchased without registering your name and address, and "swearing it is for personal or family use, and no *number* of articles can be taken from the store without, after selection, going with a list of them in your hand, to the "Board of Trade," accompanied by the clerk of the store, and there swearing on the Bible that the articles mentioned are for family use and not to be taken out of the United States. So many neces-

* Mother of the unfortunate Mrs. Maybrick.

sary articles are pronounced contraband by the United States authorities, that one is in momentary chance of being arrested, by ignorantly inquiring for them. The place is swarming with detectives who make a trade of arresting unfortunate people. They are paid by the United States Government two hundred and fifty dollars for detecting and arresting a person, and that person pays the Provost Marshal fifteen hundred to two thousand dollars to get off, that being the way matters are conducted in Memphis!"

All over the South old spinning wheels and handlooms were brought out from dusty corners, and the whirr of the wheel became a very real song to us. Every scrap of old leather from furniture, trunk, belt or saddle was saved for the manufacture of rough shoes, often made by the mother who had been fortunate enough to have hoarded them, for herself and children. I, myself, saw my aunt, Eloisa, wife of General Jones M. Withers, putting soles on the tops of once cast-off shoes of her children's, and she, who had known so well the luxuries of life, was compelled to perform her task by the meagre light of a precious tallow candle. Complaints, however, were few, from our Spartan-spirited women. Writing to my husband, in November, 1864, I said, "A lady told me yesterday that she fattened daily on Confederate fare—for, since she could obtain no useless luxuries, her health, heretofore poor, has become perfect."

The country was stripped not alone of the simpler refinements of life, but of even so necessary a commodity as salt. Scarcely a smoke-house in the South having an earthen floor, which had received the drippings from the hams or bacon sides of earlier days, but underwent a scraping and sifting in an effort to secure the precious grains deposited there. It happened that my host at "Redcliffe," just previous to the breaking out of hostilities, had ordered a boat-load of salt, to use upon certain unsatisfactory land,

and realising that a blockaded coast would result in a salt famine, he hoarded his supply until the time of need should come.   When it became known that Senator Hammond's salt supply was available, every one from far and near came asking for it.   It was like going down into Egypt for corn, and the precious crystals were distributed to all who came, according to the number in each family.

Compared with those of many of my friends in other parts of the South, our surroundings and fare at Beech Island were sumptuous.   Save at my Uncle Williams's home, I had nowhere seen such an abundance of good things as "Redcliffe" yielded.   Meats and vegetables were plenty; the river nearby was full of shad which were caught readily in seines;   and canvas-backs and teal, English ducks and game birds, especially partridges, abounded.   "Indian summer is here in all its glory," I wrote to my husband late in '64.   "The hues of the forests are gorgeous, the roses wonderful!  Millions of violets scent the air, and everything is so peaceful and lovely on this island it is hard to realise War is in the land.   Splendid crops prevail, and the spirit of the people is undaunted!"

As times grew more and more stringent, tea and coffee proved to be our greatest lack, and here, as we had done in the last days at Warrenton, we were glad to drink potato coffee and peanut chocolate.   The skin of the raw potato was scraped off—to pare it might have been to waste it—and the potato cut into slices or discs as thin as paper.   It was then carefully dried, toasted and ground, and made into what proved to be a really delicious beverage.*   Our chocolate was made in this wise: Peanuts, or pinders, or goobers, as they were variously called, were roasted and the skin slipped off.   They were next

---

* A recent writer attributes to those experiences, the coffee substitutes which now, forty years later, have "ruined the American coffee trade."   A. S.

pounded in a mortar; when, blended with boiled milk and a little sugar (a sparing use of this most costly luxury was also necessary), the drink was ready for serving, and we found it delightful to our palates.

There were spinners and weavers on Beech Island, too, and unceasing industry was necessary to prepare and weave cloth, both cotton and wool, sufficient for the clothing of the army of slaves and the family on the great plantation.    One of the island residents, Mrs. Redd, was a wonderful worker, and wove me a cotton gown of many colours which had all the beauty of a fine Scotch plaid. She spun her own cotton and made her own dyes, gathering her colours from the mysterious laboratories of the woods, and great was the fame her handiwork attained wherever it was seen.    Calico of the commonest in those days was sold at twenty-five dollars a yard;   and we women of the Confederacy cultivated such an outward indifference to Paris fashions as would  have astonished our former competitors in the Federal capital.    Nor did our appearance, I am constrained to think, suffer appreciably more than our spirits; for the glories of an unbleached Macon Mills muslin gown, trimmed with gourd-seed buttons, dyed crimson, in which I appeared at Richmond in the spring of '64, so impressed the mind of an English newspaper correspondent there, that he straightway wrote and forwarded an account of it to London, whence our friends who had taken refuge there sent it back to us, cut from a morning journal.

Not that our love for pretty things was dead; a letter preserved by Mr. Clay is fine testimony to the fact that mine was "scotched, and not killed."    It was dated Beech Island, November 18, 1864, and was addressed to Mr. Clay, now on the eve of departure from Canada.

"Bring me at least two silk dresses of black and purple. I prefer the purple to be *moire antique*, if it is fashionable. If French importations are to be had, bring me a spring

bonnet and a walking hat, for the benefit of all my lady
friends as well as myself, and do bring some books of
fashions—September, October, and November numbers
(*Ruling passion strong in war*), and bring——." The list
grew unconscionably. In after years I found a copy of it
carefully made out in my husband's handwriting, and
showing marks of having been carried in his pocket
until each article I had indicated for myself or others
had been selected, Here it is:

1. At least, 2 silk dresses, black and purple (for 'Ginie).
2. French spring bonnet.
3. Walking hat.
4. Some books of fashion.
5. Corsets—4—6, 22 inches in waist.
6. Slippers with heels, No. 3 1-2.
7. Gloves—1 doz. light coloured, 1 doz. dark.
8. Handkerchiefs, extra fine.
9. Two handsome black silk dresses for Lestia.
10. Flannel, white and red.
11. A set of fine, dark furs, not exceeding $25.
12. Set of Hudson Bay Sables, at any price, for Victoria, large cape, cuffs and muff.
13. Two Black Hernanis or Tissue dresses, one tissue dress to be brochetted for 'Ginie.
14. 3 or 4 pieces of black velvet ribbon, different widths.
15. Bolt of white bonnet ribbon; ditto pink, green and magenta.
16. French flowers for bonnet.
17. Shell Tuck comb for 'Ginie.
18. Present for little Jeff Davis, Claude and J. Winter.
19. Needles, pins, *hairpins*, tooth-brushes, coarse combs, cosmetics, hair oil, cologne.
20. Domestic, linen, muslin, nainsook, swiss, jaconet, mull muslin, each a full piece.
21. Dresses of brilliantine.
22. Black silk spring wrapping.
23. Chlorine tooth wash and Rowland's Kalydor.
24. A cut coral necklace.
25. Lace collars, large and pointed now worn.

Alas! my husband's zeal in fulfilling my commissions

all went for naught, for the boxes containing them (save two, which were deposited with Mrs. Chestnut, at Columbia, and later fell prey to the Federals or to the flames, we never knew which) were swallowed by the sea, and only he himself came home with the Government papers he had guarded, as the sole baggage he was able to save from the wreck of the *Rattlesnake* of all he had carried. And yet not all, for a long-lost pet which he had been enabled to reclaim for General Lee * was also brought safely to shore.

"Tell him," wrote my sister, from Richmond, that "General Lee's dog arrived safely. Poor dog! I'm sorry for him, for he will find the Confederacy a poor place to come to to get anything to eat! I trust for the country's sake, he knows how to live without eating!"

For the making of our toilette we discovered the value of certain gourds, when used as wash cloths. Their wearing qualities were wonderful; the more one used them the softer they became. Needles were becoming precious as heirlooms; pins were the rarest of luxuries; for the greater part of the time locust thorns served us instead. Writing paper was scarcely to be had, and the letters of that period which were sent out by private persons were often unique testimony to the ingenuity of the senders. Wall-paper, perhaps, was most frequently resorted to, and we made our crude envelopes of anything we could find. We made our own writing fluids, our commonest resource being the oak ball, a parasite, which, next to the walnut burr, is the blackest thing in the vegetable world. Or, this failing us, soot was scooped from the chimney, and, after a careful sifting, was mixed with water and "fixed" with a few drops of vinegar. Sometimes we used poke-

---

* Shortly after his arrival in Canada, Mr. Clay heard of General Lee's lost favourite. The animal, a fine Newfoundland, had been taken from the Lee home at Arlington by a Federal soldier, who sold it to a Captain Anderson (commanding an English vessel) for one hundred dollars. After some months of inquiry and negotiation, Mr. Clay secured the dog, and personally brought him back to the Confederate States. A. S.

berries, manufacturing a kind of red ink, or, made thin with water, some bit of miraculously saved shoe polish provided us with an adhesive black fluid.

Our difficulties were as great in the matter of transmitting our letters, when once they were written. We might intrust them to the mails, but these particularly were prey to our invaders; or we might charge with the care of them some traveller who was known to be making his way to the city for which the letters were addressed. Stray newspapers reached us at " Redcliffe " occasionally, from even so distant a point as our capital, and efforts were made by local editors to purvey the news of battles and the movements of the armies, but the supply of paper necessary for the issuing of a daily journal and even a weekly edition was difficult to obtain. What at first had appeared as morning papers were changed to evening editions, as the cost of candles, by which the compositors must work, had risen in '63 to three and one-half dollars a pound. Our brother, J. Withers Clay, who owned and edited the *Confederate*, turned peripatetic, and issued his paper where he could, being obliged to keep shifting, printing paraphernalia and all, with the movements of the army in the Tennessee region. Writing us from Chattanooga, on August 16, 1863, he thus described his life: " I am living in camp style. I mess with my office boys and our fare is frugal. My bed is a piece of carpet, laid on a door, with one end elevated on two bricks and the other resting on the floor. I lay my blue blanket on this, and my bones on that, with my head supported by my overcoat and carpet sack, and cover myself with a Mexican scarf when it is cool! "

On the whole, our condition was almost like that of the ancients who depended on passing travellers for gossip or news of the welfare or whereabouts of friends or kin. Thus my sister (by every tie of affection), writing from Richmond in the spring of '64, said: " Have no idea where you are, but send this letter by General Sparrow to Macon, care of Mrs. Whittle. The last intelligence I had of you was through Colonel Phillips. He told me he saw you between Augusta and Macon *somewhere.*"

Nor dared we avail ourselves of our telegraph wires, so costly had the sending of a few lines become. For the briefest message sent C. O. D. from Macon to Richmond, my sister paid sixteen dollars and implored me to send no more! The chief resource of the people was the arrival of the local train, at which time the railway stations swarmed with inquirers on foot, hedged in by others as eager, who had driven long distances in such vehicles as were at their command.

My life was one of continual suspense, notwithstanding the arrival of special couriers who came from time to time from Richmond bearing tidings of my absent husband. All lives that lie in close parallels to governments carry heavy anxieties. Mine, in those days of strife and terror, was no exception to this general rule. As negotiator at Niagara Falls with Professor Holcombe and others, the eyes of the North as well as those of the South for months had been fixed upon Mr. Clay, his interviews with Horace Greeley and the messengers sent to him by Mr. Lincoln having excited varying comments and criticisms that were anything but reassuring. Our friends in Richmond, however, wrote cheeringly:

" . . . I hear occasionally of Mr. Clay," ran a letter from the Executive Mansion, dated August 31st, '64, "but for some time past nothing has been received from him. The company he keeps * as reported by the newspapers cannot render you apprehensive of his being too happy to wish to return, though your desire to be with him may have increased his probable want of more congenial communion when the day's work is done. I am assured that his health has improved by Canadian air, and we may hope that he will bring back increased ability to labour in the cause of the Confederacy, if it should not be his portion

* Horace Greeley.

to relieve us of the need for further toil such as now is imposed. The carping spirit which prompted the criticism * on his course would have found sufficient cause whatever he might have done; or, if nothing had been done, that would have served equally. No one can hope to please everybody. You would not wish your husband to escape the reviling of those who envy such as they cannot rival, and strive to drag others down from the heights to which they cannot rise?"

Messages were numerous, urging my return to Richmond, which our President and the Mallorys assured me was the safest of places.

"Now that Sherman's barbarians are in unpleasant proximity to you," wrote Secretary Mallory, "why not come to the front where security, sympathy, mint juleps, an admiring audience, the freshest gossip and the most unselfish regard, all combine with the boom and flash of guns to welcome your coming? The correspondence between your lord and master and Holcombe on one side, and Greeley on the other, is doing good service. The parties, fragments, cliques and individuals in the United States who desire peace, but differ upon the *modus operandi* of getting it, will now learn that with Lincoln at the head of affairs, no peace is possible; while our weak brothers in North Carolina and Georgia who have clamoured so loudly that peace propositions should be made to us, cannot fail to see that, at present, peace with Lincoln means degradation. I am very glad Mr. Clay went, for I see that his presence must be beneficial to our cause."

These, and other letters as urgent and as desirous of quieting my apprehensions, came frequently. Nevertheless, my husband's stay in the severe climate of Canada caused me constant apprehension. For months my only direct news of him was through "personals," variously disguised, in the Richmond papers, which Colonel Clay was prompt to forward to me. Occasionally, however, one of

* Printed in Richmond *Enquirer*, and quoted liberally throughout the North.

the numerous letters each endeavoured to send to the other successfully reached its destination. "It gives me great pain," I wrote on November 18, '64, "to learn from yours just received that none of my numerous letters have reached you since the 30th June! I have sent you dozens, my dearest, filled with all the news of the day, of every character, and more love than ever filled my heart before! . . . My last intelligence of you was sent me from Richmond through the bearer of despatches, I presume, and bore the date of September fifteenth, more than two months ago!"

In this letter, which was dated from Beech Island, I conveyed intelligence to Mr. Clay of Senator Hammond's death, he being, at the time, a few days less than fifty-seven years of age. It occurred while all the affluent colourings of the autumn were tingeing his world at "Redcliffe." The circumstances attending his decease and burial were unique, and to be likened only to those which, in mediæval days, surrounded the passing away of some Gothic baron or feudal lord. Mr. Hammond had been failing in health for some time, when, feeling his end drawing near, he asked for a carriage that he might drive out and select his last resting-place. He chose, at last, a high knoll, from which a fine view was to be had of Augusta and the Sand Hills; and, having done this, being opposed to private burial grounds, he bequeathed the surrounding acres to the town in the precincts of which his estate lay, on consideration that they turn the plot into a public cemetery. First, however, he laid an injunction upon his wife and sons, that if the Yankee army penetrated there (the end of the war was not yet, nor came for six months thereafter), they should have his grave ploughed over that none of the hated enemy should see it.

Again and again in the remaining days he reiterated his wish. Fears were spreading of the approach of Sherman's devastating army, and the destruction of "Red-

cliffe," conspicuous as it was to all the surrounding country, seemed inevitable. Marvellous to relate, however,
when at last the spoiler came, his legions marched in a
straight line to the sea, some fourteen miles away from the
Hammond plantation, leaving it untouched by shell or
the irreverent hand of the invader.

The funeral of Mr. Hammond was solemn and made
especially impressive by the procession of two hundred of
the older slaves, who marched, two by two, into the
baronial parlors, to look for the last time upon their master's face. Save for this retinue, "Redcliffe" was now
practically without a defender, Mr. Paul Hammond being
absent much of the time, detailed upon home guard duty.
In his absence, my maid, Emily, and I kept the armory
of the household, now grown more and more fearful of
invasion with its train of insult and the destruction of
property. There were many nights when, all the rest in
slumber and a dead hush without, I waited, breathless,
until I caught the sound of Paul Hammond's returning
steps.

Just before the close of my refugee days on Beach
Island, a young kinsman, George Tunstall, who filled the
sublime post of corporal in Wheeler's Brigade in camp a
few hundred miles away, learning of my presence there,
obtained leave of absence and made his way, accompanied
by another youth, to Mrs. Hammond's to see me. The
two soldiers were full of tales of thrilling interest, of hair-
breadth escapes and camp happenings, both grave and
gay; and, rumours of Sherman's advance being rife, our
young heroes urged my cousin to take time by the fore-
lock and bury the family silver. "Redcliffe" being
almost in direct line of the Yankee general's march, the
advice seemed good, and preparations at once began to
put it into operation. Though there was little doubt of
the loyalty of the majority of the Hammond slaves, yet
it seemed but prudent to surround our operations with

GENERAL JOSEPH WHEELER
of Alabama
From a war-time photograph

all possible secrecy. We therefore collected the silver, piece by piece, secreting it in "crocus" bags, which, when all was ready, we deposited in a capacious carry-all, into which we crowded. It was at early dusk when lurking figures easily might be descried in corn-field or behind a wayside tree by our alert eyes. Declaring to those of the servants who stood about as we entered the carriage, that we were taking some provisions to Mrs. Redd, much to Lot's* surprise, we dispensed with a coachman, and drove off. We had many a laugh as we proceeded through the woods, at our absurdity in concealing our errand from the family servants and in confiding our precious secret to two of Wheeler's men. They had a terrible reputation for chicken stealing. †

When we had driven a mile or more, Mr. Tunstall produced a hatchet and began to blaze the trees. "There!" he said, after instructing us as to the signs he had made, "when you come to where the blaze stops, you'll find your valuables!" and under his directions the silver was silently sunk in the ground and the earth replaced.‡

Apropos of General Sherman, when a month or two later I was in Macon, I heard a very excellent story. A party of his men one day dashed up to the house of a Mrs. Whitehead, a fine old lady (a sister of my informant), and demanded dinner at once. The lady long since had learned that resistance to such imperative demands would be in vain, and preparations were at once begun for the meal. Notwithstanding her obliging and prompt com-

* The family coachman.

† A gentleman in the War Department—to whom I spoke of a violent protest uttered against General Wheeler's confiscations, by one Betts (who sent his complaint, long as a Presidential message, to Senator Clay, in Richmond)—smiled a little. "Well," he said, "Wheeler always would feed his men, you know!" A. S.

‡ Speaking of that episode, Mrs. Hammond said to me: "It was months before we succeeded in finding the silver again. Though we dug the ground over and over in every direction where we thought it was, we couldn't even find the blazes for a long time." A. S.

pliance, the men immediately started a forage in the poultry yard and the outhouses beyond. One of the officers penetrated the servants' quarters, and entered a cabin in which a young black woman lay sick.

"What's the matter, Sis?" he asked, in a tone that was meant to convey sympathy.

"Ain't no Sis of yourn!" was the sullen reply. "God knows I ain't no kin to no Yankee!" At that moment an infant's cry was heard.

"Hello!" said the officer. "Got a little pickaninny, hey? Boy or girl?"

"Boy chile! What's that ter you?" snapped the woman.

"What's his name?" persisted the soldier.

"Name's Wheeler, dat's what 'tis!" answered the invalid triumphantly, and the colloquy ended abruptly.

As the soldiers sat down to the table, some one, going to the door, saw Wheeler's men come tearing down the road flat on their horses. Instantly he shouted back to his companions, "Wheeler!" but they, believing the cry to be a ruse, continued to eat. The sounds of the galloping steeds soon became audible, however, and a stampede that was highly amusing to the now relieved household took place through doors and windows. When General Wheeler arrived, he found a steaming repast already prepared, and a cordial welcome from Mrs. Whitehead and her family, including "Sis."

# CHAPTER XVIII

## The Death of Abraham Lincoln

THE South was now sadly crippled. Our bulwarks were demolished and our granaries emptied, our most fertile valleys occupied by the Northern army, and Confederate money was depreciated to such an extent as to make it practically useless.* Our army was thinning daily, and even the news from Richmond, save from Mr. Davis himself, seemed to carry an undertone prophetic of coming collapse. "The enemy, yesterday and to-day," wrote Mr. Mallory, from the capital, late in October," is, in the graphic gorillaisms, 'pegging away' close at us; and the flash of his guns is visible and their roar was audible from my piazza yesterday. His approaches have been very slow, to be sure, but nevertheless, he has taken no step backward, but is 'inching' upon Richmond surely and methodically in a way that seems as gopher-like as it is certain; and he will keep up this system unless we can, by hard fighting, push him back."

Supported by the hope of Mr. Clay's return, and knowing he would seek me first among those of our kin who were nearest to the coast, I lingered on Beech Island until late in January, 1865, though I did so against the advice of Colonel Clay, who urged me to go southward, and the assurances of Mr. Davis that I might safely return to Rich-

---

* A cartoon which appeared about this time in a Richmond paper was a graphic demonstration of the shrunk value of Confederate money. It represented a man going to and returning from market. In the first scene he carried a bushel basket piled high with current bills; in the second, the basket was empty, and in his hand was an infinitesimal package, which was supposed to contain a beef steak! A. S.

mond, which city, the President was confident, would continue to prove an impregnable refuge.   In the last days of
December two such messages, equally positive and each
positively opposed to the other in its significance, sped to
me by courier from the capital.   Who was to decide when
such correspondents disagreed?   Yet the need for some
move became more and more urgent.   To return to
Huntsville was out of the question.   Northern Alabama
was overrun with Federal soldiers, to whom the name
alone of Clay, borne as it was by three men all actively
labouring for the preservation of the Confederate States,
was a challenge to the exercise of fresh authority.   I
heard distressing news of the contemplated transportation,
to Nashville, of the aged ex-Governor Clay (our uncle, Mr.
McDowell, a non-combatant full of years, had already
died in that prison under most pitiful circumstances), yet
I was powerless to send him even a line of comfort or
encouragement.   Mail routes in every direction were in
possession of the enemy, or liable to be interrupted by
them, and straggling companies of Union soldiers were on
the lookout to intercept such messengers as might
attempt to bear our letters from point to point.

My husband was in Canada, or on the seas, I knew not
where; J. Withers Clay, the second son of the ex-Governor, was active with pen and press in lower Alabama;
Colonel Clay was stationed in Richmond in the thick of
the political battle.   Our parents were left alone in the old
home, to brave the discomforts put upon them by their
sometimes cruel and sometimes merely thoughtless
oppressors.   A grandson, Clement, a mere lad, but a hero
in spirit, venturing into the town to succour the old people,
was promptly arrested.   "I wonder," wrote one who
visited our parents, "that their heartstrings have not long
since snapped!"

All through the Tennessee Valley dejection was spreading.   "If Mr. Davis does not restore General Johnston to

the army of the Tennessee," wrote J. Withers Clay, "his friends generally out here believe that he will never recover his lost popularity, or be able to get back the thousands of soldiers (now) absent without leave. I wish you would tell the President this. You have no idea of the extent of demoralisation among soldiers and citizens produced by his persistent refusal to restore him!"

For now several months I had been secretly tortured by an indecision as to what course to pursue. Though urged by a hundred generous correspondents to share their homes (for I have ever been blessed by loyal friends), I had a deepening conviction that my interests were detached from all. I was homeless, husbandless, childless, debarred from contributing to the comfort of my husband's parents, and I chafed at my separation from those to whom my presence might have proved useful. As time went on, all deprivations and anxieties were obscured by one consuming determination to join my husband at all hazards; but, despite every effort toward accomplishing this, I found myself swept helplessly along by the strong currents of the times. My sole means of communication with Mr. Clay was now through occasional "personals," which were published in the Richmond *Enquirer*, coöperating with the New York *Daily News*. One of these, which appeared early in November, 1864, indicates the indecision and anxiety which by this time was felt, also, by my husband in his exile:

"To Honourable H. L. Clay, Richmond, Virginia. I am well. Have written every week, but received no answer later than the 30th of June. Can I return at once? If not, send my wife to me by flag of truce, via Washington, but not by sea. Do write by flag of truce care John Potts Brown, No. 93 Beaver Street, New York. Answer by personal through Richmond *Enquirer* and New York *News*."

"I inclose you a 'personal' from Brother Clement, published in yesterday's *Enquirer*," Colonel Clay wrote on November 11, 1864. "I consulted Mr. Mallory, Mr. Benjamin and the President, and then sent him the following: 'Your friends think the sooner you return the better. At the point where you change vessels you can ascertain whether it is best to proceed direct or by Mexico. Your wife cannot go by flag of truce. She is well. I send you letters to-day by safe hands. H. L. C.' The reason why the earliest return is advised is that the fleet off Wilmington is not yet increased to the degree intended; and during the rough weather, before the hard winter sets in, it is much easier for vessels to run the blockade. I shall tell him that the statistics kept in the Export and Import Office show five out of six vessels, inward and outward bound, safely run the blockade, but that he must himself consider the risk from what he learns after reaching Bermuda."

Colonel Clay's prompt decision, such was my distracted state of mind, by no means satisfied me. The suggestion contained in my husband's words seemed feasible to my courageous mind. I despatched a note of inquiry at once to Richmond, begging Mr. Davis to write to Mr. Seward to secure my safe passage by land to Canada. I told him of my unrest, the increasing uncertainty that prevailed in the neighbourhood of "Redcliffe," and my desire to join my husband. The President's reply was reassuring and full of the confidence which sustained him to the end of the remaining days of the Confederacy. "There is no danger in coming here now," ran his message from the capital, dated December 29, 1864. "When he (Mr. Clay) returns he will, of course, visit this place, and can conveniently meet you here." But, when I proposed to try to make my way to this haven, Colonel Clay wrote excitedly, animated by an anxiety as great as my own:

"Don't come to Richmond! Don't send the President letters or telegrams. He is in a sea of trouble, and has no time or thought for anything except the safety of the country. I fear the Congress is turning madly against him. It is the old story of the sick lion whom even the jackass can kick without fear. It is a very struggle for life with him. I do not know that he has any reliable friends in Congress, who will sustain him upon principle, fearlessly and ably. He has less and less power to intimidate his enemies, and they grow more numerous every day. . . . If he were preëminently gifted in all respects, the present moment is perilous enough to call forth all his energies no matter how great. . . . Before this reaches you, you will have read my private letter to Hammond, in regard to the military situation in South Carolina and Georgia. I think as soon as Sherman reduces Savannah, he will move promptly up the Savannah River, and endeavour to capture Charleston by taking it in reverse. That success would be a feather in any general's cap. We cannot hope to make fight on that river, I think, but must take the Edesto as our line of defense. Now, look upon the map and you will see that the whole of Beech Island lies between the two rivers, and in the event Sherman moves up (as he will do, to cut off supplies from Charleston and Virginia), the South Carolina Railroad will fall within the line of his advance. I only give you my personal opinion; for, of course, no one can speak assuredly of Sherman's intentions. If I am right, I think you had better move in the direction of Alabama before there is any rush of travel, and as soon as you can well do so. . . . In Alabama or western Georgia there will be plenty of food; more, indeed, because of the inability to bring it east of Augusta. I write to advise you to go as far away from the line of the enemy's march as you can. . . . I dare not look into the future, after Hood's battles in Tennessee, if the Yankee accounts are verified. God knows we are pressed hard on every side by the enemy, and have no wise counsellors to give proper direction to our weak, erring efforts for independence. Passion and prejudice and personal feelings govern in many instances where patriotism should rule. Congress is discussing questions of the smallest moment while the Confederacy is in the grip of the Yankees struggling for existence. . . . I fear the pending attack upon Wilmington will prevent Brother Clement from coming in at the Port (if he should conclude not to go to Mexico) for some time yet. Until the flotilla set sail from Fortress Monroe I looked for him to come in about the last of this month or the first of the next. Now I shall not know when to expect him, for no vessels will attempt the blockade there at Washington."

It now became apparent that to wait at our exposed Island was no longer prudent. A family council was called, and it was decided that, upon the first sign of a suitable escort, I should make my way to Macon. I had not long to wait. Within a few days we learned of the presence of General Howell Cobb in Augusta. I wrote to him at once, telling him of my contemplated exodus and of my desire to place myself under his protection upon his return journey to his head-quarters at Macon. He replied with the gallant cor-diality which was ever a characteristic with him, and which I think would never have deserted him even in the midst of the roar of cannon:

"Augusta, Georgia, January 21, 1865.

"*My Dear Friend:* . . . I assure you that your threat to cling to me like the old man of the sea to Sinbad is the most agreeable threat that ever was made to me, and it shall not be my fault if it is not executed. I am here under orders from Richmond, which leave me in doubt whether I am to remain a day, a month, or a year. My opinion is that I will be ordered back to Macon in a very few days, and there is no telling at what hour I may receive the order. To make it certain, however, that I can give you timely notice, you ought to be in Augusta. I am ready to receive the acceptable trust and devote my best efforts to your comfort and happiness.  Very truly your friend,

"HOWELL COBB."

Early in February I arrived in Macon without misadventure, and here, on February 10th, my husband joined me, having learned of my whereabouts from our friends in Augusta.

Mr. Clay's experiences since leaving Nassau had been exciting. *The Rattlesnake*, a hitherto skilful blockade runner, on which he had taken passage, was bound for Charleston; but, finding an entrance at that port impossible for the moment, she had crept cautiously up to Wilmington, only to be obliged again to show her heels to the wary and enlarged blockading fleet. After numerous efforts to find a friendly harbour, the little ship, reconnoitering about the South Carolinian coast, ran aground four miles away from Fort Moultrie, grounded, it was rumoured, by the pilot. Here the little craft, which quickly became the target of the enemies' guns, was abandoned, her timbers ablaze, while passengers and crew, taking to the life-boats, bore with them such baggage as might be gathered in their haste; and now, to cap the climax of their disasters, the life-boats, too, ran aground, and sailors and passengers were compelled repeatedly to wade through the waves, which dashed throat-high about them, in an effort to rescue the pieces of baggage they had been able to save from the ship. On that cold, blustery day in early February, in garments saturated with brine, Mr. Clay was taken in a yawl to Fort Moultrie, whence, ill from the exposure he had undergone, he was carried in a sail-boat to Charleston by the Reverend Mr. Aldrich, an accidental visitor to the Fort. By that kindly man he was put to bed and to sleep under the stimulus of orange-leaf tea, while his clothing and few rescued belongings were undergoing a drying.

Upon awakening, Mr. Clay's first effort was to forward to Richmond to the care of Colonel Clay, to be held until his own arrival in the capital, a small hand-trunk addressed to Judah P. Benjamin, and to General Lee, his restored pet; his second, to find me. This accomplished, it was his intention to proceed at once to Richmond, to deliver in person his State papers, the most important of which he had carried in an oil-silk bag suspended about his neck. To the complete frustration of his plans, however, my hapless husband found the railway route between Augusta, where he supposed me to be, and Charleston, now effectually closed. It was by a roundabout road, therefore, made partly by carriage, that he reached the desired point on the seventh of February, only to learn of my departure a few days before under the escort of General Cobb. By the 10th, when Mr. Clay arrived at last in Macon, he had informed himself of the grave plight of our armies, and of the lamentable political differences existing in the capital, to which Colonel Clay, in his letter to me, had alluded. A few hurried conferences with General Cobb and others, and together we took our departure for Richmond. Everything which might become an impediment to the rough travel that lay before us was dispensed with, even my invaluable maid, Emily, being left behind at the home of Major Whittle. We proceeded first to Washington, Georgia, going, upon our arrival, to the home of General Toombs, where was sojourning Mr. Stephens, our Vice-President. The hearts of all were heavy as the gentlemen conferred together upon the outlook of our country and arms. Letters from Richmond which reached our hands at this point were excited in tone, and added to our apprehension and sorrow.

"On every side," wrote our sister, "the city rings with the cries of Rachels weeping for their children!"

"Don't come to Richmond!" urged Colonel Clay, "[or] if you think it necessary to come on, do so at once; don't delay. Leave sister; don't undertake to bring her in the present uncertain condition of the railroad connections between here and the Georgia line. . . . Our armies have been dwindling, until none is large enough to withstand an attack in the open field. There is a collapse in every department, and, worse than all, there is an utter lack of confidence by the people, in the administration, in Congress, and in the success of the cause itself. . . . Campbell *will* go out. He cannot see any benefit to be derived from his longer continuance in office as the *drudge* of the War Department, especially when the Treasury is bankrupt, and Congress cannot devise a new scheme for reëstablishing faith in the currency. That department is $400,000,000 in arrears, it is said. I know it is enormously in debt to the War Department ($32,000,000), and that the Quartermaster General and the Commissary General cannot obtain the means to pay current expenses. If we cannot have transportation and bread for the soldiers in the field, to say nothing of clothing and pay, . . . what becomes of our army? . . . As I see the present and argue thence what the future has in store for us, . . . I see nothing but defeat and disaster and ruin!"

Characterised throughout his life by a punctilious observance of everything which in his eyes appeared a duty, Mr. Clay was not to be deterred by even such grave news from carrying out his intention to deliver in person, to the President and Mr. Benjamin, an account of his stewardship in Canada. Late in February, therefore, he resumed his journey, mounted upon General Toomb's grey mare, and accompanied by the General's man, Wallace. He had not proceeded far, however, when, overtaken by an illness, the result of his exposure at Charleston, he was obliged to return to Washington. A month elapsed ere he was able again to set out for Richmond, the city which was so soon to be the theatre of our national collapse.

The roads now, in many places, were impassible. The number of Union soldiers was increasing daily in the States which Mr. Clay must cross in his northward journey. My husband, with his precious documents, would have been a rich prize to any who might have seized him. Through many vicissitudes he made his cautious way toward the capital, securing a horse, when he could, or a mule team, or following the railroad tracks where necessary. Much of the journey he made alone, but he sometimes found himself in company, and that not always wholly desirable. On one occasion he fell in with two straggling Confederate soldiers, and, being near the home of a distant kinsman, Robert Withers, upon the arrival of the trio he asked Mr. Withers' hospitality for them all. Consent was promptly forthcoming, but my husband's feelings were somewhat less cordial toward his whilom companions when one was allotted to him as a bedfellow. "Had to sleep with ———," reads his diary, "much to my dread of camp-itch!"

Eight days were consumed in that journey to the capital, by this time the scene of an excitement truly anarchistic. Mr. Clay was probably the last man in the Confederate service to seek to enter Richmond. The trend of Confederate travel just then was in an opposite direction.

Making at once for Colonel Clay's headquarters, my husband secured the trunk destined for Mr. Benjamin, to whom he shortly afterward transferred his papers. The transaction was a hurried one, and Mr. Clay pushed on to the apartment of Mr. Davis. In after days I often heard him describe the scene which there met him. He found the President engaged in hastily packing a valise, his clothing and papers scattered in little heaps about. I think he assisted his hapless friend in these preparations. An hour or two later and Mr. Clay was *en route* for Danville, on the last of the over-laden trains to draw out from the once dear but now desolated city. Of the sad journey of the President through the Carolinas, with his company of legislative friends, of which, for a portion of the way, my husband was one, I remember no particulars. I recall a hasty return to Macon, where Mr. Clay joined me, whence we hurried on in a few days to the home of former Senator B. H. Hill, at Lagrange, in western Georgia. The remembrance of the days that immediately succeeded the evacuation of Richmond, followed, as that event was, by the murder of Abraham Lincoln, is a confused one. A kind of horror seized my husband when he realised the truth of the reports that reached us of this tragedy. At first he had refused to credit them. "It's a canard!" he said; but when, at last, he could no longer doubt, he exclaimed: "God help us! If that be true, it is the worst blow that yet has been struck at the South!"

# CHAPTER XIX

## C. C. Clay, Jr., Surrenders to General Wilson

Upon leaving the home of General Toombs, we proceeded directly to that of Senator Hill, where shortly were gathered ex-Secretary of our Navy and Mrs. Mallory, Mr. and Mrs. Semmes, of Louisiana, and Senator Wigfall. We were an anxious circle, our hearts heavy with the constantly increasing testimony to our great disaster, and our minds alert to measure the ways and means of our future course. My husband and Mr. Wigfall had already determined to seek the other side of the Mississippi, there to join the gallant Kirby Smith, and make a last stand for our cause; or, if needs must be, to press on to Texas. Day by day disturbing news reached us concerning the whereabouts of Mr. Davis and his party, now making their sorry flight toward the coast of Florida, fugitives from the Federal authorities.

A Northerner would have found us a wonderful nest of "rebels," could he have looked in upon the group that one evening surrounded the table in the library of the Hill residence, upon which was spread the map of Georgia. The gentlemen were seated, the ladies standing behind them. Every eye was bent upon the road which our host was pointing out.

"If Davis would take this route"—and Mr. Hill's finger traced the way upon the diagram before us, "if he keeps to it without any detour whatsoever, he will get away," he declared. "If he turns aside a step or lingers an hour he is lost! If he crosses the river there"—and our host, who knew the topography of his State by heart, paused as he marked the spot, "no one can take him!"

Not a member of that circle but was tense in his or her desire that our chief should be spared the ignominy and pain of capture. The magnanimity of Senator Wigfall, whose antagonism to President Davis had caused a profound concern in Richmond in this hour of the Confederacy's downfall, was especially marked.

To the present, none of those assembled at the hospitable Hill home had reason to apprehend a personal danger from the conquering party. The meeting had taken place at Appomattox which, more than victories gained, has made the name of Grant immortal. The Northern General had received the proffer of Lee's sword, and peace had been proclaimed. By the terms made we had some little reason to be optimistic as to our future, despite the peopling of our Southern cities with Union soldiers. The developments of one fateful day, however, unveiled to us the actual perils we were yet to face.

As I have said, my husband and Mr. Wigfall had practically completed their arrangements to leave Lagrange and strike for the Mississippi. It was my expectation, thereupon, to return to our parents' home in Huntsville. The day agreed upon for my departure approached. At the request of my husband, I drove to the cars to ascertain what currency would be required to take me to Macon, whence I was to proceed at once to Alabama. In company with Henrietta Hill and her little brother, I drove to the station in time to see the afternoon train pull in. As it swept into the city with a shrill scream, it was crowded with men and women of both races; so overcrowded, rather, that many clung to the platforms. There were shouts and a general Babel, which I did not understand, and, as debarkation began, to these was added the bedlam of drunken laughter. When as near to the cars as the carriage would permit, I directed Benny Hill to go forward to the conductor and ask "What currency is needed to get to Macon?"

The man seemed to understand that I had prompted the question, and called to me, "Gold or greenbacks, Madam?" Then, not waiting for my reply, he hastened to add the news, "Macon has been surrendered by General Howell Cobb to the Federals, General Wilson commanding. Atlanta, as you know, is in the hands of the Yankees, Colonel Eggleston in charge!"

This was disappointing news to me, as I had but little gold and a peck of Confederate paper, which was not likely to carry me far under reported conditions. I waited until the crowd had thinned out somewhat, and then questioned the man further.

"Is there any other news than that of the proclamation for Mr. Davis's arrest?" I asked. His reply astounded me.

"Yes, Madam!" he said; "$100,000 * is offered for Clement C. Clay, of Alabama." A trembling seized me. I don't know how I made my way to the carriage. Before I was fairly seated I saw Colonel Philip Phillips, at this time a resident of Lagrange, coming toward us. In his hands he held a journal. Quickly reaching the carriage, he handed me the paper, and, pointing to the despatch, which contained the proclamation, he said, "Go home quickly and give this to Mr. Clay!"

Scarcely aware of what I did, I ordered the coachman to drive back at once, forgetting in the excitement of the moment to invite the Colonel to accompany me. Arriving at the Hill residence, I met my hostess almost at the door.

"Please ask the gentlemen to come to us!" I said

---

* The actual amount offered for Mr. Clay's apprehension was $25,000; but, in the dissemination of the proclamation through the press, the larger sum was repeatedly given as the amount offered—being so quoted by General Wilson and others. See Records of the Rebellion, series I, vol. XLIX, page 733.

faintly, "I have important news!" and I hastened upstairs.

I found Mr. Clay sitting quietly, deep in the conning of a thick volume. It was Burton's "Anatomy of Melancholy," ever a favourite with him. It lay open on his knee, steadied with one hand; the other, as was a habit with my husband, was stroking his beard, absent-mindedly. Before I could summon my voice to utter the terrible news, the others of the party had hastened upstairs. Handing the fatal paper to Senator Hill, I cried, half-hysterically, "For God's sake, read that!"

As Mr. Hill read the proclamation aloud, everyone was silent. Senator Semmes was the first to break the silence that followed the reading.

"Fly for your life, Clay!" he said, "The town is full of men from two disbanded armies, any of whom would be tempted by such a sum. Take no chances!" Then all at once everyone but my husband began to talk excitedly. As the meaning of the despatch broke upon him, Mr. Clay blanched a moment, but at Mr. Semmes's urgings he spoke.

"Fly?" he said, slowly, like one recovering from a blow, "from what?" Mr. Semmes's answer came drily.

"From death, I fear!" he said. My husband turned inquiringly to the others. Secretary Mallory, seeing the unspoken question in his face, answered it.

"I don't know what to say, Clay! One hundred thousand dollars is a glittering bribe to half-starved soldiers!" He had scarcely spoken when a knock was heard. Alarmed by the thought that some renegade was already come to arrest my husband, I flew to the door and locked it. As I did so, Senator Hill was beside me, and I remember the forceful feeling with which he spoke, even as the click of the key sounded.

"By the eternal God, Clay!" he said. "The man who dares cross my threshold to arrest you, falls on it."

Fortunately our fears were groundless, for in a moment we heard the word, "Phillips!" and, upon opening the door, the Colonel quickly entered. His calm bearing was a relief to us. Some one at once put the question to him, "What do you think Clay ought to do?"

"What does Mr. Clay think he should do?" was Colonel Phillips's reply. My husband was prompt to answer:

"As I am conscious of my innocence, my judgment is that I should at once surrender to the nearest Federal authorities!" he said.

At this announcement I could not restrain my sobs. I doubt not I troubled him much by my tears and pleadings. I begged him hysterically to fly; I would join him anywhere if he would but escape. But my ever patient husband only answered, as he tried to calm me, "Virginia! my wife! Would you have me fly like an assassin?"

I could say no more, but only listen, between the crowding fears and terrors that seized me, while those about discussed the wording of a telegram which, a short time afterward, Colonel Phillips carried to the telegraph office. It ran thus:

"*Bt. Major-General Wilson, United States Army:* Seeing the proclamation of the President of the United States, I go to-day with the Honourable P. Phillips, to deliver myself to your custody.        C. C. CLAY, Jr."

I think this resolute act, and the preparation of a letter which was immediately written to the same general, relieved my husband, for he was instantly calmer. For myself, I felt that he had signed his own death warrant. During the succeeding hours, the entire household was in consultation. Having decided to proceed to Macon by the early train the next morning, Mr. Clay retired and slept, to my surprise, as peacefully as a child, though I, less fortunate, watched and wondered at his calmness.

Early the following morning we left Lagrange, accompanied by Colonel Phillips. The world appeared very strange and worthless to me as the train hastened on to Atlanta, where a change of cars was necessary. We found that city a pandemonium; soldiers patrolling the streets, drums beating, and vans, loaded with furniture, moving up and down the avenues. In our desire to proceed as rapidly as possible we accosted a soldier.

"Where is Colonel Eggleston?" Colonel Phillips asked.

"There he is, within ten feet of you!" was the reply. The Colonel thereupon approached the officer in command and said to him, "I have a distinguished friend here, Mr. Clement C. Clay, of Alabama, who is on his way voluntarily to surrender himself."

On hearing my husband's name, Colonel Eggleston approached us and held out his hand, saying: "Is it possible, Mr. Clay, you are the man who is making such a stir in the land? I am not surprised at your surrender. I knew your record through my Senators, Pugh and Pendleton, of Ohio. You've done the right thing, sir, and I hope you'll soon be a free man."

Mr. Clay, surprised at the Federal Colonel's magnanimity, turned and presented him to me. He extended his hand. I took it. It was the first Yankee hand I had touched since we had left Minnesota, four years before. The Colonel assured us it was impossible for us to proceed that night to Macon. "It will be best for you," he said, "to spend the night at the Kimball House. But the city is in a tumult, and, as Mrs. Clay is with you, I will have a guard that you may not be disturbed." When we were ready to retire, two soldiers appeared, with muskets in hand, and took their stand, one at each side of our chamber door, where they remained until the next morning.

Shortly after breakfast, Colonel Eggleston presented himself. His manner was courteous. "As times are so turbulent," he said, "I think it best that I should detail a guard to accompany you to Macon; that is," he added, "unless you object." Upon Mr. Clay's assurance that the guard would not be unpleasant to us, the General presented Lieutenant Keck, a young officer, who, during the conversation, had been standing near. Thereupon the Lieutenant attached himself to our party and we boarded the car for Macon. Throughout the trip our guard behaved with undeviating consideration, and this, under trying circumstances; for, the wires flashing the news about the country, many of the stations along the road were crowded with friends, who, when they saw us, uttered expressions of intensest regret, even urging my husband to fly. On more than one occasion, so considerate was Lieutenant Keck's conduct, that he allowed Mr. Clay to leave the car, unguarded.

During that journey the young officer addressed me but twice; the first time to offer me a glass of water, and the second to tell me a piece of news that shocked me in double force. As we approached Macon, my husband had endeavoured to prepare me for whatever the future might hold for us. He was a prisoner, he said, and though self-surrendered, I must not be alarmed if we should find a phalanx of soldiers waiting us at the depot. The picture thus conjured had already made me sick at heart, when my husband, excusing himself, went forward into the next car for a few moments. A short time afterward Lieutenant Keck appeared. Approaching me he said, with some hesitation, "Mrs. Clay, I have some sad news for you!"

My husband's previous words suddenly rushed over me. He had been preparing me for something he knew but dared not tell me! In a moment, in my mind's eye, I saw a gibbet. "Great God," I cried. "What is it? Will they hang my husband?"

"Don't be frightened, Mrs. Clay," our guard answered. "Don't cry! Your chief was arrested yesterday!"

"My chief," I echoed. "You mean General Lee?"

"No!" was his response, "Mr. Davis! He is now at the Lanier House, in Macon!" The loosening of the tension to which I first had been keyed was so great that I was scarcely able to utter a comment, nor had I recovered from the shock when the train pulled into Macon. Notwithstanding my husband's brave counsels, the news of Mr. Davis's arrest added a hundredfold to our depression. When I told Colonel Phillips and Mr. Clay, who shortly returned, my husband's face grew graver. "If that is true," he said, "my surrender was a mistake. We shall both perish!"

In an indistinct way I felt my husband to be right; and surely after events demonstrated how nearly truly he had prophesied. The almost instantaneous appearance of Mr. Clay and Mr. Davis as prisoners produced a confusion in the press statements and telegrams that flew over the country, and coloured the feeling of the public to such an extent that those in high places who were seeking sacrificial victims were enabled, without exciting a protest, to overlook the fact that Mr. Clay, scorning arrest, had confidently and voluntarily committed himself into the Government's hands, to court its fullest investigation. "The arrest of Clement C. Clay," was the heading under which my husband's courageous act was buried in so far as it might be; and so generally was the fact of his voluntary surrender overlooked, that a Southern historian, whose books have been circulated among schools, took up the phrase and incorporated it among the "historic" facts which children con.

Arrived at Macon, we found a single transfer wagon at the station.. To this we were conducted, and our party of four, with our grips and valises, completely filled the vehicle. As we drove away from the station I felt much as must have felt the poor wretches in the French Revolution as they sat in the tumbrels that bore them to the guillotine.

We drove at once to the residence of our friends, Colonel and Mrs. Whittle, whence Colonel Phillips proceeded to General Wilson's headquarters to deliver my husband's letter announcing his surrender. It was a beautiful afternoon. The trees were in full foliage and the air delicious with sweet odours of Southern blossoms. Dusk was approaching as, without previous announcement, we drove up to the Whittle home. The family were seated on the veranda. With them was our brother, J. Withers Clay. As they recognised us they rushed down the steps to meet us, full of eager questioning.

"What does it mean?" they cried. "Why have you come here?" and every eye was full when my husband answered, "I have surrendered to the United States Government. Allow me to present my guard, Lieutenant Keck!" Never shall I forget how dear Mrs. Whittle (who was slightly deaf), with eyes full of tears, reached out her hand to that representative of our triumphant antagonists, as if, by a forbearing kindness, she would bespeak his favour for my husband.

As we entered the house, we were all in tears, and Colonel Phillips, glad of an excuse to leave the painful scene, hastened to deliver his message to the General in command. Returning in the course of an hour, he reported General Wilson as approving Mr. Clay's course. He sent word that he was awaiting instructions in regard to Mr. Davis's party, "Whom, I presume, you will accompany. Meanwhile, I request that you will not talk of the surrender!" He further directed that Lieutenant Keck be sent immediately to him. I think this young soldier had a tender heart, for, seemingly touched at our sorrowful situation, he lingered about a moment as if unwilling to leave us without a farewell. Seeing his hesitation, I offered him my hand and thanked him for his humane treatment of my husband, which, I assured him, I should ever remember. If his eyes, or those of others to whom he was dear should see this acknowledgment they will know I did not speak lightly.

General Wilson's request was scrupulously observed by us, and though friends came in numbers to sympathise with us and encourage us, we were silent on the forbidden topic of my husband's surrender. A day or two later, word came that we must hold ourselves in readiness to leave Macon. Meantime, I had addressed a note to General Wilson, begging that I might be allowed to accompany my husband on his journey to his destination, wherever it might be. The Commanding General promptly acceded to my request, though, he assured me, the trip before us would be a rough and disagreeable one, and advised me to consider well before I took it.

Of course, I was not to be deterred. I made instant preparation for the journey. My available wardrobe was small, being limited to a few Perodi's (which in those days served the same purpose as the shirt-waist of 1900) and a rusty black skirt, a veritable war-relic; but my friends in Macon, knowing the impossibility of getting my own possessions together, quickly came to the rescue. The results of their generosity were not in all cases strictly what donor or recipient might have wished, from the point of view of fashion or art. For example, Mrs. Lucius Mirabeau Lamar sent me a treasured foulard silk gown, of a pretty brown and white pattern; but she, being both shorter and stouter than I, the fit was not one that even the deliberately courteous would have ventured to call a good one; nevertheless, I received it gratefully and courageously adapted it to serve as travelling attire. Mrs. William D. Johnston, too, sister of our loved General Tracy, likewise urged a gift upon me of several changes of Parisian *lingerie*, which she had but just acquired. With this borrowed finery (which afterward carried its own penalty) stowed in my valise, when the announcement of the time appointed for our departure came to us, it found me ready.

It was set for the late afternoon. We arrived at the railway station a half-hour before train time. At the last, we hastened away from the friends whose sorrow and sympathy threatened to disturb the composure it was so necessary to preserve against our coming ordeals. We were surprised to find the city in a kind of uproar. Cavalry clattered through the streets and gazing sightseers thronged the sidewalks. Our passage to the station proceeded without mishap or adventure of any kind; nevertheless, we had scarcely alighted from our carriage when, looking back, up the street we saw a company of cavalrymen approaching. There was an increasing activity in the gathered crowds, which were composed of silent citizens of Macon, elbowed by Freedmen and Union soldiers, who lounged among them.

As the cavalry approached the station, the significance of the scene became plain to us. They were a guard, flanking on each side an old "jimber-jawed, wobble-sided" barouche, drawn by two raw-boned horses. In the strange vehicle were seated Mr. and Mrs. Davis. Mr. Davis was dressed in a full suit of Confederate grey, including the hat, but his face was yet more ashen than was his garb. Behind them, completing the pitiful cortège, came a carryall, in which were Miss Howell, the Davis little ones and nurses; and, as the procession drove by, the alien and motley crowd along the walks yelled and hooted in derision. But not all—one heartless Union soldier tried the patience of a sorrowful "rebel" onlooker.

"Hey, Johnny Reb," shouted the first, "we've got your President!"

"And the devil's got yours!" was the swift reply.

As the procession arrived at the station, two soldiers approached Mr. and Mrs. Davis, and escorted them at once to the cars. The interest of everyone for the moment being centred on the party of the late President, my excitement grew. Wild thoughts filled my mind. I could not restrain them. "Oh! if they would only forget you!" I said impetuously, to my husband. Alas! scarcely had I uttered the words when two guards approached. "This is Mr. Clay, I presume?" and with a hasty farewell to our kind friends, the Whittles, we were soon aboard the cars.

As we entered, Mr. Davis rose and embraced me.

"This is a sad meeting, Jennie!" he said, as he offered me a seat beside him, for Mrs. Davis and my husband, already deep in conversation, had established themselves nearby. As I seated myself I became aware that the car had filled up with soldiers. I heard the doors slam, and the command, "Order arms!" and in the dull thud of their muskets as the butts struck the floor, I realised for the first time that we were indeed prisoners, and of the nation!

# CHAPTER XX

DAWN found us haggard and ill. Our night ride to Augusta was a fatiguing one. Of our party, only the children slept. The air in the car was of the foulest, and the discomforts of the trip were consequently most trying to our invalids, of whom there now were three—Mr. Davis, Mr. Clay, and our venerable Vice-President, Mr. Stephens, we having taken the latter aboard during the night; also, our late Postmaster-General Reagan, ex-Governor Lubbock, and General Wheeler and staff. Nor were we again permitted to leave the car until our arrival in Augusta. Telegraphic orders having been sent ahead for our meals, these were brought to the train and eaten *en route*.

Upon our arrival in Augusta, I asked Colonel Pritchard for the privilege of driving in the carriage assigned to us to the home of a beloved friend, Mrs. George Winter. Upon my promise that at the hour appointed I would be responsible for Mr. Clay's appearance on the boat which was to take us to Savannah, Colonel Pritchard gave a somewhat reluctant consent and we drove rapidly away. As had been the case in Macon and Atlanta, the town was in commotion. This visit to our friends was almost an error; for, greatly excited at our appearance among them, they embraced us in hysterical alarm, and begged my husband even yet to fly. To add to the distress, neighbouring friends, hearing of our presence, hastened in and joined their pleadings to those of our hostess. The scene was unendurable to Mr. Clay, and, literally tearing ourselves from their embraces, we re-entered the carriage. The

258

horses heads were turned at once toward the river where our custodians awaited us. Arrived there, though I cannot admit that it was our intention or impulse to board the boat with a fond alacrity, our embarkation was not without a misleading appearance of eagerness. The bank of the river was both steep and slippery, and, notwithstanding I was assisted in my descent by two officers, my approach was neither stately nor awe-inspiring. In fact, it was precipitate, and I found myself, most unexpectedly, in the arms of a soldierly little figure in undress uniform who stood close to the crude gang-plank. As I opened my lips to apologise for my unexpected onslaught, he turned and raised his hat. It was "little Joe!"

An episode of that trip in connection with General Wheeler fixed itself indelibly in my mind. I was in conversation with this hero on one occasion, during which he leaned against the side of the boat in a half-recumbent position. Presently a young officer, rude in the display of "his brief authority," approached us, and rapping General Wheeler sharply with his sword, said, "It is against the rule to lean on the guard-rail!"

To my amazement, our hero, who had fought so nobly against his peers and whose name alone had been a menace to his foes, merely touched his hat and said quietly, "I did not know the rule, sir, or I would not have infringed it." I was thrilled with admiration.

"General!" I exclaimed, "you have taught me a lesson in self-control and courtesy I can never forget! Had I been a man, that Yankee would have been exploring the bottom of the Savannah River, or I, one!"

The discomforts to which we had been subjected during our journey to and from the headquarters of General Wilson culminated in the wretched little craft on which we now were. Not a chair was in the cabin for our invalids, nor an available couch. For Mr. Davis, who suffered intensely during the trip from pain in his eye (for years a chronic disability), two valises were stacked one on top of the other, being the nearest approach to a seat it was possible to improvise. On these he rested during much of the journey, Mrs. Davis, Miss Howell or myself in turn acting as support in lieu of a chair-back. From time to time we bathed his temples with cologne in vain attempts to lessen his tortures.

Our journey from Savannah may best be pictured by reference to my pocket-diary, carried throughout those momentous weeks. We boarded the *William P. Clyde* on the fifteenth of May, our destination still unknown to us, as we steamed out into the Atlantic. These are some of the brief records I made of ship and passengers:

"May 16, 1865. *William P. Clyde* is a brig-rigged steamer, quite comfortable. The Fourth Michigan is with us, and an armed convoy, the *Tuscarora*, escorts us. Her guns bear directly upon us, day and night. Fears are entertained of the *Stonewall* or *Shenandoah*. My husband keeps well and heroic. God in mercy give us grace for the fiery ordeal."

"May 17th. Fairly at sea, and considerable fear of the *Stonewall* evinced by the ship's crew. All the axes of the vessel are removed from their usual positions to the Colonel's room. Mrs. Davis sent ashore for oranges for Miss Howell, who is ill. Poor girl!"
["It was Mr. Davis who called my attention to the removal of the battle-axes. 'Cowards!' he said, 'They're afraid of this handful of Confederate men!'"]

"May 19. Nearing Fortress Monroe. We are boarded by Captain Fraley, Commander of the *Tuscarora*, the man-of-war which has been our escort, her guns bearing directly on us from Hilton Head. The Captain called on Mr. and Mrs. Davis, and husband and myself, and renewed an acquaintance of former years. He proffered any attentions in his power. Just to our left is seen Fort Calhoun, built by Mr. Davis, while Secretary of War. . . ."

"May 20. Anchored off Fort Monroe awaiting orders. General Halleck to arrive on board at 11 A. M. I sadly fear they will land my darling at this fort.   God forbid!   In sight are many vessels, some bearing the English and some the French flags.   The fort presents the same appearance as years ago, when I went to visit the spot.   One week this day since we bade adieu to friends.   Two days have we been anchored.   General Halleck said to be on *Tuscarora*."

"May 21.   Last night at dark a tug was hailed.   She replied, "General Halleck!"   She was alongside in a few moments with orders which were quickly known.   Governor Lubbock, Colonel Johnston and General Wheeler and staff left at six this A. M. for Delaware.   At ten, Mr. Stephens and Judge Reagan were put aboard the *Tuscarora* for Fort Warren. Mr. Stephen's servant detained.   We are still in doubt, but Monroe is probably our destination."

"May 22.   Mr. Davis, Mr. Clay and Burton Harrison are all left!   Preparations are going on at Fortress Monroe for them, 'tis said.   Colonel Pritchard says I will not be allowed to land or go to Washington or Baltimore or abroad!!! Terrible firing from a man-of-war!"

"May 23.   Wrote letter to Judge Holt, and note to General Miles.   At ten we were boarded by Major Church, and two Yankee women and four guards, and all hands, luggage, berths and persons thoroughly searched.   A 'comico-serio-tragico' scene!   Sailors our friends.   Both nurses leave. Mrs. Davis's [man] Robert only left."

Our journey on the *Clyde*, though sorrowful, apprehensive as we were concerning the fate to which the prisoners were being led, was otherwise uneventful.   Mr. Davis was exceedingly depressed, and moved restlessly about, seeming scarcely ever to desire to sit down.   Always an intellectual cosmopolite, however, he made observations on the natural phenomena about us, commenting from time to time on the beauty of sea or sky.   Our meals, which were served at a table reserved for the prisoners, by no means represented the fare of the coastwise steamers of to-day, but few of us were in a mood to take note of culinary deficiencies.

On the morning of May 22d a sultry, drizzling rain fell. It was a day exactly calculated to induce melancholy even in the stoutest-hearted. To us, eagerly alert to learn what we might of our fate, it was unspeakably distressful. Shortly after breakfast my husband came quietly into our stateroom. "There is no longer any doubt," he said, "that this fort is the one destined for Davis and me! I have just been notified that we are expected to take a ride on a tug. I am convinced we shall be taken to Fortress Monroe. I can't imagine why they do not come out boldly and tell us so, but be sure this is our farewell, my wife!" We took leave of each other in our stateroom, nor did I leave it to follow Mr. Clay to the deck. I stood, instead, at the fourteen-inch window of my cabin, alone with my thoughts.

As Mr. Davis passed the aperture, he stopped for a second to say good-bye to me, then he, too, disappeared. A few moments passed, and then the weeping of children and wailing of women announced the return of the stricken family. I heard a soldier say to Mr. Davis's little son, "Don't cry, Jeff. They ain't going to hang your pa!" and the little fellow's reply, made through his sobs.

"When I get to be a man," he cried, "I'm going to kill every Yankee I see!"

When the child approached my door and I caught him in my arms and tried to cheer him, his resentment quickly changed to a manly tenderness; and, putting his baby lips up for a kiss, he said, "My papa told me to keep care of you and my Mamma!"

I referred in my diary to the serio-comic incidents of the search of our party. The event occurred early in the morning of the day following that of my husband's removal. While gazing sadly across the waters toward the grim fort, I espied what seemed to be a pretty shallop, dancing lightly over the waters, in which were seated two women, brightly dressed. The little vessel seemed to be making for the *Clyde*. When I observed this, I called Mrs. Davis's attention to the approaching party, saying, "Thank God! Here, I do believe, are two Virginia ladies come to give us some comfort."

In a few moments one of our unknown visitors was at my cabin door. In my eagerness to meet a friendly face, I had almost extended my hand, when something in the appearance of the person before me struck me as peculiar. My surprise and curiosity was soon relieved, for my visitor said glibly, "We've been sent by the Government to see if you have any treasonable papers on board!" I looked at her in amazement.

"Is it possible," I asked, "that the United States Government thinks we are such simpletons as to have carried treasonable papers aboard this ship?" My indignation grew.

"I frankly confess that if I could sink the whole Yankee nation in Hampton Roads I would do so; but carry valuable papers *here*? Pshaw!" and I turned away from her, full of contempt.

It was a hot, sultry day; one of those May days when the sun strikes the water vertically, and even breathing becomes a fatiguing effort. Despite the weather, the women who had thus unexpectedly presented themselves were greatly overdressed. Each wore an immense chignon on the back of her head, and was rouged and powdered and befrizzed to an extent that was altogether unusual in ordinary circles. Bustles of the largest size, high-heeled shoes, conspicuous stockings, and as freely revealed gay petticoats completed the gaudy costumes of these remarkable agents of the Government. The person who had addressed me entered my cabin and proceeded to strip the pillow-case from the by no means immaculate pillow. She shook and felt carefully each article of bedding; then opened my valise and as minutely examined every article of borrowed finery therein. She commented on their quality as she did so, but I speedily put an end to this. "Proceed with your work, Madam!" I said, and I turned from the unpleasant sight before me.

As she emptied my gripsack, I heard her utter a half-shriek of alarm.

"Oh!" she cried, "you have a pistol!"

"Of course I have," I said, complacently reaching for it and taking it in my hand; and, a spirit of mischief seizing me (it has often been my salvation), I twirled the alarming firearm in the air, taking care that the barrel should fall pointing toward her, saying, as I did so, "You may take everything in the stateroom but this. If necessary, I shall use it!" As I marked the effect of my words, her shrinking and ejaculations of fear amused me more and more, nor did she resume her work until, tired of the farce, the pistol was once more safely bestowed in my bag. When she renewed her search, her manner was somewhat more timid.

Upon completing the overhauling of my belongings she turned to me. "Will you please take off your dress, Madam?" she said. My answer was forceful and prompt.

"I will not! If you wish it taken off, you may disrobe me!" And I added, in my indignation, "I've heard that white maids are as good as black ones!"

And now the comedy moved rapidly. The lady began by taking off my breastpin and my collar. She unfastened my bodice and removed it, examining every seam with a microscopic care. She then proceeded to remove my clothing piece by piece, submitting each to the same scrupulous examination. Coming at last to my stays, she attempted to unclasp them.

The situation was so amusing I could not resist the growing desire to accentuate it. I have alluded to the prevailing sultry weather. In the close little cabin, the heat was scarce bearable. Already perspiration was trickling in streams down the cheeks of my unwelcome visitor. Smiling within myself as the lady came forward to remove the last-named garment, I took a full, deep breath and held it, expanding my form to the very utmost, tightening my clothing for the time being to such an extent that I think she could scarcely have pried open the garments with hammer and chisel. The efforts of my tormentor (?) were entertaining. Every now and then between a straining on my part and a futile tugging on hers, she would run out of the cabin, fanning herself and gasping to the guards, "Oh! I am nearly dead!"

At first, I utilised these intervals "to gird on my armour" still tighter; but, at last, when I was myself almost exhausted from holding my breath, I relaxed and allowed her to proceed. By the time her examination of my apparel and belongings was completed, the lady's face was striped, and the path of the perspiration, wending its way through layers of cosmetics, had quite destroyed her erstwhile dazzling appearance; but though I, too, was almost fainting from the heat, and would gladly have been left alone, my determination to tease her was by no means appeased. I, therefore, demanded that, having undressed me, the lady complete her work and put my clothing on again. This, with various delays, amusing and otherwise, she at last accomplished, much to her satisfaction if not wholly to mine. Once rehabilitated, I stepped to Mrs. Davis's stateroom, mine being between those of Mrs. Davis and Miss Howell. I found the former in tears and reduced to the lightest of deshabille. I tried to comfort her, but she still wept, saying:

"Oh, 'Ginie! What humiliation!"

"But I would die before they should see me shed tears!" I declared.

"Ah, you haven't four little children about you," said Mrs. Davis. Nor did this search end the trials that befell us while we lay in Hampton Roads. Upon leaving my stateroom the following morning I met Mrs. Davis, baby Winnie in arms. She was greatly agitated.

"What has happened?" I asked.

"That man!" she replied, pointing to an officer near by, "has come to take away my shawl. It's the last wrapping I have! He declares it is part of Mr. Davis's disguise!"

"You're not going to let him have it?" I asked, my indignation rising at once.

"What can I do?" asked Mrs. Davis, wringing her hands.

"Tear it into shreds as fine as vermicelli!" I cried, "and throw it into Hampton Roads!"

As I spoke the officer stepped toward us. Raising his hand and shaking his finger in my face, he asked, threateningly, "You dare counsel resistance, Madam?"

"Yes!" I retorted, returning the finger-shaking, "To the shedding of blood, and I'll begin with you!"

The scene must have been a ludicrous one to all save the two participants. Mrs. Davis's spirits certainly rose in contemplating it, for, as the officer strutted off, his sword dragging at his side, she smiled as she said, "Puss-in-boots!" In a second, however, her anxiety returned.

"What shall we do?" she asked. "He will surely come back for the shawl." Bent upon foiling him, I quickly suggested an expedient.

"My shawl," I said, "is almost a counterpart of yours. Let's fold them both up and make him guess which is which. Perhaps he'll take mine!" and we laughed heartily at the device.

It was not long ere Lieutenant Hudson returned, this time with another shawl, a coarse thing such as the small stores nearby afforded. Upon his repeated demand we complacently handed him Mrs. Davis's shawl and mine.

To our amazement he took them both.    Then, as the old saying puts it, we "laughed on the other side of our faces."    For, by the aid of one of Mrs. Davis's former maids, Lieutenant Hudson was enabled to identify Mrs. Davis's shawl, which he retained, returning mine.    The first, for many years, was preserved among the curios of the Smithsonian Institution.

During the morning of the day made memorable by the visit of the Government's searching party, General Miles and his staff boarded the *Clyde*.    It was my first meeting with the handsome young officer who was destined to incur so much odium in the near future for his treatment of the unfortunate ex-President of the Confederate States.    I can recall no particulars of that first meeting with my husband's jailor, save that he and his staff made an impressive group as they stood bowing respectfully, while a few civil words were spoken by their leader.

Upon the question of the latter, as to whether he might serve me in any way, I answered, "Yes! let me know, from time to time, whether my husband lives or is dead.    If you will do this it will relieve me from an insupportable suspense!"    To this he kindly agreed.

In the interim, I had sent to my husband his valise, containing some gold and my Bible, which, being set in a specially large type, I knew he would be glad to have. These were brought back to me shortly after General Miles's visit, by an officer who found us still at the mess table.    My Bible was returned to me because of the following "communication from Mrs. Clay, written on the fly-leaf."

"2 P. M.  Ship-board.  May, '65.  With tearful eyes and aching heart, I commend you, my precious husband, to the care and keeping of Almighty God.  May He bless you, and keep you, and permit us once again to meet, shall be my unceasing prayer.  Farewell,                          WIFE."

As the officer dropped the gold upon the table beside me, he said, "Please count it, Madam!" I instantly declined to do this, however, saying, "If General Miles sent it, I presume it is correct," and swept it into my lap without further examination.

# CHAPTER XXI

## RETURN FROM FORTRESS MONROE

By the second day after the incarceration of Mr. Davis and Mr. Clay we were a heartsick company, and I was glad when, in the late afternoon of the twenty-fourth of May, our sailing orders came. During the last day we were anchored off Fortress Monroe, two hundred paroled prisoners had been taken aboard the *Clyde*, a small and stuffy boat at best, and the five days spent upon the return trip added to our anguish of mind by much physical discomfort. The sea was exceedingly rough. Often during the voyage a hundred or more passengers at a time were confined below. Those who were well found their cabins unendurably warm. In mine, the gossip of the negroes and sailors on the lower deck was clearly audible; and, as their themes ran principally upon the probable fate of the prisoners, questionable as I knew the source to be from which flowed the conversations, the gossip did not serve to lessen my melancholy, though it keyed my alertness to a higher pitch.

Some hours previous to our departure from Hampton Roads, in sheer exhaustion from the experiences that had crowded upon us, I lay down in my cabin, a prey to mingled heart-aching and bitterness; when, looking toward the door, I perceived a sentinel on guard. What I took to be an added indignity made me resentful. I spoke to him.

"You are a brave man, standing there with bayonet in hand to terrorise a wretched woman!" I said. He turned slightly, "Mrs. Clay," he answered, "You ought to be glad to have me here guarding you, for this boat is full of rough soldiers!" In a moment my wrath was turned to gratitude. I thanked him, and I felt that in him, thereafter, I had a friend; indeed, we had reason to feel that all aboard who dared to show it felt pity for and kindness toward our desolate party.

During the trip, as Mrs. Davis, Miss Howell and I sat at night on deck, looking out over the seas, I thought the swish of the waters against the *Clyde's* side was as melancholy a note as I had ever heard. One evening we had sat thus, discussing our situation and the dangers that surrounded us, when, rising to return to my state-room, I felt my dress slightly pulled. Thinking my skirts had become entangled in the rope coils or rigging near us, I reached out to detach them, when, to my alarm, I found my hand in contact with another, and into mine was thrust a bundle of newspapers. I could not have thanked the sailor who handed them to me had I had the presence of mind to do so, for, passing swiftly on his way, he was lost in the darkness ere I could identify him. The roll was in my hand, however, and I made my way quickly to the cabin with it. They were the first news-papers we had had since arriving at the Fortress. By the light of the dim cabin lamp I read them. The aggregation of "opinions of the press" was so awful in its animosity that they stunned my very power of thought. One extract burnt itself into my brain. It ran, "We hope soon to see the bodies of these two arch traitors, Davis and Clay, dangling and blackening in the wind and rain!"

The horror of these printed words for the moment overbalanced my reason. I hastened with it to Mrs. Davis; a great mistake, for her agony of mind upon reading it was such that restoratives were necessary to prevent her from fainting. I never knew who the sailor was who gave the papers to me, though I was more fortunate in regard to the author of another kindness which, happily, was less reactionary upon me.

Immediately upon my husband's incarceration I had busied myself in writing letters to a list of distinguished public men which had been prepared for my use by Mr. Clay. It included the name of Joseph Holt, who, once our friend, had deplored the possible loss to the nation of my husband's counsels. My list comprised thirteen names, the number that has been accounted unlucky since thirteen sat at the table of our Lord and one betrayed him. In view of the months of persecution, which followed my husband's surrender, directly traceable to malice or fanatical zeal in the Judge Advocate's office, an analogy is unavoidable. My list included the names of T. W. Pierce, of Boston, Ben. Wood, owner and editor of the New York *Daily News*, R. J. Halderman, Charles O'Conor, the great jurist, Judge Jeremiah Black and others. To Mr. Holt I wrote as follows:

"OFF FORTRESS MONROE ON STEAMER *Clyde*,
"May 23, 1865.

"JUDGE ADVOCATE GENERAL HOLT.

"*My Dear Sir:* The circumstances of my husband's voluntary surrender to the Federal authorities, to meet the charges against him, doubtless have reached you, as General Wilson, commanding at Macon, promised to telegraph as well as write you immediately of it. We left Macon on the 13th, in company with other prisoners, General Wilson permitting me to accompany Mr. Clay without orders or restrictions. For five days we have lain at this spot awaiting events. Yesterday morning, with five minutes' warning only, my husband was taken to Fortress Monroe. As no communication is permitted, I am denied appeals to Generals Miles or Halleck, but entertain strong hope that one or the other may arrive to-day to relieve my suspense.

"But the object of this letter is to appeal to you, in this moment of dire necessity, on behalf my dear husband. You, Judge Holt, now the embodiment of the 'majesty of the law,' were once pleased to subscribe yourself my 'sincere friend.' I will not believe that time or circumstances have changed your feelings toward one who reciprocated that friendship and was beloved by your angelic wife. So, into your hands, my dear sir, I commit my precious husband's case, begging that you will see to it that he receives proper counsel and a fair and impartial trial, from which he will surely come forth vindicated. Of course, you have some appearance of testimony in your courts or the proclamation would not have been issued, but I also believe that you esteem Mr. Clay as innocent of that horrid crime, as I know him to be. Hold the scales of mercy and justice as our great and final Judge will hold them in your and my cases when we stand at the Bar, and I shall fear no evil. Write me a line at Macon, if you please, and, if possible, permit me to visit my husband. With kindest regards to . . . believe me,

" ETC."

With the exception of the Archbishop of Bermuda, who was away from his post, as I learned some time later, only Mr. Holt, of the thirteen written to, ignored my appeal.

Having taken the precaution to give to each correspondent an address at which, under cover, replies might reach me, I sealed and addressed each letter preparatory for posting; but now I found myself in a quandary as to how I should accomplish this important feat. I held them for several days uncertain as to whose care I might intrust them. As we were approaching Hilton Head, however, a soldier, whom I had observed passing and repassing the open door of my cabin, tossed in a slip of paper on which was written, "I will mail your letters. Trust me." As there was nothing treasonable in them, and the need was urgent for getting them swiftly to their several destinations, I concluded to accept the offer so miraculously made.

I therefore rolled them up, and, putting a gold dollar in a bit of paper, awaited the reappearance of my unknown messenger. In a few moments he came, and I slipped the little parcel into his hands.   That afternoon I heard a careless whistler pass my door and the bit of gold was tossed into my stateroom, and with excellent aim, too, for it fell directly upon my berth.   The friendly stranger had refused to retain sufficient coin to pay for the postage. Before leaving the *Clyde* I ascertained his name.   He was Charles McKim, of Philadelphia.

Such kindly aid unexpectedly extended to us by a stranger now and then had its own part in stimulating and encouraging us during a voyage in which a thousand hopes and fears and memories tortured us.   The very coast-line, there in the distance, seemed to write on the horizon the story of our disasters.   We passed on our way within one hundred yards of desolate, historic Sumter, over which the Union flag floated, and the solitary sentinel pacing his rounds was visible to us. Beyond lay Charleston, her outlines placid, though we knew she was scarred within.

Our journey, as I have stated, was full of discomfort. Our cabins were far from clean, and chamber service we had none save that performed by Mrs. Davis's coloured servant, Robert, who attended to our needs; and so soiled were the pillows that we were obliged to pin over them our white petticoats before retiring, these being our only protection against the nocturnal invaders that thronged in the bedding.   It will be concluded, therefore, that, upon our arrival in Savannah, we were a rather bedraggled and travel-stained party.   Our original supply of clothing for the trip had been small, and the service demanded of it thus far had been in exactly an inverse ratio.   It required some courage, therefore, as well as ingenuity, to arrange our toilettes in such manner as would help us to a condition of outward composure.   I, having no little ones to care for, was most abundantly provided, and was, therefore, enabled to contribute to my less fortunate companion, Mrs. Davis, my black silk

Talma, a loose garment of those days much used in travelling.

We heard at once, upon stepping ashore at Savannah, that the Federal authorities had prohibited our party the use of carriages, and the absence of friendly faces at the wharf told us that the date of our arrival had also been kept a secret. We were, therefore, obliged to begin our walk up the acclivity that led to the Pulaski House without the moral support of a friendly presence. Those of the young children who could toddle did so; but the infant, Winnie, was carried by Miss Howell, Robert following behind with such luggage as he could "tote." We were a sad procession!

We had nearly reached the hotel, when a party of gentlemen, seeing us, stopped in the midst of a conversation and eyed us a second. Among them were our friends, Mr. Frederick Myers and Mr. Green. Upon recognising our party, first one and then another of the group caught up the children and bore them on their shoulders into the Pulaski House.

The news of our arrival spread over the city at once, and an impromptu levee was begun which lasted until late in the night. It was followed, the next day, by gifts of flowers and fruit, and, what was immediately needful, of clothing of every description. The people of Savannah acted as by one great impulse of generosity, all eager to demonstrate their devotion to the prisoners now in the hands of the United States Government, and to us, their representatives. We found in the city many of our former Washington and Richmond friends, among whom were ex-Senator Yulee, of Florida, and General Mercer. Savannah was in a state of continual disquiet. The air rang with sounds of fifes and drums of Federal soldiers, and bands of triumphant music were encountered in every direction. Drills were constant and innumerable, and fully as unpleasant to our eyes as our conquerors could wish; but, to my Southern mind, no sight was so sad, and none presented so awful a travesty on the supposed dignity of arms, as the manœuvres of a regiment of negroes in full dress!

However, I was in no mood to think resentfully upon these minor evils of our times; for, notwithstanding the kindnesses shown our party on every side, my apprehensions for my husband's safety increased as the journals of each day gave out their horrors. The news that Mr. Davis, saddened, ill, strengthless, as we knew him to be, had been put in chains, startled us. Not a soul in the South but was horrified at the wanton act, and none, I think, will ever forgive the deed though its authorship has remained unacknowledged to this day. The press, both North and South, was filled with alarming prognostications and with news of the gathering testimony which would fix the crime with which the ex-President and my husband were charged, upon them. Items which I might not otherwise have seen were clipped from Northern papers and sent to me by friends eager to acquaint me with news of every development which might warn or strengthen. From mysterious purlieus, witnesses were being brought forward on whose awful testimony were to be formulated, it was said, charges of heinous crime against the prisoners of state. What this testimony was to be, who was to give it, were mysteries to me. I tried in vain to communicate with Mr. Clay, and on the 8th of June, unable longer to endure the suspense, I wrote to General Miles, imploring him to send me at least one line to assure me of Mr. Clay's welfare; at the same time inclosing a second letter to Judge Advocate General Holt.

To add to my distress of mind, the interest of the newspapers, being now concerned with the Surratt and other trials, became silent for the time being on the cases of Messrs. Davis and Clay, and, until the receipt of a letter from General Miles, I was uncertain of my husband's whereabouts, rumours having reached me of his having been transferred to Fort Warren. A letter received at this time from General James H. Wilson records that he, too, was under this impression. Waiting from day to day in the hope of ascertaining some definite information concerning Mr. Clay, and having established communication with friends in various quarters, I now began to shape my plans for a return to Huntsville, meanwhile offering such consolations to my companions as was in my power. Only the uncomprehending children of our party seemed happily free from the weight of trouble everywhere besetting us. I remember an amusing incident in connection with the little Jeff., our manly protector, just previous to my leaving the hotel to accept the hospitality of friends. He had scarcely arrived, when he formed an attachment for a fine Newfoundland dog, a regular attaché of the popular hostelry. While Mrs. Davis and I were entertaining some of Savannah's kind people, we heard Jeff.'s voice shouting every now and then in uproarious good humour, "Bully for Jeff.! Bully for Jeff.!" At last I went out to reason with him. I found him successfully mounted on his canine acquaintance, a strong bridle in one hand, a switch in the other.

"You shouldn't say 'Bully for Jeff.,'" I remonstrated. "It isn't nice. You must remember whose boy you are!" The little fellow looked nonplussed.

"Well!" he said, ruefully, "Mis' Clay, if a fellow don't bully for hisself, who's going to bully for him?" I gazed at him, puzzled. This was a Waterloo for me. I answered, "Well, bully for yourself! but don't bully so loud," and retreated to the parlour, leaving the little lad to cogitate on whether he or I was master of the situation.

I lingered in Savannah, eagerly awaiting letters which I hoped would meet me there, until the middle of June, when I proceeded to Macon, *en route* for Huntsville, and I am amused now at the contrariety of the human memory, when, into the woof of the thoughts of those strenuous days, there is thrust a thread of comedy.   Just before leaving the hospitable coast city, I was the guest of Mrs. Levy, mother of the brilliant Mrs. Philip Phillips, of Washington, of Mrs. Pember, and of Miss Martha Levy, one of the readiest wits I have ever known.

During the evening first referred to, many guests were introduced, among them some of Savannah's prominent Hebrews.   For an hour Miss Martha had been busy presenting her friends, both Christian and Jew, when, one after another, came Mr. Cohen, Mr. Salomon, Dr. Lazarus and Dr. Mordecai.   At this remarkable procession my risibles proved triumphant.   I glanced slyly at Miss Martha.   Her eyes shone with mischief as she presented Dr. Mordecai.

"And is Haman here, too?" I asked.

# CHAPTER XXII

## RECONSTRUCTION DAYS BEGIN

UPON leaving Savannah I proceeded by boat to Augusta, reaching that city on the fifteenth of June, going thence to Macon, escorted to Atlanta by Colonel Woods. During the last half of my journey I was under the care of General B. M. Thomas, who saw me safely into the hands of our kind friends, the Whittles, whose hospitable home became my asylum until I proceeded on my way to Huntsville. The necessity for procuring passports through the several military districts made my journey a slow one. To add to my discomforts, my trunks, recovered at Macon, were several times rigorously searched ere I reached my destination. At every transfer station my baggage was carefully scrutinised, and the small value in which passports were held may be conjectured from the following incident.

At a certain point in my homeward journey a change of cars became necessary at a little wayside town. Night was already upon us when we reached the station of Crutchfield, where the transfer was to be made. The little structure was surrounded by hangers-on, threading their lazy way through a small company of black and white soldiers. I was alone, save for the little five-year-old son of my maid, Emily, who, being ill, I had left at the home of Mrs. Whittle. No sooner had my trunk been deposited on the platform than it became the object of rough handling and contumely. The train on which I was to continue my journey was already in position, but the close-pressing crowd about were heedless alike of my protest and appeals to allow my baggage to be put aboard. I begged them not to detain me, saying I had General Croxton's passport with me; but their only answer was a gruff rebuke. "You have passed his jurisdiction, Madam," said one of the military near by.

It was a black night, and but few of those about me carried lanterns. The scene was fear-inspiring to a lonely woman. My alarm at the thought of a detention had reached its height, when, by the fitful lights about, I saw a tall young man break through the crowd.

"By what right do you detain this lady?" he cried, angrily. Then, turning to the black figures around us, he commanded, "Put that trunk on board the car!" and almost before I realised it my difficulties were over, and I had myself stepped aboard the waiting train, rescued from my unfortunate dilemma by John A. Wyeth, since become a surgeon of national distinction. Mr. Wyeth had come to the station for the purpose of boarding this train, which proved a happy circumstance, for it gave me his protection to Stevenson, a few hours distant from Huntsville. His father had been the long-time friend of my husband; moreover, Dr. Allen, grandfather of the young knight-errant, had been one of Senator Clay's earliest instructors. Thus, the circumstance of our meeting was a source of double gratification to me.

While a guest at the home of Colonel Lewis M. Whittle, being unceasing in my efforts to secure all possible aid for and to arouse our friends in behalf of my husband, I made several trips of a day or so to other homes in the vicinity. During such an absence, the Whittle home was invaded by a party of soldiers, headed by one General Baker, who made what was meant to be a very thorough search of all my belongings, despite the protests of my gentle hostess. But for her quick presence of mind in sending for a locksmith, the locks of my trunks would have been broken open by the ungallant invaders. I returned to find my friends in deep trouble and anguish of mind on my behalf. They repeated the story of the search with much distress of manner. From the disorder in which I found my room when, shortly afterward, I entered it, these agents of the Government must have hoped to find there the whole assassination plot. Clothing of every description was strewn over the floor and bed and chairs; while on mantelpiece and tables were half-smoked cigar stumps and ashes left by the gentlemen who took part in that memorable paper hunt. After a thorough examination of my wardrobe, piece by piece, they had taken possession of numerous letters and photographs, almost purely of a private character, among them the picture of my dead infant, treasured beyond any other. My hostess informed me that, during the process of searching, General Baker, regardless of her presence, personally had commented on the quality of my lingerie and the probable avoirdupois of its owner, saying, among other things, "I see none of the destitution I've heard tell of in the South!" In his eagerness to discourse on the beauty of a lady's apparel, he overlooked a recess in one of my trunks which contained the only written matter that, by any turning of words, might have been designated treasonable.

Great, indeed, was my surprise, when, seated on the floor surveying the disorder about, overwhelmed with a conviction of desolation to come, I opened one secret little slide and looked within the pocket. Now my chagrin and disappointment were changed to joy; for there, within, lay the sermon-like, black-covered book that contained my husband's careful copies of his State correspondence while in Canada, together with other important original papers! The sight was almost too good to be true! Immediately I began to see all things more hopefully. I remember even a feeling of merriment as I gazed upon one of my husband's boots standing just where it had been thrown, in the middle of the floor, while hung around it was a wreath of once gorgeous pomegranate flowers, which I recognised as those I had worn at one of the last functions I had attended in the Federal City.

Many months passed, in which repeated demands were made for the letters carried away by these emissaries of the Government, ere they were returned to me. Though taken thus forcibly from me for Governmental examination, I have no reason to conclude that those in authority at the War Department detained them for so serious a reason or purpose. On the contrary, I have ground for believing that my letters and other possessions lay open for seven or eight months to the gaze of the more curious friends of the department authorities; for, my friend, Mrs. Bouligny,* early in '66, wrote warning me in regard to them, "I heard a lady say the other day that she knew of a person who had read your journal at the War Department!" By this time I was again in the North, pleading with President Johnson for the release of my husband and the return of my papers. When, at last, I received them, they were delivered to me at the home of Mrs. A. S. Parker, at 4½ and C Streets, Washington, by a Federal officer, who came in a United States Mail wagon with his burden!

My home-coming after the eventful trip to Fortress Monroe was a sore trial. Ex-Governor Clay, now an old man of seventy-five years, and Mrs. Clay, almost as aged (and nearer, by six months, to the grave, as events soon proved), were both very much broken. For more than three years they had waited and wept and prayed for the loved cause which, in its fall, had borne down their first-born. The Clay home, every stone of which was hallowed to them, was now occupied by Captain Peabody

* Then widow of Congressman Bouligny, of Louisiana, and now Mrs. George Collins Levey, of London, England.

and his staff. Servants and all other of their former possessions were scattered; and Mother Clay, whose beautiful patrician hands had never known the soil of labour, who, throughout her long life of piety and gentle surroundings, had been shielded as tenderly as some rare blossom, now, an aged woman, within but a few months of the tomb, bereft of even her children, was compelled to perform all necessary household labour. The last and bitterest pain, that of my husband's incarceration, fell crushingly upon her. Her son, who had added lustre to his distinguished father's name, who in private virtues had met every wish of her heart, now lay a prisoner in the nation's hands, and the nation itself had gone mad with the desire to wreak a vengeance on some one for the deplorable act of a madman. The knowledge came to her as a very death-dealing blow, the climax of years of unintermitting anxiety, deprivations, and the small tyrannies practised by our many invaders during the investment of Huntsville. Friends and kindred had been cut down on every side. For three years our little city had been in Union hands. None of her formerly affluent citizens but had been impoverished or ruined. By the summer of '65, the country about was completely devastated.

The crops were inconsiderable; scarcely any cotton had been planted, and the appalling cotton tax had already been invented to drain us still further. All over the South "Reconstruction days" had begun. Confusion of a kind reigned in every town or city. It was no longer a question of equality between the Freedmen and their late masters, but of negro supremacy. On every side the poor, unknowing creatures sought every opportunity to impress the fact of their independence upon all against whom they bore resentment. The women were wont to gather on the sidewalks of the main thoroughfares, forming a line across as they sauntered along, compelling their former masters and mistresses who happened to be approaching to take the street; or, if not sufficiently numerous or courageous to do this, would push their way by them, bumping into them with a distinct challenge to the outraged one to resent it.   As if to encourage this spirit of "independence," the agents of the conquering Government were there to protect their protégés from the indignant resentment such conduct might well awaken, though they seemed not to be equipped to instruct them in better things.

Upon my return to Huntsville, after Mr. Clay's incarceration, having been absent from it now nearly four years, I found the metamorphosis in the beautiful old town to be complete.   Indignation at the desecration about us was the one antidote to despair left to the majority of our neighbours, who, their property seized, their fields unplanted, their purses empty, had small present peace or ground for hope in the future.   Indignities, petty and great, multiplied each day at the hands of often wholly inexperienced Federal representatives, who, finding themselves in authority over the persons and property of men distinguished throughout the land, knew not how to exercise it.   Looking back upon those frightful years, I am convinced that these agents, far more than our enemies who strove with our heroes upon the field, are responsible for a transmitted resentment that was founded upon the unspeakable horrors of "Reconstruction days."   Happy, indeed, was it for us that the future was hidden from us; for, bad as the conditions were that met my husband's family then, there were to be yet other and worse developments.   Our home, opposite to that of Governor Clay, was now occupied by one Goodlow, head of the Freedmen's Bureau.   From the one wing of the parental house to which ex-Governor and Mrs. Clay were now limited, only the sorry sight met our eyes of the desecration of our once lovely residence,

—the galleries and portico of which were now the gathering place for protégés of the Government. Daily I saw Alfred, the former dining-room servant of Governor Clay, revelling in his newly acquired liberty, dash by our dwelling, seated in a handsome buggy behind a fine trotter. He was a handsome copper-coloured negro, with the blood of red men in his veins. His yellow gauntlets were conspicuous two streets away, and as he passed he left on the evening air the odour of the Jessamine pomade with which he had saturated his straight Indian locks in his effort to outdo his late master.

Poor Alfred! He was a child with a toy balloon. A few years passed. In tattered attire, and with the humblest demeanor, he eked out a scanty living at a meagre little luncheon-stand on the corner of a thoroughfare. His former respect and regard for his old master now returned, and with it, I doubt not, a longing for the days when, in his fresh linen suits, laundered by the laundress of the Governor's household, a valued servant, he had feasted on the good things he himself had assisted in concocting !

Ground to the earth as we were by the cruelties of the times, that Freedman's Bureau was frequently, nevertheless, a source of amusement. Its name bore but one meaning to the simple-minded follower of the mule-tail who appealed to it. He knew but one "bureau" in the world, and that was "ole Missus's" or "Mis' Mary's," an unapproachable piece of furniture with a given number of drawers. Bitter was the disappointment of the innocent blacks when they failed to see the source whence came their support.

"Whar's dat bureau?" was sure to be the first question. "Whar all dem drawers what got de money an' de sugar an' de coffee? God knows I neber see no bureau 't all, an' dat man at de book-cupboard * talked mighty short ter me, at dat !"

* Desk.

While letting my thoughts linger for a moment on those dreary days, I cannot refrain from recalling one of the occasional instances of humane conduct shown us by those placed in authority over the citizens of Huntsville, associated, as it is, with a bit of genuine negro blundering. The generosity of Dr. French, Medical Director, there stationed, toward the family of our brother, J. Withers Clay, in giving his medical services freely to them, greatly touched us all. Appreciating his obvious desire to administer to our wounded spirits a true "oil and wine," my sister one morning gathered a bunch of fragrant camomile blossoms, and, calling her ebony *femme de menage* to her, she said, "Take these flowers over to Dr. French and say Mrs. Clay sends them with her compliments. Tell him that these camomile blossoms are like the Southern ladies—the more they are bruised and oppressed the sweeter and stronger they grow! Now," she added, "tell me, Sally, what are you going to say?" Sally answered promptly:

"I'se gwine tell de doctor dat Mis' Mary Clay sont her compliments an' dese cammile flowers, an' says dey's like de Southern ladies, de harder you squeezes an' presses 'em de sweeter dey gits!"

It is perhaps unnecessary to relate that the message which reached the kind doctor was put in written form.

# CHAPTER XXIII

## News from Fortress Monroe

To minister to my husband's aged parents dulled in some degree my own alarms, yet the wildest rumours continued to multiply as to the probably early trial and certainly awful fate of Mr. Davis and Mr. Clay. Controversies were waging in the press, both condemning and approving the actions of the Military Commission in Washington; yet, even in those still early days of his imprisonment, voices were raised in many localities to declare Mr. Clay's incapability of the crimes imputed to him.*

Meantime, reputable men in Canada, who adduced indubitable proof of the truth of the accusations they made, had already assailed the characters of the witnesses upon whom the Bureau of Military Justice so openly relied to convict its distinguished prisoners—witnesses by whose testimony some had already perished on the gallows. How true these accusations were was proved a year later, when, his misdoings exposed on the floor of the House of Representatives, a self-confessed perjurer, Conover, the chief reliance of the Bureau of Military Justice, the chief accuser of my husband, fled the country. At this *dénouement*, Representative Rogers openly averred his belief that the flight of Conover, one of the most audacious of modern criminals, had been assisted by some one high in authority, in order to make impossible an investigation into the disgraceful culpability of the high unknown!

* "It were as easy," wrote one editor, "to suspect General Lee of duplicity, or General Butler of magnanimity, as to think Mr. Clay guilty of the crimes imputed to him!"

So early as June 10, 1865, a pamphlet had been printed and circulated throughout the country by the Rev. Stuart Robinson, exposing *seriatim* the "Infamous Perjuries of the Bureau of the Military Justice." It took the form of a letter to the Hon. H. H. Emmons, United States District-Attorney at Detroit, and was quoted, when not printed in full, by many leading newspapers. Throughout the closely printed pages the paper presented an exposé of the unworthy character of the most prominent witnesses on whose testimony the hapless Mrs. Surratt and her companions had been condemned to the gallows; witnesses, moreover, who were known to be the accusers of Mr. Davis and Mr. Clay, who, it was announced, were soon to be tried for complicity in the murder of the late Federal President. In his pamphlet, Mr. Robinson did not content himself with refuting the statements made by the miscreant witnesses. He went further and accused Mr. Holt (by name), head of the Bureau of Military Justice, of being *particeps criminis* with the evil men whose testimony he so credulously or maliciously employed.

"If any one supposes," wrote Mr. Robinson, "I have judged Mr. Holt uncharitably in making him *particeps criminis* with this villain"—a notorious witness—"whom he parades and assists in the work of lying himself out of his previous perjuries by still more preposterous lies, let him carefully ponder this letter. . . . This is the man whom Judge Advocate Holt, after his perjuries have been exposed, brings back to the stand and assists in his attempts to force his lies down the throat of the American people. Who now," Mr. Robinson continued, "is the base criminal—Judge Holt, or the men whom he seeks by such base and impudent perjuries, under the garb of sworn testimony, to defame?"

Such a brave challenge might well have been expected to give the Government pause. To the increased agony of our minds, its agents took no cognisance of Mr. Robinson's fearless exposure, but ignored the protest with its startling array of charges, which easily might have been verified, and continued to rely upon its strange allies to assist in the persecution of its prison victims.

Instinct with the zeal of the fanatic, and intrenched behind the bewildered Mr. Johnson, the Head of the Bureau of Military Justice was indifferent alike to contumely and the appeals of even the merely just. In so far as the country at large might see, its Judge Advocate was imperial in his powers. The legality of the existence of the Bureau had been denied by the greatest jurists of the times; yet its dominating spirit was determined, despite the gravest warnings and condemnation, to railroad, by secret trial, the more distinguished of the prisoners to the gallows. "Thoughtful men," Reverdy Johnson had said in his argument in the trial of Mrs. Surratt, "feel aggrieved that such a Commission should be established in this free country when the war is over, and when the common law courts are open and accessible. Innocent parties, sometimes by private malice, sometimes for a mere partisan purpose, sometimes from a supposed public policy, have been made the subjects of criminal accusation. History is full of such instances. How are such parties to be protected if a public trial be denied them, and a secret one in whole or in part be substituted?"

"The Judge Advocate said, in reply to my inquiries," said Thomas Ewing, "that he would expect to convict *under the common law of war*. This is a term unknown to our language, *a quiddity* incapable of definition." And, again, "The Judge Advocate, with whom chiefly rests the fate of these citizens, from his position cannot be an impartial judge unless he be more than man. He is the Prosecutor in the most extended sense of the word. As in duty bound before this court was called, he received the reports of detectives, pre-examined the witnesses, prepared and officially signed the charges, and, as principal counsel for the Government, controlled on the trial the presentation, admission and rejection of evidence. In our courts of law, a lawyer who heard his client's story, if transferred from the bar to the bench, may not sit in the trial of the cause, lest the ermine be sullied through the partiality of the counsel."

To our sad household at distant Huntsville, each day, with its disquieting rumours and reports of these trials, added to our distress of mind. There was scarcely a man or woman in the South who did not prophesy that, the popular cry being "Vengeance," and full military power in the hands of such men as Stanton and Holt, our former President and Mr. Clay would surely meet the fate of Mrs. Surratt.

Under the domination of such knowledge, my condition of mind was a desperate one. We were nearly a thousand miles removed from the seat of Government and from my husband's prison. The Bureau of Military Justice, it was well known, was industriously seeking to convict its prisoners; while the latter, ignorant even of the charges against them, and denied the visits of counsel or friends, were helpless to defend themselves, however easy to obtain the proof might be. It were impossible for a wife, knowing her husband to be innocent, and resenting the ignobleness of a government which would thus refuse to a self-surrendered prisoner the courtesies the law allows to the lowest of criminals, to rest passively under conditions so alarming.

From the moment I stepped upon the soil of Georgia I renewed my appeals to those in the North of whose regard for my husband I felt assured. Among the first to respond were Charles O'Conor, of New York, T. W. Pierce, of Boston, R. J. Haldeman, and Benjamin Wood, editor and proprietor of the New York *Daily News*. Mr. Wood wrote spontaneously:

"I beg you to have full faith in my desire and exertions

to relieve your noble husband from persecution, and to secure for him a prompt and impartial trial, and consequently an inevitable acquittal of the charge that has been infamously alleged against him. I will communicate immediately with Mr. O'Conor, Mr. Carlisle, Mr. Franklin Pierce, and Judge Black. Let me request you to accord me the pleasure of advancing to Mr. Clay, until his liberation, whatever sum may be necessary for the expenses attendant upon legal action for his defense, as, owing to his imprisonment and the present unsettled condition of your neighbourhood, there might be a delay that would prove prejudicial to his interests."

"I have no idea he will be brought to trial," wrote Mr. Pierce, on June 16th, "as the evidence on which the Government relies is a tissue of wicked fabrication, from the perjured lips of the lowest upon the earth! No one who knows him (Mr. Clay) can for a moment believe him guilty or even capable of crime. I have written to Judge Black and requested him to make effort to have you come to the North. I hope your application to Judge Holt* will secure for you this liberty."

Mr. O'Conor's letter ran as follows:

"NEW YORK, June 29, 1865.

"*My Dear Madam:* I do not believe that any attempt will be made to try Mr. Clay or any other of the leading Southern gentlemen on the charge of complicity in the assassination † of Lincoln.

"Such of them as have, through mistaken confidence in the magnanimity of their enemies, surrendered themselves into custody, may be obliged to suffer imprisonment, until it shall be determined, as a matter of policy, whether they ought to be tried for treason. . . .

* Neither this application, nor any communication sent by Mrs. Clay to Judge Holt, met with the recognition of acknowledgment. A. S.

† A reference to Holt's Report, dated December 8, 1865, will show how little either Mr. Pierce or this great legal light apprehended the audacity of the inquisitorial Military Commission, of which the Secretary of War and Joseph Holt made two. A. S.

"Mr. Jefferson Davis is, of course, the first victim demanded by those who demand State prosecutions.  His will be the test case.  .  .  .  I have volunteered my professional services in his defense, and although I have hitherto been refused permission to see him, and his letter in reply to my offer has been intercepted and returned to him as an improper communication, I am persuaded that, if a trial shall take place, I will be one of his defenders.  In performing this duty, you may fairly consider me as in compliance with your request, defending your husband.  .  .  .  I sympathise most sincerely with yourself and your husband in this cruel ordeal, and shall be most happy if my efforts shall have any influence in mitigating its severity or in shortening its duration.

"I am, my dear Madam, with great respect and esteem,
" Yours truly,
" CHARLES O'CONOR."

This epistle, coming from so wise a man, was calculated to calm us; one from Mr. Haldeman inspired us equally to courage.

" HARRISBURG, July 24, 1865.
"MRS. C. C. CLAY.

"*My Dear Madam:* Your exceedingly affecting letter did not reach me until long after it was written.  .  .  .  So soon as it was practicable, I visited Honourable Thaddeus Stevens at his home in Lancaster City.  I selected Mr. Stevens more particularly on account of his independence of character, his courage, and his position of intellectual and official leadership in the lower house of Congress, and in his party.  It is not necessary for me to tell you, Madam, that, knowing your husband, I never had a suspicion of his complicity in the assassination of Mr. Lincoln, but you will be gratified to learn that Mr. Stevens scorned the idea of either his guilt or that of any of the prominent sojourners in Canada.*

"Mr. Stevens holds, that as the belligerent character of the Southern States was recognised by the United States, neither Mr. Davis nor Mr. Clay can be tried for treason.  .  . That, if tried, Mr. Clay should be tried in Alabama.  You will perceive, then, my dear Madam, that connected with the proposed trial of your husband, there are profound questions

* Several years later Mr. Stevens reiterated these statements to one of the editors of the New York *Tribune*, who again quoted Mr. Stevens's remarks in an able editorial.   A. S.

of statesmanship and party. On this account, Mr. S. would not like to have his name prematurely mentioned. He is using his great political influence in the direction indicated, and it is, of course, much greater when he is not known as the counsel of Mr. Clay. . . . I promised to see Mr. Stevens so soon as the form and place of trial are announced. . . . Mr. Stevens will be a tower of strength, and command attention and respect from President, Secretary and Congress. . . .

"Hoping, Madam, that when I address you again, it will be under happier auspices, I am,

"R. J. HALDEMAN."

Nor were these all. Ex-Attorney General Black wrote me early in July these brief but kind words of sympathy:

"I hasten to assure you that I will do all that in me lies to secure justice in Mr. Clay's case. I have written to the President, Secretary of War, and Mr. Davis. You may safely rely upon me to the extent of my ability to do you good!"

Letters as positive and cordial came also from Messrs. George Shea and J. M. Carlisle. I had written meanwhile to Mr. Clay in prison, hoping thereby to give him courage; to the Secretary of War, beseeching for kindness to his self-surrendered and delicate prisoner; to General Miles, begging him to keep his promise and tell me of Mr. Clay's condition. It was three months ere I heard from my husband. The Secretary of War ignored my letter, and three weeks passed ere the general in command at Fortress Monroe made reply. His letter was judicially kind. It saved me, at least, from apprehension lest Mr. Clay, too, should be submitted to the horrible indignity which had been put upon Mr. Davis, the news of which was still agitating the country. General Miles's letter was as follows:

"HEADQUARTERS MILITARY DISTRICT OF FORT MONROE.
FORT MONROE, Virginia, June 20, 1865.

"*Dear Madam:* Your letter of the 8th inst. * is at hand.

* The letter reads "ult.," but, being obviously an error, is here changed. A. S.

In answer, I am happy to say to you, your husband is well in health and as comfortable as it is possible to make him under my orders. He has not at any time been in irons. His fare is good. (I think Mr. Davis's health better than when he left the *Clyde*.) He has pipe and tobacco. The officers in charge are changed every day. Your husband was pleased to hear you were well. Wished me to say that he was well and comfortable and under the circumstances quite cheerful. Has every confidence that he will be able to vindicate himself of the charge. He sends much love, and hopes you will not make your [self] uneasy or worry on his account, as his only concern is about you. Your letter was sent to Judge Holt.

"Your husband has not been allowed any books except his Bible and prayer-book, although I have requested provision to allow him one other, but have received no answer as yet. You may be assured that while your husband is within the limits of my command he will not suffer. Hoping this will find you well, I remain

"Very respectfully,
"NELSON A. MILES,
" Brevet Major-General United States Volunteers."

On the face of it this communication was kind. But, to offset its statements as to my husband's comfort, rumours quite the reverse reached us from many reliable sources. How well these were founded, how grievously the life in prison told upon my husband's spirit, may be adjudged from the following excerpts from a running letter from Mr. Clay which reached me late in the autumn. It was designed for my eyes alone, in the event of some sudden termination of his present awful experiences. In part it was a solemn charge and farewell to me, and this portion was guarded; for Mr. Clay had supposed he must commit the letter, at last, to the care of General Miles for transmittance to me. In part, it is evident hope was reviving him; by this time permission had been given to him to write to me through the War Department; also, he perceived the way opening for a private delivery of the letter, and therefore, at the last, he spoke more unreservedly.

"CASEMATE NO. 4, FORTRESS MONROE, VIRGINIA.
                    " FRIDAY, August 11, 1865.

*"My Dearly Beloved Wife:* After repeated requests, I am permitted to address you this communication, which is only to be delivered to you by General Miles in case of my death before we meet on earth. . . . This letter is written in contemplation of death; for, although trusting through God's goodness and mercy to see you again on this earth, yet, as my health is much impaired and I am greatly reduced in flesh and strength, and never allowed a night's unbroken rest, I feel I am in greater peril of my life than is usual. Under the solemn reflection that I may not see you again before I am called hence to meet my Judge, I shall try to write nothing that I would erase at that day when I must give an account of the deeds done in the flesh. God bears me witness that I am unconscious of having committed any crime against the United States or any of them, or any citizen thereof, and that I feel and believe that I have done my duty as a servant of the State of Alabama, to whom alone I owed allegiance, both before and since she seceded from the Federal Union. I have not changed my opinion as to the sovereignty of the States and the right of a State to secede; and I am more confirmed by my reflections and our bitter experience that the Northern people were so hostile to the rights, interests and institutions of the Southern States, that it was just and proper for these to seek peace and security in a separate government. I think the utter subversion of our political and social systems and sudden enfranchisement of four million slaves a great crime, and one of the most terrible calamities that ever befell any people; that generations yet unborn will feel it in sorrow and suffering; and that nothing but intense hatred and vindictive rage could have so blinded the North to its own interests and [to] those of humanity, as to induce the consummation of this act of wickedness and folly. I look for nothing but evil to both blacks and whites in the South from this sudden and violent change in their relations; intestine feuds and tumults; torpid indolence and stealthy rapacity on the part of the blacks; jealousy, distrust and oppression of them on the part of the whites; mutual outrage and injury, disquiet, apprehensions, alarms, murders, robberies, house-burnings, and other crimes; the blighting of hearts and homes and the destruction of industry, arts, literature, wealth, comfort and happiness. No people, save

the Jews, have ever been more oppressed and afflicted than those of the South, [and] especially the blacks, will be, in my opinion. *Their professed deliverers will prove the real destroyers of the negroes in the end.*

"Had I foreseen this, I should doubtless have been in favour of enduring lesser evils and wrongs from the North and postponing this calamity, for it would have come sooner or later, but, perhaps, not in our day. I never doubted . . . that our interest would be best served by preserving the old Union, under which I might have enjoyed wealth and honour all my life. I felt that I was acting against my own interest in favouring Secession, but thought it my duty to my State and the South. Hence, I have nothing to reproach myself for as to my course in that respect. I only regret that we did not defer the evil day or prepare longer, better maintaining our independence. I still think we might and would have maintained it, with more wisdom in council and in the field, and with more virtue among our people. I feel it due to my character, to my family and friends, to say this much on public affairs. . . .

"Now in regard to your own course and that of my kindred, I would advise you, if able, to remove from the South; but, impoverished as you all are, or soon will be, it is improbable that you can do so. Hence, you had best make your home in some city or large town, where the white population prevails. I think populous negro districts will be unsafe. You will be obliged to cast off our former slaves, if they should desire to live with you, for you have no means of supporting or of employing them. . . . Do what you can for the comfort of my parents. . . . Try to exercise charity to all mankind, forgiving injuries, cherishing hatred to none, and doing good even to enemies. . . . This is true wisdom, even if there was no life beyond the grave, because the best way of securing peace of mind and of promoting mere worldly interests. *But when I remember that Christ commands it and enforced it by His example, and promised, 'if you keep my commandments, you shall abide in my love,' the inestimable great reward should stimulate us to the performance of the duty.* . . . Nothing has convinced me of the divinity of Christ so much as His superhuman morality and virtue. . . .

"SATURDAY, August 12, 1865.

". . . I hope and sometimes think that my confinement here is to end in good to me. I have tried and am

still trying to turn it to my incalculable profit. I have searched
my own heart, and reviewed my life more earnestly, prayer-
fully, and anxiously than in all my days before coming in
here. I have read The Book through twice; much of it more
than twice. . . .

"You will see from my Bible and prayer-books that I have
been assiduous and earnest in their study. I confess that
this has been from necessity rather than choice. I have
never been allowed to see any word in print or manuscript
outside of them, until 3d inst., when a copy of the New York
*Herald* was brought me, and I was informed that I was [to be]
allowed to see such newspapers as General Miles would daily
send me.

"September 10, 1865.

"I dropped my pen in the delusive hope that I was to be
allowed to see you soon, or at all events to correspond freely
with you, and that in the meantime I would be allowed a rea-
sonable hope of living, by granting me opportunity to sleep.
For I must now tell you what I have heretofore thought I
would conceal till my liberation or death, *that I have endured
the most ingenious and refined torture ever since I came into this
living tomb; for, although above the natural face of the earth, it
is covered with about ten feet of earth, and is always more or less
damp like a tomb. With a bright light in my room and the
adjoining room, united to it by two doorways, closed by iron
gates, which cover about half the space or width of the partition,
and with two soldiers in this room, and two and a lieutenant in
the adjoining, until about 30th June; with the opening and
shutting of those heavy iron doors or gates, the soldiers being
relieved every two hours; with the tramp of these heavy, armed
men, walking their beats, the rattling of their arms, and still
more the trailing sabre of the lieutenant, the officer of the guard,
whose duty is to look at me every fifteen minutes, you may be
sure that my sleep has been often disturbed and broken. In
truth, I have experienced one of the tortures of the Spanish
Inquisition in this frequent, periodical and irregular disturb-
ance of my sleep.* During the one hundred and twelve days
of my imprisonment here I have never enjoyed one night's
unbroken sleep; I have been roused every two hours, if asleep,
by the tread of soldiers, the clank of arms and the voices of
officers. . . . I have never known the feeling of refresh-
ment from sleep on arising any morning of my imprisonment.
Besides, I have never been allowed retirement from sight,

actual or potential, of my guards; having to bathe and do all the acts of nature in view of the guard, if they chose to look at me. I have never been allowed an interview with any one alone, not even with a minister of God, but have always been confronted with two or more witnesses, whenever minister or physician come to see me. I have never been allowed any clothes save those in present use. . . . Where my other clothes are I do not know, as several of those who were represented as masters of my wardrobe denied the trust. I have found out that some things I valued have been stolen, together with all the little money I kept. I think it probable that you will never see half of the contents of my valise and despatch bag. The inclosed letters* present but a glimpse of my tortures, for I knew that the grand inquisitors, the President and Cabinet, knew all that I could tell and even more; and, besides, my debility of body and of mind was such that I had not power to coin my thoughts into words. . . . And to be frank, I was too proud to confess to them all my sufferings, and also apprehended that they would rather rejoice over and aggravate than relent and alleviate them. I now feel ashamed that I have complained to them instead of enduring unto death. My love for you, my parents and brothers, prevailed over my self-love, and extracted from me those humiliating letters. I have been reluctant to humble myself to men whom I regarded as criminals far more than myself, touching all the woes and wrongs, the destruction and desolation of the South.

"If you ever get my [Jay's] prayer-book, you will see scratched with a pencil, borrowed for the occasion, such items in my monotonous prison life as I felt worth recording.

"October 16th.

"On the 19th of August I wrote my second letter to the Secretary of War, and was then in hopes of removal of the guard from the adjoining room in a day or two. Besides, I was so enfeebled and my nerves so shattered by loss of sleep that I could scarcely write. Hence I quit this painful labour of love. The guard was not removed till the 12th of September, and then because my condition, from loss of sleep, was become really very critical. Since then I have improved very much in health and have slept as well as I ever did. But I have been deluded with the hope of my enlargement on

* Copies of those addressed by Mr. Clay to the Secretaty of War and to President Johnson. A. S.

parole, and thought I would not dwell on so painful a theme. I now learn that I am to be moved to-day to Carroll Hall, where Mr. D—— is. . . . Hence I avail myself of a chance to send you these sheets lest they should never reach you if I die in prison. I must impress on you the propriety of *concealing this communication while I live and never alluding to it,* for, if found out, I should suffer for it. . . . I dare say I should be turned out on parole but for the charge against me of concerting Lincoln's murder. They are loth to confess the charge to be false, which they would do by releasing me. I am made to suffer to save them from the reproach of injustice. I should be willing to brave them out by stubborn endurance and refusal of anything but legal justice. I should not fear that. But I am never to be tried for murder, nor, I think, for treason. They know there is no pretext for charging me with murder, and they doubt their ability to convict me of treason before a jury of Southern men, and such only could legally try me. . . .

"Now excuse any incoherence or want of method and the bad writing, as it is all done under great disadvantages, which I may explain hereafter. You can write to me under cover to Captain R. W. Bickley, Third Pennsylvania Artillery, Fortress Monroe, Virginia. He will be here till 10th of November, and then go out of service. After that I'll find some one else through whom you can write to me. He is from Philadelphia. He, Captain J. B. Tetlow, Philadelphia, Captain McEwan, Lewisburg, Pennsylvania, and Dr. John J. Craven* of this place, have been very kind to me; also Lieutenant Lemuel Shipman, Sunbury, Pennsylvania. The last made me a wooden knife to eat with during the time I was denied knife and fork and spoon, which was till thirtieth of June.

"They would, too, shake hands (which was forbidden) and treat me as an equal when they could do so unobserved. Take care you don't allude to this letter in yours through War Department. . . . —————— —————— *has no sensibility or refinement, and hence Mr. Davis and I have suffered more than we should have done. Mr. Davis was ironed without cause, and only grew violent when they offered to iron him. I*

---

* Dr. Craven was already in communication with Dr. Withers, of Petersburg, Va., Mr. Clay's cousin, who, through the courtesy of his fellow-practitioner, was enabled to contribute occasionally to Mr. Clay's comfort and welfare. A. S.

*know this from one who was present.    Facts are, General M——*
*was authorised to iron us if necessary for safety, and deemed it*
*necessary with Mr. D——, or mistook the authority as an order*
*to do it.    But Mr. Davis is petulant, irascible, and offensive in*
*manner to officers, as they tell me, though they say he is able,*
*learned, high-toned, and imposing in manner."*

Before this heartrending letter reached me, however,
another, couched purposely in terms more guarded (as
befitted matter which must run the gauntlet of Secretary
Stanton's, the Attorney-General's and General Miles's
scrutiny), had reached me.    In my endeavours to comfort our enfeebled parents, I had already discussed with
them the advisability of making my way to Washington,
and in the first letter from me that reached my husband's
hands I spoke of my hope of doing so.    Unknown to me,
Mr. Clay, so early as June 30th, had written an urgent
appeal to Secretary Stanton that I might be allowed to
see or communicate with him.    To this he had received
no reply.    Upon learning, therefore, of my intention
through my letter, his first impulse was to dissuade me.

"If you come North," he wrote, on August 21st, "you
must come with a brave heart, my dear 'Ginie   .   .   .
prepared to hear much to wound you, and to meet with
coldness and incivility where you once received kindness
and courtesy.    Some will offend you with malice, some
unwittingly and from mere habit, and some even through
a sense of duty.    Many religionists have, doubtless, found
pleasure and felt they were doing God service in persecu-
ting heretics.    If rudely repulsed, remember, in charity,
that such is human nature.    The Jewish priests drove off
the lepers with stones.   .   .   ."

# CHAPTER XXIV

## Again in Washington

By September I had reopened correspondence with many Washington friends. As will have been seen by a perusal of certain preceding letters, the question of giving me permission to return to the capital already had been broached to the President and Secretary of War, by Judge Black and others. It was now again brought to the attention of Mr. Johnson, by Mr. Duff Green, a long-time friend of ex-Governor Clay, of my husband, and of the President's. It was the first application of all that had been sent to the Government to bring a response. The Executive's reply was couched as follows:

"I am directed by the President to say that an application for permission to visit Washington, made by Mrs. C. C. Clay, Jr., over her own name, will be considered by him.                                        R. Morrow,

                                "Major and A. A. G., Secretary."

In forwarding this communication to me, Mr. Green wrote:

"We think there is nothing to prevent your coming at once. To wait for permission may delay you weeks, and perhaps months. Your coming would not prejudice either yourself or your husband, and you can do more by a personal application to the President than by an application 'over your own name.'"

Two months dragged by, however, ere I could complete arrangements for the journey and detach myself from our clinging parents, who, deprived of all of their other children, now placed their dependence upon me. Notwithstanding their hearts ached for some assurance of Mr. Clay's safety, they were ill-disposed to look upon my projected trip with favour. Huntsville was in complete subjugation to the Federal representatives. We had numerous reasons to realise the pitiless and cruel policy that had been inaugurated by our conquerors, and few to lead us to look for kinder things at the hands of the powers at Washington. The reports that reached us of the treatment accorded to those Southerners who had already proceeded to the capital, even allowing for the prejudice of editors unfriendly to us, were not of a kind to encourage a hope for clemency or justice there. The efforts of the wives of other prisoners to communicate with their husbands, their applications to the Government to grant them the right of trial, not only had been of no avail, but, in some instances, had made them the direct objects of attack from those inimical to them. "I have had a weary time," one wrote late in October, "but of that, if you knew how weary, you would cry out 'No more an' you love me,' rather than bear the infliction of the retrospect, so I will not torment you." . . . President Johnson's remarks to the South Carolina Delegation, concerning Mrs. Davis's efforts, became the talk of the country. I was astonished when I learned that she had never written a line without consultation with Mr. Schley and his, in turn, consulting General Steedman upon the tenor of her letters, and receiving the approval of both on the manner of presenting the subject. It was the old fable of the lamb whose grandfather muddied the stream.

Such news served further to convince my husband's parents of the futility of the trip I was contemplating. They urged that I would be attacked on every side so soon as I entered the Federal capital; they pleaded, too, alas! the stringency of our present means, a very vital objection just then to us whose every possession had either been "confiscated" or otherwise rendered useless to us. Nevertheless, every moment anxiety was consuming me. I resolved to act while I had the strength, and made known my resolve to our parents.

The middle of November had arrived ere, by the aid of Mr. Robert Herstein, a kindly merchant of Huntsville ("may his tribe increase'"), who advanced me $100 in gold (and material for a silk gown, to be made when I should reach my destination), I was enabled to begin my journey to the capital. Under the escort of a kind friend and neighbour, Major W. H. Echols, of Huntsville, who, having in mind the securing of a certain patent, arranged his plans so as to accompany me to Washington, I bade father and mother "good-bye" and stepped aboard the train. My heart sometimes beat high with hope, yet, at others, I trembled at what I might encounter. Fortunately for the preservation of my courage, I had no forewarning that I had looked, for the last time, upon the sorrowful face of our mother. Her closing words, in that heartbreaking farewell, were of hope that I would soon return bringing with me her dearest son. With the desire to cheer them both, I wrote back merrily as I proceeded on my way; but, indeed, I had small need to affect a spirit of buoyancy; for, from the beginning, I was the recipient of innumerable kindnesses from fellow-travellers who learned my identity. In many instances my fare was refused by friendly railroad conductors.

"I have paid literally nothing thus far," I wrote from Louisville, Kentucky, which city I reached early in the morning of November 15th. "At Nashville," my letter added, "we took sleeping cars, which were as luxurious as the bed that now invites me. I had, however, an amusing, and, at first blush, an alarming nocturnal adventure. I was waked by the rattling of paper at my head, and, half unconsciously putting out my hand, it lighted on the hairy back of some animal! I sprang out of bed, raised the curtain, and there sat, in the corner of my berth, the most monstrous *coon* you ever saw! The black around his eyes at first made him appear like an owl, but he proved to be a genuine old 'zip coon.' So I got out one of 'Mammy 'Ria's' nice biscuit, which have been greatly complimented by my friends, and asked him please to come out of my bed and eat some supper. But he wouldn't! And I had to wake Major Echols in the gentlemen's apartment, who forcibly ejected him after a good laugh at me!"

A day later and we reached Cincinnati, where, owing to the late arrival of the boat, the *St. Nicholas*, on which we had travelled from Louisville, through banks of fog, we were delayed some twelve hours. Our trip on this river steamer was, in its way, a kind of triumphal progress, very reassuring to me at that critical moment. As I wrote back to father, "We found the captain a good Southerner and a noble old fellow! Had one son in the Federal Army and lost one at Shiloh! Mr. Hughes, of the Louisville *Democrat*, was aboard; he said his paper had been suppressed, but he would now be permitted to go South. He is a rabid secessionist, and promised to copy the *News* * articles concerning my husband." On board, too, was Mrs. Gamble, of Louisville, a wealthy woman whose name was associated with innumerable kindnesses to our soldiers, and generous gifts to our cause. She was a sad woman, but sympathised greatly with Mr. Davis and Mr. Clay, and begged that upon my return from Washington we would make our home with her "until better times."

Upon learning the length of time we must spend in Cincinnati, I went at once to the Spencer House, whence I wrote and immediately despatched notes to my old friends, Mrs. George E. Pugh, wife of the ex-Senator, and to Senator and Mrs. George H. Pendleton (the first a

* New York *Daily News*.

resident of the city, the last-named residents of Clifton, a suburb), telling them of my unexpected presence in the city, and hoping to see them during the day. On my way to the hotel, I had looked about the city with increasing interest and pleasure. How different it was from our devastated country!

"You never saw the like of the fruit!" I wrote enthusiastically to mother. "Grapes, oranges, apples; such varieties of nuts—cream, hazel, hickory, and English walnuts—as are on the beautiful stall just at the entrance of the hotel! The Major has just entered, laughing heartily at Yankee tricks and Yankee *notions!* He says a man said to him, 'Insure your life, sir?'

"'For what?' says the Major.

"'For ten cents!' replies the man. 'And if you are killed on the cars, your family gets $3,000 cash!'

"'Three thousand?' rejoins Major Echols, contemptuously. 'What's that to a man worth a *million!*' at which all stare as if shot. I laugh, too, but tell him I fear we will be made to pay for his fun, if they think us *millionaires!*"

The day was half gone when dear Mrs. Pugh, only a few years ago the triumphant beauty of the Pierce and Buchanan administrations, but now a pale, saddened woman, clad in deep mourning, appeared. God! what private sorrows as well as national calamities had filled in the years since we had separated in Washington! The pathos of her appearance opened a very flood-gate of tears, which I could not check. But Mrs. Pugh shed none. She only put out a restraining hand to me.

"No tears now, I beg of you. I can't endure it. Tell me of yourself, of your plans. Where are you going? What of Mr. Clay? How can I aid you?" she asked, turning away all discussion save as to the object of my journey.

The afternoon was already nearly spent when Senator

and Mrs. Pendleton arrived, having driven in from their suburban home upon the receipt of my note, sent at midday. Their welcome was cordial and frank as in the old days. They had come to take me home to dinner, where, they assured me, we might talk more freely than at the hotel. They would take no refusal, but agreed with Major Echols, who was unable to accompany us, to see me safely to the station in ample time to take the midnight train for Washington. In the hours that followed, I learned somewhat of the experiences in the North, during the bloody strife of the four years just closed, of Southern sympathisers, even where their sympathy was restrained from announcing itself by an open espousal. Senator Pendleton's known friendliness for Clement L. Vallandigham, whose fearlessness and outspoken zeal in our behalf had cost him so dearly, had brought its own penalties. At times, he told me, when feeling ran highest, neither his home nor that of Senator Pugh had escaped certain malodorous missiles of the lawless !

We spent much of the evening in scanning the problems that lay before me. I told my host of the numbers of brilliant men who had volunteered their aid to Mr. Clay, mentioning among others the name of Judge Hughes, of Washington, whose friendly proffer of counsel had reached me just previous to my departure from Huntsville.

"By all means," said Senator Pendleton, as we drove at last to the station, "see Judge Hughes first ! He is strictly non-partisan, is a friend of the President's, and, moreover, is under obligations to Mr. Clay, which I know he would gladly repay !"

It was already a late hour when we rejoined the waiting Major Echols. With a warm "God bless you, dear friend !" Senator and Mrs. Pendleton bade me "good-bye," and I stepped aboard the train for Washington.

What that name called up, what my thoughts were, or what my sensations, as I realised our approach to the city once so attractive, but now seeming to represent to me a place of oppression and the prison in which for six months Mr. Clay had been incarcerated, may better be imagined than described. Early the following morning our train began to thread its way through familiar country. By mid-day we had reached war-scarred Harper's Ferry, and passed over into old Virginia! A short journey now, and I found myself once more driving up Pennsylvania Avenue in the company of tried friends, *en route* to Willard's.

# CHAPTER XXV

## Secretary Stanton Denies Responsibility

From the hour of my arrival in the capital, Friday, November 17th, my misgivings gave place to courage. I went directly to Willard's, which, being near the Executive Mansion and the War Department, and my purse very slender, I believed would save me hack hire. I had scarcely registered when General Clingman called. He was followed shortly by Senators Garland and Johnson, of Arkansas, the vanguard of numerous friends, who within a few hours came to extend their sympathies and wishes for the success of my mission. During that first day I sent a note to Colonel Johnson, Mr. Johnson's Secretary, asking for an interview with the President at the earliest possible date. To my great relief of mind, within a few hours there came an answer, telling me the President would see me the following Wednesday!

For the next few days I knew no moment alone. The list of callers noted in my small diary necessarily was but partial, yet even that is wonderfully long. Among them, to my surprise and somewhat to my mystification, were General Ihrie, Major Miller and Colonel Ayr of Grant's staff. Their friendliness amazed me. I could imagine no reason why they should call. General Ihrie, moreover, assured me of his chief's kind feeling toward my husband, and advised me to see the Lieutenant-General at an early date.

The Sunday after my arrival, callers began to arrive before breakfast, the first being Colonel Ogle Tayloe, bearing an invitation from Mrs. Tayloe to dinner the following evening. Before church hour had arrived, dear old Mr. Corcoran came, intending to give me welcome on his way to St. John's. He forgot to leave again until services were over, and others returning from church crowded in. Mr. Corcoran's manner was full of the old-time charm, as he bade me good-bye at last; and, as he took my hand in parting, he said, "You've not forgotten the little white house round the corner?" (referring to the banking-house of Riggs & Corcoran).

"No," I answered, smiling sadly, "You are my bankers still, but, alas! where are my deposits?"

Mr. Corcoran's glance was full of kindness. Laying his hand upon his heart, he replied, "They are here, my friend!" and he pressed my hand reassuringly.

I remember that Sunday as one in which tears of gratitude rose to my eyes again and again, until at last I exclaimed, "It is all very strange to me! There appears to be none of my husband's enemies here! It seems to me as if everyone is his friend!"

The following morning, however, I had an experience calculated to arouse in me a feeling somewhat less secure. I was still in the bath when a tap came at my door.

"A lady wishes to see you," was the reply to my question.

"Who is she?" I asked.

"Don't know, ma'am. She wouldn't give her name!"

"Very well," I answered. "Explain to her that I am dressing; that unless her business is imperative, I would prefer to have her call later."

In a few moments I heard light tapping again. Upon my inquiry, a name was whispered through the key-hole, which I recognised as that of the wife of a well-known public official. I at once admitted her. The purpose of her visit was a peculiar one. She had come to warn me of the presence in the city of James Montgomery, *alias* Thompson, one of the hireling witnesses whose "testimony" against Mr. Davis and Mr. Clay had been registered with the Bureau of Military Justice. By some unfortunate connection of her own family with this miscreant, my visitor had learned that Montgomery, upon hearing of my object in visiting Washington, had been heard to make a threat of violence against me. The lady, who shall continue to be nameless, was so convinced some harm threatened me that she begged me to promise that while in the capital I would go armed, and especially be cautious with unknown callers. Montgomery, she added, was likely to disguise himself; but, further to aid me in guarding against some injury at his hands, she had brought with her a photograph of the wretched man. Whether or not some crime was projected against me by this man I never knew, but the wild nature of the times warranted me in exercising, thereafter, a prudence which otherwise would not have occurred to me. I took counsel with friends, and, with one exception, later to be mentioned, no occurrence during my stay in the capital served to arouse in me a further apprehension from that quarter.

In the days that intervened until my appointment with the President, my hours were spent in advantageous interviews with Judge Hughes, of Hughes & Denver, with Judge Black, Senator Garland, Frederick A. Aiken and others, during which I gleaned much knowledge of what had transpired since my husband's incarceration, and of the public feeling concerning the distinguished prisoners at Fortress Monroe, whose trials had been so mysteriously postponed. It was now six months since the imprisonment of Messrs. Davis and Clay; but in so far as might be learned, definite charges against them had not yet been filed at the War Department. On every side I heard it declared that the situation was unprecedented in English or American jurisprudence. Leading lawyers of the country were ready and eager to appear in the prisoners' behalf, but every effort made by friends to see them thus far had been futile. In those first weeks, reiterated proffers of legal aid continued to reach me daily from distinguished quarters.

Upon my arrival in the capital I had put myself at once into communication with Judge Hughes, as advised by Senator Pendleton. His kindness was unceasing, not only in the matter of legal advice to guide me through the intricacies of my undertaking, but in his generous placing at my disposal his horses and carriages, and the services of his coachman and footman. Mrs. Hughes was absent in the West, and the hospitality of their home, therefore, was barred; but all that a thoughtful nature could suggest was done by the Judge to facilitate success in my mission.

From the first, too, Judge Jeremiah S. Black, ex-Attorney-General, and Secretary of State under President Buchanan, with whom I now became, for the first time, personally acquainted, proved a bulwark of sympathy that thereafter never failed my husband and self. He was a peculiar man in appearance, with shaggy brows, deep-set eyes, and a cavernous mouth, out of which invincible arguments rolled that made men listen. This feature was large when he spoke, but when he laughed, the top of his head fell back like a box cover, and looked as if it must drop over the other way. Happily for the unfortunate, his heart was modelled on a scale as large, and for months he gave his time and advice unstintedly to me.

On the Wednesday appointed by the President, accompanied by Judge Hughes, I proceeded to keep my appointment at the White House. One of the first familiar faces I saw as I entered was that of Mrs. Stephen A. Douglas, now widowed. A wait of some moments being imminent, with the affectionate warmth so well-known to me in other and happier days, Mrs. Douglas at

once volunteered to accompany me in my call upon
"the good President," and in a few moments we were
shown into his presence. Mr. Johnson received us
civilly, preserving, at first, what I learned afterward
to know was an habitual composure, though he softened
somewhat under the ardent appeal of Mrs. Douglas
when she urged upon him the granting of my request.

My first impression of the President, who, while a
Senator, in the fifties, had seldom been seen in social
gatherings in the capital, was that of a man upon whom
greatness, of a truth, had been thrust; a political accident,
in fact. His hands were small and soft; his manner
was self-contained, it is true, but his face, with "cheeks
as red as June apples," was not a forceful one.

From the beginning, as Judge Black had declared he
would do, Mr. Johnson clearly wished to shirk the responsibility of my husband's case, and to throw it upon
the shoulders of his Secretary of War. His non-committal
responses to my reasons why I should have access to
my husband, why he should be tried or liberated, dis-
heartened me greatly. When Mrs. Douglas perceived
this, she added her pleadings to mine, and, as the President's shiftiness became more and more apparent, she
burst into tears, and, throwing herself down on her
knees before him, called upon me to follow her example.
This, however, I could not comply with. I had no
reason to respect the Tennesseean before me. That he
should have my husband's life in his power was a monstrous wrong, and a thousand reasons why it was wrong
flashed through my mind like lightning as I measured
him, searing it as they passed. My heart was full of
indignant protest that such an appeal as Mrs. Douglas's
should have been necessary; but that, having been made,
Mr. Johnson could refuse it, angered me still more. I
would not have knelt to him even to save a precious
life. This first, memorable one of many, unhappy

scenes at the White House, ended by the President inviting me to call again after he had consulted his Cabinet. At the same time he urged me to see Mr. Stanton.

"I think you had best go to him," he said. "This case comes strictly within the jurisdiction of the Secretary of War, and I advise you to see him!"

Realising the futility of further argument with Mr. Johnson at the time, I followed his advice, going almost immediately, and alone, to the War Department. It was my first and last visit to Secretary Stanton, in that day of the Government's chaos, autocrat of all the United States and their citizens. Varying accounts of that experience have appeared in the press during the last thirty-seven years. The majority of them have exaggerated the iron Secretary's treatment of me. Many have accused him of a form of brusque brutality,* which, while quite in keeping with his reputation, nevertheless was not exhibited toward me.

The Secretary of War was not guilty of "tearing up in my face and throwing in the waste-basket," as one writer has averred, the President's note of introduction, which I bore him, even though I was a declared "Rebel" and the wife of a so-called conspirator and assassin. He was simply inflexibly austere and pitiless.

Upon arriving at the War Department, I gave my card and the President's note to the messenger in waiting, which, from across the room, I saw handed to the Secretary. He glanced at them, laid them on the desk at which

---

* To pass by less irreproachable witnesses, the following incident illustrative of Mr. Stanton's *brusquerie* to women was told by the Reverend Elisha Dyer. "While sitting in Mr. Stanton's private office, a well-dressed lady entered. She was rather young, and very captivating. Approaching the Secretary, she said, 'Excuse me, but I *must* see you!' My old friend at once assumed the air of a bear. In a stern voice he said, 'Madam, you have no right to come into this office, and you must leave it! No, Madam,' he continued, when she tried to speak, 'not one word!' And, calling an orderly, he said, 'Take this woman out!'" A. S.

he sat, and continued in conversation with a lady who stood beside him. In a second the messenger returned, and desired me to take a seat on a sofa, which, as it happened, was directly in line with Mr. Stanton's desk. In a few moments the lady with whom he had been in conversation withdrew. As she passed me I recognised her. She was Mrs. Kennedy, daughter of ex-Secretary Mallory, then a prisoner in Fort Lafayette. Her face was flushed and very sad, which I interpreted (and rightly, as it proved) as meaning that her request had been denied. The sight filled me with indignation. I resolved at once to retain my seat and let the Secretary seek me, as a gentleman should do. I was strengthened in this determination by the conviction that he would ignore my plea also, and I was resolved to yield him no double victory.

After a delay of a few moments, in which the Secretary adjusted first his glasses and then his papers, he slowly approached me, saying, "This is Mrs. Clay, I presume?"

"And this Mr. Stanton?" I replied.

I at once briefly, but bravely, proceeded with my story. I told him that my object in visiting Washington was to obtain the speedy release of my husband, who was dying hourly under the deprivations and discipline of prison life; or, failing this, to obtain for him an early trial, which he desired not to shirk, but to hasten; of the result of which we had no fear, unless "he be given up to that triumvirate called the 'Military Bureau of Justice,' of which you are one, Mr. Stanton!" This I said with inward trembling and with eyes brimming, but looking him fully in the face. His own gaze fell.

"Madam," he answered. "I am not your husband's judge——"

"I know it!" I interrupted. "And I am thankful for it; and I would not have you for his accuser!"

"Neither am I his accuser!" he continued. I could

scarcely believe I had heard him aright. His manner was gravely polite. I remember thinking at that moment, "Can this be the rude man of whom I have heard? Can I have been misinformed about him?"

"Thank you, Mr. Stanton, for those words," I said. "I had not hoped to hear them from you. I thought you were the bitterest of my husband's enemies! I assure you your words give me fresh hope! I will tell the President at once of this cheering interview!"

At these expressions Mr. Stanton seemed somewhat confused. I wondered whether he would modify or recall his words. He did not, however, and thanking him again for even that concession, I withdrew.

The legal friends to whom I gave an account of this conversation were less confident as to its significance. If Mr. Stanton was neither Mr. Clay's judge nor accuser, who was? Some one was surely responsible for his detention; some one with the power to obstruct justice was delaying the trial, which the first legal minds in the country for months had sought to bring about. If not Mr. Stanton, could it be Mr. Holt, whose name was already become one of abhorrence among the majority of Southerners? Judge Black felt sure it was. But accusation against the Judge Advocate General without proof was impolitic, with my husband's safety still in the balance. In a situation so serious as the present, I should have preferred to conciliate him.

"Have you tried to interest Judge Holt in your husband's behalf?" wrote our old friend ex-Speaker Orr. "Would not some little kind memory of the past steal over him when you revive the morning reminiscences of the Ebbitt House, when his much-adored wife was a shining luminary in that bright circle? He would be more or less than man if such a picture did not move him. Will you try it?"

Great, indeed, was Mr. Orr's surprise when he learned

that I had written to Mr. Holt three times, only to meet with complete silence at his hands!

Under such circumstances it was wiser to adhere to my first purpose; namely, to sue for the privilege of seeing Mr. Clay and for his release on parole, or for a speedy trial. I was urged by Judge Black not to cease in my appeals to the President; to tell the Executive of my interview with his Secretary of War, and in the meantime to secure from General Grant, if possible, a letter to the President, advocating my plea. I had already been assured by General Ihrie of his chief's ability and willingness to serve me. On the evening of the second Sunday after my arrival in Washington, therefore, I drove from Willard's at seven o'clock, accompanied by Major Echols, to Lieutenant-General Grant's headquarters in Georgetown. I found these to be established in what was formerly the home of our friend Mr. Alfred Scott,* of Alabama, now deceased. Soldiers guarded the entrance, as became a military headquarters, and one came forward to take my card as we drove up. Upon his return, Major Echols and I were shown at once to the General's reception parlour. Dismissing the officers in uniform who stood about, General Grant received me courteously, tendering his hand frankly. I at once presented Major Echols, saying that "my friend, like yourself, is a graduate of West Point; but, feeling bound to offer his allegiance to his native South, he had served with distinction at Fort Sumter," which introduction, I imagined, pleased the General, though it disconcerted my modest escort.

I now briefly, and in some trepidation at finding myself face to face with the "Hero of the Hour!" the "Coming Man," "Our next President" (for by these and many other titles was the hero of Appomattox already crowned), explained as succinctly as I could my motive in calling

---

* Mr. Scott's daughter is the wife of the widely known Dr. Garnett, of Hot Springs, Arkansas.

upon him, closing my remarks with the assurance that the one circumstance prompting me to ask his aid was not his army victories, but his noble conduct to our beloved General Lee in his recent surrender. I was convinced, I added, that the man who had borne himself so magnanimously toward a brave soldier whom he had vanquished, possessed the soul to espouse and sustain a cause, if just, though all the world opposed. It was in this faith I had come to him.

The Federal General listened very gravely. When I had finished he responded in his characteristic, quiet way: "If it were in my power, Mrs. Clay, I would to-morrow open every prison in the length and breadth of the land. I would release every prisoner unless——" (after a pause) "unless Mr. Davis might be detained awhile to satisfy public clamour. Your husband's manly surrender entitles him to all you ask. I admire and honour him for it, and anything I can say or do to assist you shall be done. I heartily wish you success."

I asked him, in the course of our conversation, if he would go with me to the White House the next day, at any hour, day or evening.

"That is impossible," he said. "I leave at midnight for Richmond."

"Would you be willing to write what you have spoken?"

"With pleasure!" he replied. Going to the door he called, "Julia!"

In a moment Mrs. Grant entered the room. She shook my hand with the cordiality of a friend, saying, as she did so, "We have many mutual friends in St. Louis." She then expressed her deep sympathy for me, and hoped her husband could serve me with the President.

In a few moments General Grant returned with the promised letter. I thanked him from a grateful heart. Upon rising to go, he accompanied me half down the steps, where, with a hearty shake of the hand, we parted.

# CHAPTER XXVI

## Mr. Holt Reports Upon the Case of C. C. Clay, Jr.

Armed with General Grant's letter, my hopes at once rose high. It seemed to my eager and innocent mind that an ally so really great could not fail to convince the President and his Cabinet of the wisdom of granting my plea in whole or in part. I began to feel that the culmination of my husband's troubles was now approaching. I hastened to send the letter to Mr. Johnson. It read as follows:

"Washington, D. C., Nov. 26, 1865.

"His Excellency A. Johnson,
"President of the United States.

"*Sir:* As it has been my habit heretofore to intercede for the release of all prisoners who I thought could safely be left at large, either on parole or by amnesty, I now respectfully recommend the release of Mr. C. C. Clay.

"The manner of Mr. Clay's surrender, I think, is a full guarantee that if released on parole, to appear when called for, either for trial or otherwise, that he will be forthcoming.

"Argument, I know, is not necessary in this or like cases, so I will simply say that I respectfully recommend that C. C. Clay, now a State prisoner, be released on parole, not to leave the limits of his State without your permission, and to surrender himself to the civil authorities for trial whenever called on to do so.

"I do not know that I would make a special point of fixing the limits to a State only, but at any future time the limits could be extended to the whole United States, as well as if those limits were given at once.

"I have the honour to be,
"Very respectfully, your obedient servant,
(Signed.)     "U. S. Grant, Lieutenant General."

\* The letter here given is from a copy furnished Mrs. Clay by Robert Morrow, Secretary in 1866.

In my note accompanying the General's recommenda-tion, I begged to repeat my request that I be allowed to visit Mr. Clay at Fortress Monroe, and that I be furnished with copies of the charges against him, in order that I might consult with him as to the proper means to disprove them, in the event of his being brought to trial. After a two days' silence on the part of the Executive, I wrote a note of inquiry to Mr. Johnson. The reply that reached me was not calculated to stimulate my erstwhile hope-fulness.

"I cannot give you any reply to your note of this inst.," wrote Colonel Robert Johnson, on the 30th of November, "except that the President has the letter of General Grant. No action has yet been had. I will bring the matter before the President during the day, and will advise you."

And now, indeed, I began to be aware how all-powerful was the hidden force that opposed the taking of any action on my husband's case. Again and again there-after I called upon President Johnson, pleading at first for his intervention on my behalf; but, upon the third visit, when he again suggested that I "see Mr. Stanton," I could refrain no longer from an outburst of completest indignation. I was accompanied on this and on almost all my innumerable later visits to the White House by Mrs. Bouligny, who witnessed, I fear, many an astonishing passage at arms between President Johnson and me. On the occasion just touched upon, aroused by Mr. Johnson's attempt to evade the granting of my request, I answered him promptly:

"I will *not* go to Mr. Stanton, Mr. President! *You* issued the proclamation charging my husband with crime! *You* are the man to whom I look for redress!"

"I was obliged to issue it," Mr. Johnson replied, "to satisfy public clamour. Your husband's being in Canada while Surratt and his associates were there made it neccessary to name him and his companions with the others!"

"And do you believe, for one moment, that my husband would conspire against the life of President Lincoln?" I burst out indignantly. "Do you, who nursed the breast of a Southern mother, think Mr. Clay could be guilty of that crime?"

Mr. Johnson disclaimed such a belief at once.

"Then, on what grounds do you detain one whom you believe an innocent man, and a self-surrendered prisoner?" I asked.

But here the President, as he did in many instances throughout those long and, to me, most active days in the capital, resorted to his almost invariable habit of evading direct issues; yet it was not long ere I was given reason to feel that he, personally, sincerely wished to serve me, though often appearing to be but an instrument in the hands of more forceful men, whom he lacked the courage to oppose, and who were directly responsible for my husband's detention. Before the end of December the President gave me a valuable and secret proof that his sympathies were with rather than against Mr. Clay.

Until the sixth of December, nearly seven months after my husband's surrender, no formal charges had been filed against him with a view to placing him on trial, or on which to base his continued imprisonment. During that time, the visits of counsel being denied him, there was not in the capital one who was vitally concerned in his or Mr. Davis's case, though certain unique aspects of the cases of the two distinguished prisoners of the Government had invited a more or less continuous professional interest in them.

At the time of my reappearance in Washington, though the city was filled with distinguished pardon-seekers, and with Southerners who had been summoned on various grounds, to explain their connection with the late Confederate States' Government, interest in the prisoners at Fortress Monroe became quickened. The Legislature of the State of Alabama drew up and forwarded a memorial to the President, asking for Mr. Clay's release. Prominent lawyers besides those whose letters I have quoted wrote volunteering their aid, Senator Garland, Mr. Carlisle, and Frederick A. Aiken, counsel for Mrs. Surratt, among them. Through Mr. Aiken, already familiar with the means employed by the Military Commission to convict their prisoners, I gained such information as was then available as to the probable charges which would be made against Mr. Clay.

"I send you the argument of Assistant Judge Advocate General Bingham, in the Surratt trial," he wrote on November 25th. . . . "This argument has been distributed broadcast over the country, and the opinion of the Republican party educated to think it true! It seems to me," he added, "that a concisely written argument in favour of Mr. Clay, on the evidence as it stands, would be useful with the President."

In the midst of this awakening of our friends on Mr. Clay's behalf, the Government's heretofore (from me) concealed prosecutor, Mr. Holt, presented to the War Department his long-delayed and elaborately detailed "Report on the case of C. C. Clay, Jr." On the face cf it, his action at this time appeared very much like an eitort to checkmate any influence my presence might awaken on the prisoner's behalf. Upon learning of this movement I at once applied to the War Department for an opportunity to examine the Report. It was not accorded me. After some days, learning of Mr. Stanton's absence from the city, and acting on the suggestion of Mr. Johnson, on the 20th of December I addressed Mr. Holt by letter for the third and last time. I asked for a copy of the charges against my husband, and also for the return of my private correspondence, which had been taken from me, in part, at Macon, and part from my home in Huntsville. Days passed without the least acknowledgment from the Judge Advocate.

It was at this juncture that Mr. Johnson's friendliness was exhibited toward me; for, happening to call upon him while the document was in his hands, I told him of my ill success and growing despair at the obstacles that were presented to the granting of my every request at the War Department.* I begged him to interpose and assist me to an interview with Mr. Clay, but, above all, at this important moment, to aid me in getting a copy of the charges now formulated against him. Thereupon, exacting from me a promise of complete secrecy, the President delivered his official copy of the "Report" into my hands, that I might peruse it and make such excerpts as would aid me. I did more than this, however; for, hastening back with it to the home of Mrs. A. S. Parker, which had been generously thrown open to me, I spent the night in copying the document in full.

The list of accusations against my husband was long. It represented "testimony" which the Bureau of Military Justice had spent six months, and, as later transpired, many thousands of dollars, in collecting, and was a digest of the matter sworn to in the Judge Advocate's presence.

* For months Mr. Holt's Report was steadily refused to the public. Referring to this secretive conduct, in July, 1866, A. J. Rogers said, in the House of Representatives, "Secrecy has surrounded and shrouded, not to say protected, every step of these examinations. In the words of the late Attorney-General, 'Most of the evidence upon which they [the charges] are based was obtained *ex parte*, without notice to the accused, and whilst they were in custody in military prisons. *Their publication might wrong the Government.*' . . . The Secretary of War, February 7, 1866, writes to the President that the publication of the Report of the Judge Advocate General is incompatible with the public interests. This report," continues Mr. Rogers, "in the testimony it quotes, will show that the interests of the country would never have suffered by the dispensing with illegal secrecy, but that the interests and fame of the Judge Advocate General himself would suffer in the eyes of all the truth-loving and justice-seeking people on earth." A. S.

As I read and copied on during that night, the reason for Mr. Holt's persistent disregard of my letters became obvious. No official, no man who, for months, against the protests of some of the most substantial citizens, the most brilliant lawyers of the country, had been so determinedly engaged in secret effort to prove a former friend and Congressional associate to be deserving of the gallows, could be expected to do anything but to avoid a meeting with the wife of his victim. In December, 1860, when Mr. Clay's position as a Secessionist was known to be unequivocal, Mr. Holt, whose personal convictions were then somewhat less clearly declared, had written, on the occasion of my husband's illness, "It is my earnest prayer that a life adorned by so many graces may be long spared to our country, whose councils so need its genius and patriotism!" In December, 1865, basing his charges against his former friend — a former United States Senator, whose integrity had never suffered question; a man religious to the point of austerity; a scholar, of delicate health and sensibilities, and peculiarly fastidious in the selection of those whom he admitted to intimacy —, Mr. Holt, I repeat, basing his accusations against such a one-time friend upon the purchased testimony of social and moral outcasts, designated Mr. Clay in terms which could only be regarded as the outspurting of venomous malice, or of a mind rendered incapable of either logic or truth by reason of an excessive fanaticism.

Under this man's careful marshalling, the classes of "crimes which Clay is perceived to have inspired and directed" were frightful and numerous. The "most pointed proof of Clay's cognisance and approval of" [alleged] "deeds of infamy and treason" lay in the deposition of G. J. Hyams" (so reads the Report), "testimony which illustrates the treacherous and clandestine character of the machinations in which Clay was engaged," to the complete satisfaction of Mr. Holt.* One of the most curious pieces of evidence of the Judge Advocate's really malignant design in that virulent "Report" lies in his wilful perversion of a statement which Mr. Clay had made by letter to the Secretary of War. My husband had written that, at the time of seeing Mr. Johnson's Proclamation for his arrest (during the second week in May), he had been nearly six months absent from Canada, a fact so well known that had Mr. Clay ever been brought to trial a hundred witnesses could have testified to its accuracy. Mr. Holt, to whom the Secretary of War, while denying the access of counsel to his prisoner, had confided Mr. Clay's letter, now altered the text as follows:

"In connection with the testimony in this case, as thus presented, may be noticed the assertions of Clay in his recent letters to the Secretary of War, that at the date of the *assassination*, he, Clay, had been absent from Canada nearly six months."

The substitution of the word "assassination" for "proclamation" made a difference of one month, or nearly so, in the calculations by which Mr. Holt was attempting to incriminate and to preclude a sympathy for his defenseless victim, my husband. After thus subtly manipulating Mr. Clay's statement in such way as to give it the appearance of a falsehood, Mr. Holt next proceeded to stamp it as such, and decreed that this "remain as the judgment of the Department upon the communications of this false and insolent traitor!"

"It is to be added," this remarkable Report continues, "upon the single point of the duration of his stay in Canada, that it is declared by two unimpeached witnesses†

---

* Hyams, alias Harris, was one of the witnesses who, six months before the date of Mr. Holt's Report, had been exposed by the Rev. Stuart Robinson, and who, six months later, or less, himself confessed his perjuries to the Judiciary Committee. A. S.

† But not *unimpeachable*, as later events proved. They were afterward denounced by Mr. Holt as unprincipled, perjurers and *the cause of all his trouble*. A. S.

that he was seen by them in Canada in February last. It may be said that this Bureau has now "no doubt that it will be enabled, by means of additional witnesses, to fix the term of Clay's stay in Canada even more precisely than it has already been made to appear."*

Having now carried, through many pages, his charges of numerous and basest crimes against Mr. Clay, Mr. Holt sums up his Report thus:

"It may, therefore, be safely assumed that the charge against Clement C. Clay, of having *incited the assassination of the President, is relieved of all improbability by his previous history and criminal surroundings!*"

It must not be supposed that my woman's mind at once recognised the real atrocity of these charges in that first reading, or identified the palpable inaccuracies in them; nor that fortifying deductions immediately made themselves plain to me. As was said of another Holt document, sent later to the House by the Judge Advocate General himself, every sentence of the Report before me was "redolent with the logic of prosecution, revealing something of the personal motive. There was certainly nothing in it of the *amicus curiae* spirit, nothing of the searcher after truth; nothing but the avidity of the military prosecutor for blood."

At that time, denied access to my husband, his papers and journal scattered, my own retained by the War Department, I possessed nothing with which to combat Judge Holt's accusations, save an instinctive conviction

---

* In fact, as will have been seen elsewhere, Mr. Clay arrived in South Carolina on the fourth of February, 1865, after a full month's journeying by stormy sea from Nova Scotia to Bermuda; thence on the ill-fated *Rattlesnake*, which, failing to make its way into port at Wilmington, now in the hands of the Federals, with delay and circumlocution, ran the blockade at Charleston, only to perish under the very ramparts of Fort Moultrie. His return, therefore, was sufficiently dramatic, and known to hundreds of *truly unimpeachable* witnesses, had the Judge Advocate allowed Mr. Clay to know the charges against him or given him an opportunity for denial. A. S.

that when once the charges were made known to Mr. Clay, he would be able to refute them.

That this elaborately detailed, this secretly and laboriously gathered category of crime was destined months hence to be turned to the open contempt and shame of the Judge who drew it up, I had no consoling prescience, and not even the most astute of my counsellors foresaw. Three months after Mr. Clay's conditional release, in April, 1866, however, Representative Rogers, in his report to the Judiciary Committee appointed by the House, revealed to the body there assembled the "utterly un-American proceedings of the Military Bureau" and the strange conduct of its head.

After a detailed report on the testimony which, having been given to the Bureau of Military Justice, the witnesses now acknowledged before the House Committee to have been false, Mr. Rogers continued:

"Who originated this plot I cannot ascertain. I am deeply impressed that there is guilt somewhere, and I earnestly urge upon the House an investigation of the origin of the plot, concocted to alarm the nation, to murder and dishonour innocent men, and to place the Executive in the undignified position of making, under proclamation, charges which cannot . . . stand a preliminary examination before a justice of the peace. . . . But that no time was left me to pursue to the head the villainies I detected in the hand, I might have been able plainly to tell Congress and the country that if, in this plot, we had a Titus Oates in Conover,* so also we had a Shaftesbury somewhere."

Many newspapers, the *New York Herald* and Washington *Intelligencer* in the lead, also began to reiterate the demand for a public inquiry into the strange workings of

---

* Conover was the chief witness in the cases of Mrs. Surratt and her companions, and Mr. Holt's charges against Mr. Clay were based on his testimony and that of others who had been drilled in their parts by Conover. A. S.

the Bureau of Military Justice.  Rumours ran over the country that "persons in high places who deemed it for their best interest to show complicity on the part of Davis and others in the assassination of Lincoln, by false testimony or otherwise, will find themselves held up to public gaze in a manner they little dream of." *

Two months later Mr. Holt issued a pamphlet which, under the heading, "Vindication of Judge Holt from the Foul Slanderers of Traitors, Confessed Perjurers and Suborners acting in the interest of Jefferson Davis," was scattered broadcast over the country.  It is improbable that any parallel to this snarl of defiance was ever sent out by a weak but, by no means, an apologetic offender in high office.  The pamphlet covers eight full pages of admissions as to the deceptions which he claimed had been practised upon *him*, but contains no line of regret for the tyranny he had exercised, and which had condemned distinguished and innocent men to lie for months in damp dungeons, prey to a thousand physical ills and mental torments.  Mr. Holt's vindication began as follows: "To all loyal men !   In the name of simple justice   . . . your attention is respectfully invited to the subjoined article † from the *Washington Chronicle*,‡ of yesterday,

* The public, however, was not destined to be treated to a spectacle so likely to react to the Government's dishonour.  Mr. Holt, who for a year caused to be denied to the prisoners (one of whom had been a Cabinet Minister, the other a United States Senator) even the visits of counsel, now, for some forever unexplained reason, instead of arresting the perjurer Conover, after his admissions in the Committee room of the House, talked to him kindly, and extended him the courtesy of a trip to New York, in order that he *might procure further testimony.* Once arrived, the polite swindler excused himself to his companion, and, bowing himself out, "was not seen by him thereafter," said Mr. Holt; and he adds naïvely, "and up to this time he has not communicated with me, nor has he made any effort, as I believe, to produce the witnesses !"   A. S.

† In part an interview with Mr. Holt, and the whole most obviously inspired by him.

‡ Practically the only voice now raised in an attempt to explain or justify the Advocate General's unique methods.  While denying his knavishness, it had the singular appearance of developing his foolishness.  A. S.

as representing a perfectly true vindication of myself from the atrocious calumny with which traitors and suborners are now so basely pursuing me.   Joseph Holt."

"It is clear," says this "vindicatory" excerpt, "that a conspiracy has been formed to defame the Judge Advocate General and the Bureau of Military Justice.  .  .  .  At the bottom of this conspiracy, or actively engaged in executing its purposes, is Sanford Conover, who, after having been fully proved guilty of subornation or perjury,* has unquestionably sold himself to the friends of Davis † and is seeking with them to destroy the reputation of a public officer ‡ whose confidence he gained, as we shall hereafter see, by the same solemn protestations, and which confidence he subsequently most treacherously abused.  .  .  .  A more cold-blooded plot for the assassination of character [*sic*] has never been concocted in any age or country!'"

It will be seen, Mr. Holt now overlooked the months in which he, supported in his secret work by the Secretary of War, and with almost unlimited powers vested in him, had been engaged in plotting with *the same tools, though warned of their evil careers*, against the lives of gentlemen of irreproachable character and antecedents; against my husband, who had with confidence in its integrity placed himself in the hands of the Government in the expectation of a fair and impartial trial.

Mr. Holt's "Vindication" continues: "Conover, though now wholly degraded, was then, so far as was known to the Government, without a stain upon his character."

---

* Conover had obviated the necessity for proving, by confessing, his own infamy.  A. S.

† Now for sixteen months a prisoner in Fortress Monroe, and denied trial or counsel!  A. S.

‡ It is hard to believe that, if Mr. Holt's reputation had survived the doubt thrown upon it by the House Committee, in the preceding July, it could be seriously injured by anything that might be averred by so vile a man as his former ally, Conover.  A. S.

(The thoughtful reader must naturally turn to the accusations of the Reverend Stuart Robinson, made publicly to the Government representative, Hon. H. H. Emmons, and, by the press, scattered through the country fifteen months previous to this declaration in Mr. Holt's "Vindication.") "Hence, when he wrote me," continues the aggrieved Judge Advocate General, "alleging the existence of testimony implicating Davis and others, and his ability to find the witnesses, and proffering his services to do so, I did not hesitate to accept his statements and proposals as made in good faith and entitled to credit and to consideration."

In the "Report" on the case of Mr. Clay, dated December 6, 1865, which, by the courtesy of the President, I was enabled to see, Mr. Holt's willing adoption of the fabrications of his unscrupulous "witnesses" was apparent in every phrase. In fact, its spirit of malice terrified me. I kept faith with Mr. Johnson and told no one of the knowledge I now possessed; but I communicated some of the main points of the "Report" to Judge Black and other advisers, and, resolving that I would never cease until I attained my point, I redoubled my pleadings with the President for the permission to visit my husband, which request I now knew it would be useless to make at the War Department. When I returned the "Report" to the President, I was keyed to a high pitch of alarm by the spirit shown by the Advocate General, and my requests now took another form.

"It is said, Mr. Johnson, that you have refused to allow the Military Court, composed of Messrs. Holt, Speed and Stanton, to try Mr. Davis and Mr. Clay." The President bowed affirmatively.

"Then I pray you to give me your solemn oath in the presence of the living God, that you will *never*, while in this Presidential chair, yield those two innocent men into the hands of that blood-seeking Military Commission!"

I was greatly agitated, and weeping. Mr. Johnson, however, was calm and seemingly deeply in earnest as he answered me,

"I promise you, Mrs. Clay; trust me!"

"I will; I do!" I cried, "but I would like you to emphasise this sacred oath, remembering the precious lives that hang upon it."

Upon this Mr. Johnson raised his hand and repeated his promise, adding again, "trust me!"

After this interview I felt a sense of security which gave me comparative repose of mind, but, nevertheless, I called almost daily, to fortify Mr. Johnson against the continued machinations of those officials whose influence was so inimical to my husband and Mr. Davis. I now began to perceive that Judge Black, Senator Garland and others had said truly when they remarked to me that Mr. Johnson might be moved, if at all, by his heart rather than by his head. He had already given me a strong proof of this; soon he gave me others.

The Christmas season was approaching, and while all about me were arranging their little gaieties and surprises, the realisation of Mr. Clay's isolation and discomforts and peril became more and more poignant. To add to the sadness of our situation, letters from Huntsville containing pathetic allusions to the failing health of my husband's mother now began to follow each other rapidly. I was urged to act quickly if she and her son were to meet on earth again. In my letters to Mr. Clay I dared not tell him of this approaching disaster, for between himself and his mother an unusually tender relationship existed. I dreaded the alarm such news might give him, alone and ill in his dismal prison, exhausted as he was with waiting for direct communication with me. I had already been a month in Washington without having effected a meeting with him. Under the circumstances, the headway gained seemed inappreciable. With a copy of Holt's "Report" in my possession, I resolved to go on to New York for consultation with Mr. O'Conor, Mr. Shea, and Mr. Greeley, so soon as I should receive some definite concession from the President.

I now told Mr. Johnson of Mrs. Clay's condition, and begged him to release my husband, if only to permit him one interview with his probably dying mother, to return again to custody if the President so wished; or, failing the granting of this, to allow me to visit him in prison.   At last, after much reiteration on my part, Mr. Johnson yielded; he promised that he would issue the permit for my visit to Fort Monroe on his own responsibility in a few days; that I might rely upon receiving it upon my return from the metropolis.

Hastening to New York, I was soon made aware by Messrs. O'Conor, Shea and Greeley, who called upon me severally, that my one course now was to persist in my effort to precipitate a trial for my husband, or to procure his release on parole, in which these gentlemen stood ready to supplement me, and, upon the announcement of a trial, to defend Mr. Clay.

My interview with Mr. Greeley took place in one of the public corridors of the New York hotel, now thronging with Southern guests, and, as I sat beside him on a settle, in earnest conversation with the fatherly old man, his bald "temple of thought" gleaming under the gaslights, which threw their fullest brilliancy upon us, I remember seeing several prominent Southern generals then registered at the hotel glance repeatedly at us, and always with a look of surprise that said very plainly, "*Well!* If there isn't Mrs. Clem. Clay hobnobbing with that old Abolitionist!"

# CHAPTER XXVII

## President Johnson Interposes

Mr. Johnson kept his word. Late in December I found myself on my way to Baltimore with the President's autographed permit in hand, that would admit me to my husband's prison. I left Washington on the afternoon of the 27th of December, going by train to Baltimore. Here, crossing the city in an omnibus with other passengers, to the wharf of the "New Line Steamers," I was soon on board the boat, the *George Leary*, bound for Norfolk and Fortress Monroe. I was so keenly alive to my own lonely condition that I could not bring myself even to register my name among the list of happier passengers. Everywhere about me gaily dressed people thronged. I saw among them General Granger and wife, his staff, and ladies of the party. As the *George Leary* pulled out from her moorings, the brass band of a company of soldiers bound for Norfolk began to play sweet, old-time airs. I had no desire to linger among the carefree throng, and, calling the stewardess, handed her a gold-piece, saying, "Can you sign for me or get me a stateroom? I only go to Fortress Monroe."

In a few moments she returned, regarding me inquiringly.

"Lady!" she asked, "ain't you the wife of one of those gentlemen down at the Fort?"

"Yes!" I answered. "I am the wife of Mr. Clay, the prisoner!"

Thereupon she opened her hand, displaying my gold-piece, saying, "The captain says he can't take any fare

from you.   He'll be here in a little while!"   And she
moved away.

In a few moments the tall, gaunt Captain Blakeman
stood before me.

"Are you Mrs. Clay?" he asked.   "Wife of the prisoner
at Fortress Monroe?"

Upon receiving my affirmative answer, the Captain
spoke earnestly.

"Mrs. Clay, you have my deep sympathy.   I'm a regular
Down-Easter myself—a Maine man; but for forty years
I've plied a boat between Northern and Southern cities;
and I know the Southern people well.   I think it is a
damned shame the way the Government is behaving
toward you and Mrs. Davis!"

For a moment the tears blinded me, seeing which the
Captain at once withdrew, comprehending the thanks he
saw I could not utter.   However, when the gong sounded
for supper, he returned, and with kindly tact led me to a
place beside him at the table, though I assured him I
wanted nothing.   At my obvious lack of appetite he
showed a very woman's thoughtfulness, himself preparing
the viands before me while he urged me "to drink my
coffee.   You *must* take something," he said from time to
time, whenever he perceived a lagging interest in the
dishes before me.   Nor did this complete his kindnesses,
for on the following morning, as I left the boat, Captain
Blakeman handed me a slip of paper on which was written:

"New Line Steamers, Baltimore, December 27, 1865.
"Will please pass free Mrs. C. C. Clay, rooms and meals
included, to all points as she wishes, and oblige,
              "S. Blakeman,
        "Commanding Steamer *George Leary*."

"I hope you will use this pass as often as you need it,"
he said.

We arrived at Fortress Monroe at four o'clock the next
morning.   As I stepped from the gangplank, the scene

about me was black and bleak, the air wintry. Save for a few dozing stevedores here and there, whom I soon perceived, the wharf was quite deserted. It had been my intention, upon my arrival, to go directly to the little Hygeia Hotel just outside the Fort, but upon the advice of Captain Blakeman I accepted the shelter offered me by the clerk in charge of the wharf, and rested until daylight in his snug little room just off from the office.

Just before leaving Washington I had written to Dr. Craven, telling him of my intended visit to the prison, and asking him to meet me at the little hotel. I now, at the first streak of dawn, still acting upon the suggestions of the kind captain, found a messenger and sent him with a note to General Miles, telling him of my arrival with the President's permit to see my husband, and asking that an ambulance be sent to convey me to the Fort; and I despatched a second to Dr. Craven to tell him my whereabouts. Unknown to me, that friendly physician, whose humane treatment of Mr. Davis and my husband had brought upon him the disapproval of the War Department, had already been removed from his station at the Fort. My messenger found him, nevertheless, and upon receipt of my message he came and made himself known to me. His words were few, and not of a character to cheer one in my forlorn condition.

"Look for no kindness, Mrs. Clay," he said, "at the hands of my successor, Dr. Cooper. He is the blackest of Black Republicans, and may be relied upon to show the prisoners little mercy."

Our interview was brief, and, as the Fort ambulance was seen approaching, the Doctor left me hurriedly. "For," said he, "it will do neither you nor the prisoners any good if you are seen talking with me." He had scarcely disappeared in the grey morning when the escort from the Fort arrived. The vehicle was manned by two handsome Union soldiers, one, Major Hitchcock of

General Miles's staff, and the other Lieutenant Muhlenberg, a grandson, as I afterward learned, of the author of "I would not live alway." Months afterward, when Mr. Clay left the Fortress, he carried with him the little volume containing Bishop Muhlenberg's verses, a gift from the young lieutenant.

Arrived at the Fort, I was taken at once to the headquarters of General Miles, and conducted to a room commodiously and even luxuriously furnished. In a short time the General made his appearance. He was polite and even courteous in the examination of my passport, which he scanned carefully; but his manner was noncommittal as he politely asked me to "be seated." I seated myself and waited. The General withdrew. After the lapse of a few moments, an orderly appeared, bearing upon a salver a tempting breakfast; but I, who had spent months in seeking the privilege I had now come to claim, could touch nothing. I declined the food, saying I would wait and breakfast with my husband. The orderly looked perplexed, but removed the tray; and now a dreary and inexplicable wait began, interbroken with first a nervous, then an indignant, and at last a tearful inquiry. During the morning I affected a nonchalance wholly at variance with my real feelings. Picking up a book that lay at my elbow on the table, I was surprised to see a familiar name upon the fly-leaf. I commented upon the luxury of the apartment when next General Miles entered, and added, "These books seem to have been Governor Wise's property." The General was quick to defend himself from any suggestion that might lie in my words. He replied at once. "These headquarters were furnished by General Butler before I was sent here!"

Midday came and still the President's autographed permit, which to me had seemed so powerful a document, was not honoured. A savoury luncheon was now brought in, but a nausea of nervousness had seized me and I could

DR. HENRY C. VOGELL

Fortress Monroe, 1866

not eat a morsel. My excitement increased momentarily, until the distress of mind and apprehension were wholly beyond my control. I now implored General Miles to let me see my husband, if only for a moment; to explain this delay in the face of the President's order. I begged him to allow me to telegraph to Washington; but to all my pleadings his only reply was to urge me to "be calm." He assured me he regretted the delay, but that "his orders" were such that he could neither admit me to my husband's room, nor allow me to use the Government wires at present.

By the middle of the afternoon, faint with pleadings and worn with indignation and fears at the unknown powers which dared thus to obstruct the carrying out of the President's orders, not knowing what might yet be before me, my self-possession entirely deserted me. I remember, during my hysterical weeping, crying out to General Miles, "If you are ever married, I pray God your wife may never know an hour like this!"

In the midst of an uncontrollable paroxysm which seized me at last, Dr. Vogell, who has been variously designated as the private secretary and instructor of General Miles, entered. During the day General Miles had presented the Doctor to me, and, in his subsequent passing and repassing through the room, we had from time to time exchanged a remark. He was a tall, picturesque man, of possibly sixty years. At the sight of my culminating misery, Dr. Vogell could bear the distressful scene no longer. He cried out impulsively, "Miles, for God's sake, let the woman go to her husband!"

Unhappily, this manly outburst, though it had its own message of sympathy for me, failed as utterly to move the commanding General Miles as had my previous urgings. In the months that followed, Dr. Vogell often called upon me clandestinely in Washington (announced as "Mr. Brown"), to say that "a friend of yours was quite well this morning, and desired his love given you!" The recollection of his kindnesses lives imperishable in my memory, but especially vivid is that first upwelling sympathy during the painful waiting at the Fort.

General Miles seemed not untouched by my pleadings, but, it was evident, he felt himself subject to a superior power which forced him to refuse them. His manner throughout, in fact, was courteous and apologetic. Despite my agony of mind, it was late in the afternoon ere the President's order was honoured. Then General Miles entered, and, with an appearance of completest relief, consigned me, tear-stained and ill, to the care of Lieutenant Stone, who conducted me to Mr. Clay's prison.

All day my husband, to whom there had penetrated a rumour of my coming, had been waiting for me, himself tortured by fears for my safety and by the mystery of my delay. The gloomy corridors, in which soldiers patrolled night and day, guarding the two delicate prisoners of State, were already darkening with the early evening shadows when, at last, I saw my husband, martyr to his faith in the honour of the Government, standing within the grating, awaiting me. The sight of his tall, slender form, his pale face and whitened hair, awaiting me behind those dungeon bars, affected me terribly. My pen is too feeble to convey the weakness that overcame me as Lieutenant Stone inserted and turned the key in the massive creaking lock and admitted me; nor shall I attempt to revive here the brief hours that followed, with their tumultuous telling over of the happenings of the past months and our hurried planning for the future.

I returned to the capital full of sorrow and indignation. My adventure at Fortress Monroe had revealed to me, far more fully than I previously had suspected was possible, the struggle for power that was now going on between the Secretary of War, Mr. Stanton, on the one side, and on the other, President Johnson, by whose courtesy or timidity this official still retained his portfolio. I resolved to relate my entire experience at Fortress Monroe to the President at the first opportunity.

In the meantime, my husband, with whom I had left a digest of Holt's report, upon a careful perusal of it, had been greatly aroused. By the courtesy of a secret friend, he hastened to send me a list of persons who could, if called upon, readily testify to his whereabouts during certain periods described in the charges against him. He urged me to see the President, and not to cease in my efforts to obtain his release on parole. His condition of mind as expressed in this communication was, it was evident, one of intense excitement.

"You must not get discouraged!" he wrote. "*My life depends upon it, I fear!* Since the days of Cain and Judas, men may take life for money or some other selfish end. As innocent men as I am have been judicially murdered, and I do not feel secure from it, although God knows I feel innocent of crime against the United States or any citizen thereof. As to my declaring my purpose to surrender to meet the charge of assassination, my unwillingness to fly from such charge, my preferring death to living with that brand on me, my desire to exculpate Mr. Davis, myself and the South from it, you know as well as I do.

"Judge Holt is determined to sacrifice me *for reasons given you.** He may do it if I am not allowed liberty to

* In the preparation for the publication of these Memoirs, I found myself continually lighting upon evidences of irregularity in the Government's proceedings against Mr. Clay. I was met constantly by what appeared to be a persistent and inexplicable persecution of Messrs. Davis and Clay (if not a plot against them, as hinted by Representative Rogers) at the hands of the War Department, acting through Mr. Joseph Holt. I encountered charges, not ambiguously made against Mr. Holt, of malice, and of rancour which would be satisfied only with the "judicial murder" of the prisoners in his hands. Charges of malice and meanness have been made against him by living men as frequently as by those who have passed away; men, moreover, whose

seek witnesses and prepare my defense; or, if I am subjected to the mockery of trial by Military Court, when
all the charges he can make may be brought against me
in a great drag-net."

As a step toward securing an early interview, and also
because the President's daughters, Mrs. Stover and

integrity of purpose has never been challenged.    A rather general condemnation of Mr. Holt appears in certain correspondence of the sixties.    It was uttered publicly in the press in the early and middle portion of that decade.    In the pamphlet alluded to and quoted from in
Chapter XXII. of these "Memoirs," the Rev. Stuart Robinson had
quoted Mr. Crittenden, of Kentucky, and another, to show the peculiar
estimate in which Mr. Holt was then held.    "I know little," wrote Mr.
Robinson, in June of '65, "either of the personal or public character of
Mr. Holt. . . .    The only well-defined impression I have of his personal character is gained from two remarks concerning him in 1861–'62.
The first, that of a venerable Christian lady, of the old-fashioned country type, made to me: 'Joe Holt, Sir, is the only young man I ever knew
that left this country without leaving one friend behind him in it!'
The other, the fierce retort of the venerable Crittenden, to a Cabinet
officer, reported to me by Governor Morehead: 'Joseph Holt, of *Kentucky*, did you say, Sir?    I tell you, Sir, by Heaven! there is no such
man as Joseph Holt, of *Kentucky!*'"

In addition to such contemporaneous public utterances concerning
Mr. Holt, I have learned much that is corroborative by word of mouth
from men whose opinions have been softened by time, and whose conspicuous positions in national affairs establish their utterances as both
weighty and trustworthy.    Said one of these, a United States Senator,
within the year (1903), "Joseph Holt was the meanest man of his
time.    He was both unscrupulous and ambitious ; and the *smartest*
man I ever knew!"

Another as prominent in the nation's affairs, said, using the same
adjective as did the Senator just quoted, "He was a peculiarly mean
man.    I don't know the true circumstances of Mr. Davis's and Mr.
Clay's imprisonment, but the suspicions that attached to Holt were
never proven, nor, so far as I know, investigated.    After he went out
of office he seemed to have no friends.,    He remained in Washington.
I often saw him.    Every morning he would get into a shabby old
buggy and drive to market, where he would buy his meat and vegetables, potatoes, etc., for the day.    These he would carry back to the
house in his buggy, and his cook would prepare his solitary meals for
him.    I never felt anything but dislike for him," said this gentleman,
"and I don't know any one else who did!"

"True!" responded another gentleman, whose word has balanced
national opinion to a large extent for many years, "Mr. Holt was
repugnant to me.    I think he was generally regarded as a man who
had forsaken his own section for gain.    I thought him a heartless man.
When he left office he went into utter obscurity!"

These remarks, coming from sources so authoritative, lent strength
to the supposition that Mr. Holt's behaviour toward his self-surrendered

Mrs. Patterson, now presiding at the White House, had been courteous to me, I resolved, as a stroke of policy, to attend the Presidential reception to take place on the ninth of January. Naturally, since my arrival in Washington, I had not participated in the social life about me. In acknowledgment of Mr. Johnson's concessions, and, with my husband's life at stake, with a desire further to win the President's good offices, I now prepared to attend his levee. My toilette was complete save for the draw-

prisoner and former friend, Clement C. Clay, if it might be traced to its source, would, indeed, reveal a persecution at once vengeful and malicious, springing from some personal animus. For a year I made continuous effort to find this motive, but without success. Pitiless enmity, supported by almost unlimited powers (vested in Mr. Holt as Judge Advocate General, when the Government was in an unprecedented condition of chaos), this officer surely exercised toward Messrs. Davis and Clay; but, where was the *raison d'être*?

By an accident, "at the eleventh hour," the paper in Mr. Clay's handwriting containing the sentence quoted in the preceding text came to light. I wrote promptly to Mrs. Clay-Clopton concerning it, urging her to try to recall, if possible, the "reasons" which Mr. Clay, in his prison in Fortress Monroe, on the night of December 29, 1865, had given her in explanation of Mr. Holt's animosity toward him. Her reply ran as follows:

"I *can* give you, in regard of Mr. Holt's persecution of my husband, one very important reason! On the breaking out of the war, I think on the secession of Mississippi, Holt, who had won both his fame and his fortune in that State of his adoption, espoused the Southern cause. Whether this was known to others than Mr. Davis and Mr. Clay, I do not know. From the impression that remains on my memory, Holt communicated in confidence to those two gentlemen alone his intention of standing by the South. Possibly, it was said to Mr. Davis alone, as the latter was Mississippi's leading Senator, and by Mr. Davis repeated to Mr. Clay. It was a common thing in those days to keep secret one's intentions." [See visit of Admiral Semmes, Chapter IX.] "Whether Holt's decision was known to others than Mr. Davis and Mr. Clay, his friend," continues the letter, "I do not know. I remember Mr. Clay telling me that Mr. Holt was a renegade and a traitor, *who had pledged himself to the South;* but when, in his selfish ambition, he received a higher bid from the Federal Government, he deserted our cause and went over to the opposition. I do not recall the position offered Mr. Holt by the Federal Government, but it was a plum he coveted.

"You ask whether Mr. Clay and Mr. Holt ever had any dealings with each other, political or business:

"None of any kind! Mr. Clay only knew of Holt's base defection from our cause and condemned him for it. My husband told me (in the Fortress), 'Mr. Holt knows the estimate Mr. Davis and I have of his defection and would fain get us out of the way!'" A. S.

ing on of my gloves, when, while awaiting the call of my hostess Mrs. Parker and her daughter Mrs. Bouligny, whose preparations were somewhat more elaborate than my own, I broke the seal of some letters from home. The news they contained was of a nature well calculated to divert me from the thought of appearing at a public gathering, even at the Executive Mansion.

The first told me, in hurried lines, of the illness of my husband's mother; the second, posted a few hours later, announced her death. "I write beside mother's dead body," began my sister, Mrs. J. Withers Clay. "Her constant theme was brother Clement, and the last thing I remember hearing her say was 'What of my son?' in so distressed a tone that her heart appeared broken. . . . I trust you have seen your dear husband ere this. I hope he will be released before poor father leaves us. He is very distressed, very gentle and subdued in his trouble. . . . I can never forget mother's heart-thrilling question 'What of my son?' She was very unhappy about your last letter—it was rather low-spirited—and said, 'I have no hope; I shall never see my son!'"

Within the next day I called upon Mr. Johnson. He received me with his usual urbane manner, quite in contrast with my own indignant mood.

"Mr. Johnson," I began, "Who *is* the President of the United States?"

He smiled rather satirically and shrugged his shoulders.

"I am supposed to be!" he said.

"But you are *not!*" I answered. "Your autographed letter was of little more use to me when I reached Fortress Monroe than blank paper would have been! For hours it was not honoured, during which time your Secretary of War held the wires and refused to allow me either to see my husband or to communicate with you!" Then, in as few words as possible, I related the circumstances of my

visit to the Fort.   Mr. Johnson, though constrained to
preserve his official reserve, was unable to repress or
disguise his anger at my recital.

"When you go there again you'll have no difficulty,
I assure you!" he said.

"When may I?" I asked eagerly.

"When you wish," he answered.

I now pictured to him my husband's position; I re
lated the sad news I had just received, and which, under
present conditions, I knew I dared not tell Mr. Clay.
implored the President, by every argument at my command, to exercise his Executive power and release Mr.
Clay on his parole.   Every moment of his incarceration
under the discipline invented by the unscrupulous
military authorities, I felt his life to be imperilled.   As
our interview proceeded, however, I perceived the old
indecision of manner returning.   The President's replies
were all to one effect; viz.: that the Secretary of War
must decide upon the case.   He freely made out another
permit to the prison, this time to cover a longer stay,
but about a parole for Mr. Clay, or the naming of a day
for an early trial, he could promise nothing.   He would
consult his Cabinet; he would see Mr. Stanton.   At
last, my importunities for an authoritative action growing greater, the President burst out with every evidence
of deep feeling:

"Go home, woman, and write what you have to say,
and I'll read it to my Cabinet at the next meeting!"

"You will not!" I answered hotly.

"Why?" he asked, cynically.

"Because," I replied, "you are afraid of Mr. Stanton!
He would not allow it!   But, let *me* come to the Cabinet
meeting, and *I* will read it," I said.   "For, with my
husband's life and liberty at stake, I do not fear Mr.
Stanton or any one else."

The President assured me I need have no misgivings;

if I would write my plea and send it directly to him, he would, he promised me, have it read at the next Cabinet meeting (on the morrow). Actuated by the hope, however meagre, of gaining a possible sympathy from the President's Governmental associates, even though the dictator Stanton was so coercing a personality in that body, I prepared my letter. I afterward secured an official copy of it. It ran as follows:

"WASHINGTON CITY, January 11, 1866.
" *To His Excellency, President of the United States :*
". . . How true it is that all conditions of life, however seemingly extreme, are capable of augmentation! I have thought and so told you, that for eight months past I have been, and God knows with what cause, at the Nadir of despair; that my cup, bitterer than the waters of Marah, was brimming, my heart breaking. A letter received two evenings ago announces the death of my husband's beloved mother, wife of ex-Governor Clay. Deeply distressing to me; oh! Mr. Johnson, what a blow to my husband, your unhappy prisoner! He was her idolised son, her first-born; bears the name of her lover-husband, and upon whose lineaments she had not rested her longing eyes for three long, weary, desolate years.

"On the morning of the first she swooned, and expired on the second, inquiring, 'What of my son?' Oh, Mr. President, what an agonising reflection to my husband! How can I summon nerve to tell him the news? I cannot write so great a grief, nor can I tell it and leave him in his gloomy prison to struggle with it alone! Will you not pour in the oil of healing? I beg of you, permit me to bear with me, along with my 'weight of woe,' the antidote. Issue the order for my husband's release on his *parole d'honneur*, with bail if desired, and let him once more see our father, who lies (now) on a bed of illness. My sister writes, 'Father cannot long survive.* God grant that he may see dear brother Clement ere he goes. Cannot he come?'—I repeat, cannot he come?

"Mr. President, you hold many noble prisoners in your forts, but Mr. Clay's case is *sui generis*. General Grant, the whole-souled soldier, in his letter to you in his behalf, says, 'His manly surrender is to me a full and sufficient guarantee

* Governor Clay died the following autumn.

that he will be forthcoming at any time the civil authorities of the land may call for him.'   Even Mr. Stanton, who is not considered partial to so-called 'Rebels,' told me, in my only interview, that 'he was not my husband's judge,' as if he, Pilate-like, were willing to wash his hands of innocent blood. I replied tremblingly, 'I would fain not have you for his accuser, Sir.'   To which he rejoined, not unkindly, 'I am not his accuser, Madam.'   I thanked God for even that cold comfort as harbinger of better days.

"And now, Sir, may I ask you who are those opposed to my husband's release on parole?   I have yet to find the first man, Federal or other, who does not express admiration at the high sense of honour and chivalric faith, in the prompt and manly surrender; and astonishment at the detention.   To-day we might have been far away in some peaceful spot, united at least, and happy, but for that sense of unsullied honour, which 'feeling a stain like a wound,' remained to wipe it out.   Can you longer refuse him the privilege?

"The law supposes all men innocent till proven guilty, and if it will allow me, I, alone, can disprove, *in toto*, the testimony of the conspiracy case, implicating him.   Mr. Clay, always delicate, is dying daily.   He told me he was resigned to God's will and perfectly willing to perish in those four walls if his country would be benefited thereby.   Mr. President, my husband is my world, my all, and 'dear to me as are the ruddy drops that visit this sad heart.'   Give him to me for a little while, at least long enough to glad the dim eyes of the eager and aged watcher at home and close them; and he shall return to you, on his honour and my life, at any moment called for by the Government.   Let me bring him to you to prove to you the truth of my statement in point of health, and to afford him the right of personal appeal.   .   .   .   That God may incline you to grant my prayer and soften 'the hearts of our enemies,' restore Peace indeed to the land, and bless and guide and guard you in public and private life to your journey's end, is the prayer of her who hopefully, trustfully, and truthfully subscribes herself,

"Your friend,
(Signed.)                                        "V. C. CLAY."

I sent this epistle to Mr. Johnson, but, despite the haste in which I had written and despatched it, I was too late for the promised reading, which fact I learned from the following message, that reached me the next day. It was written on the back of the President's card in his (by this time) familiar, scrawling hand.

"Your letter," it read, "was too late yesterday. It does your heart and head credit. It is a most powerful appeal. You have excelled yourself in its production!"

At the next Cabinet meeting Mr. Johnson made his promise good. The letter was then read, by Mr. Evarts, too late, however, even had it produced immediate results, to enable me to carry the parole I had hoped for to my husband. I was again with Mr. Clay at the Fortress when this meeting took place, but, having no balm to soothe the wound, I could not tell him of the blow that had befallen him, nor did he hear of it until, nearly four months later, he left the prison. In the interim, in order that my husband should not remark upon the sombreness of my attire, I wore a red rose in my bonnet and red ribbon at my throat whenever I visited the Fort.

I learned the particulars of that (to me) eventful Cabinet reading from Mr. Johnson later. Upon the conclusion of the letter Mr. Stanton asked for it. He scanned it closely and put it into his pocket without comment. Nor was the missive again returned to Mr. Johnson until weeks had elapsed and several requests had been made for it.

# CHAPTER XXVIII

## The Nation's Prisoners

On the twenty-first of January, 1866, a few days after my last conversation with President Johnson, I found myself a second time within the ramparts of America's most formidable military prison. This time, unhindered, I was led directly to my husband's gloomy room. In this and the several succeeding visits I paid Mr. Clay in prison, I learned to comprehend, where before I had but imagined, the terrible sufferings my husband had undergone for now eight months. When I parted from General Miles on May 24th, of the preceding year, he gave me his promise that Mr. Clay should have every comfort he could allow him.

I found, upon my admission to Fortress Monroe, in January, 1866, that his prisoner, for three or more months, had been confined within a narrow cell, grated and barred like a cage in a menagerie, into which the meagre daylight crept through the long, thin opening in the thick walls. An unwholesome sweat had oozed through the bare walls which surrounded him, at times, it was said, increasing until it flowed in streams. For weeks after entering the prison (I now learned) Mr. Clay had been denied not only the use of his clothing, but his toilet brushes and comb, and every item calculated to preserve his health and self-esteem had been taken from him. His only food for weeks had been a soldier's rations, until Dr. Craven, at last, felt obliged to order a hospital diet. These rations had been passed through the prison bars in tin cup or plate, unaccompanied by knife, fork or spoon.

For forty days at a stretch he had not been permitted to look upon the sun; for months, though debarred from communication with or visits from his own family, he was exhibited to strangers, civilian or military, who from time to time were brought into his cell, conversing among themselves, or to the gratings to stare at him with curious gaze. "I have been treated as if already convicted of an infamous crime," wrote my husband in a paper sent out by one who proved trustworthy. "Indeed, one of my warders told me that the orders from Washington required I should be subjected to the same prison discipline that the assassins of Abraham Lincoln underwent. While the Third Pennsylvania Artillery (volunteers) were on duty (till October 31st), I scarcely ever walked out without being greeted with 'Shoot him! Hang him! Bring a rope! The damned rascal!' But since the regulars came in nothing like this has occurred. . . . Mr. Davis and I are not allowed to communicate with each other. We have met but a few times, in walking contrary to the intention of officers and orders, but only saluted each other and asked of health."

Once, my husband told me, upon thus meeting, Mr. Davis and he greeted each other in French, whereupon the soldiers, scenting some further "treason," rushed at them, pointing their bayonets.

"I have been subjected," continued my husband's statement, "to the most refined but severe torture of body and soul; my health considered in order to preserve the sensibility of the body to pain. . . . I have been allowed irregularly some newspapers, but never one alluding to any evidence against me, or mentioning me, unless in terms of reproach. I am cut off from the world, except its reproaches!"

During none of my visits to the Fort was I permitted

to speak with Mr. Davis, between whom and my husband, as I have said, even an occasional word, for a long time, was interdicted; but, when sending to him a tray of good things from among gifts to my husband or brought with me from Washington, I managed often to send, with an extra segar or two, a twisted paper lighter on which I had scribbled "Mrs. Davis and children are well," or some (as I hoped) equally cheering greeting.

In later days, when a fuller liberty of walking about the Fort was granted the prisoners, they were occasionally able to pass to each other some brief message, written, it might be, on the inch-wide margin of a bit of newspaper or wrapping. Two or three times a scrap of writing-paper, written all over in the finest possible hand, was passed from one to the other. Two such messages, uttered under the impression that Mr. Clay was soon to be liberated, are expressive of the unflinching spirit which Mr. Davis at all times showed, even under torments as humiliating, and, in one instance, even more cruel, than those endured by my husband. The first would seem to have reached Mr. Clay shortly after my first visit to the Fort. A lengthy note, in finest script and compressed within the dimensions of a single six-by-eight sheet of paper, it read as if it had been written sentence by sentence, as mood dictated or opportunity offered.

A second note, in even more diminutive script,* was passed to my husband in the early winter of '66, when at last it seemed assured that Mr. Clay would be liberated. It was written in this belief, and gave my husband directions as to friends whose influence might be awakened on our late President's behalf. Mr. Davis reiterated his loyalty to the cause for which he was now suffering, but

---

* On the back of this scrap, Mr. Davis wrote in pencil, "If you get this, say I've got the tobacco and will give you a puff." Long afterward, lest the identity of the little slip should be lost, Mr. Clay added this comment beneath the original inscription: "Preserve! Mr. Davis to me in prison! C. C. C." A. S.

declared his anxiety for his wife's and children's fates. He felt that there was a bloodthirsty hate against him, the strong motive being to degrade the lost cause in his person.

In all of his communications, however short, Mr. Davis wrote with dignity and conviction, as became a man who had been the Chief Magistrate of a people. Once only, and that during my first stay in the Fort, I saw the tall figure of our late Chief. "I saw Mr. Davis walking on the ramparts," I wrote to ex-Governor Clay. "His beard and hair are white, and he is thin to emaciation, but walked like a President still."

Upon my arrival at the Fortress early in '66, I found Mr. Clay established in Carroll Hall, in what, in view of his earlier surroundings, was a comfortable room. It was perhaps sixteen feet square, and was lighted by two fairly large windows which opened toward the front of the building, but were heavily barred with iron, as was also the entrance. The cot upon which my husband slept was much too short for his comfort, and a stool was the only seat at his disposal.

After a survey of Mr. Clay's quarters, I at once called the attention of General Miles to the shortcomings of the cot and the absence of a chair, and in a few hours a mattress sufficiently long and two chairs were brought in. I also requested that a drugget be placed upon the floor of Mr. Davis's room, in order that the noise caused by the change of guard might be diminished; for, in his nervous state, it was said, he suffered greatly by reason of it. This, I believe, was also conceded. My husband had converted the window-sills of his room into a buffet and book-shelf, respectively, on one of which were kept his medicines and such tidbits and delicacies as were now from time to time sent to him by Dr. Withers, our cousin, or which I carried in with me from Washington friends. On the other, his meagre supply of books, the Bible and Jay's Prayers being the principal volumes.

But for his own scrupulous cleanliness, Mr. Clay's life must long ago have succumbed to his unparalleled deprivations in that cruel imprisonment. So neatly had he kept his cell and room, however, that they were the wonder of all his attendants. It was his custom, when he took his morning bath (he told me), to stand the basin first in one and then another position in the room, splashing the water about as far as he could, after which he would take the broom with which he was provided and brush the wet portions clean! To such depths of cruelty did the agents of Mr. Stanton and Mr. Holt condemn a delicate scholar —a former friend, recently a United States Senator, whose name throughout the land was the synonym for unfailing integrity, against whom the United States as yet seemingly had not found a single charge on which he might be brought to trial!

I learned of many instances of insult offered to Mr. Clay by his rude first custodians. Upon one occasion, reminded of it by the sound of the dull-splashing waters without the walls of his cell, my husband conceived the idea that a salt bath would assist in strengthening him. He therefore asked the attendant for the day if, instead of the fresh water usually supplied to him, he would bring him some salt water. The man's reply was emphatic.

"You damned Rebel!" he said. "You may thank God you get any water. You don't deserve to have any!"

My husband, whose nature was of the tenderest and most patient, especially with the ignorant, answered very quietly, "I *am* thankful for any water!" His reply illustrated anew the magic of the soft answer, for the soldier, looking very much ashamed, spoke in a moment in a very different manner.

"Forgive me, Mr. Clay," he said, "I don't know why I did it. I've got nothing against you. Guess it's a kind of habit of damning Johnny Rebs! I'll get you the water. I believe you're a Christian gentleman!"

On the evening of the first day of my second visit to the Fortress, I encountered Dr. Cooper, against whom, it will be recalled, Dr. Craven had warned me. To the prisoner he had always revealed himself as a man of strictly unsocial manner, not to say an austere and pitiless one. During the first day of my visit to the Fort, I saw nothing of him. It was dark when I left my husband's cell and set out, escorted by Lieutenant Stone, for the little hotel outside the ramparts. Once outside of the prison, the air was chill, and so silent, save for a strong wind, that I was conscious of no sound save it and the swashing of the waters against the stone walls of the Fort. Its cadence was weird and full of melancholy. As the doors of the prison closed behind us, I saw in the shadows a curious figure coming directly toward us. It was clad in a long, loose, flapping dressing-gown, and in its mouth was a pipe in which glowed a live spark of tobacco. I observed my guard looking straight ahead and apparently unobservant; but he said, under his breath and in a tone only audible to me, "Here comes Dr. Cooper!"

Another moment and the figure was beside us.

"Stone," said a gruff voice, "present me to Mrs. Clay!"

My escort complied promptly, and then, to my alarm, hastened away at once, leaving me dismayed and apprehensive, in the care of the "blackest of Black Republicans" and one who would "show me no mercy!"

"Madam!" said the Doctor, whose features I could scarcely discern in the dusk, "my wife wishes you to accept the hospitality of our house to-night!"

Had the man turned suddenly and clasped manacles about my wrists, I could scarcely have been more startled.

"I beg your pardon!" I stammered. "I am on my way to General Miles's headquarters for my passport with which to leave the Fort. I have not the privilege of remaining within the ramparts over night."

"Nonsense, Madam!" replied the Doctor, almost rudely.

DR. GEORGE COOPER
Fortress Monroe, 1866

"My wife expects you! We soldiers have no luxuries and but few comforts, but we can give you shelter and save General Miles some trouble in sending you to and fro!" And he started rapidly across the stone walk. I followed him in silence for some distance, hardly knowing why I did so, my mind busy conjuring up the possible significance of his conduct, and alert to meet the unknown perils into which it was possible I was being led. Presently the Doctor, between puffs of tobacco, asked, "Ever been here before?"

"Yes!" I answered, sorrowfully enough, but with some pride, too, unless at that moment I proved untrue to myself, which I know I did not. "Yes! I was here during President Pierce's administration, when my husband was an honoured Senator, and I, beside Secretary Dobbin, looked on the brilliant rockets that wrote the names of Pierce and Davis across the night sky!" I was sad at the thought of that joyful occasion and the contrast the present afforded me. Suddenly the Doctor, who had been chewing most ostentatiously at his pipe, edged up to me and said, in a low voice:

"Cheer up! Cheer up! Cheer up! Madam!" He spoke so rapidly that I hardly realised the significance of his words. They sounded exactly like "chirrup, chirrup, chirrup, Madam." "My wife," he added, still in that low-guarded voice, "is the damnedest Rebel out, except yourself, Madam!"

I was dumbfounded! He, Dr. Cooper, the blackest of Black Republicans, etc., against whom I had been warned so emphatically? A flood of gratitude rushed over me. Half crying, I turned to grasp his hand and thank him, but seeing my intention, he drew away, saying sharply, "None of that, Madam! None o' that!" and, increasing his gait suddenly, almost flew before me, his long gown rising in his wake most ludicrously, as he made for a dark cottage that now began to shape itself out of the gloom. It was so small that until we were almost upon it I had not perceived it. Every window it boasted was mysteriously dark.

My guide pushed open the door, however, and entered, I following him mechanically. The door closed behind me, and it seemed automatically, as the Doctor disappeared from view; but, in a moment, I found myself in the friendly embrace of the Doctor's wife, one of the loveliest of women, Elva Cooper.

"Be of good cheer, my sweet sister!" she said, as her tears flowed in sympathy with mine. "You are in the right place. There is nothing under heaven you would do for Mr. Davis or Mr. Clay that I will not do. I am an Old Point Comfort woman, born here. My mother is a Virginian," she continued, "and is with me; and you must know my little Georgette. We are all Rebels of the first water!" and this I found to be true.

This strangely God-given friend, Elva Jones Cooper, with whom I remained four days and nights, never flagged in her devotion to me and the prisoners. I saw her many times in my several visits to the Fort, and on numberless occasions had reason to note the womanly expression of her sympathy. Quite frequently she would prepare with her own hands a dainty breakfast, write on a card, "By order of Dr. C——," and send to one or the other of the prisoners.

I once saw her gather from a box of growing violets a small bunch of flowers, tie them with a strand of her shining hair, and drop them into her husband's hat, saying, "Put that hat where Mr. Clay can see it. He shall smell violets, even though he is a prisoner!"

Mrs. Cooper was young, not thirty; beautiful in form and face; snowy skin and raven hair and eyes; tall, commanding, and graceful. My husband, on seeing her, exclaimed, "Maid of Saragossa!" And very appropriately did he transfer to her this poetic title.

Outwardly, Dr. Cooper's deportment to me was barely civil, and so continued. I dared not ask one favour, so stern and seemingly implacably did he deport himself toward my husband and me, toward our section and the cause for which we were suffering; yet, in the months to come, as on that memorable night of January 21, 1866, many an occasion arose to convince me that Dr. Craven's successor, after all, was actuated by a genuine feeling of humanity toward the State prisoners, and I soon grew to recognise in him a lamb in wolf's clothing.

# CHAPTER XXIX

Upon my return from the Fort on the 30th of January I redoubled my pleadings for Mr. Clay's release, both by correspondence and by visits to the White House. The President's bearing toward me was courteous and friendly, though it was apparent the confusion of the times and the pressure which was being brought upon him on every side was troubling him; but, notwithstanding that he listened and with every evidence of sympathy, Mr. Johnson continued irresolute, deferring from time to time on what, in fact, seemed the most trivial excuses, the issuing of the release papers. If I called once at the White House during the weeks that followed, I called fifty times, incessantly suing for my husband's freedom, and adding sometimes a plea for the pardons of friends and neighbours in Huntsville who were eager to resume their normal positions in the community. In the middle of February I was enabled to write home as follows:

"*My Dear Father:* I send your long-sued-for pardon. Act upon its requirements at once! I am pressing my husband's case and *never* mean to stop until success crowns my efforts. I am emboldened to hope the day not far distant when he will be a free man! Great political excitement now reigns. . . . The President is very kind to me always."

Notwithstanding there were times when my own heart sank to an almost hopeless state, I wrote thus hopefully to the patriarch at home, for each post told me of his increasing feebleness, and I longed to sustain him, at least until my husband's release was accomplished.

"God bless you!" wrote my sister, Mrs. J. Withers Clay, early in March, "and give you success! I asked father to send you some special message. He replied, 'Give her my best love, and tell her for God's sake to tell me when my poor boy will be pardoned!'"

These appeals, as will be understood, were the private agonies which acted like a lash to spur me to the end of the task of securing my husband's freedom, and to stimulate me, even in the face of the continued delays which now were become so inexplicable.

Early in February a change in public feeling began to be made manifest in the press. The mystery of the detention of the prisoners at Fortress Monroe without trial was arousing curiosity. The New York *Herald*, thanks to the intervention of our friend, Colonel Robert Barnwell Rhett (of the doughty and fearless Charleston *Mercury*), who had presented Mr. Clay's case to Mr. Bennett, now began to make inquiry in the cases of the unjustly treated prisoners.

"Dear Mrs. Clay," wrote Colonel Rhett, late in December, "having the opportunity of a good talk with Mr. Bennett, of the New York *Herald*, day before yesterday, I urged him to come out for the release of your husband. He said he did not know much about the business! I told him Mr. Clay was universally recognised to be one of the purest and most high-minded public men in the country—one wholly incapable of anything criminal or questionable; and that he had gone to Canada at the solicitation of Mr. Davis to communicate with the Peace Party of the North. I reminded him that, after the collapse of the Confederate Government, when a reward was offered for his arrest, Mr. Clay had voluntarily and promptly surrendered himself, asking an investigation; and that no intelligent man in the country who knew anything of our public men believed the charges to be other than frivolous and absurd. I added that Mr. Clay's prolonged captivity was regarded simply as an outrage on propriety, and that if he, Mr. Bennett, would take the subject in hand, he would greatly gratify the Southern people.

"He showed an interest in the matter, and said he would take it up in the *Herald*. That paper, you are aware, *aims to reflect the current public opinion*, irrespective of parties, and now warmly supports President Johnson against the Radicals. It is a great power, and by preparing the public mind and strengthening the President, may aid you efficiently."

The results of this interview by no means met the hopes of Colonel Rhett, however; for the utterances of Mr. Bennett's paper were few and guarded. But they were as a straw showing the veering of the wind.

"I was disappointed in Mr. Bennett's fulfilment of his promise to speak in Mr. Clay's behalf in the *Herald*," ran a second letter from our friend. "A few incidental expressions of opinion and a communication published did not come up to my expectations. If you feel disposed to write, Mrs. Bennett is the channel by which to reach him. She told me she sympathised with the South in her feelings, and admired Southerners. . . . In failing to deal with the case as you present it, the President must be very feeble in the article of nerve, touching his War Secretary and other Radical adversaries. Yet the widow prevailed with the unjust Judge, and I trust your importunity may weary the cautious Tennesseean into decided steps for Mr. Clay's release!

"Yours, etc.,

"R. BARNWELL RHETT."

Early in the month of February two important letters reached me through Mr. R. J. Haldeman. They were addressed to the President, and bore the signature of Thaddeus Stevens and R. J. Walker, respectively. Since my letter addressed to him in May, 1865, Mr. Haldeman's efforts had been unremitting to interest in my husband's behalf those whose recommendations were likely to have most weight with the President and his advisers. He now wrote me as follows:

"MRS. C. C. CLAY, JR.

"*My Dear Madam:* I inclose you a very handsome letter from the Honourable R. J. Walker to the President. I also sent you the letter of Mr. Stevens, which has become of some importance in view of Mr. Stevens's recent utterances. Mr. Walker considers it of the *highest* importance, and wonders how I obtained it.

"After seeing you, I called on Mr. S—— in reference to the proposed visit (to you), but found him brooding over the violent speech which he has since made. I did not therefore deem it prudent to insist upon the performance of his promise, and am confirmed in my judgment by events.

"During the day I heard something which convinced me the President would not then act. This I could not bring myself to tell you, and therefore obeyed a hasty summons to New York by an unceremonious departure from Washington. As the future unfolds, I hope to be again at Washington, and at the propitious moment. I hope you will keep up your good spirits, for, upon the faith of a somewhat phlegmatic and never over-sanguine Dutchman, I think the period of Mr. Clay's release approaches rapidly. . . . Mr. Walker, however, desires me to say to you that 'as we must all go to Clay at last, why not go at once?' I think this pointed witticism would bear repetition to the President. I am, very respectfully, Madam,          Yours,

"February 3, 1866.          "R. J. HALDEMAN."

As I had done in the case of General Grant's letter, I now hastened to send to the President the letters from Thaddeus Stevens and Judge Walker, both of whom recommended the prompt release of Mr. Clay. The letter from R. J. Walker was what might have been expected from an old friend of Mr. Clay's; that from Mr. Stevens, the most radical of Radicals, was a source of some astonishment. It was not the only surprise of those weeks, however.

"I have had strange visitors lately," I wrote to father. "Some extremists of the Radical party have called upon me to assure me of their belief in my husband's innocence!" And in my diary of the 14th of that fateful February, I find entered: "When will wonders cease? Who but the Honourable Mr. Wilson, of Massachusetts, has called, and voluntarily, to say he will do anything in his power for me or Mr. Clay; knows he is innocent; believes Mr. Davis to be also innocent! It is the goodness of God!"

The circumstances of Mr. Wilson's unexpected visit were altogether dramatic. I was seated at the dinner-table with the family of Mrs. Parker, when, it being still early in the evening, a visitor was announced who declined to give his name or the purpose for which he had called.

"Tell Mrs. Clay that a friend wishes to see her," was his message. A sudden remembrance flashed over me, and, indeed, over the friends around me, of the secret warning I had received just after my arrival in Washington, viz.: that I must be on my guard against strange visitors. After a few moments' consultation with the family, I decided to see the stranger. Doctor Maury, Mrs. Parker's son-in-law (who had been Chief of Staff on General Longstreet's medical staff, and was a brave and charming man), accompanied me to the drawing-room door, encouraging me by telling me to have no fear, as he would remain near by. As I entered the room the Doctor drew back into the hall. He was prepared, he assured me, for any emergency.

Great, indeed, was my astonishment upon entering, to see, rising to meet me, Senator Wilson, Vice-President of the United States! To that moment I had had no acquaintance with the Massachusetts Senator, though I had seen him often on the floor of the Senate. Though seized with an inward panic of apprehension that he was the bearer of some dreadful tidings, I took the proffered hand of my strange visitor, obeying mechanically an instinct of responsive courtesy. For a moment, however, fear made me speechless. At last, Mr. Wilson broke the painful silence.

"You are doubtless surprised to see me," he said.

"Unutterably so!" I rejoined. "Please tell me quickly why you have come, and end this agony of suspense!" And I burst into tears.

"Do not weep, dear Madam!" said Mr. Wilson. "Mr. Clay is well, and I have come to tell you that I deeply sympathise with you and desire to help you to obtain his release!"

"Mr. Clay's surrender," Mr. Wilson continued, "reflects great honour upon him. He is a brave and good man. Though he and I were opposed in politics, I have always respected Mr. Clay. Even his enemies on my side of the Chamber always knew where to find the Senator from Alabama!"

My heart was so full as I listened to these words, I could not make answer to this tribute to the worth of my suffering husband but by a fresh flow of tears. Somehow, as he stood before me, the erstwhile shoemaker of Nantucket seemed stamped with the seal of nobility from God! I did not then know his kindly nature, and those to whom I related the incident of this visit said nothing to impress me with the sincerity of Senator Wilson's act. On the contrary, many assured me that some selfish and sinister motive impelled the interview, and that Mr. Wilson would not commit himself by writing what he had spoken. A friend to whom I wrote an account of the visit, replied, counselling me as follows:

"I do not personally know Mr. Wilson, but believe him, from report, to be tricky, unscrupulous, and only hypocritically fanatical. Mr. Stevens may have spoken to him, or Mr. Sumner (whom, you remember, I saw); or he may have wished to approach the President through an opening which he supposed congenial to the President's wishes. However, your course is clear. Commit Mr. Wilson by a letter to the President, so that when the fight waxes furious he may not be able to take advantage of what the President may do. I consider it a good sign that the President desires to keep the letters of Messrs. Stevens and Walker."

In the meantime I had spoken of the incident with warm enthusiasm to Mr. Johnson. He replied very much as others had done; to wit., that Mr. Wilson would not commit to writing the sentiments he had expressed verbally to me.

"He fears the Radical press too much," said the President.

Nettled somewhat at this distrust, I assured Mr. Johnson of my faith in his Vice-President; that I would get the letter from him, and voluntarily. "If not," I added, somewhat stung by his cynicism, "I will extort it!"

Shrugging his shoulders, and casting up one eye, a characteristic habit of the President, he asked, "How?"

"Simply," I replied, "by an avowal that I will give to the *Herald* and other papers the whole affair, telling how the Honourable Senator had come, secretly, by night, like Nicodemus, to deceive by false promises a sorrowful woman, for some base reason best known to himself!"

Leaving the President still with an incredulous smile upon his face, I returned to my asylum at Mrs. Parker's, and shortly addressed Mr. Wilson a note, expressive of my wish. A reply, under his own frank, reached me early in March, and I bore it in some triumph to the President. The Vice-President's letter, a copy of which I afterward secured, was dated from the "United States Senate Chamber, Washington, March 3, 1866." It was addressed to

"HIS EXCELLENCY, THE PRESIDENT OF THE UNITED STATES.

"*Sir*" [the letter began]: "Mrs. Clay, the wife of Clement C. Clay, is now in the city, and has requested me to obtain permission for her husband to go to his home on parole. His father is said to be at the point of death, his mother recently deceased, and, if there be no objections or reasons unknown to me why the request of Mrs. Clay should be denied, I have no hesitation in recommending its favourable consideration, if only from motives of humanity, as I have no doubt Mr. Clay will be forthcoming when his presence is again required by the Government.

"I have the honour to be,
"Very respectfully, your obedient servant,
(Signed.) "H. WILSON."

Some six weeks later, when Mr. Clay's release was at last accomplished, and the press was busy with comments upon it, the names of the gentlemen who had written to the President on my husband's behalf being enumerated, some of the Radical papers attempted to deny the probability of Mr. Wilson's intercession; which was, as it appeared to me, a singularly useless thing to do, since his letter was already filed among the Government's archives. But the air everywhere was full of political revolution, and parties and partisans did not hesitate to resort to such means in their endeavour to effect the desired feeling in the public mind.

Every step taken by the President in those days was opposed or attacked. In my efforts to accomplish my husband's release, I came in contact with many good and earnest men, anxious to serve Mr. Clay and me, though often wholly disapproving of Mr. Johnson's weak course The retention of Mr. Stanton in the Cabinet was peculiarly offensive to a great many. Wherever a political meeting was held, Mr. Johnson was liable to vituperative assault. Private conversation teemed with rumours of a growing and increasingly violent opposition.

In view of Mr. Johnson's demonstrated kindliness to me, it was not only loyal to the President, but, I hoped, would prove protective to Mr. Clay's interest, that I should give the Executive the benefits of some of the warnings I had heard by no means privately uttered. I, therefore, spoke to him fearlessly, and wrote to him no less unrestrainedly.

A few days after Mr. Wilson's visit, I wrote to Mr. Johnson in this wise, my letter being dated February 16th:

"MR. PRESIDENT.

"*Dear Friend:* Fearing I may not see you this morning, I fortify myself with this note. I go up [to the War Department] hoping for my father's correspondence. If I get neither, may I beg to remind you of your promises? I have some strange things to tell you. . . . Rumour says that 'the people say,' 'If Mr. J—— does not support them versus the Radicals, they will call on General Grant!' I know you will not falter, and are not to be intimidated by threats from brave men, far less cowards. . . . Will you not send me one line? Do! and say the wheel has advanced one notch toward the day of deliverance!'"

A letter received after sending the above missive, in addition to the conferences I held daily with Judges Black and Hughes, and with others calculated by their established judicial and political worth to aid me, had its share in stimulating me to press my arguments home more and more confidently in my future interviews with Mr. Johnson.

"I was spectator yesterday in a Democratic Convention in an adjoining County (Harrisburg)," ran the letter, "when the news of the veto was brought. A resolution of approval was immediately adopted, and I, being seen in the crowd, was called out. I raised such a storm in fifteen minutes as would have done the President's heart good to have witnessed. The people are palpitating with eagerness to have the battle-ground defined, foggy constructions and platforms removed, so that they may charge upon the foes to a restored and tranquil Union.

"*Alea jacta est:* Mr. Johnson has put his hand to the plow, and cannot look back. . . . He has shown the very highest order of statesmanship in that command of himself and ability to bide his time, amid unexampled embarrassments, which have won for him the confidence of reflecting men. But could you not gently insinuate some day that, hereafter, the great debate, on appeal, is to be carried before the Tribunal of the American people in the case of the President versus Congress? . . . Many of Mr. Lincoln's acts, wrong in themselves, were nevertheless pardoned or applauded, because they evinced energy, courage or willingness to shoulder responsibility. . . .

"As one of the people, . . . and accustomed to 'pulse' the public, I think I may unhesitatingly assert that Mr. Johnson would gain immensely by no longer waiting to be attacked and undermined, but boldly striking his country's and his own enemies. If he would break out before witnesses into indignant denunciation of Mr. Stanton for having attempted to sap the foundation of liberty, and that, therefore, he is unfit to be in the Government of a free people, a thrill of joy would course like electricity through the land. Let the contest be only strictly defined; let the President, with a cabinet of friends, stand forward as the defender of peace and Union against a Congress which seeks to perpetuate strife, discord, and disunion, and we will, by meetings held in every county of the North, so arouse the people in support of our constitutional and law-abiding President against a lawless and usurping Congress, that it would be comparing small things to great to compare it with the pressure which General Monk and the people of England brought to bear upon the fanatical Parliament in behalf of Charles II."

A few days after the receipt of this letter, while on my way to call upon the President, and in the company of my faithful friend, Mrs. Bouligny, I met Mr. Stanton descending the stairs of the White House. I saw by the Secretary's manner that he recognised me. Indeed, there was a half-inclination of the head, as if he had expected me to bow to him. I did not do so. The innate contempt I felt for this despotic Secretary of War, whom I knew to be the power upholding Mr. Holt, who was so cruelly detaining my husband, froze my manner into a hauteur I could not easily have assumed. I went angrily to my appointment.

As I entered the parlour in which the President stood ready to receive me, I immediately broke into the subject to which I so continually had returned at each of my many visits during the past three months. But the President interposed a question.

"Did you meet Stanton as you came in?" he asked.

"I did!" I replied. "And he had the audacity to bow to me!"

"The scoundrel!" ejaculated the President. "He has been here an hour clamouring for the blood of Davis and Clay!"

"But you will release them?" I asked.

"You must be patient," answered Mr. Johnson. "I must detain them a little longer to satisfy public clamour!"

At this my indignation rose. In augmenting emotion I recapitulated the letters and indorsements I had brought to him urging my husband's release. I reiterated my reasons why the recommendations of these gentlemen should have weight with him. I referred to my husband's inability to combat the charges that had been made against him, while denied trial, the access of counsel, or his release from custody. I described his ill-health and the aged father at home, now so near to death; I rehearsed my husband's past services to his country and the dishonourable way in which the Government had acted toward this self-surrendered prisoner. I spoke the thoughts that rose in my heart, irrespective of the consequences, and, having massed my arguments in this way, I summed them all up in one uncontrollable protest:

"And now, Mr. President," I asked, "in the name of God, what doth hinder? In view of all these things, does it not seem that you are the lion in the path? Please tell me who was benefited by Mr. Lincoln's death? Was it Clement C. Clay? What good accrued to him from the murder? He was the loved representative of a proud constituency. He is now pining in solitary confinement. You, Mr. Johnson, are the one man benefited! You have succeeded to the highest office in the gift of the people! You, through this elevation, have become the centre of a nation's hopes, the arbiter of life and death!" I paused in my plea, at a movement of deprecation made by the President, but I would not be halted.

"You have promised me," I continued, "and Heaven knows how I thank you for it, that never while you sit in the Presidential chair will you surrender to the Military Commission the two prisoners in Fortress Monroe. In that, you have saved their lives! I have not the shadow of a doubt but that execution, and that in chains, as in Mrs. Surratt's case, might have taken place. But, when, notwithstanding the recommendations of such men as General Grant, Thaddeus Stevens, Judge Walker, and Henry Wilson, I see you waiting for 'public clamour' to subside, and, at the same time, in counsel with your Secretary of War, I am afraid. Again I implore you to stand firmly, my friend; thus far, at least, by not yielding to the desires of that wicked Commission and staining your soul with innocent blood!"

Turning, my eyes rested upon the marble bust of the late President, and I said, "Whose bust is that?"

"Mr. Lincoln's," was the surprised reply.

"I know it!" I answered. "But is he not a dead President? And why, may I ask, do you, a living one, stand surrounded by his Cabinet? Why do you not reach out to the great conservative heart of this Nation and select your own Cabinet? Why not become the popular head, as you can become? So long as you stand, Mr. President, as the barrier between your Military Commission and my husband and Mr. Davis, so long will I dare to be your friend to the extent of telling you what the people say of you!"

"Well, what do they say?" asked the President, with an air of indifference which, it was obvious, was assumed.

"They say," I replied, "that you should get rid of Mr. Lincoln's Cabinet; that you should surround yourself with a Cabinet of your own! Why do you hobble yourself with a dead man's advisers? They say, too, you are swinging in too circumscribed a circle! I have even heard," I added, "hints of 'impeachment' uttered in connection with the dissatisfaction resulting from your administration!"

During my bold speech the President gave evidence of being deeply moved, if not irritated, by my revelations; and, feeling that I had said enough, if, indeed, not too much, in the intensity of my feelings, Mrs. Bouligny and I withdrew. Ere we left him, however, the President assured me, as he so often had done (though he said the words over each time with an earnest gravity that was void of consciousness of his repetition), that he would "confer as to the release in our next Cabinet meeting!"

# CHAPTER XXX

## The Government Yields Its Prisoner

By the early spring of '66 the faces of old friends began to reappear in the Northern cities. New York, which I necessarily visited at times during those eventful months, when not at the Fort with Mr. Clay or beseeching the President on his behalf, was crowded with Southern people, many of whom were returning from abroad, or were industriously seeking to reëstablish business connections. In the capital one met on every hand friends of the ante-bellum days, saddened and changed, it might be, in fortune, but brave-spirited and walking with heads upright and hearts strong to meet the future. "I am persuaded that our States and people are to be prosperous, despite the portentous clouds which are now around us," wrote Mr. Mallory, from Bridgeport, Connecticut, where, now an invalid, he was constrained to remain; "and that the day is not far distant when you and your incomparable lord, with other congenial spirits, will smile at fate and look back to the paths we are now treading with more of pride than of sorrow! My love to Clay. God love him! What would I not give to be able to serve him!"

A spirit as loyal and comforting to us pervaded the circle of old-time associates in Washington, and permeated the newer ones who had gathered about me in my adversity. Mrs. Parker, the brilliant hostess of the Buchanan days, who now so hospitably had thrown open her home to me, proved an unsparing and faithful friend. Her hospitality to me and to the legion of other friends who flocked to offer their sympathy and services to me was unstinted, and the several members of her family vied with each other in extending their kindnesses and protection to me.

Among the friends who reappeared in Washington about this time, my diary notes the calls upon me early in '66 of fair Constance Cary and her fiancé, Burton Harrison,* long since released from the imprisonment which, for a time, he shared with Mr. Davis; of my kinswoman, Mrs. Polk, of North Carolina, and of Madame Le Vert, the brilliant Octavia Walton, who, almost three decades before, had led all other fascinating beauties in the capital. Accompanied by her daughters, Mme. Le Vert had returned to the North to intercede for the pardons of General Beauregard and others of her kin and friends. Her comings and goings were heralded everywhere. She was the distinguished member of the Southern coterie in New York, whence frequent trips were made to the capital, and it was commonly remarked that the charm of her personality had suffered no diminution with the increase of years.

Our beloved General Lee, who had been summoned to Washington to appear before the Reconstruction Committee, was the lion of the day. I saw him several times, surrounded by hosts of admirers, the ladies begging for mementoes, buttons—anything, in fact, he might be persuaded to give up, while he, modest and benevolent, yielded helplessly to their demands. It was during these months that I became acquainted with the lovely Mme. de Podestad, General Lee's kinswoman, who was both witty and beautiful. For a number of years, as the wife of one of the Spanish Minister's suite, she was a conspicuous member of Washington society. Going thence to Spain, she became lady-in-waiting to the Queen. Madame de Podestad was a devoted admirer of

* Mr. Harrison died in Washington, March 29, 1904. A. S.

MRS. A. S. PARKER
of Washington, D. C.

her heroic kinsman, and I saw much of her in those memorable days of '66.

It was a time of intense political excitement. The strife over the Civil Rights bill was the absorbing topic everywhere. The "returning good sense of the people," upon which the President so long had appeared to depend, was less apparent than he had hoped, and to many astute minds the air seemed to vibrate with premonitions of the Government's overthrow. Cabinet changes were so earnestly desired that a discussion of that body became part of every conversation. Mr. Johnson's absorption in the progress of the Civil Rights bill was so great, that, upon my return from a visit to my husband, early in April, realising the inadvisability and the inconsiderateness of pressing my demands at that moment, I yielded to the urgings of my friends and entered upon a short season of diversion. I remember to have visited, in company with Senator Bright and Mr. Voorhees, the studio of Vinnie Reames, whose vogue in Washington was then at its height; and I indulged in a pleasure trip to Baltimore, where a great fair was in progress which had been arranged by the patriotic ladies of that city. Contributions had poured in, and half the capital was in attendance.

"Mrs. Johnson sent a superb basket of flowers," reads the account I sent home, "which was raffled for sixty dollars! A portrait of the President was bought and sent to her. Also General Johnston's and General Lee's were bought and sent to their wives. Mr. Corcoran won the portrait of 'Stonewall' Jackson. Admiral Semmes was present one day, and he and I promenaded the rooms together. Though not the 'Pirate's Bride,' I was proud of his company. A *robe de chambre* for Mr. Davis and a superb pillow for Mr. Clay are in my possession. Will take them soon! Ross Wynans," I added, in describing the more generous donations sent to the energetic ladies, "has sent one hundred thousand dollars, and an English gentleman twenty-five thousand!"

Admiral Semmes was the most recent of the State prisoners to be released, and his appearance at the fair was the signal for a lively enthusiasm. By this time Mr. Stephens, our late Vice-President, was a free man, and thrice had called upon me in Washington to offer sympathetic suggestions concerning the case of my husband, so inexplicably detained. Our dear friend, ex-Secretary of the Navy Mallory, had been given his liberty early in March.

"Deeply anxious about your good husband," Mr. Mallory wrote, early in April, "I have deferred writing to you from day to day since my release, confident that I would soon be able to congratulate you upon his release. Persuaded that he will never be called upon seriously to respond to the charge upon which he was incarcerated, and unable to perceive any reason or motive for discriminating between him and others, myself included, who laboured in the Confederate cause, I am at a loss to conceive why this confinement *continues*. Of course, I fully appreciate the character of the struggle between the two great departments of the Government, and the embarrassments which it throws in the President's path; and hence I attribute to this cause all which affects Mr. Clay, and which I cannot otherwise account for. But the restoration of civil law throughout the country opens a way which his friends may very properly take . . . and I have been prepared to learn it has been entered upon!"

A resort to the *habeas corpus* proceedings thus suggested by Mr. Mallory had already been discussed by Judge Black as a step to be taken when all other efforts had proved unsuccessful. By the fourteenth of March, Mr. Johnson's courage to act in behalf of Mr. Clay had risen to the point of procuring for him the liberty of the Fort without guard, from sunrise to sunset, which order I had carried at once to General Miles.

"I have not yet called upon the President," I wrote father upon my return from Fortress Monroe, on the 29th of March, "but will report myself to-morrow and ask of him that no revocation of the late order shall be made. I shall urge Mr. Clay's release, if only temporary, that he may come and see you and help you arrange your business. . . . The Radical pressure on the President is fearful. They have expelled Foote, and have persuaded Stewart, of Nevada, his son-in-law, to desert his colours and cause, and they may pass the veto over the President's manly veto of the Civil Rights bill. But President Johnson will fall, if fall he must, battling!"

The records of my calls upon the Executive during the weeks that followed almost might be traced by the many pencilled cards sent me by Mr. Johnson from time to time.

"It will be impossible for me to see you until it is too late. I am pressed to death!" reads one. "There is a committee here in consultation; I cannot tell what time they will leave. I fear too late, but see if in twenty minutes," runs another. And a third, "Some matters of importance are now transpiring. I will see you at any time, but would prefer passing the answer until Saturday." Weeks passed thus in futile calls and beseechings, until, having tested every expedient to hasten the President to the fulfilling of his promise, my patience was exhausted.

"Again I am under the necessity of writing," I began in a letter to my sister, dated the fourteenth of April, "without announcing my husband's release! Nor can I give you any definite information save what I mean to do and wish others to do. I am at this moment from the President's; did not see him, but left a note inquiring when I could, and [asked] to be informed by note, which he often does in my case. He *shall* tell me in this inter-view whether he means speedily to release Mr. Clay. If not, then I will have issued the writ of *habeas corpus*, unless Judge Black oppose it!"

At eleven o'clock at night, however, I added, "The President sent for me to-night, and I have strong hopes that Mr. Clay will be released in a few days! I will telegraph you immediately when it occurs. I pray Heaven it may be ere this reaches you!"

Three days later, accompanied by my faithful friend, Mrs. Bouligny, I again called upon the President. It was eight o'clock in the evening. Having detected, as I believed, a disposition on Mr. Johnson's part yet further to procrastinate, notwithstanding his recent promises that he would order Mr. Clay's release, I was resolved not to leave the White House again without the requisite papers. I announced this intention to the President as he greeted us, asking him at the same time whether he would not spare me another moment's anxiety and write me the long-petitioned-for order for Mr. Clay's release.

Mr. Johnson's mood was light. He repeated some of the *on dits* of the day, trying in various ways to divert me from my object, to which, however, I as often persistently returned. From time to time other visitors entered to claim the President's attention; or, he excused himself while he went into a Committee meeting which was being held in an adjoining room. During such an interval I sat at the President's desk and scribbled a short letter in pencil to Mr. Clay. It was dated:

"EXECUTIVE MANSION, WASHINGTON, D. C.,
April 17, 1866.

"My precious husband!" I wrote. "Behold me seated in the library of this house, in the President's chair, writing you the 'glad tidings of great joy!' The President has just gone in for a few moments to see some gentlemen, and will bring me your *release papers* when he returns! He told me on the fourteenth that he would try to have them, but not to be too hopeful. So I came with some misgiving, to be relieved and rejoiced. Ere this will reach you, you will be informed by telegram of the release. I will telegraph you to-night. . . . Judge Black anxiously desires to see you, also Judge Hughes, both kind friends to me!'"

It was still early in the evening when I wrote this buoyant epistle, which immediate after-events scarcely bore out. The President returned again and again to my companion and me, but ten o'clock arrived and still the papers had not been given me. I was growing more and more impatient, but upon reiterating my intention not to leave without the papers, the President became somewhat jocular. He invited Mrs. Bouligny and me to make ourselves comfortable, his words being accompanied by an evasive smile. My soul rose up in resentment at this!

"You seem to be inclined to treat this matter lightly, Mr. President," I said hotly. "I am indignant! I want the paper!" Alas! my protest did not win me a direct compliance. The hands of a nearby clock already pointed to eleven when, the President having seated himself at a desk or writing-table that stood at hand, I rose and stepped to his side.

"Mr. President," I said, "are you going to give me that paper? I will not go until you do!" My words were hurled at him angrily. He looked up at me curiously, and the half-cynical smile on his face changed. It was as if, notwithstanding the ardour with which I had urged my demand throughout the evening, he now for the first time realised I was not to be put off.

"Give me the paper, Mr. Johnson!" I urged. "I am resolved to have it!"

My imperative demand at last proved effectual. The President turned without further demur and wrote a brief note, which, upon calling an attendant, he sent out immediately. In a few moments the messenger returned, bearing a paper which read as follows:

> "WAR DEPARTMENT, WASHINGTON, D. C.,
> "April 17, 1866.

"ORDERED:

"That *Clement C. Clay, Jr.*, is hereby released from confinement and permitted to return to and remain in the *State of Alabama*, and to visit such other places in the United States as his personal business may render absolutely necessary, upon the following conditions, viz.: That he takes the oath of allegiance to the United States, and gives his parole of honour, to conduct himself as a loyal citizen of the same, and to report himself in person at any time and place to answer any charges that may hereafter be preferred against him by the United States.

> "By order of the President,
> "E. D. TOWNSEND,
> "Ass't Adgt. General."

The paper, prepared by the hand of an amanuensis, had been written at and dated from the Executive Mansion, and a space beneath had been reserved for the name of the Secretary of War. When it reached my hand, however, the words at the top, viz.: "Executive Mansion," had been crossed out and "War Department" substituted; the space for signature had been filled in with the name of Mr. Stanton's assistant, General Townsend, and the words "Secretary of War" (below) had been crossed out. The changes were made in a different ink from that used in the body of the paper. The document was a curious additional proof of Mr. Stanton's personal indisposition to release his illegally detained prisoner, and of Mr. Johnson's equal evasion of the responsibility of freeing him. As neither name appeared upon the document, it would seem as if a "muddle" had been intended in the event of some later complications arising.

It was already toward the midnight hour when this document was handed to me. I seized it eagerly, and,

JEFFERSON DAVIS and CLEMENT C. CLAY, JR.
(after release from Fortress Monroe)

thanking the President for at last performing the act for which I had so long pleaded, I hurried to the carriage which had been in waiting and ordered the coachman to drive with all haste to the telegraph office.   As I parted from the President he expressed the warmest good wishes for Mr. Clay's health and our future, and pressed upon me an autographed *carte de visite*, which I took with no less surprise than pleasure, being glad to see in the politician before me this evidence of the inner, sympathetic man.   Though our horses dashed down the avenue at breakneck speed, it was within a few moments of twelve o'clock when I hurried into the telegraph office.

"Can you send a telegram to-night?" I asked.

"Yes, Madam," was the reply.

Inexpressibly relieved, I dictated these words:

"HONOURABLE C. C. CLAY, Fort Monroe.

"You are released!   Have written you to-night.

"V. C. C."

The President's telegram to the Fortress having been sent simultaneously with mine, my husband was given his freedom the next day.   There remained, however, yet a few duties to perform ere I might join him at Petersburg, whence we together were to return to our beloved home; to Alabama, with its purple and russet mountains and spreading valleys, its warm hearts and loyal friends, and where waited the feeble and eager father, ex-Governor Clay, whose remaining tenure of life was to be so short.   There were kindnesses to be acknowledged ere I left the capital, and on every side I met detaining hands overwhelming me with congratulations on my success at last.   The evening before my departure, the venerable former Vice-President of the Confederate States called upon me to extend his good wishes for the future.   Being deterred from coming in person, Judge Black wrote several notes full of his characteristic impulsiveness.

"Dear Madam," his messages ran, "tell your great and good husband I could do nothing for him, because his magnificent wife left nobody else a chance to serve him! I would have been proud to have some share in his defense, but circumstances have denied me the honour. I rejoice none the less in his happy deliverance, and I have no right to envy you the privilege which you have used so grandly, of vindicating his stainless name. His liberation under the circumstances is a full acknowledgment that the charges against him in the proclamation are infamously false. . . . Your note of yesterday evening literally took my breath away. After you had done so much for yourself and I had done so little, nay, less than nothing, you address me as if I had been your benefactor merely because I rejoiced in your success. . . . If I say but little, you must not, therefore, suppose that I shall ever forget your amazing eloquence, your steadfast courage under circumstances which might have appalled the stoutest heart; your unshaken faith where piety itself might almost have doubted the justice of God; the prudence with which you instinctively saw what was best to be done, and the delicacy which never allowed the charms of the lady to be lost in the great qualities of the heroine. These things are written down at full length in the book of my memory, where every day I turn the leaf to read them. . . . I cannot forget your sad look when I saw you at Mrs. Parker's the last time. Do not allow yourself to doubt the ultimate triumph of justice. *God has recorded among His unalterable decrees that no lie shall live forever!*

"Remember, if I can serve you it will always seem like a privilege to do it. In feudal times, when the liege man did homage to his suzeraine, he put his head between her hands (if it was a queen or a lady) and declared himself hers to do her commands; to be the friend of her friends, and the enemy of her enemies, for life and limb and earthly honours. Imagine the homage vowed in proper form, and claim your authority as suzeraine whenever you please. I ought to add that Mrs. Black was so wrought upon by your conversation that she has longed to see you again, and her whole heart, an honest and good one as ever beat, is yours."

"You went to work like a true wife," was the message sent by my dear old mess-mate, Mrs. Fitzpatrick ,"and God blessed you for it. Did you see Mr. Holt? I have heard he was our bitterest enemy. Can it be so?"

"Ten thousand thanks to God, my dear friend, for your release!" wrote Mr. Mallory to my husband. "May He punish with rigorous justice   .  .  . your unjustifiable and most cruel incarceration! My wife and I, if indescribables would permit us, would dance for joy to-day at the news of your release. Love to your wife! God bless her bright spirit and noble heart; and may we meet in Florida, one acre of whose barrens I would not give for all New England!"

From Mr. Lamar, "dear old Lushe," the following tender word came: "Ah, my friend, you know not how often, how constantly my heart has been with you! Often in the watches of the night, when all around was hushed in sleep, have I wept over your fate!  .  .  . I have not time to write now, except to beg you to come right here and make your abode with me. We have a large house. Oh, do, Mr. Clay, do come and see me! I would share the last dollar I have with you. Come, my friend, *and live with me*, and let us henceforth be inseparable. Please come. I believe the sight of you will restore my health; at least, if anything can.

"Your devoted brother, L. Q. C. LAMAR."*

* Mr. Clay's response to this letter is printed in Mayes' "Life of Lamar." (Page 122.)

The sight of these letters of long ago sets the tears gushing, and awakens a thousand tender memories of kind hearts that long since ceased to beat to the emotions of pain or pleasure. Oh! the vast army of men and women who, by their sympathy in those last crucial days of my experiences in the capital, were a buoy to my courage, and that of my husband, broken in health, and heart, and spirit, as we turned back to our home in Alabama!

The news of his mother's death, which came to Mr. Clay a few days after his release from Fortress Monroe, fell upon him like a pall. I could not induce him to visit Washington, to which city powerful friends had invited him. He had but one wish; to return to his stricken father, far from the turbulent political centre, where a man's life and honour were but as a pawn in the hands of the unscrupulous politicians of that day.

A few months and his father had passed away, gladdened, despite the vicissitudes of his later days, that his cherished son at last was restored to him. We laid the tired body beside that of the little mother. Together they sleep in the valley that smiles up so perennially to the crest of Monte Sano. A few years of effort for my sake, to retain an interest in the world which to his broken heart appeared so cruel and hollow, and my husband withdrew to our mountain home, sweet with the incense of the cedars; to his books and the contemplation of nature; to the companionship of the simple and the young. Yet a few more years, and he, too, fell wearily to sleep, and was put to rest beside those he had so well loved. I can think of no more fitting close to this portion of my memories than these brief quotations, from some of the hundreds of tributes which came from all quarters of the land, like the upwelling of healing springs in the desert, when at last I was left alone.

One who sat in the Senate Chamber in Washington,

scanning a later generation of his fellows, all eager in the strife for the fame that is the guerdon of the true statesman, wrote thus of Mr. Clay, his predecessor:

"You knew him best, having proved him, by a long association in the sacred character of wife, in many years of trial filled with memorable vicissitudes, as a true and knightly gentleman, a devout Christian, a loyal husband and friend, a patriot of the sternest type, a statesman of great ability, and the devoted son of Alabama. *In my course of thought and conduct, as his successor in the Senate, I have thought it well to accept his standard as that which would best help me worthily to represent our beloved State. Mr. Clay left a character here which stands greatly to the credit of the State, and will be quoted long after we have passed away, in proof of the character of the people he so worthily represented. His name and public history in the Senate are a cause of pride to our people.*

"Your sincere friend,

"JOHN T. MORGAN."

And one who had been our intimate friend for more than thirty years, Bishop Henry C. Lay, wrote of my dear one thus:

"How gentle and kind he was! How fond of young things, and how tender to the weak and helpless! Especially was he a singularly devoted husband, giving you his admiration and his confidence. . . . Life seemed very full of promise to him in those days. It was a sad change when the storm arose, with its exile, imprisonment, disappointed hopes, retirement into seclusion and inaction! Truly your life, with its opposite poles in Washington and Alabama, has been a varied one!"

## THE END

# ANNOTATIONS

We used several criteria in selecting items for notes. We generally avoided identification for well-known persons such as Jefferson Davis or for persons, events, or other items that are adequately described in the text. We are not always consistent in limiting notes to items that illuminate the context, but Virginia Clay "drops" so many names that consistency sometimes seems less important than illustrating the richness and diversity of her world. Finally, we must confess that sometimes our search for information came to a dead end.

Another aim of these notes is to correct errors, most of which involve minor matters such as misspelled names or misinformation about such things as Mary Chesnut's schooling. We are continuing (not completing) the process that Ada Sterling began. "There are," she wrote to Virginia Clay on June 13, 1903, "some notable inaccuracies in the book. . . . Don't be discouraged if these things keep bobbing up to the very day of publication. . . . And so, even when I have put *my* grey matter to the keenest test, in all probability they [the publisher] will assume the responsibility of having some expert throw a search light over it for errors which I have not detected" (Ada Sterling to Virginia Clay, Ada Sterling Letters, Clement Claiborne Clay Papers, Duke University Library). But if they did, not all errors were caught.

## CHAPTER 1

### Page 3

General William Arrington (1766–1812) was only sixteen

when the Revolution ended. His rank was acquired later in the militia. By Mary Ann (Williams) Battle (1768–1816), he had not only Virginia Clay's mother but also a son, Nicholas William Arrington (1807–1865) of "The Cedars," Nash County, North Carolina.

Dr. Peyton Randolph Tunstall became an army surgeon after his wife's death in 1828. His second marriage proved childless. He died in Pensacola in 1847.

## Page 4

Major Drake has not yet been identified. A Francis Drake was father-in-law of Virginia Clay's uncle N. W. Arrington. A John Hodge Drake stood in the same relationship to *his* uncle, John D. Arrington.

Mary Ann Williams Battle (1803–1867), half-sister of Virginia's mother, had married Henry Watkins Collier (1801–1855). Her sister Martha Williams Battle (1799–1876) married, first, Elias Bolivar Fort and, after his death, Elisha Hunter Sharp, from whom she was later divorced. Her two oldest daughters were Mary Ann Fort, later Mrs. William Mayo, and Martha Williams Fort, later Mrs. William Bilbo.

Henry W. Collier, Virginia's uncle by his marriage to Mary Ann Battle, was governor of Alabama from 1849 to 1853. A respected attorney from Tuscaloosa, he served on the Alabama Supreme Court. The Collier-Clay family alliance strengthened both families in Alabama politics.

The Forts, Virginia's aunt and uncle, would be traveling to their plantation in Mississippi, which became a state in 1817; Virginia made her journey to Alabama with them about 1831.

## Page 6

Virginia lived with Alfred Battle (1821–1877) and his wife, née Millicent Bradley Beadle (d. 1872).

## Page 7

In the early morning hours of Wednesday, November 13, 1833, thousands of shooting stars showered down on Alabama. The two-hour display had such an effect on the people that from that time on events were often dated as before or after the "stars fell on Alabama."

William Augustine Battle (1825–1909) was a lawyer and writer.

## Page 9

Maria Brewster Brooks was born in Westmoreland, New Hampshire, in 1809. In 1833 she was invited by Reverend Williams to go to Tuscaloosa, Alabama, and take the position of assistant teacher at the Alabama Female Institute. She became a central figure in the school where she continued teaching after her marriage to Professor Samuel Stafford of the University of Alabama.

Hilary Abner Herbert (1834–1919), congressman, diplomat, and rival of Yancey on the stump, married Ella Bettie Smith, a woman known for her beauty, intellect, accomplishments, and charities.

Thomas Barker Tunstall (1788–1842) was Alabama's secretary of state from 1836 to 1840 and clerk of the state house of representatives in 1836 and from 1840 to 1842.

## Page 10

For Sir Brian Tunstall, see note 3 in the introduction. His illegitimate half-brother, Cuthbert Tunstall (1474–1559), was successively bishop of London and of Durham under Henry VIII, deprived under Edward VI, and restored under Mary I. No bishop has belonged to the Order of the Garter, though the bishop of Winchester is its prelate, and the bishop of Oxford (formerly of Salisbury) is its chancellor. There was no Bishop Tunstall in Queen Anne's time.

*The Gamester* (1753) was a play written for David Garrick by Edward Moore (1712–1757). Charles Kean (1811–1868) was the son of the great Edmund, the first major English actor to visit America in his prime. Charles Kean married the actress Ellen Tree (1805–1880) in 1842.

Robert Macaire was the villain of the melodrama *l'Auberge des Adrets* (1823) by Saint-Amand and Paulyanthe. The play was converted into farce and Macaire into the type of the businessman as swindler by the genius of Frédérick Lemaître (1800–1876), then at the outset of a great acting career. Macaire was also a favorite in the cartoons of Daumier.

### Page 12

Madame LeVert (1810–1877) was born Octavia Walton. In 1836 she married Henry Streckey LeVert, a distinguished and wealthy Mobile physician. It was in this home (at Government and Emmanuel Streets) that she established her salon, which subsequently brought her fame as the hostess of the great and near great of two continents. She was also the author of one book, *Souvenirs of Travel* (1857).

### Page 13

Torquato Tasso (1544–1595) was an Italian epic and pastoral poet whose personal life was the theme of a tragedy by Goethe.

### Page 14

Jeremiah Clemens (1814–1865), senator from 1849 to 1853, was a brilliant but erratic figure in Alabama politics. A Unionist who signed the Ordinance of Secession, he later defected from the Confederacy. Jeremiah Clemens had cousins in Hannibal, Missouri.

### Page 15

Virginia Clay's diploma from the Female Academy, Nashville is dated December 9, 1840.

Alexander Keith McClung (1812?–1855) would probably have been a much less manageable husband than the gentle and equable Clement Claiborne Clay. Disappointed in politics as well as in love, he committed suicide.

Rob Roy (Robert Macgregor, alias Campbell, 1671–1734) was a famed Scottish outlaw and title character in a Walter Scott novel published in 1817. Scott describes him in the introduction as "blending the wild virtues . . . and unrestrained license of an American Indian," his name thus being appropriate for McClung's "wild and untamable" horse.

### Page 16

William Lowndes Yancey (1814–1863), fieriest of the "fire-eaters" (early and extreme secessionists) was eventually Clement Clay's colleague in the Confederate Senate.

### Page 17

William Capers (1790–1855) was a bishop of the Methodist Episcopal Church from 1846 to his death.

### Page 18

The stagecoach route from Huntsville to Tuscaloosa passed through Elyton. About fifteen miles south of Elyton the road crossed a rocky ridge, an area known as Stone Mountain and Stoney Lonesome.

## CHAPTER 2

*Page 20*

Benjamin Fitzpatrick (1802–1869) and his second wife (née Aurelia Rachel Blassingame) were from Autauga County ("Jasmine Hill"). He had been governor from 1841 to 1845 and had filled out an unexpired term in the Senate in 1848–1849. He would be Clay's colleague there until secession, save for a few months in 1855 when the legislature was deadlocked over his reelection. Virginia Clay passes over the suspension of the two couples' friendship in 1860. See Ruth Ketring Nuermberger, *The Clays of Alabama: A Planter-Lawyer-Politician Family* (Lexington, Ky.: University of Kentucky Press, 1958), 166.

James Ferguson Dowdell (1818–1871), then of Chambers County, served in the House from 1853 to 1859. Later he was a Confederate colonel and then president, from 1868 to 1870, of the East Alabama Male College (Methodist) at Auburn.

James Lawrence Orr (1822–1873) of Anderson District, South Carolina, was in the House from 1849 to 1859. The last antebellum Democratic Speaker, he was later a Republican governor—after having served in the Confederate Senate. He was Grant's minister to Russia at the time of his death.

*Page 21*

Williamson Robert Winfield Cobb (1807–1864), a Tennessean by birth, grew cotton in Jackson County, which was part of the congressional district that included the Clays' own Madison County. In the House from 1847 to 1861 and chairman, during Orr's speakership, of the Committee on Public Lands, he was a strong supporter of what would later be the Homestead Act, the subject of his song. Expelled by the Confederate House of Representatives as disloyal (he had failed to take his seat), he is supposed to have been killed accidentally by his own pistol while putting up a fence.

### Page 22

Virginia Clay is confused. Clay was defeated by W. R. W. Cobb for the congressional seat in a bitter race in 1853. Clay never ran against Cobb again, but was elected to the U.S. Senate by the Alabama legislature several months later.

### Page 25

Baron Alexandre de Bodisco (1786–1854) was Russian minister to the United States at the time of his death.

### Page 26

The *Richmond Enquirer,* edited by Thomas Ritchie from its foundation in 1804 to 1845 and controlled by him until his death in 1854, was widely regarded as the standard of Jeffersonian orthodoxy. It had been the one paper subscribed to at Monticello.

### Page 27

The Pierces were actually about a mile out of Boston, en route to their Concord, New Hampshire, home at the time of this calamity on January 6, 1853. Little Benjamin Pierce was nearing the end of his twelfth year.

### Page 28

Hugh Lawson Clay (1823–1890) was the youngest of the three sons born to Clement Comer and Susanna Withers Clay. Like his brothers he studied law, and he began a practice in 1845. In 1855 he married his second cousin, Harriet Celestia Comer (1835–1902), the Celeste whom Virginia Clay loved as a sister. Lawson Clay served both in the Mexican War and as a Confederate officer in the Civil War. See Nuermberger, *Clays of Alabama,* 78–79, 184.

Virginia and H. L. Clay had descended on Concord without warning in May 1852.

### Pages 29–30

Mrs. Slidell, née Mathilde Deslonde (1815–1870), was the wife of John Slidell (1793–1871), a New Yorker who had risen to political power in Louisiana and was senator from 1853 until secession. He was subsequently Confederate commissioner to France.

Jacob Thompson (1810–1885) and his wife (née Catherine Jones) had left Washington in 1851 when he retired from the House of Representatives; they returned from Mississippi when he became Buchanan's secretary of the interior in 1857. Thompson would later be Clement Clay's colleague as a Confederate agent in Canada.

### Page 30

Miss Isabella ("Belle") Cass was a daughter of the veteran senator from Michigan, Lewis Cass (1782–1866). Democratic presidential nominee in 1848, Cass had been secretary of war and then minister to France under Jackson and would be Buchanan's secretary of state. Belle was married, before March 1853, to the Dutch minister, Baron von Limburg, and thereafter spent about half of her time abroad.

James Guthrie of Kentucky (1792–1868) was Pierce's secretary of the treasury. His daughters, both widows, were Mrs. Polk and Mrs. Coke.

Robert Toombs (1810–1885) and his wife (née Julia Du Bose) were enjoying his new status as senator from Georgia after eight years' service in the House.

Benjamin Ogle Tayloe (1796–1868), scion of great Virginia and Maryland families, was the inheritor of Washington's famous Octagon House where the Madisons had resided after the White House was torched. He was one of the richest Americans of his day. His second wife (née Phebe Warren, 1804–1881) was from Troy, New York.

George Washington Riggs (1813–1881) had been succeeded in 1848 by his brother Elisha as junior partner in the Washington banking firm of Corcoran and Riggs; in 1854 he would buy out the senior partner and reverse the order of their names. Since 1896 it has been simply the Riggs Bank.

Eugène, comte de Sartiges, was Napoleon III's minister. His wife was the former Miss Thorndike of Boston.

Howell Cobb (1815–1868) returned to the House in 1855; he had been Speaker during the crisis of 1850 and subsequently governor of Georgia. Under Buchanan he would head the Treasury Department and go on to preside over the Provisional Congress (and Constitutional Convention de facto) of the Confederate States. His wife (née Mary Ann Lamar, 1818–1887) spent much more of her time at home in Georgia.

Francis, tenth Lord Napier of Merchistoun (1819–1889) was British minister from 1857 to 1859. He and his wife (née Ann Jane Charlotte Lockwood) enjoyed, for British representatives, an unprecedented popularity. The term "embassies" used here should, of course, be "legations." It is worth noting that Washington was his first post of ministerial rank after service as secretary of legation at St. Petersburg and of embassy at Constantinople.

Virginia Clay's spelling is not always to be trusted. Mrs. Slidell (as already noted) was Mathilde Deslonde.

Stephen Russell Mallory (ca. 1812–1873) was a Florida senator from 1851 to 1861 and was best known as the Confederate secretary of the navy.

*Page 35*

Adèle Cutts (1835–?) married Senator Stephen Arnold Douglas (1813–1861) in November 1856 as his second wife. Her maternal aunt was Mrs. Robert Greenhow (née Rose O'Neal), later famous as the Confederate spy whose success in extracting information from amorous Yankees (especially Virginia Clay's later champion, Senator Henry Wilson of Massachusetts) contributed greatly to the Southern victory of First Manassas (Bull Run). Adèle's father, James Madison Cutts, was the son of former congressman Richard Cutts of Massachusetts and Dolley Madison's sister, née Ann Payne. Adèle Cutts Douglas eventually took as a second husband Robert Williams (1829–1901), a Virginian who had stayed with the Union, serving mostly in the office of the adjutant general. A brigadier by brevet at the end of the war, he would eventually become adjutant general in 1892, retiring the following year. The original index to *Belle* confuses him with the better-known A[lpheus] S[tarkey] Williams.

*Page 36*

John Francis Twisleton Crampton (1805–1886) had been secretary of the British legation from 1845 to 1852, twice serving as chargé d'affaires; he was minister from 1852 to 1856 when pronounced persona non grata for his disregard of American neutrality in recruiting for Crimean War service. At home he was made knight commander of the Bath, succeeded to a baronetcy, and was posted as minister, successively, to St. Petersburg and Madrid. His bachelorhood was temporarily interrupted by marriage to a singer, Victoria Balfe.

*Page 37*

Adelina Patti (1843–1919), born to Italian parents who were

also singers, was one of the greatest coloratura sopranos of the nineteenth century. She made her official American debut in New York in 1859, though she had made a few earlier appearances in this country.

### Page 38

William Henry Palmer (ca. 1830–1878), an Englishman by birth, later used the name Robert Heller and performed both as pianist and as magician. He was an organist in Washington when Virginia Clay knew him.

Giuseppe Bertinatti (1808–1881) represented Victor Emmanuel II, soon to be king of Italy.

### Page 40

The opéra bouffe was a French comic opera constructed on too trivial a scale to entitle it to rank as an opéra comique.

## CHAPTER 3

### Page 43

John Bell (1797–1869), a former Speaker of the House and secretary of war, was senator from Tennessee 1847 to 1859. He would be the nominee of the Constitutional Union Party for the presidency in 1860.

A former Ohio congressman, John B. Weller (1812–1875) was senator from California from 1852 to 1857. He would later serve as governor of that state and as minister to Mexico.

Richard Brodhead (1811–1863) was senator from Pennsylvania from 1851 to 1857.

John Renshaw Thomson (1800–1862) was senator from New Jersey from 1853 until his death.

Andrew Pickens Butler (1796–1857) was a senator from South

Carolina best remembered as one of the principal objects of Charles Sumner's invective in the notorious "Crime against Kansas" speech.

Judah Philip Benjamin (1811–1884) was a senator from Louisiana from 1853 to 1861 and later was attorney general, secretary of war, and secretary of state, successively, in the Davis cabinet.

James Murray Mason (1798–1871) was elected to the Senate in 1847 from Virginia and served until 1861. He later became Confederate commissioner to the United Kingdom.

William Osborne Goode (1798–1859) was a Virginia congressman from 1841 to 1843 and again from 1853 until his death.

Eli Sims Shorter (1823–1879), a native of Georgia, graduate of Yale, and lawyer in Eufaula, Alabama, served in the House from 1855 to 1859 and was later colonel of the Eighteenth Alabama Volunteer Infantry.

John Milton Sandidge (1817–1890) was a Louisiana congressman from 1855 to 1859 and later was a Confederate colonel.

Miles Taylor (1805–1873) was a congressman from Louisiana from 1855 to 1861.

George Ellis Pugh (1822–1876), Democratic senator from Ohio from 1855 to 1861, was a leader in opposing extreme Southern demands at the Charleston convention in 1860, but he was ruined politically in Ohio by his opposition to the war. His beautiful wife, née Thérèse Chalfant, died in 1868.

Advocates of the various reforms associated with the name Amelia Jenks Bloomer (1815–1894) were generally considered ill-mannered cranks.

Lucius Quintus Cincinnatus Lamar (1825–1893), congressman from Mississippi from 1857 to 1860, would draft his state's ordinance of secession and serve the Confederacy in both military and diplomatic capacities. His postwar career was the most brilliant, politically, enjoyed by any Confederate of such prominence. He would serve with distinction in both houses of Congress, as Cleveland's secretary of the interior, and as a United States Supreme Court justice from 1888 until his death. His wife, née Virginia Longstreet, whose father, Augustus Baldwin Longstreet, was president of the University of Mississippi and author of *Georgia Scenes,* died in 1884.

David Clopton (1820–1892), later Virginia Clay's second husband, was a resident of Tuskegee, Alabama, and a member of the House from 1859 to 1861. Later he was a Confederate congressman and served on the Alabama Supreme Court from 1884 until his death.

Jabez Lamar Monroe Curry (1825–1903), a lawyer in Talladega, served in the House from 1857 to 1861. Later he was a Confederate congressman and lieutenant colonel, a Baptist preacher, a president of Howard College, a professor at Richmond College, and an apostle of public education in the South as the agent for the Peabody Fund, which was established in 1867 by banker George Peabody to promote education in the southern states. Cleveland made him minister to Spain. He and Clement Clay would become very hostile, politically, during the war years.

James Chesnut Jr. (1815–1885) was senator from South Carolina from December 1858 to November 1860 and later was a Confederate brigadier. The literary gifts of his wife, née Mary Boykin Miller (1823–1886), have made her the most famous Southern woman of her time.

## Page 44

George Hunt Pendleton (1825–1889), an Ohioan of Virginia extraction, had studied at the University of Cincinnati under O. M. Mitchel, later the nemesis of the Clays in Huntsville, and had gone on to Heidelberg University. He was a congressman from 1857 to 1865, but *not* senator until the period 1879 to 1885. McClellan's running mate in 1864, author (as senator) of the basic civil service law known as the Pendleton Act, "Gentleman George" was a survivor. Cleveland made him minister to Germany. His wife, née Alice Key, was a daughter of Francis Scott Key. Chief Justice Roger Brooke Taney was her uncle by marriage.

Chevalier Johann Georg Hülsemann was the Austrian chargé d'affaires and later minister plenipotentiary who complimented the future Mrs. Pugh.

### Page 47

Henry Watterson (1840–1921) was the son of Harvey Magee Watterson (1811–1891), who was a congressman from Tennessee from 1839 to 1843. His son Henry was famous as "Marse Henry," longtime publisher of the *Louisville Courier-Journal* and as an oracle in Democratic Party affairs.

### Page 49

Louis Moreau Gottschalk (1829–1869) was an American pianist and composer (born in New Orleans) who enjoyed great success as a performer before his untimely death in Rio de Janeiro.

### Page 50

Mary Boykin (Miller) Chesnut was not educated abroad but in Charleston, at Mme Talvande's French School for Young Ladies.

The "lovely Preston girls," daughters of John Smith Preston, were Mary Cantey (Mamie) and Sally Buchanan (Buck), who are familiar to readers of Mrs. Chesnut's diary.

Muscoe Russell Hunter Garnett (1821–1864), a nephew of

Virginia senator R. M. T. Hunter, served in the U.S. House of Representatives from 1856 to 1861 and in its Confederate counterpart from 1862 until his death. His wife (née Mary Picton Stevens) was from a wealthy and distinguished family in Hoboken, New Jersey.

### Page 51

Preston Smith Brooks (1819–1857), representative from South Carolina's Edgefield District since 1853 and a veteran of the Mexican War, is remembered for his furious caning of Charles Sumner, whose "Crime against Kansas" speech had included studied insults to Brooks's kinsman, Senator A. P. Butler, and to the state of South Carolina itself. Brooks is said to have lived long enough to form some idea of the harm he had done the South.

Frederick John May (1812–1891) was professor of the practice of surgery at Columbian College, predecessor of George Washington University.

### Pages 52–53

Daniel Edgar Sickles (1819–1914) was a representative from New York in Congress from 1857 to 1861. The tragedy that Virginia Clay alludes to on page 53 and which is specified on page 97 was the murder of Philip Barton Key (1818–1859), the son of Francis Scott Key. Sickles, whose wife had confessed to an affair with Key, shot Key in a jealous rage. Edwin M. Stanton defended Sickles, who was acquitted on the ground of temporary insanity. Sickles later achieved the rank of major general in the Union army, and after his retirement served in other positions in New York State and in the federal government. In a letter to Virginia Clay (January 17, 1904) Ada Sterling reported that she had recently had the occasion to talk with General Sickles and that when she told him that "your memoir [Virginia Clay's] had been done and would appear in the course of time, he looked most interested, and as if he had been awakened from some dream" (Sterling Letters, Clay Papers, Duke).

"Another much-talked-of lady" was Mrs. Judah Philip Benjamin (née Natalie St. Martin). It was the Stephen Decatur House (not Stockton House) that Mr. Benjamin had furnished so elaborately for his wife and daughter; nonetheless, they returned to Paris after a short stay in Washington.

## Page 54

Mrs. Davis is Mrs. Jefferson Davis (née Varina Howell, 1826–1906).

The Wickliffe sisters were daughters of Charles Anderson Wickliffe (1788–1869), a Kentucky congressman and governor and postmaster general under Tyler. Their brother, Robert Charles Wickliffe (1819–1895), was governor of Louisiana from 1856 to 1860. Their husbands were David Yulee (né Levy) (1810–1886), senator from Florida from 1845 to 1851 and from 1855 to 1861 and later a Confederate congressman; William Matthew Merrick (1818–1889), associate justice of the U.S. Circuit Court for the District of Columbia from 1854 to 1863 and of the District of Columbia Supreme Court from 1885 to 1889; and Joseph Holt (1807–1894) who, from being a friend, was destined to become the Clays' archenemy.

Joseph Holt, who was to play an important role in the lives of Virginia and Clement Clay (see especially Ada Sterling's note on pages 337–339), was a Kentuckian who, as postmaster general in 1859, opposed Northern efforts to coerce the South on the issue of slavery. Nevertheless, he became secretary of war during the last weeks of the Buchanan administration, adhered to the Union, and was made judge advocate general by Lincoln.

## Page 55

The first Mrs. Clopton was sister to Robert Fulwood Ligon (1823–1901), a Georgian who had settled in Tuskegee, Alabama. He served as a captain in both the Mexican War and the Civil War and was Alabama's last lieutenant governor under the constitution of 1868, the first to recognize such an officer. He served from 1877 to 1879, after which he served two years in the national House of Representatives.

Clifford Anderson Lanier (1844–1908) and his brother, the much better known poet, Sidney Clopton Lanier (1842–1881), would encounter Virginia Clay during the coming war.

## CHAPTER 4

## Page 58

Fanny Fern was the pen name of the popular writer Sarah Payson Willis (1811–1871), sister of Nathaniel Parker Willis and successively married to Charles H. Eldridge (d. 1846) and to the biographer James Parton (1822–1891). The saying quoted here is often ascribed to Talleyrand on the eve of the revolution of 1830.

Fusion presumably refers to a coalition of Whigs, Americans ("Know-Nothings"), and "Black Republicans," which prevented the Democrats from electing a speaker (their first choice was not Orr but his fellow South Carolinian William Aiken) and eventually placed Nathaniel Prentiss Banks of Massachusetts (1816–1894) in the chair. Virginia Clay has obviously misdated her letter here; it must have been in 1855.

Joshua Reed Giddings (1795–1864) was a representative from

Ohio who was elected in 1838 as an antislavery Whig. In 1842 his resolutions against slavery brought a formal House censure; he resigned and was overwhelmingly reelected by his constituents.

Thurlow Weed (1797–1882) was a New York journalist and politician. He founded the *Albany Evening Journal* in 1830 to support the Anti-Masonic Party, and he later was a Whig and a Republican. Weed had a political alliance with William H. Seward and managed Seward's unsuccessful campaign for the Republican presidential nomination in 1860.

Charles Sumner was a Free-Soil Democrat and senator from Massachusetts (1851–1874) who was an early convert to the Republican Party.

William Henry Seward (1801–1872) began his political career as a Whig in New York. He was elected governor in 1838 and went to the U.S. Senate in 1849. He was an early supporter of the Republican Party and was reelected to the Senate as a Republican in 1855. He was Lincoln's and Johnson's secretary of state.

Salmon Portland Chase (1808–1873) was elected governor of Ohio in 1855. He began his political career as a Whig and was later associated with the Liberty, Free-Soil, and Republican Parties. Lincoln appointed him secretary of the treasury in 1861. In 1864 he was appointed chief justice of the Supreme Court. He presided over the impeachment trial of President Andrew Johnson.

### Page 62

In maintaining the same cabinet unchanged throughout his term Pierce was actually unique. John Quincy Adams changed secretaries of war in the last year of his term, replacing James Barbour of Virginia, who wanted the English mission, with Peter B. Porter of New York. Garfield lived out less than seven months of his own term, and the only member of his cabinet who served the rest of the term (under President Arthur) was the secretary of war, Robert Todd Lincoln, who, as his father's son, was not expendable.

William Learned Marcy (1786–1857), former New York senator and governor, had been secretary of war in the Polk administration. His (second) wife was the former Cornelia Knower.

### Page 63

Randolph Barnes Marcy (1812–1887), a kinsman of the secretary, was a captain in the Fifth Infantry and already a distinguished explorer. He would rise to be inspector general of the army (1878–1881) with rank of major general but is best known as chief of staff to Major General George Brinton McClellan (1826–1885), who had married his daughter Mary Ellen (Nellie). George Brinton McClellan Jr. (1865–1940) was mayor of New York from 1908 to 1910.

George Brinton McClellan (1826–1885), a native of Philadelphia and a graduate of West Point, became one of the best known Union commanders. He was commanding general of the U.S. Army after Winfield Scott's retirement, organizer of the Army of the Potomac, and Democratic nominee for the presidency in 1864 against Lincoln.

### Page 64

James Campbell (1812–1893), a former Pennsylvania judge and attorney general, was postmaster general under Pierce.

Robert McClelland (1807–1880), former Michigan congressman and governor, was Pierce's secretary of the interior.

Caleb Cushing (1800–1879) of Newburyport, Massachusetts, was one of the most intelligent and widely mistrusted politicians of his time. He had already served as congressman, first minister to China, Mexican War brigadier, and unsuccessful

Democratic nominee for the governorship of his native state before becoming Pierce's attorney general.

Faneuil Hall, in Boston, was completed in 1743. It was a gift from Peter Faneuil, for whom it was named. This hall is labeled the "Cradle of Liberty" because of the stirring and influential speeches made there calling for American independence from England.

James Cochrane Dobbin (1814–1857), former North Carolina congressman, played a leading role in the nomination of President Pierce.

### Page 65

William F. Spicer rose from midshipman to master in 1853 and became a lieutenant the following year. By the end of the war he had risen to commander, and a year before his death he became a commodore. He died in 1878.

### Page 68

Here Virginia Clay's memory tricked her. That Davis was at Fortress Monroe on this occasion is disproved by his personal annotation on Craven's *Prison Life of Jefferson Davis* (1866). See Edward K. Eckert, ed., *Fiction Distorting Fact: Prison Life, Annotated by Jefferson Davis* (Macon, Ga.: Mercer University Press, 1987), 9. Craven's passage contrasts the past, when, as secretary of war, Davis was an honored visitor at Fortress Monroe, with the miserable present. Davis wrote in the margin next to this passage that "never was at Ft. Monroe until brought to it as a captive." For information about Craven's *Prison Life of Jefferson Davis,* see our note pertaining to page 298.

### Page 69

Actually Davis's illness came in February 1858, eleven months after his swearing in as a senator.

Aaron Venable Brown (1795–1859), sometime law partner

of James K. Polk, had been a Tennessee congressman and governor before becoming Buchanan's postmaster general. His wife (née Cynthia Holland Pillow) was the widow of John W. Saunders; her daughter was Narcissa Pillow Saunders (misspelled as Sanders in the text). Gideon Johnson Pillow (1806–1878) had been made a major general for his Mexican War service by his close friend Polk; peculiarly obnoxious to the regulars, he never rose above brigadier under President Jefferson Davis. See also a reference to General Pillow on page 172.

## CHAPTER 5

### *Page 73*

John George Nicolay (1832–1901) had been Lincoln's private secretary, and John Milton Hay (1838–1905) was Nicolay's assistant. The latter combined careers in literature, journalism, and diplomacy and became secretary of state under McKinley and Theodore Roosevelt. Nicolay and Hay were coauthors of *Abraham Lincoln: A History,* 10 vols. (New York: Century Co., 1890), an indispensable but highly partisan work that Southerners were apt to find distasteful.

Roger Brooke Taney (1777–1864) of Maryland had served Andrew Jackson as attorney general and interim secretary of the treasury, removing the federal deposits from the Bank of the United States. He became chief justice in 1836 as successor to John Marshall; his intellectual superiority to Marshall and other luminaries such as Joseph Story was less generally recognized than Virginia Clay supposed. His great qualities as a judge, on the other hand, have usually been obscured by his disastrous opinion in the Dred Scott case. Two of his six daughters would be employed in the Treasury Department after his death. Their mother (née Ann Phoebe Key) was an aunt of Barton Key and Mrs. George Pendleton.

*Page 74*

John Catron (ca. 1786–1865), a native of Tennessee, was appointed to the U.S. Supreme Court by Andrew Jackson. His efforts to keep Tennessee from seceding in 1861 were fruitless.

John Archibald Campbell (1811–1889) was a Georgia native who rose to prominence as a Mobile, Alabama, attorney. He was appointed to the U.S. Supreme Court in 1854 and resigned in 1860. He was a mediator between Confederate and federal authorities in March and April 1861. He served as assistant secretary of war in the Confederate government, and he was sent to confer with President Lincoln at Hampton Roads in 1864.

*Page 75*

Reverdy Johnson (1796–1876), a native of Maryland and an eminent constitutional lawyer who served in the Senate from 1863 to 1868, opposed the harsh reconstruction measures imposed on the South and defended many Southerners who were charged with disloyalty to the Union.

Robert J. Walker (1801–1869) of Natchez, Mississippi, was a U.S. senator from 1835 to 1845. He served as secretary of the treasury under President Polk and was appointed governor of the territory of Kansas by President Buchanan. He practiced law in Washington, D.C., when he was not holding office.

Robert Mercer Taliaferro Hunter (1809–1887) had been Speaker of the House from 1839 to 1841. He became a senator from Virginia in 1847 and was chairman of the powerful Committee on Finance. Considered a presidential possibility in 1860, he would serve briefly as Confederate secretary of state and then as senator from Virginia for the duration of the Confederacy.

Thomas Francis Bayard (1828–1898) was at this time a Delaware attorney in private practice. As one of the chief Northern

Democrats of his generation, he would serve from 1869 to 1885 in the Senate, as secretary of state during Cleveland's first term, and as ambassador (technically the first) to Great Britain from 1893 to 1897. The nickname "Chevalier"—in honor of the sixteenth-century French hero of their name—seems to have been almost hereditary in the Bayard family.

## Page 76

The Smithsonian Institution was founded in 1838 with a bequest of James Smithson to increase and diffuse knowledge among people. The first building was started in 1847 and was finished in 1855.

Matthew Fontaine Maury (1806–1873) was the great oceanographer, author of *The Physical Geography of the Sea,* director of the Naval Observatory, commander in the United States Navy, and later commander in the Confederate States Navy.

## Page 77

Lewis Cass (1782–1866) was a brigadier general in the War of 1812, governor of the Michigan Territory, and U.S. senator (1845–1848 and 1849–1857). He was the Democratic nominee for president in 1848, but was defeated by Zachary Taylor. He served as secretary of state in the Buchanan administration.

Thomas Hart Benton (1782–1858) was a senator from Missouri from 1821 to 1851 and was a representative from 1853 to 1855. He was a staunch champion of Andrew Jackson and was the author of *Thirty Years' View; or A History of the Working of the American Government for Thirty Years from 1820 to 1850,* 2 vols. (New York: D. Appleton, 1856).

James Moore Wayne (1790–1867), a former Jacksonian congressman from Georgia, had been on the Supreme Court since 1835. Like Catron, and unlike Campbell, he would stay with the Union.

John McLean (1785–1861), former Ohio congressman and postmaster general under Monroe and J. Q. Adams, had been named to the Court by Jackson in 1829. A prominent Methodist, he was repeatedly mentioned for the presidency but was never nominated.

John Jordan Crittenden (1787–1863), long the most eminent of Kentucky Whigs save for his friend Henry Clay, served in the Senate from 1817 to 1819, from 1835 to 1841, and again from 1855 to 1861. He had been attorney general under Harrison and Fillmore and governor of Kentucky from 1848 to 1850. After the failure of his compromise proposals in the winter of 1860–1861, he served out the remainder of his life in the House of Representatives. Crittenden's family well represented the split in Kentucky between North and South: one son was a Confederate general, and another was a Union general. Crittenden's (third) wife, whom he called "Lady Crittenden," was Elizabeth Moss (1804–1873), widow, successively, of Dr. Daniel Pinchbeck Wilcox and of the fur trader, explorer, and sometime Missouri congressman William Henry Ashley (1778–1838). She was a conciliator, like the senator, and her admirers included even Black Republicans such as Congressman Owen Lovejoy (1811–1864) of Illinois. We are told that "from early maidenhood to old age, the fascinating beauties of her person and character were conspicuous" (Alexander Brown, *The Cabells and Their Kin: A Memorial Volume of History, Biography, and Genealogy,* 2d ed. [1939; reprint, Harrisonburg, Va.: Carrier, 1978], 635).

George Wallace Jones (1804–1896) was a native of Kentucky and a graduate of Transylvania University, but his various careers are associated with the states of Wisconsin, Michigan, and Iowa. In 1848 he was one of the first senators from Iowa and represented the state for twelve years, during which period he favored compromising with the South.

*Page 78*

Benton's second daughter, Jessie Ann (1824–1902), was the wife of the "Pathfinder," John Charles Frémont (1813–1890), first Republican presidential nominee. Her sister Elizabeth was married not to Thomas Benton Jones but to William Carey Jones. Susan (1835–?) married Gauldrée de Boileau, French secretary of legation, on June 2, 1855.

*Page 79*

William Crowninshield Endicott (1826–1900) of Massachusetts was secretary of war in Cleveland's first administration.

*Page 81*

With regard to Mrs. Bouligny, see reference on page 119.

Jones, having served as Buchanan's minister to New Granada (now Colombia), had been arrested on Secretary Seward's order on returning to New York in 1861 and transferred to Fort Warren. He was charged with conspiring against the Union for continuing a correspondence with his old friend Jefferson Davis. Jones was never brought to trial and was released after fifty-four days.

*Page 82*

Edmund Pendleton Gaines (1777–1849) was brevet major general, U.S. Army; a hero of the War of 1812; and long the rival and bitter personal enemy of Winfield Scott. His second wife, formerly Myra Davis (1807–1885), was the widow of William W. Whitney. She claimed to be the daughter of Daniel Clark (ca. 1766–1813), Irish-born merchant, planter, land speculator, and sometime delegate in Congress from Orleans Territory, and she declared herself the heiress to his great estate. The courts found in her favor—in 1891.

*Page 84*

"My cousin, Miss Comer" is a reference to Loula Comer, a sister of Celeste Comer Clay. In 1858 Loula Comer married Paul Fitzsimons Hammond, the youngest son of James Henry Hammond, who was elected governor of South Carolina in 1842 and U.S. senator in 1857. There is further information about Hammond in chapter 16.

## CHAPTER 6

*Page 86*

Senator William McKendree Gwin served in Congress from Mississippi from 1841 to 1843, and then he moved to California and was elected to the U.S. Senate, where he served California from 1850 to 1855. He was reelected and served from 1857 to 1861. He was recognized as a Southern sympathizer.

Albert Gallatin Brown (1813–1880) represented the state of Mississippi in the House from 1839 to 1841 and from 1847 to 1853 and in the U.S. Senate from 1854 to 1861, the last few years there serving with Jefferson Davis.

*Page 87*

James Gordon Bennett (1795–1872) was founder and editor of the *New York Herald*. The younger Bennett took over in 1867.

*Page 90*

Tom Tait Tunstall (1823–?), lawyer and consul, was the son of Virginia Clay's paternal uncle George Brooke Tunstall.

*Page 98*

Amelia Jenks Bloomer (1818–1894) married Dexter Bloomer in 1840. Although a reformer in various areas—e.g., temperance, education, women's rights movements—she is chiefly associated with a new type of dress, which consisted of a full bodice, short skirt, and full trousers.

Sam Houston (1793–1863) represented Tennessee in the U.S. Congress, then moved to Texas. He fought in the Texas war for independence and was twice elected the president of the Republic of Texas (1836–1838 and 1841–1844). He was in Washington, D.C., as a Texas senator from 1846 to 1859 when he was associated with the Clays. As governor of Texas (1859–1861), he opposed secession.

## CHAPTER 7

### Page 101

Giulia Grisi (1811–1890) was a celebrated Italian soprano who toured the United States in 1854 and whose second marriage (in 1856) was to Giovanni Matteo Mario (1810–1883), the greatest operetta tenor of his generation.

Bozio [sic] is perhaps a misspelling for Angelina Bosio (1830–1859), Italian soprano.

Jenny Lind (1820–1887), famous Swedish soprano, came to America in 1850 and remained two years before returning to Europe.

Castle Garden is now a national monument under its original name, Castle Clinton, a fortress built in 1811 for the protection of New York at the Battery. Leased as a place of public entertainment in 1824, it was the scene of welcomes for, among others, Lafayette and Kossuth; Presidents Jackson, Van Buren, and Tyler; and Jenny Lind. It later became the principal New York clearing house for immigrants and still later the city's aquarium.

### Page 102

Julia Dean (1830–1868) was an American actress noted for

her golden hair and deep blue eyes. She was hailed as a child of nature after her New York debut.

Mrs. Jarley is a character in Dickens's *The Old Curiosity Shop* who owned a traveling wax works exhibit.

## Page 103

Charlotte Cushman (1816–1876), the first great tragedienne of the American stage, was born in Boston of distinguished New England families.

Meg Merrilies, a character in the popular dramatization of Scott's *Guy Mannering*, was regarded by many as Cushman's most popular role.

The actress Mrs. Gilbert may be Anne Hartley Gilbert (1821–1904), the English-born character actress and dancer. According to the *Dictionary of American Biography*, however, she began her American acting career in what is now the Middle West and did not make a formal debut on the East Coast until September 1864.

John Brougham (1814–1880), a native of Dublin, Ireland, and author of more than one hundred plays, spent much of his working life in the United States. *Pocahontas,* or *The Gentle Savage,* was a musical burlesque by Brougham and the most popular of its genre.

## Page 104

William Makepeace Thackeray (1811–1863), the distinguished English novelist, made two visits (lecture tours) to the United States (November 1852–April 1853 and October 1855–April 1856). He was in Washington in February 1856.

Ann Bishop (1814–1884) was born in London and began her career as a vocalist after distinguishing herself as a student at the Royal Academy of Music. Her first American tour occurred in 1847. After an eventful international career, she settled in New York and died there. She was often referred to as Madame Anna, but she was not French, as Virginia Clay supposes her to be.

Blind Tom (1849–1908) was Thomas Greene Bethune, an American pianist born blind and a slave in Columbus, Georgia. His owner, a Colonel Bethune, exploited his uncanny musical gift, and among his many engagements was his performance in the White House for President Buchanan.

Regarding Miss Lane, see pages 114–115.

### Page 105

George Maynard (1813–1891) had a distinguished career as a dentist in Washington, D.C., where he settled in 1836. He was a researcher and innovator as well as a practitioner, but he is best known for his role in the development of firearms, the Maynard rifle especially.

Thomas Wiltberger Evans (1823–1897) was a highly successful dentist in Paris whose practice included the most important royal families in Europe. His fabulous life is recounted in the *Memoirs of Dr. Thomas W. Evans: The Second French Empire,* ed. by Edward A. Crane (New York: D. Appleton, 1905).

### Page 107

William Hammond Garrett (1819–1863) represented Cherokee County in the Alabama legislature from 1843 to 1849. He was the Indian agent responsible for supervising the move of Creeks and Seminoles to the Indian Territory in the 1830s, and in the 1850s he continued to serve the Creeks. In 1861 he was a secessionist who tried to influence the Creeks to enter the Civil War on the Southern side.

### Page 108

The name of the Creek chief is Opothle Yahola (not Apothleohola). This "brilliant young Tuckabatchee, said to have been a son of David Cornell," was a leader of the Creek nation in Alabama. He reluctantly led his people west in the relocations of the 1830s, and with several thousand Creeks he camped outside Tuscaloosa in 1836. He traveled to Washington, D.C., to represent his people and died during the Civil War. See Angie Debo, *The Road to Disappearance* (Norman: University of Oklahoma Press, 1941), 101–102.

### Page 110

When Virginia asked about Chief Nea Mathla she probably meant Chief Eneah Emarthla, a Creek warrior who fought in the Red Stick War of 1812–1813 and who escaped to live for some years with the Seminoles in Florida. He eventually was taken by the U.S. government to Indian Territory where he lived into his eighties.

### CHAPTER 8

### Pages 114–115

Harriet Lane was born in Mercersburg, Pennsylvania, in 1830. Her mother was James Buchanan's sister, and when Harriet became an orphan in 1841, her uncle adopted her. She accompanied him to London when he was minister to Great Britain, and when he was elected president in 1856 she became the White House hostess for her bachelor uncle. In 1866 she married Henry Elliott Johnston, but by 1884 she had lost her two sons and her husband. Her last years were spent in Washington, where she devoted her life to philanthropic causes. She died in 1903.

### Page 118

James Gordon Bennett (1841–1918), referred to as a handsome, courtly youth, was the son of the founder of the *New York*

*Herald.* The younger Bennett assumed management of the *Herald* in 1867 and financed Stanley's famous search for Dr. Livingston (1869–1871).

The German is an elaborate social dance resembling a cotillion, or it is a party where only this dance is danced.

### Page 119

Regarding "Mrs. A. S. Parker," Virginia Clay seems to be mistaken about the initials A. S. Her generous friend is cited as the wife of George Parker, "a wealthy merchant of Washington" in Nuermberger, *Clays of Alabama,* 292 n. 75. Mrs. Pryor, who was also a guest at the wedding of Mary E. Parker to John Edward Bouligny, refers to Mr. Parker (without initials or first name) as a wealthy grocer. See Mrs. Roger A. Pryor [Sara Rice Pryor], *Reminiscences of Peace and War* (New York: Macmillan, 1904), 10–12. It was at this wedding, according to Mrs. Pryor, that President Buchanan received word of the secession of South Carolina from the Union, which took place December 20, 1860. Bouligny (1824–1864) was the one Louisiana congressman who refused to withdraw when his state seceded, and he remained in Washington until his untimely death.

### Page 120

William Wilson Corcoran (1798–1888), a native of Georgetown, was for a long time Washington's leading banker. He also was a philanthropist and supporter of conservative politicians. He endowed the Corcoran Gallery of Art and was a benefactor of Columbian College (now George Washington University) and of the University of Virginia.

"And lo! Ben Adhem's name led all the rest" is the last line of the poem "Abou Ben Adhem" by Leigh Hunt (1784–1859), friend of Shelley, Keats, and other distinguished writers of the Romantic period. Mr. Corcoran, so Virginia is saying, loves his fellow man, like Abou Ben Adhem, whose name therefore leads the list of those who love the Lord.

## Page 121

The *Greek Slave* (1843) is a famous piece of sculpture by Hiram Powers (1805–1873) that circumvents the problem of exhibiting female nudity in Victorian America by representing this shackled figure as Christian virtue. The context is the effort of the Greeks to free their country from Turkish occupation.

## CHAPTER 9

### Page 127

John de Havilland (1826–1886) was, apparently, the unofficial poet laureate of the capital. The complete title of the poem alluded to by Virginia Clay is "A Metrical Description of a Fancy Ball Given at Washington, 9th April, 1858." It was first published in the *Washington Evening Star,* May 10, 1858.

### Page 128

Aunt Ruthy Partington is the comic heroine of Shillaber's *Life and Sayings of Mrs. Partington* (1854), which was very popular and obviously well known to the guests at the Gwin ball.

Benjamin Perley Poore (1820–1887) was born in Massachusetts, but he lived most of his life in Washington, D.C., where he began his distinctive career as a Washington correspondent in 1854. One of his best-known books is *Perley's Reminiscences of Sixty Years in the National Metropolis,* 2 vols. (Philadelphia: Hubbard Brothers, 1886).

Major Jack Downing is a character created by humorist and American editor Seba Smith (1792–1868) who founded the *Portland (Maine) Courier* in 1829 and began in 1830 the humorous letters on the subject of politics signed by "Major Jack Downing."

## Page 133

Mrs. Partington does not see horns on the head of "Old Buck" Buchanan, who quickly replies that he is not a married man. He therefore cannot be a cuckold, that is, a man whose wife is unfaithful and who will be so identified for public ridicule by horns on his head. It may be surprising that this hoary old joke was still turning up in the mid-nineteenth century.

## Page 134

Mme Germaine de Staël (1766–1817), daughter of Jacques Necker, Louis XVI's famous minister of finance, was the wife of the Swedish ambassador to France and the hostess of the most brilliant salon in Paris. She expressed her liberal views in such novels as *Corinne* and was banished from Paris by Napoleon in 1807. Because she supported women's rights and was well known for her love affairs, one wonders how much of her persona Varina Davis borrowed for her disguise at the Gwin ball.

## Page 136

The galop is defined by the *Oxford English Dictionary* as a "lively dance in 2-4 time," and the earliest illustrative citation in the *OED* is 1832.

## CHAPTER 10

## Page 139

Richard Bickerton Pennell Lyons (1817–1887), second Lord Lyons of Christchurch, previously British minister plenipotentiary at Florence, would serve at Washington from 1859 to 1864.

He would later be ambassador at Constantinople from 1865 to 1867 and at Paris for the last twenty years of his life.

## Page 140

There was, of course, no British embassy, nor any other in Washington, but merely a British legation; there was no ambassador, just a minister plenipotentiary. This resulted from the republican parsimony that prevented the United States, until 1893, from conferring the highest diplomatic rank on any of its own representatives abroad.

## Page 142

Anson Burlingame of Massachusetts (1820–1870) was a Free-Soil supporter and member of the House of Representatives (1855–1861). He was an effective debater known for his impassioned denunciation of Preston S. Brooks after Brooks attacked Senator Charles Sumner.

## Page 143

Ebenezer Rockwood Hoar (1816–1895) was successively a judge of the Massachusetts Court of Common Pleas and of its supreme court and briefly was attorney general at the start of Grant's administration. He was blocked from the Supreme Court by senators he had disobliged.

## Page 144

Raphael Semmes (1800–1877) was appointed midshipman in the U.S. Navy in 1826. He resigned his commission as commander in February 1861 and assumed the same rank in the Confederate navy. His exploits as captain of the CSS *Alabama* made him a naval hero in the Confederacy, and he rose to the rank of rear admiral.

## Page 145

Edmund Ruffin (1794–1865) was a Virginia agricultural reformer, an extreme secessionist, and a voluminous and important diarist. He believed himself, as a volunteer, to have fired the first gun at Fort Sumter. He killed himself two months after the surrender at Appomattox.

## Page 146

"Out of this nettle, danger, we pluck this flower, safety" is a line, slightly misquoted in *Belle*, spoken by Hotspur in Shakespeare's *Henry IV, Part I* (act 2, scene 3). Hotspur, the son of Henry Percy, earl of Northumberland, leads a rebellion against Henry IV, and although he is not Shakespeare's hero, he embodies a concept of honor that, a few centuries later, will play a prominent role in the culture of the Old South. See, for example, Bertram Wyatt Brown's *The House of Percy: Honor, Melancholy and Imagination in a Southern Family* (New York: Oxford University Press, 1994).

Virginia Clay consistently writes of her friend George Hunt Pendleton as a senator from Ohio. He did not attain that position until 1879. Pugh's colleague was actually the Radical Republican Benjamin F. Wade. Pendleton was in the House from 1857 to 1865.

Clement Vallandigham, the "ardent member from Ohio," was the leader of the peace Democrats. His vigorous opposition to the war had caused Lincoln to banish him to the Confederacy in May 1863 (see Nuermberger, *Clays of Alabama,* 239). In June he embarked for Canada, and in February 1864 he became commander of the Sons of Liberty, a secret society in the Midwest (the old Northwest) that opposed the war and promoted the idea of a separate republic for that section of America. Jacob Thompson and Thomas Hines, two of the members of Clay's

Canadian commission, conferred with Vallandigham, but nothing came of the association.

Regarding "We have piped and they would not dance, and now the devil may care," the "distinguished colleague" who wrote the letter containing this memorable sentence was Jefferson Davis. See Clay Papers, Duke.

### Page 148

Virginia Clay does not comment, retrospectively, on the astounding about-face that is to take place in Joseph Holt's future relationship to the Clays. To add emphasis to the inexplicable vindictiveness that characterizes Holt's treatment of Clay as a prisoner of state, Virginia Clay might have quoted the following passages from a letter Holt wrote to her on August 28, 1860, containing news of the death of his wife, one of the Wickliffe sisters (see *Belle*, 54): "You know her generous and affectionate appreciation of your husband's character. . . . I should add that she cherished for yourself the warmest and tenderest affection. You were indeed for her the breathing embodiment of all that is graceful, noble and true in woman" (Joseph Holt to Virginia Clay, Clay Papers, Duke).

### Page 151

Eugenia Levy Phillips was one of six daughters of Mr. and Mrs. Jacob Levy of Charleston, South Carolina. She married Philip Phillips, an Alabama congressman from 1853 to 1855. She became widely known and admired during the Civil War for her defiance of General Benjamin Butler during the occupation of New Orleans and her subsequent banishment to Ship Island.

### Page 152

Major General John Bankhead Magruder (1807–1871) was

in command of troops in the Confederate defense of Richmond during the Seven Days' Battles.

Joseph Eggleston Johnston (1807–1891) resigned as quartermaster general on April 22, 1861, and became one of the Confederacy's first full generals.

Sydney Smith Lee (1802–1869), Robert E. Lee's elder brother, was chief of the U.S. Navy's Bureau of Coast Survey when Virginia seceded from the Union. He resigned his commission, apparently with reluctance. According to Mary Chesnut, "Captain Smith Lee wishes 'South Carolina could be blown out of [the] water.' He does hate so the disrupting of his dearly beloved (navy?) country" (C. Vann Woodward, ed., *Mary Chesnut's Civil War* [New Haven: Yale University Press, 1981], 26).

The long letter from Mrs. Phillips dated May 4, 1861, refers to the Blairs with heavy sarcasm (see Eugenia Levy Phillips to Virginia Clay, Clay Papers, Duke). These would be Francis Preston Blair (1791–1876) and his sons Montgomery (1813–1883), whose wife, Minna, had been a close friend of Varina Davis in the 1850s, and Francis Preston Blair Jr. (1821–1875). The elder Blair was a Democrat and a friend of Andrew Jackson, but as the crisis over slavery grew, he and his sons left the Democratic Party and supported Lincoln. Montgomery Blair was postmaster general in Lincoln's cabinet but was later dismissed to appease the Radicals. The "fanatical Mrs. Lee" is Montgomery Blair's sister, Elizabeth (1818–1906), who married a cousin of Robert E. Lee, Samuel Phillips Lee (1812–1897), later a rear admiral in the U.S. Navy. Francis and Montgomery Blair were not fanatics or Radical Republicans, however, and they provide a poignant example of Union loyalists who did not want war with the South, who had many Southern friends, and who were damned by the Republicans as well as by Southerners such as Mrs. Phillips and probably Virginia Clay. It was at the Blair House that Francis Preston Blair, at the request of Lincoln, offered Robert E. Lee command of the Union forces. Today, Blair House, located at 1651 Pennsylvania Avenue, is owned by the federal government and is used as a guest house to accommodate distinguished state visitors.

## CHAPTER 11

### Page 153

John Tyler Morgan (1824–1907), Dallas County (Alabama) attorney and Confederate brigadier veteran, was elected a U.S. senator in 1876 and served until his death in 1907.

### Page 154

General Edmund Kirby Smith (1824–1893) is best remembered as the nearly autonomous commander of the Confederacy's Trans-Mississippi Department from February 1863 until May 1865. He was a brigadier under J. E. Johnston in 1861.

### Page 155

Edward Dorr Tracy (1833–1863) moved from his birthplace, Macon, Georgia, to Huntsville in the late 1850s, where he practiced law. During the Civil War, he rose from the rank of captain to brigadier general. He was killed in action at Port Gibson, Mississippi, in May 1863.

### Page 157

The "Yorick of the Glade" is the mockingbird that seems to imitate or mock other bird songs. The metaphor in quotation marks suggests a local source for the comparison of the mockingbird to the dead jester, Yorick, whose skull Hamlet addresses in act 5, scene 1 of *Hamlet*: "Where be your gibes now? . . . your songs?"

LeRoy Pope Walker (1817–1884), a native of Huntsville, Alabama, and closely associated with the secession movement, did serve briefly (February 21–September 16, 1861) as the first Confederate secretary of war. As brigadier general, he saw no action, and from April 6, 1864, to the end of the war, with the rank of colonel, he presided as judge of a military court in north Alabama. His second wife was Eliza Pickett of Montgomery.

### Page 158

The letter Virginia Clay quotes on pages 158–159 is addressed to her and signed Varina Davis.

Hannibal Hamlin (1809–1891) was a senator from Maine from 1857 to 1861 and was elected vice president in 1860; Charles Durkee (1805–1870) was a congressman from 1849 to 1853 and a U.S. senator from Wisconsin from 1855 to 1861; James Rood Doolittle (1815–1897) of Wisconsin served in the U.S. Senate from 1857 to 1869; Joseph Ripley Chandler (1792–1880) from Pennsylvania served in Congress from 1849 to 1855.

### Page 160

Colonel LeRoy Pope (1765–1844), a wealthy planter, was one of the founders of Huntsville and a powerful political influence in his community.

"The birthplace of the immortal poet" is a reference to Twickenham, where the English poet Alexander Pope (1688–1744) lived. This name was briefly conferred on the settlement established by LeRoy Pope in northern Alabama, but the town's name was changed to Huntsville.

William Smith (1762–1840), a former senator from South Carolina, moved to Huntsville after 1833. As Virginia Clay notes, he declined an appointment to the United States Supreme Court that had been offered him in 1836 and in the same year was elected to the Alabama House of Representatives.

## Page 163

The son of Anak, to whom Virginia Clay compared the black candidate for baptism, is one of many references, usually plural (sons of Anak or Anakim), to these foes of the Israelites. She may have had in mind a passage from Numbers 13:30–31 in which their large size is emphasized, as reported by Moses' spies: "We seemed like grasshoppers, or so we seemed to them."

## Page 164

Andrew Barry Moore (1807–1873) of Perry County, Alabama, was governor when Alabama seceded. He took action to protect the state by ordering federal installations seized and by commissioning agents to travel to the North to buy arms for the state's militia.

## Page 165

Pierre Gustave Toutant Beauregard (1818–1893), a native of Louisiana and a graduate of West Point (1838), resigned his commission in February 1861 and was appointed brigadier general in the provisional army of the Confederate States of America on March 1, 1861, and later named full general in the regular army.

It might be of interest to note that nine General Smiths are cited in Ezra J. Warner, *Generals in Gray: Lives of the Confederate Commanders* (Baton Rouge, La.: Louisiana State University Press, 1959).

## Page 166

Harriet Celeste Comer Clay (1835–1902) married her second cousin Hugh Lawson Clay on May 13, 1855. The Clay correspondence reveals that Virginia believed her sister-in-law to be a kindred spirit.

Manassas Junction, Virginia, was a strategic railroad junction near Bull Run where important battles were fought in 1861 and 1862. Winchester, Virginia, was the scene of battles in 1862, 1863, and 1864.

## CHAPTER 12

### *Page 169*

John Hunt Morgan (1825–1864) was born in Huntsville, Alabama. He was not a West Point graduate, but had organized the Lexington (Kentucky) Rifles in 1857 and joined the forces of General Simon B. Buckner after the Civil War began. His daring exploits, including raids into Indiana and Ohio, made him one of the legendary figures of the Confederacy. He was killed in Greenville, Tennessee, on September 4, 1864, in a surprise attack by Union cavalry.

### *Page 170*

Dr. Oliver Wendell Holmes (1809–1894), a native of Massachusetts and a professor of anatomy at Harvard Medical School, was during his life one of the most popular of American poets. In the poem to which Virginia Clay alludes ("On Lending a Punch Bowl") the complete and correct line is "The little Captain [Miles Standish] stood and stirred the posset with his sword."

James Ewell Brown ("Jeb") Stuart (1833–1864) graduated from West Point in 1854, resigned his commission when Virginia seceded from the Union, was Lee's chief of cavalry, and by the time of his death—he was mortally wounded on May 11, 1864, and died the next day—was the best-known cavalry commander in America.

### *Page 171*

Joachim Murat (1767–1815) was created marshal of France

and king of Naples by Napoleon, whose sister, Caroline Bonaparte, married Murat. He is best remembered as a brilliant and dashing cavalry leader, hence an exemplar for subsequent cavalry commanders such as Jeb Stuart.

Fort Donelson fell to Union troops in February 1862, and the battle of Nashville occurred December 15–16, 1864. Both were severe losses for the Confederate army.

### Page 172

Felix Kirk Zollicoffer (1812–1862) was a Tennessee newspaperman and politician who served in Congress from 1852 to 1859. He was commissioned brigadier general in the provisional army of the Confederate States on July 4, 1861, and was killed in action on January 19, 1862.

Albert Sidney Johnston (1803–1862) was a West Point graduate who had achieved the rank of brevet brigadier general in the U.S. Army when he resigned his commission on May 3, 1861, and was appointed second ranking general in the regular army of the Confederacy. He was mortally wounded during the battle of Shiloh (April 6, 1862).

Union General Don Carlos Buell (1818–1898) arrived in Huntsville on June 29, 1862, and set up his headquarters there. Because of Confederate raids on his lines of communication, however, Buell left Huntsville on August 31 for Murfreesboro, Tennessee.

### Page 173

Simon Bolivar Buckner (1823–1914), a native of Kentucky and a West Point graduate (1844), was appointed brigadier general in the Confederate army on September 14, 1861. Before the end of the war he was a lieutenant general and the last survivor of the Confederate army above the rank of brigadier.

John Cabell Breckinridge (1821–1875) (name misspelled in the text), a native of Kentucky, was a lawyer and successful politician, who, at the age of thirty-five, was vice president during the Buchanan administration. He accepted a commission as Confederate brigadier general on November 2, 1861. In February 1864 he was appointed by Davis as secretary of war. After the fall of the Confederacy, he left for England and then Canada, but returned to Kentucky and his law practice in 1869.

Mrs. George Wythe Randolph was Mary Elizabeth Adams (1830–1871). Her first husband had been William B. Pope of Mobile; her second, Randolph (1818–1867), Thomas Jefferson's youngest grandson, was Confederate secretary of war during most of 1862.

Mrs. Joseph Christmas Ives, née Cora Semmes, sister of the Confederate senator from Louisiana and cousin of the Confederate naval hero Raphael Semmes, was the organizer and producer of that version of *The Rivals* in which Virginia Clay so brilliantly excelled.

## Page 174

"I recall the great amateur performance of 'The Rivals,' which made that first winter in Richmond memorable" seems to be a chronological error. Mary Chesnut remarks on this production and Virginia Clay's remarkable performance in a diary entry dated February 5, 1864 (see Woodward, *Mary Chesnut's Civil War,* 553–554). Constance Cary Harrison also recalls the play, in which she acted the role of Lydia Languish, as occurring late in the war, when Confederate prospects were dismal. See Mrs. Burton Harrison [Constance C. Harrison], *Recollections Grave and Gay* (New York: C. Scribner's Sons, 1911), 176–177. There was widespread disapproval of theatricals and other entertainments as frivolous and worse during these critical times, and perhaps

Virginia preferred to remember an earlier and happier period of the Confederacy for the time context.

Constance Cary (1843–1920) and two of her Cary first cousins were noted belles in wartime Richmond where they had moved with their widowed mother after the destruction of Vaucluse, their Fairfax estate. It was in Richmond that Constance met Burton Norvell Harrison, Jefferson Davis's secretary, whom she married November 26, 1867. They were among the Southerners who went to New York City after the war and prospered. Mrs. Harrison's literary career began in 1876, and of her works (novels, plays, and essays) probably the only one still read today is *Recollections Grave and Gay,* her autobiography.

Paduasoy is a rich, corded silk cloth of a kind used in hangings, vestments, and garments, for example.

### Page 176

Mrs. John Drew (1820–1897) was born in London, the daughter of performers with a long theatrical heritage. She made her theatrical debut in 1827, and her most celebrated role was playing Mrs. Malaprop in *The Rivals.* She is also famous as the successful manager of Philadelphia's Arch Street Theatre (1861–1892) and as the grandmother of Lionel, Ethel, and John Barrymore.

*Bombastes Furioso* was a highly successful farce (1810) written by a British bank teller, William Barnes Rhodes (1772–1826).

### CHAPTER 13

### Page 181

Union brigadier general Ormsby McKnight Mitchel (name misspelled in the text), a former math professor at West Point and astronomy professor at Cincinnati College, commanded a small detachment of the Army of the Ohio, which captured Huntsville on April 11, 1862. Mitchel was ordered to take the

Memphis and Charleston Railroad. Blamed for his troops' sack of Athens, Alabama, Mitchel was later reassigned to a less important command at Hilton Head, South Carolina.

### Page 183

Philip Dale Roddey (1826–1897) (last name is misspelled in the text) was a native of north Alabama and spent the Civil War years chiefly in that area, fighting under both Forrest and Wheeler. He was promoted to brigadier general on August 3, 1863.

### Page 184

John Alexander Logan (1826–1886), perhaps the most distinguished Union general who lacked professional training, was known as "Black Jack" because of his swarthy (Virginia Clay's word) complexion, but he was not an African American, as Mrs. Spence supposed. Longtime senator from Illinois, he was James G. Blaine's vice presidential running mate in 1884.

### Page 187

The battle of Seven Pines, or Fair Oaks, Virginia, was fought east of Richmond from May 31 to June 1, 1862. Union general George B. McClellan had split his large army on the Chickahominy and was attacked by Confederate general Joseph E. Johnston, who was wounded during the battle and replaced on June 1 by General Robert E. Lee.

Confederate general James Longstreet attacked federal troops on June 1, but the battle of Seven Pines was over. Longstreet continued as a division and a corps commander under Lee for the rest of the war.

### Page 188

Thomas Jonathan "Stonewall" Jackson (1824–1863) was the most famous Confederate general except for his commander,

Lee. He was known for flanking maneuvers and swift marches. He was wounded at the battle of Chancellorsville and died on May 10, 1863.

On June 25, 1862, a week-long battle began to dislodge the federal troops on the peninsula southeast of Richmond. Jackson brought his troops by rail from the Shenandoah Valley to reinforce Lee's army. The resulting Seven Days' Battles saved Richmond for the Confederacy.

James Johnston Pettigrew (1828–1863) survived the severe wound he received at the battle of Seven Pines. Following a prisoner exchange two months after his capture, he was back in combat and was fatally wounded on July 14, 1863, during the retreat from Gettysburg.

## CHAPTER 14

### Page 195

Alfred Holt Colquitt (1824–1894) served one term as a congressman from Georgia (1852–1854) and was both governor of Georgia and U.S. senator after the war. He was an obliging friend of the Clays.

### Page 196

Joseph Evan Davis, the son of Jefferson and Varina Davis, was born April 18, 1859. His tragic death on April 30, 1864, resulted from a fall, as described by Varina Davis: "The most beautiful and brightest of my children . . . had, in play, climbed over the connecting angles of a bannister and fallen to the brick pavement below. He died a few minutes after we reached his side. This child was Mr. Davis's hope, and greatest joy in life" (Ishbel Ross, *First Lady of the South: The Life of Mrs. Jefferson Davis* [New York: Harper and Brothers, 1958], 199).

*Page 197*

Henry Lyndon Flash (1835–?) was born in Cincinnati but reared in New Orleans. During the war he served on the staffs of Generals Hardee and Wheeler. He published a small volume of lyrics in 1860; his collected poems appeared in 1906 (Henry Lyndon Flash, *Poems* [New York: Neale, 1906]).

Brigadier General Felix Kirk Zollicoffer was killed at the battle of Fish Creek, Kentucky, on January 19, 1862. The final of four stanzas of "Zollicoffer" suggests the tenor of much of Confederate war poetry:

> But a handful of dust in the land of his choice,
> A name in song and story,
> And fame too short, with her brazen voice
> "Died on the Field of Glory."

Sidney Lanier, poet, musician, critic, and teacher, whose family traced musical talent back to the Elizabethan period, joined the Macon (Georgia) volunteers in April 1861, and in 1863 he and his brother Clifford served as mounted scouts along the James River. His poetic career began in 1875.

*Page 199*

"Cimmerian darkness" is a proverbial expression for perpetual darkness deriving from a fabled people, the Cimmerii, supposed by the ancients to live in perpetual darkness. See, for example, book 11 of Homer's *Odyssey*.

"General French, Franklin, Virginia" may well be Major General Samuel Gibbs French (1818–1910), a northern-born West Point graduate who quit the army in 1856 to supervise his wife's Mississippi plantation. French was serving in the Virginia area until he was sent to Jackson, Mississippi, in 1864.

### Page 201

Emily Mason (1815–1909), who edited the collection titled *The Southern Poems of the War* (Baltimore: J. Murphy, 1868), was the daughter of John Thomson and Eliza (Moir) Mason. Her only brother was Stevens Thomson Mason, the first governor of Michigan. John Y. Mason and James M. Mason were not related to each other, although the latter was Emily's second cousin.

Mrs. Phoebe Pember (1823–1913) was one of the six daughters of the Jacob Levy family and a younger sister of Eugenia Phillips. She married a Northerner who died of tuberculosis in July 1861, and in spite of the opposition of her family she accepted in November 1862 an appointment as chief matron of Hospital 2 in the huge Chimborazo Hospital complex in Richmond. She published an account of her experiences there in *A Southern Woman's Story* (New York: G. W. Carleton, 1879).

## CHAPTER 15

### Page 203

Although chapter 15 is titled "C. C. Clay, Jr., Departs for Canada," very little is actually written about his mission or accomplishment between May 19, 1864, when he reached Halifax, and February 2, 1865, when, as a passenger aboard the *Rattlesnake,* he waded ashore after the ship ran aground in Charleston Harbor. Perhaps the most accessible account of this confusing period can be found in Nuermberger, *Clays of Alabama,* chapter 11 ("Canadian Adventure"). Little or nothing was accomplished, according to Nuermberger: "In seven months of activity the Confederates had spent over half a million dollars and had employed, directly or indirectly, several hundred persons. But no revolution had occurred in the Northwest; no Confederate prisoners had been released; no peace had been made;

and no Democratic victory had come in the election. The Confederates had succeeded only in carrying on a 'war of nerves'" (260).

In March 1864 Ulric Dahlgren led a raid against Richmond, but it was defeated, and Dahlgren was killed. Dahlgren was trying to free federal prisoners in Libby Prison, but papers reportedly found on his body indicate that the assassinations of President Jefferson Davis and his cabinet were also intended. He was the son of Rear Admiral John A. Dahlgren, USN.

Clay was not reelected by the Alabama legislature to his Confederate senate seat in November 1863. Politics in the legislature, the growing strength of the peace party, which advocated ending the war, Clay's unpopular votes against a pay increase for Confederate soldiers, and the election of new men to the legislature—men whom Clay said he had never heard of—all cut into his traditional power base.

### Page 205

Leroy Augustus Stafford (1822–1864), whose death Celeste Clay refers to in her letter to Virginia, was mortally wounded in the Battle of the Wilderness, May 5, 1864, and died three days later. Of the eight Confederate General Walkers, the most likely candidate here is Henry Harrison Walker (1832–1912), who was wounded in the battle of Spotsylvania Court House, which followed immediately after the Wilderness battle.

Henry Lewis Benning (1814–1875), a noted lawyer and jurist in Columbus, Georgia, before the war, was a brigadier general from January 17, 1863, to the end of the war; he was nicknamed "Old Rock." The largest infantry post in the United States bears his name.

### Page 206

James Byron Gordon (1822–1864), a brigadier general as of September 28, 1863, received a mortal wound during the Wilderness campaign and died in Richmond on May 18, 1864.

## Page 207

Augusta Jane Evans (1835–1909), who in 1868 married Colonel Lorenzo Madison Wilson of Mobile, was one of the most popular novelists of the nineteenth century. Although she was born in Columbus, Georgia, she spent all of her writing life in Alabama. Her best-known novel, *St. Elmo,* was published in 1866.

## Page 208

O. V. would be the initials of the badly wounded Captain Octave Vallette (see page 207).

## Page 209

James Philemon Holcombe (1820–1883), a Confederate congressman and former law professor at the University of Virginia, was involved in the Canadian mission and already in Canada when Clay and Jacob Thompson arrived in Halifax.

## CHAPTER 16

### Page 212

George Frisbie Hoar (1826–1904), brother of E. R. Hoar, was a Republican senator from Massachusetts from 1877 until his death.

### Page 213

Redcliffe, the plantation home of James Henry Hammond, was built on a ridge overlooking the Savannah River.

Virginia Clay is wrong on several points in her account of the Hammond family. Catherine Hammond's maiden name was

Fitzsimons (not Fitzsimmons), and her sister Ann had married Wade Hampton II (1791–1858), not his father (1751 [or 1752]–1835), who had been a major general in the War of 1812 but did not serve with Jackson at the battle of New Orleans. Wade Hampton II became a bitter enemy of his brother-in-law after it was revealed that Hammond had sexually molested Hampton's daughters. Hampton succeeded in temporarily blocking Hammond's political career by threatening exposure. See Carol Bleser, ed., *The Hammonds of Redcliffe* (New York: Oxford Press, 1981), 9–10. Virginia Clay may never have known of this episode, but she probably did know that he kept at least one slave mistress. In any case she obviously chose to be discreet about Loula's father-in-law, whom she apparently liked and admired. General Wade Hampton (1818–1902), the famous Civil War cavalry general, was the son of Wade Hampton II.

### Page 214

On March 4, 1858, Senator James Henry Hammond delivered a speech in the U.S. Senate on the "Kansas question," but turned it into a defense of slavery, saying that slaves were the "mud-sill" class of society.

## CHAPTER 17

### Page 222

Macon Mills refers to a textile mill in Macon, Georgia, a city that prospered in the 1850s as a commercial and manufacturing center and cotton market.

General Stephen Augustus Hurlbut (1815–1882) was a Southern-born Union major general whose career in the army during the war and his subsequent activities were marked by corruption. Virginia Clay misspells the name.

*Page 226*

This list of personal items that Virginia Clay asked her husband to bring back from Canada is an unfortunate revelation of vanity and selfishness. Professor Bell Wiley, for one, sees it this way: "Virginia's repeated requests were not for medicines to relieve the suffering but for finery with which to adorn herself" (Bell Irvin Wiley, *Confederate Women: Contributions in American History*, no. 38 [Westport, Conn.: Greenwood Press, 1975], 79).

*Page 228*

John Withers Clay (1820–1896), the middle son of Clement Comer Clay and Susanna Withers Clay, was the first out-of-state student to receive an M.A. degree from the University of Virginia. He read law "in a desultory fashion and later practiced it with indifferent success" (Nuermberger, *Clays of Alabama*, 76). He married Mary Fenwick Lewis (1825–1898) in 1846, and in later years Withers turned to journalism and was best known as the editor of the *Huntsville Democrat*. The Withers Clay family included eleven children, seven of whom survived infancy, which made life especially difficult following the war. See Nuermberger, *Clays of Alabama*, 299–300.

*Page 229*

Mrs. Whittle (née Sarah Michael Powers of Monroe County, Georgia, 1822–1871) was the wife of Colonel Lewis Neale Whittle (1818–1883), a Virginia native, prominent attorney, and ardent secessionist of Macon, Georgia. Many Southerners who during the war were not able to reach their homes because of Union occupation were welcomed at the white clapboard Whittle house at the corner of College Street and Georgia Avenue. The Clays stayed at the Whittles' home on several occasions.

Horace Greeley (1811–1872) was best known as the editor of the *New York Tribune,* where he used his influence to oppose slavery, including, among other issues, forcible resistance to the Fugitive Slave Act. Although he was a Radical Republican in his views, he favored general amnesty and, as one will see, befriended Virginia Clay. On May 13, 1867, he signed Jefferson Davis's bond in Richmond, with adverse consequences to his popularity in the North.

*Pages 232–233*

Virginia Clay does not specify the date of her departure from Beech Island (misspelled "Beach" in the text), but it was after the death of James Henry Hammond on November 13, 1864, whose funeral she attended. Sherman's march to the sea began November 16. General Joseph Wheeler (1836–1906), after the fall of Atlanta, had the task of opposing General Sherman's famous (or infamous) march across Georgia. The comment about Wheeler's men stealing chickens reflects, humorously, on the reputation his cavalrymen had for a lack of discipline. Although not a native of Alabama, as the caption under his photograph suggests, Wheeler moved to Alabama in 1868 and served eight terms as an Alabama congressman. Later he served as a major general of United States volunteers against Spain in 1898. Redcliffe did not lie in Sherman's path and was saved from destruction.

CHAPTER 18

*Pages 236–237*

Withers Clay, in his letter to Virginia, refers to one of the most controversial decisions that Jefferson Davis made as president of the Confederacy: the replacement of General Joseph E.

Johnston on July 17, 1864, with General John Bell Hood as commander of the Army of Tennessee. Johnston's failure to prevent Sherman's relentless drive to Atlanta was the immediate cause of this decision. Hood, however, was unable to save Atlanta, which only added to the demand by Johnston's proponents such as Withers Clay and more influential allies such as Texas senator Louis Wigfall that Johnston be restored to his command.

*Page 245*

Benjamin Harvey Hill (1823–1882) practiced law in Lagrange, Georgia, and represented his state in the Confederate Senate. After the war, he served in the U.S. House of Representatives (from 1875 to 1877) and in the Senate (from 1877 to 1882).

## CHAPTER 19

*Page 246*

Louis Trezevant Wigfall (1816–1874) was born in South Carolina and became a controversial politician in that state and in Texas, where he moved in 1846. A duelist, Democrat, and fire-eater, he defeated Sam Houston for a U.S. Senate seat in 1859. During the war, he was briefly a Confederate brigadier general and then a senator and became one of the bitterest critics of President Davis.

*Page 249*

*The Anatomy of Melancholy* (1621) was written by Robert Burton (1577–1640), a student of Christ Church, Oxford, whose treatise is a compendium of seventeenth-century learning. That Clement Clay should have been reading such a book at such a time is indeed a witness to his scholarly tastes.

### Page 250

Union general James Harrison Wilson (1837–1925) had defeated Nathan Bedford Forrest at Selma, Alabama, in the spring of 1865. Wilson then moved through Montgomery to the Alabama-Georgia line with an overwhelming force of cavalry. He reached Macon, Georgia, on April 20, 1865. It was to this general that Clay wrote his letter of surrender on May 11, 1865.

### Page 256

The Miss Howell who was with the Davis children waiting for the train was Varina Davis's younger sister Maggie (Margaret Graham Howell [1842–1930]), who married Carl de Wechmar Stoess. She was a great consolation at the time of Davis's incarceration in Fortress Monroe.

## CHAPTER 20

### Page 258

John Henninger Reagan (1818–1905) was a Texas congressman who served as postmaster general of the Confederacy. He was imprisoned after the war at Fort Warren in Boston Harbor. Later he was a Democratic congressman and senator.

### Page 260

General Henry Wager Halleck (1815–1872), the successful administrator and mediocre field commander (alternately referred to as "Old Brains" and "Old Wooden Head"), served as commander of the Military Division of the James after Appomattox, and presumably in this capacity he arrived at the *William P. Clyde* on May 21, 1865, to give orders as to the disposition of the prisoners aboard.

*Page 261*

According to Dr. John Craven (see our note pertaining to page 298), the disposition of the prisoners aboard the *William P. Clyde* differed from the account in *Belle*. General Wheeler and his staff were placed aboard the *Maumee* for Fort Warren in Boston Harbor, and Stephens and Reagan were placed aboard the *Tuscarora* bound for Fort Delaware, near Philadelphia. Shelby Foote's account is the same as the account in *Belle*. See Shelby Foote, *The Civil War: A Narrative,* 3 vols. (New York: Random House, 1974), 3: 1012.

*Page 267*

Brigadier General Nelson Appleton Miles (1839–1925) was not yet twenty-six years old when he took Jefferson Davis by the arm on May 22, 1865, and led him into Fortress Monroe. Miles had just arrived that day to relieve the commanding officer, Colonel Roberts. It seems obvious that Miles was handpicked for his new position. Not being a West Pointer, he would not be swayed by any sense of respect or collegiality for his distinguished prisoner from carrying out the most odious of Stanton's orders. Indeed, his compliance earned him a promotion to major general the following October. He was, according to Shelby Foote, "Horatio Alger in army braid and stars" who knew how to please his superiors and who "before the century was out . . . would succeed Grant, Sherman, and Sheridan as general-in-chief," a promotion not necessarily unconnected to his marriage to Sherman's niece (Foote, *Civil War,* 3: 1034).

CHAPTER 21

*Page 271*

Joseph Holt, appointed judge advocate general of the army

on September 3, 1862, was the first incumbent of an office created by Congress designed to forward Lincoln's policy of placing political prisoners such as Clay and Davis under executive or military control. "The assassination of Lincoln aroused in the War Department an added zest for military trials of civilians. . . . Holt's credit with the Radical group soared in proportion to the certainty of obtaining a conviction" (Allen Johnson and Dumas Malone, eds., *Dictionary of American Biography* [New York: C. Scribner's Sons, 1928–1936], 5: 182). Holt retained his position until 1875, though not with the same powers. For a more detailed account of Holt's office as head of the Bureau of Military Justice, see William Hanchett, *The Lincoln Conspiracies* (Urbana, Ill.: University of Illinois Press, 1983), 62 ff.

Benjamin Wood (1820–1900), a brother of Fernando Wood, the Tammany Democratic leader, purchased the *New York Daily News* in 1860 and edited it until his death. He served in Congress during the Civil War (1861–1864) and again was elected to the U.S. House of Representatives for one term in 1881.

Richard Jacobs Haldeman (1831–1886) served in U.S. legations in Paris, St. Petersburg, and Vienna. After returning home, he purchased the *Harrisburg (Pennsylvania) Daily and Weekly Patriot and Union* and served as its editor until 1860. Later, from 1869 to 1873, he was a Democratic congressman from Pennsylvania. Of the four times Haldeman's name occurs in the text, including the index, it is misspelled only once, on page 271, a reference that is inadvertently omitted in the original index.

Charles O'Conor (1804–1884), New York attorney, possessed one of the most brilliant legal minds in the nation. This respected leader of the American bar was senior counsel for Jefferson Davis on his indictment for treason and was one of his bondsmen.

Jeremiah Sullivan Black (1810–1883), Pennsylvania lawyer and judge, had been successively attorney general and secretary of state under Buchanan. Along with Reverdy Johnson and Charles O'Conor, he was one of the leaders of legal opposition to the continuation of martial law as an instrument of Reconstruction. At this time he was in the confidence of President Johnson, though later they broke off their relationship.

### Page 274

General Hugh Weedon Mercer (1808–1877), a West Point graduate, commanded the Confederate regiments at Savannah until 1864, when he took part in the defense of Atlanta.

### Page 275

The "authorship" of this disgraceful episode was a directive from the War Department authorizing General Miles "to place manacles and fetters upon the hands and feet of Jefferson Davis ... whenever he may think it advisable in order to render [his] imprisonment more secure," an authority that Miles used on the second day of Davis's incarceration. See Foote, *Civil War,* 3: 1034.

### Page 277

The story of Haman is the subject of the Book of Esther. A Persian courtier who was enraged when a Jew, Mordecai, refused to bow down to him, Haman became an enemy of the Jews and was hanged in consequence.

### CHAPTER 22

### Page 278

General Bryan Morel Thomas (1836–1905), a native of Georgia and a West Point graduate, resigned from the U.S. Army in 1861 and was appointed a lieutenant in the Confederate army. He was commissioned a brigadier general on August 4, 1864.

## Page 279

Union general John Thomas Croxton (1836–1874) was with General James H. Wilson's cavalry, which rode into central Alabama in March 1864. Croxton led the raiders who burned the University of Alabama in April.

Dr. John Allan Wyeth (1845–1922) was a surgeon with the Fourth Alabama Cavalry who spent the last years of the war (October 1863 to April 1865) in northern prisons. His father was Louis Wyeth, and his mother, Euphemia Allan, was the daughter of Dr. John Allan (name misspelled in text) (1788–1843), a noted teacher who was pastor of the Huntsville Presbyterian Church from 1820 until his death. The younger Wyeth went north after the war for additional medical training and later became a national leader in medical education. His autobiography, *With Sabre and Scalpel,* was published in 1914.

Stevenson, in Jackson County in north Alabama, was an important station where the Nashville and Chattanooga and the Memphis and Charleston Railroads met.

Colonel Whittle's middle initial should be "N" for Neale. This Macon railroad investor and attorney was a strong supporter of the Clays. His wife, Sarah, was known for the steadfastness of her friendships, but perhaps this time she was sorely tested when the federal soldiers invaded her house to search Virginia's possessions.

In La Fayette Curry Baker (1826–1868), Virginia Clay encountered another pocket-lining Union general. She undoubtedly rejoiced when "he came to grief as a star witness against President Andrew Johnson during the latter's impeachment trial, when he could not produce damaging letters he had alleged to exist" (Ezra J. Warner, *Generals in Blue: Lives of the Union Commanders* [Baton Rouge: Louisiana State University Press, 1964], 17).

*Page 283*

Established by Congress on March 3, 1865, the Bureau of Refugees, Freedmen, and Abandoned Lands "was armed with a broad mandate of responsibility over all matters relating to the former slaves. Its role in the process of Reconstruction was controversial at the time and has been controversial among historians ever since" (William Warren Rogers, Robert David Ward, Leah Rawls Atkins, and Wayne Flynt, *Alabama: The History of a Deep South State* [Tuscaloosa: University of Alabama Press, 1994], 234). Major General Wager Swayne (1834–1902), assistant commissioner for the Freedmen's Bureau in Alabama and later military governor, ordered the Clay property restored to Clement Clay, which transpired in January 1867. Clay's indictment for treason was also suspended at this time. See Nuermberger, *Clays of Alabama,* 302–303.

## CHAPTER 23

*Page 287*

Mary Surratt was a forty-five-year-old widow and proprietor of a boarding house when Booth supposedly met there with some of his confederates to plan Lincoln's assassination. The case against the widow was flimsy at best; nevertheless, she was tried, convicted as a conspirator, and hanged July 7, 1865, as were three others: Lewis Paine (Powell), George Atzerodt, and David Herold.

Stuart Robinson (1814–1881) was pastor of the Second Presbyterian Church in Louisville, Kentucky, when the Civil War erupted. Suspected of disloyalty and facing persecution, he went to Canada in July 1862 and aided Southern refugees there.

*Page 288*

Virginia's reference to Thomas Ewing was probably Thomas

Ewing Sr. (1789–1871), former senator from Ohio, secretary of the treasury under Harrison, and secretary of the interior—an office that he was first to hold—under Taylor. A staunch supporter of Lincoln, he was later Johnson's nominee to succeed Stanton at the War Department, an appointment that the Senate failed to ratify. He was father to two Union brigadiers and father-in-law to William Tecumseh Sherman.

### Page 292

George Shea was a New York attorney and a protégé of Horace Greeley.

### Page 298

Brevet Lieutenant Colonel John J. Craven, M.D. (1822–1893) was the chief medical officer at Fortress Monroe from May 25, 1865, to December 25, 1865. He was relieved of his duty because of his efforts to mitigate the inhumane treatment to which Davis and Clay were subjected during their imprisonment. In 1866, Dr. Craven published an account of this period of his life titled *The Prison Life of Jefferson Davis* (New York: G. W. Dillingham, 1866) in which his purpose was not only to describe the facts of Davis's imprisonment but also to convey his respect for the man (not his opinions) in the hope of improving the chance of a fair trial for Davis. According to Craven, "This is absolutely the first statement in his favor . . . [in] the Northern Press" (315). Craven's account of the harsh treatment of Jefferson Davis at Fortress Monroe made the Confederate ex-president a folk hero in the South.

Captains Titlow (the correct spelling), Bickley, and McEwan in their capacity as overseers of prison guards and prisoners would have had regular contact with Davis and Clay. Captain Bickley informed Dr. Craven that his regiment, the Third Pennsylvania Artillery, was being mustered out of service and would be leaving the fort at the end of the month. Davis and Clay regarded the officers of this regiment as more friendly than hostile.

## CHAPTER 24

### Page 300

Duff Green (1791–1875) was a Kentucky-born newspaperman. He was a strong supporter of Andrew Jackson while Calhoun was a Jackson ally, but after the break between Calhoun and Jackson, Green's paper, the *United States Telegraph*, ceased to be the organ of the Jackson party and was replaced by Frank Blair Sr.'s *Washington Globe*.

### Page 301

"'I have had a weary time,' one wrote in late October" refers to a letter from Varina Davis dated October 29, 1865, from Augusta, Georgia. The rest of the paragraph comes from this letter, although the reader would not suspect this from the text. Varina wrote, "I presume you have seen the gentlemanly attacks which Mr. President Johnson made upon me to the So. Ca. Delegation. You will be somewhat astonished when I tell you that I have never written him a line without consulting with Mr. Schley [the family friend with whom Varina was staying] and his consulting Genl Steedman [James Blair Steedman, the Union general who was in charge of that area in Georgia] upon the tenor of the letters and receiving the approval of both the manner of presenting the subject and the words used" (Varina Davis to Virginia Clay, Clay Papers, Duke). A brief version of Aesop's fable "The Wolf and the Lamb" follows with this appropriate moral, not included in the letter: a tyrant will always find pretext for his tyranny, so it is useless for the innocent to seek justice through reasoning when the oppressor intends to be unjust. According to Ishbel Ross, Johnson "deplored her [Varina's] letters and called her an angry woman" (*First Lady of the South*, 273).

## Page 302

Robert Herstein, a German-born merchant who arrived in Huntsville in 1855, became the father of seven children and the head of one of the city's most prominent Jewish families.

William H. Echols, who escorted Virginia to Washington, D.C., was a former civil engineer with the Memphis and Charleston Railroad. A leading citizen of Huntsville after the war, he operated the Bell Factory cotton mill (1874–1884) and was president of the First National Bank of Huntsville. He died in Huntsville in 1909.

## Page 306

Willard's is a Washington hotel long favored by politicians.

## CHAPTER 25

### Page 307

Thomas Lanier Clingman (1812–1897) was a North Carolina congressman (1843 to 1845 and 1847 to 1858) and senator (1858 to 1861). He was appointed a Confederate brigadier general in 1862.

Augustus Hill Garland (1832–1899) had represented Arkansas in both houses of the Confederate congress. He was denied a seat in the United States Senate in 1867, but entered it a decade later, having served in the meantime as governor of Arkansas. He was attorney general in the first Cleveland administration.

Robert Ward Johnson (1814–1879) had been a congressman

from 1847 to 1853, a U.S. senator from Arkansas from 1853 to 1861, and a Confederate senator from 1862 to 1865.

### Page 308

We have not been able to identify Virginia's secret visitor.

### Page 309

Frederick Aiken was a junior lawyer in the firm of the distinguished lawyer Reverdy Johnson.

### Page 312

"The Secretary of War . . . as one writer has averred" is probably a reference to a passage in Perley's *Reminiscences:* "He [Clement Clay] was taken ill in prison with asthma, and his wife came to Washington to solicit his release. She went to President Johnson, and he gave her the necessary order, which she took back to Secretary Stanton. Stanton read the order, and looking her in the face, tore it up without a word and pitched it into his waste-basket" (239).

## CHAPTER 26

### Page 318

Robert Johnson (1834–1869) was the president's thirty-year-old son who had come to Washington from Tennessee to serve as his father's assistant and secretary.

### Page 320

John Armor Bingham (1815–1900) represented Ohio in the U.S. House of Representatives from 1855 to 1863 and was appointed judge advocate of the Union army by President Lincoln. Bingham returned to the House and served from 1865 to

1873. As chairman of the Judiciary Committee, he was one of the House managers of the impeachment proceedings against President Johnson. He was an outstanding orator and had a reputation for great wisdom.

*Page 325*

Andrew Jackson Rogers (1828–1900), a Democrat from New Jersey and a minority member of the House Judiciary Committee, was instrumental in uncovering the perjury committed by witnesses who had been paid and rehearsed for false testimony. According to Nuermberger, the most notorious perjurer was Sanford Conover—or Charles A. Dunham, to use his real name. (See Nuermberger, *Clays of Alabama,* chapter 12, for a concise account of Clement Clay's ordeal during his imprisonment.) In 1866 the courageous Rogers was defeated for reelection to Congress.

Titus Oates (1649–1705) was the infamous perjurer who, with others, fabricated a document of eighty-one articles purporting to describe a plot by Pope Innocent XI to condemn King Charles II to death as an infidel and to appoint Jesuits to positions of power. Oates's power was at its height in 1684, and few dared challenge him for fear of being accused in turn as a Catholic conspirator. Oates was condemned to prison in 1681. Between 1679 and 1681 the first earl of Shaftesbury took advantage of the popular anti-Catholic sentiment, fomented by Titus Oates and his confederates, to undermine the power of Charles II in order to advance his own political agenda. Virginia Clay is quoting U.S. Representative Rogers, who seems to suggest Secretary of War Stanton as an American Shaftesbury seeking to usurp the power of President Andrew Johnson.

*Page 328*

Messrs. Holt, Speed, and Stanton, to whom Virginia Clay

refers bitterly, comprised the Bureau of Military Justice of which Joseph Holt, as judge advocate general of the army, was the head. The other two men were members by virtue of their offices: James Speed as attorney general and Edwin Stanton as secretary of war. It was they who appointed the members of the military courts, notably in the trial of the persons accused in the plot to assassinate Abraham Lincoln, which terminated June 30, 1865, with the verdict of guilty for all eight conspirators, and in the trial of Captain Henry Wirz, commandant of Andersonville Prison, found guilty of deliberate cruelty to prisoners and hanged November 10, 1865. James Speed, less well known than Stanton, was, like Joseph Holt, from Kentucky. He was elected to the state senate in 1861 as a Union man and appointed attorney general in 1864. He joined forces with Radical Republicans after Lincoln's assassination.

## CHAPTER 27

### *Page 331*

General Robert Seaman Granger (1816–1894), although a West Pointer, did not see much military action in the war. His service was largely confined to camp and garrison duty, which included commands in Huntsville, Decatur, and Stevenson.

### *Page 334*

William Augustus Muhlenberg (1796–1877), a native of Pennsylvania, was an Episcopal clergyman whose life, according to the *Dictionary of American Biography,* was "a series of experiments in broadening and enriching the work of the church. . . . He also influenced strongly the development of hymnody in the Episcopal Church. Of his composition, the sentimental 'I would not live alway' [sic] (written in 1824) was the best known" (7: 313–314).

Henry Alexander Wise (1806–1876) was governor of Virginia from 1856 to 1860. The allusion to his books is Virginia Clay's way of exposing the widespread theft of property belonging to Southerners by Union soldiers. In this case, the looter is General Benjamin Franklin Butler (1818–1893), who was a dictatorial commandant of conquered New Orleans and who "lined his own pockets and those of his family" (Warner, *Generals in Blue*, 61).

### Page 342

The "waters of Marah" is a reference to the bitter water that the Israelites, fleeing from Egypt, could not drink until God showed Moses how to make the water sweet. See Exodus 16:22–25.

### Page 344

William Maxwell Evarts (1818–1901) was the Boston-born attorney who served as one of President Andrew Johnson's counsel during the impeachment trial and as U.S. attorney general from July 1868 to March 1869. Later he was secretary of state under President Hayes.

## CHAPTER 28

### Page 348

Carroll Hall, a building near the main sally port of the fort, had long been used as officers quarters. Dr. Craven had recommended that Davis be moved from the dark, damp, and unhealthy casemate in which he was confined. This change of habitation took place October 5, 1865, after a reluctant Miles made changes to convert quarters to a prison on the second floor. According to Craven, "It is a tradition in and around Old Point Comfort, that both Grant and Sherman occupied in their day the very chambers selected for the second incarceration of Mr. Davis." See Craven, *Prison Life of Jefferson Davis*, 265–266.

"Jay's Prayers" probably refers to *Prayers for the Use of Families* by William Jay (1769–1853), first published in London in 1820.

## Page 351

"Yes! I was here during President Pierce's administration, when my husband was an honoured Senator," Virginia Clay told Dr. Cooper. Apparently Davis was not there, however. See page 68.

## Page 352

"Maid of Saragossa" is probably a reference to the dauntless woman described in Byron's *Childe Harold's Pilgrimage* (canto 1, stanzas 55–57) who foiled a French attack on Saragossa during the Peninsular War.

## CHAPTER 29

### Page 358

Henry Wilson (né Jeremiah Jones Colbaith, 1812–1875), the "Natick Cobbler," was, of course, not yet vice president because, until the adoption of the Twenty-fifth Amendment, that office would remain vacant for the remainder of the term to which its holder, now president, had been elected. Wilson had been senator from Massachusetts since 1855; he would be Grant's running mate in 1872 and would die in office as vice president. As chairman of the Senate Committee on Military Affairs he might have expected to have some influence in a matter of "military justice." As a thoroughgoing Radical Republican he was a most unlikely ally for the Clays.

### Page 360

Nicodemus, the Pharisee and "ruler of the Jews" who came at night to question Jesus (John 3:1–13) may be judged in several lights, but in the present context he represents a hypocrite. That is, if Henry Wilson, who pays a call—incognito and in the evening—to offer Virginia Clay his help and fails to fulfill his promise, then she will publicly expose him as a Nicodemus, "deceiving by false promises."

## Page 363

"*Alea jacta est,*" that is, "The die is cast." The meaning is obvious in the context.

Secretary of War Edwin M. Stanton again is the subject of one of Virginia Clay's last interviews with President Johnson, and again she accuses him of weakness in not dismissing Stanton. Actually, Stanton had refused to resign when so ordered by Johnson and had for a time virtually lived in his office in noncompliance. He resigned only after the effort to remove Johnson from office had failed.

General Monk is George Monck (or Monk) (1608–1669/70). He was the Commonwealth general who prevailed in the power struggle that followed the death of Oliver Cromwell and subsequently arranged the restoration of Charles II. He was created duke of Albemarle and remained in command of the army until his death.

## CHAPTER 30

## Page 369

In March 1866 Congress passed the Civil Rights Act over President Johnson's veto. This act guaranteed the rights of American citizenship for freedmen and struck down the black codes enacted by Southern states to control the ex-slaves. These rights were later incorporated into the Fourteenth Amendment to the Constitution, which was adopted in 1868.

Vinnie Ream (not Reames), sculptress, was later a mistress of the most famous Union general except for Grant. See Michael Fellman, *Citizen Sherman: A Life of William Tecumseh Sherman* (New York: Random House, 1995).

"The Pirate's Bride" is probably Virginia Clay's playful allusion to Medora, bride of the pirate Conrad in Byron's "The Corsair." Admiral Semmes and other Confederate naval personnel were often referred to as pirates in the Northern press.

### Page 371

Virginia Clay erred in saying that Solomon Foote [Foot] (1802–1866), Republican senator from Vermont since 1851, had been expelled. He had died on March 28, 1866. It was John Potter Stockton (1826–1900), newly elected Democratic senator from New Jersey, who had been unseated on March 27 on a technicality as votes were being rounded up to override Johnson's veto of the Civil Rights Bill. William Morris Stewart (1827–1909) was Republican senator from Nevada from 1864 to 1875 (and again from 1887 to 1905).

### Page 377

In response to Lamar's offer of hospitality, Clement Clay regretfully declined for several reasons, one of which sheds additional light on his sense of honor. "I confess to you that my interest and my inclination both incline me to go elsewhere; but as I feel in some measure responsible for the suffering of the people of this State, and as I have been honored by them beyond deserts, I am persuaded that it is my duty to share their fate." See Edward Mayes, *Lucius Q. C. Lamar: His Life, Times, and Speeches, 1825–1893* (Nashville: Publishing House of the Methodist Episcopal Church, 1856), 122.

### Pages 378–379

Virginia Clay passes summarily over Clement Clay's last years because her purpose in *Belle* ends with her husband's release from Fortress Monroe. Nevertheless, her summation is misleading in that his life during the following years had necessarily to be active as he struggled to provide for himself and his wife. And he lived almost sixteen years after his release from prison, dying on January 3, 1882, after an illness (pneumonia). Virginia Clay made her first and only trip to Europe in the summer of 1884 and became the third wife of longtime friend Judge David Clopton of the Alabama Supreme Court on November 29, 1887. See Nuermberger, *Clays of Alabama,* chapter 13.

# INDEX TO THE 1905 EDITION

453

# INDEX TO THE ANNOTATIONS